Edmund J. Davis *of* Texas

CIVIL WAR GENERAL, REPUBLICAN LEADER,
RECONSTRUCTION GOVERNOR

EDMUND J. DAVIS
of TEXAS

CIVIL WAR GENERAL,

REPUBLICAN LEADER,

RECONSTRUCTION

GOVERNOR

by CARL H. MONEYHON

THE TEXAS BIOGRAPHY SERIES ★ NUMBER 2

A Joint Project of the Center for Texas Studies at TCU
and TCU Press ★ Fort Worth, Texas

Library of Congress Cataloging-in-Publication Data

Moneyhon, Carl H., 1944-
Edmund J. Davis of Texas : Civil War general, Republican leader,
Reconstruction governor / Carl H. Moneyhon.
p. cm. — (The Texas biography series ; no. 2)
ISBN 978-0-87565-405-8 (cloth : alk. paper)
1. Davis, E. J. (Edmund Jackson), 1827–1883. 2. Governors—Texas—
Biography. 3. Texas—Politics and government—1846–1865. 4. Texas—
Politics and government—1865–1950. 5. Republicanism—Texas—History—
19th century. 6. Reconstruction (U.S. history, 1865–1877)—Texas.
7. Unionists (United States Civil War)—Texas—Biography. 8. Generals—
United States—Biography. 9. United States. Army—Biography. 10. United
States—History—Civil War, 1861–1865—Biography. I. Title.
F391.D257M66 2010
976.4' 05092—dc22
[B]
                                                              2009033717

TCU Press
P. O. Box 298300
Fort Worth, Texas 76129
817.257.7822
http://www.prs.tcu.edu

To order books: 800.826.8911

Designed by Margie Adkins Graphic Design

THIS BOOK IS DEDICATED TO
NICHOLAS JOHNSTON ADNEY

He watched the book mature over the last ten years and was always
encouraging, pushing Grandaddy to finish that "soldier book."

AND TO THE MEMORY OF PATRICIA MONEYHON,
WHOSE PRESENCE IS SORELY MISSED.

CONTENTS

EDITOR'S FOREWORD

Through its rich and colorful history, Texas has been home to countless fascinating figures. Some of the state's great works of historical literature, such as Eugene C. Barker's biography of Stephen F. Austin and Marquis James's study of Sam Houston, have chronicled the lives of Texas's larger-than-life leaders. Yet there remain many important personalities who have not yet found their biographer, and many more whose stories are in need of fresh examination in a scholarly biography. The Texas Biography Series, published by the TCU Press and the Center for Texas Studies at TCU, offers a venue for telling their stories. Another major goal of the series is to broaden the body of biographical literature in Texas historiography beyond its traditionally heavy emphasis on the "great men" (which has often meant "great white men on horseback"). While the series will certainly include biographies of nineteenth-century political and military leaders, it will strive to encourage biographers to examine the full range of historical actors who have shaped the destiny of the Lone Star State, including women, members of racial and ethnic minorities, as well as figures from the worlds of business, the arts, science, religion, and even sports. In doing so, the series will contribute to keeping the field of Texas history vital and relevant as it moves into the twenty-first century.

As the second volume in the series, Carl H. Moneyhon's biography of Edmund J. Davis fulfills one of the series' principal aims, which is to place well-known Texas personalities in modern historiographical context utilizing recent scholarly knowledge. Professor Moneyhon, one of the leading scholars of Reconstruction in Texas, presents a finely drawn portrait of Davis, one of the most controversial figures in the state's history. Reviled by his Democratic contemporaries and condemned by generations of historians with thinly veiled pro-Confederate sympathies, Davis championed the rights of African Americans, sought to create Texas's first meaningful system of public education, and tried to restore law and order and bring economic development to the war-ravaged state. Rather than being the unprincipled political opportunist portrayed in traditional works, Moneyhon's Davis emerges from these pages as a courageous visionary whose virtues far outweighed his mistakes. Along the way, we learn a lot about the entire era of the Civil War and Reconstruction in Texas. This, then, is "revisionist" history in the finest sense of the term—history that takes a fresh look at a topic and reaches conclusions that move our understanding in new directions.

This book and its successors in the Texas Biography Series owe their existence to three important institutions. The TCU Press and its staff have furnished the editorial and production expertise to create books equal to those of the leading national publishing houses. The Center for Texas Studies at TCU is a critical partner in launching, funding, and publicizing the series. And finally, Houston Endowment has provided a generous grant underwriting much of the cost of *Edmund J. Davis* and the next several titles in the series. As series editor, I am grateful to all of these partners who have made the series a reality.

Gregg Cantrell
Erma and Ralph Lowe Chair in Texas History
Texas Christian University

PREFACE AND ACKNOWLEDGMENTS

I first encountered Edmund J. Davis nearly fifty years ago when taking a course in Texas history taught by Llerena B. Friend at the University of Texas at Austin. The analysis of Davis that I heard in that class was not favorable to him, but, even so, I was struck by what appeared to me to be his determination a hundred years before to accomplish the changes taking place around me in the 1960s. My interest in him grew while working with John Hope Franklin at the University of Chicago on a dissertation about the Republican Party in Texas during Reconstruction, and that curiosity refused to diminish in the years afterwards as I have continued researching the history of Texas during that period of such great change. Davis was a puzzle. He was a man who was part of the state's political elite prior to the Civil War, yet he vigorously opposed secession. He not only refused to follow the path taken by most of the state's leaders, he left the state, actively opposed the Confederacy, and attempted to bring Texas back into the Union. After the war, he became a leader among the men trying to reconstruct the state on the basis of true free labor; then, as governor, he pursued policies that were progressive and egalitarian. In the face of extreme hostility, he maintained his course through Reconstruction and, even after leaving the governor's mansion, remained dedicated to changing Texas. He continued on that course until the day he died.

For me, the besetting question concerning Edmund Davis was why he took the path he did. What moved this man to take stands so out of step with those around him? This book seeks to answer that question. I hope to provide insights into his life and his public positions and perhaps reveal him to be the hero he most certainly was. While so little of the change that he envisioned for Texas survived his administration, the goals he fought for proved to better reflect the ideals of the nation than those of so many of his contemporaries. In the end, however, this study does not and cannot provide a complete picture of the man. While possibly more of his public letters survive than for any other mid-nineteenth century Texas politician, nothing remains of his private correspondence. A particularly frustrating discovery was that at one point such materials existed, but they were not part of the papers placed in the state archives, nor were they passed on to his family. Thus, the private Davis, particularly his relationship with his family, remains something of an enigma. Even accepting this shortcoming, it is my wish that the pages that follow do justice to a man I have come to admire all the more in the years that I have pursued some understanding of his life.

A project that has covered over four decades inevitably produces many obligations. Unfortunately, there are simply too many who have assisted me to mention all. I do wish, however, to thank those who provided special help. Among these, the two people to whom I perhaps owe the greatest debt are Harriet and David Condon. David is the great-great grandson of Governor Davis and the great-grandson of Britton Davis. The Condons possess what is the only collection of personal items from the Edmund Davis family, including the clipping files that Lizzie Davis kept on the history of her family and her husband from the 1850s into the 1880s. They generously shared their family history and their treasure of family documents. These allowed me to personalize Davis in ways that would not otherwise have been possible.

There are many friends who also have kept their eye out for Davis and pointed me towards materials that I otherwise might not have encountered. Jerry Thompson of Texas A&M International discovered references to Davis in the Samuel Heintzelman Papers that offered a clearer picture of Davis's actions during the Cortina War. Rick McCaslin at the University of North Texas ran across important letters at the Rosenberg Library that added to the story of Davis's life during the Civil War. Michael Parrish, at Baylor University, shared material that he encountered doing Internet research. Donaly Brice provided inestimable help in accessing Davis material in the Texas State Library and Archives. Others willingly endured my telling of Davis's story, offering suggestions and corrections. These include the late Barry Crouch of Gallaudet University, Mike Campbell at the University of North Texas, James Smallwood now retired from Oklahoma State University, Alwyn Barr at Texas Tech, and Patrick Williams at the University of Arkansas at Fayetteville. I also would like to give special thanks to Lewis Gould, now retired from the University of Texas at Austin, for his encouragement in the early stages of my research on Texas Republicans and Governor Davis.

There are two people who deserve special recognition. I can never repay my debts to John Hope Franklin. He provided me with an example of scholarship I still seek to follow. And, as always, I owe a special thanks to my wife Patricia for her unending support and encouragement.

A SOUTHERN BORN MAN

"A young gentleman of steady habits and good attainments."
—Brigadier General W. J. Worth and the Officers
of Fort Marion on Edmund J. Davis, 1844

The House chambers in the Texas State Capitol attracted a large crowd on Friday afternoon, 9 February 1883, despite the steady fall of a cold drizzling rain. They came for the funeral of possibly the most controversial politician who ever held office in the state, their former Republican governor, Edmund J. Davis. Davis's body lay in state through the afternoon, watched over by the Austin Grays, a company of local militia. At four o'clock, an Episcopal clergyman conducted funeral services. Following the rites, a large cortège of state and local officials, the city's bar, and many friends followed the coffin to the state cemetery for burial. Only the day before, Governor John Ireland, one of Davis's bitterest political enemies, had invited Davis's family to bury him in the state cemetery, a place reserved for the state's distinguished dead. The parties appeared to put aside their political differences. The Democratic legislature even adjourned, resolving that "we bury all past political differences and recognize in the character of the deceased those qualities that marked him as an honorable, honest man; a kind and obliging neighbor, and a tried and faithful friend."[1]

The honors and the resolutions of respect shown that day were typical of public funerals of the day. Political leaders did what was expected of them. On the other hand, an outpouring of grief and a demonstration of respect by everyday people and especially African Americans gave a special meaning to the events on that bleak day. For three

1

hours, according to at least one report, an unbroken stream of citizens, black and white, flowed by the casket. They came from all walks of life. Their presence honored a man who had attempted to make a better world for them; his goals once fed their hopes for a brighter future. Indeed, he was very different from many who had held the gubernatorial office. Davis was Texas's first Republican governor and he went on to be a Republican leader for a decade after leaving office. Throughout his life Davis worked to create a different Texas, one that gave hope and protection to the poor of both races.

The positive memory of Davis faded quickly in the years that followed his funeral. When Oran Roberts, a Democratic leader who opposed Davis, wrote the first history of the era in 1898, the man he depicted seemed little like the one honored that cold day in Austin. Instead of showing the good Davis had done, Roberts devoted his pages to condemning Davis for presiding over a government that the author charged had exercised a "tyranny" and inflicted "tenfold more aggravating and oppressive injuries than those suffered under the military government" of Reconstruction. He said that Texans had rightly thrown him out of office to save themselves from the "ignominy and ruin which was threatened by a continuance of such Republican rule." Roberts's characterization of Davis and his administration quickly became part of Texas's historical canon. Twelve years later, professional historian Charles Ramsdell gave Roberts's interpretation the imprimatur of scholarly authority in the first study of the Davis years. Agreeing with Roberts, Ramsdell observed that "the administration of Davis was responsible for more of the bitterness with which the people of Texas have remembered the reconstruction era than all that happened from the close of the war to 1870." He went further to conclude that "the name of no Texan has gone down to posterity so hated as his."[2]

The conflicting accounts raise a critical question about this important figure. Who was Edmund J. Davis? Was he an honorable man, deserving the recognition given him by those who filed by his coffin on the day of his funeral? Was he the tyrant described by Roberts and Ramsdell? His life tells us much about Texas in the years prior to the Civil

War, during the war, and the years that followed. It also shows why Davis provoked such widely varying reactions among those who knew him.

His story began in Florida on 2 October 1827, when he was born to William Godwin Davis and Mary Ann Channer Davis. His father was a native of Virginia who had moved to South Carolina as a child with his mother and stepfather. At Charleston, William owned a blacksmith shop and operated a business transporting cotton from the back country into the city. There he met Mary Ann Channer, an immigrant from England, and married her on 5 July 1812. The couple ultimately had nine children. Edmund was the sixth.[3]

William was a man who reflected much of the speculative spirit of the early nineteenth-century United States. In 1817, he moved from Charleston to St. Augustine, Florida, where Edmund was later born. William initially became involved in a scheme to secure land from the government on Key Largo for the purpose of creating a town and developing coffee plantations. Nothing came of that idea, but he and Mary Ann also speculated to secure the land in St. Augustine. Their first major land purchase was in St. Augustine near the old fort, five hundred acres secured for $50, an acquisition confirmed by the United States government in May 1824. In addition, the family became involved in the development of the proposed town of North City on the outskirts of St. Augustine.[4]

A more ambitious plan evolved when the family acquired 175 acres on the south end of Key Biscayne. The couple planned to develop a town and a port there, and to further their plan they sold three acres to the United States government in 1824 to construct the Cape Florida Lighthouse. Their plans for Key Biscayne island darkened after American Indian attacks forced the lighthouse to be abandoned in 1836. Plans then brightened when United States troops landed there in 1838 and used the lighthouse as a staging area for General William S. Harney's campaign into the Everglades in 1840. The presence of the army encouraged them to plan a resort town to be called Key Biscayne. They even prepared a map, naming the streets of their proposed community after their children, including their son Edmund.[5]

Throughout these years, besides any profits he may have made through his land speculation, William's only sources of income were the salaries he received from a number of public offices. He secured his first position in December 1822 when Mayor Waters Smith named him city marshal of St. Augustine. After that he secured other appointments, including those of city scavenger and jailer. William Davis's career as a public official appeared closely tied to Smith. When Smith was named United States Marshal for western Florida, William Davis received an appointment as a deputy. It was not surprising that Davis ultimately named one of his sons Waters after the man who appeared to be his political patron.[6]

Despite the speculative side of Edmund's parents, they provided a home life that appears to have been orderly and to have afforded opportunities to the children that many did not possess. Edmund emerged from a household in which religion was important. William and Mary married at Charleston's Independent Congregational Church; however, the family became Episcopalian after moving to Florida. Edmund was baptized at St. Augustine's Trinity Church, and he would continue to be a regular churchgoer through the rest of his life. His family also valued education. In the 1840s, Edmund attended a school run by Edward A. DeCottes. At the school Davis secured a background in mathematics, studying algebra and geometry, and completing the course of "trigonometry, mensuration, [and] conic sections" offered in *Hutten's Mathematics.* DeCottes also offered a class in surveying that Davis attended. In addition to math and math-related work, Davis's studies included philosophy, history, English grammar, and chemistry. He studied languages with courses in Latin and, beginning in 1843, French. DeCottes's evaluation of him provided the first insight into the character of the young Edmund. The teacher considered him to be "both studious & attentive."[7]

The bright young Davis determined at an early age that he wanted to be a professional soldier. What provoked this interest is unclear, although the soldiers he met at the nearby garrison at Fort Marion, headquarters for the third military department, may have influenced him. The commander, Brigadier General W. J. Worth, and the officers at the fort knew the young Davis and possibly encouraged his ambitions. Unquestionably other local boys felt the call of the military, including Edmund's friend, Edmund Kirby Smith, future Confederate general. In 1841 Smith went to West Point, following his brother Ephraim. Two years later, Davis decided he wanted to go West Point as well. In 1843, at the age of sixteen, he made his first attempt to become an officer in the army.[8]

Davis's father actively supported his son's desire to enter the military and to attend West Point. Unfortunately for the ambition of both, Edmund was at a disadvantage because of his father's political hostility to David Levy, the Florida territorial delegate to the U.S. Congress at that time. In 1843 William wrote to the superintendent at West Point asking for a special at-large appointment for his son, thus side-stepping the usual recommendation of a member of Congress. The letter provided some insights into the ideological world of the Davis family, indicating one with strong nationalistic feelings. William explained that he would not ask Levy to support his son's ambition to enter West Point noting not only his opposition to Levy's politics, but also to his background. "I believe he is an alien," William wrote, "& I would not condescend to solicit the interference of any foreigners for any appointment under our government. I solicit the place for my son as an American citizen who is proud of his birthright." Noting his father's death in the Revolutionary armies and his own work in fortifying the city of Charleston during the War of 1812, William assured the superintendent of his strong nationalism and consciousness of "having done only my duty for my country."[9]

Edmund did not receive the at-large appointment to West Point in 1843, but his father did not give up. The next year Davis enlisted the help of the officers stationed at Fort Marion, who provided a glowing endorsement, indicating that men other than his teacher thought he was a promising youth. In a letter signed by eighteen officers, including General Worth, they described the seventeen-year-old candidate as a "young gentleman of steady habits and good attainments." They believed that if admitted, he would "acquit himself with honor to the Institution and become a useful officer in the service of his country." This time William appealed directly to the Secretary of War, who had the power to make additional appointments. Despite Davis's education and strong support from teacher and officers, however, the second effort also failed.[10]

The world of the Davis family changed with the end of the American-Indian wars. The army closed Fort Dallas in Florida. This meant that Key Biscayne would not be the immediate center of a thriving economy and that William and Mary Ann never moved forward with the development of the town they proposed to build. Along with the departure of the army, a dispute with the family of a previous owner over the title of that land developed. A lengthy court fight ultimately left the land in family hands, but the suit sealed the fate of any development on Key Biscayne and William Davis's future in Florida. Sometime in the early 1840s William left his family in St. Augustine and headed for Texas, seeking fresh opportunities in the new Republic.[11]

He began his search for a new future in Galveston. It is unclear when he arrived, but scholars believe that he was there before 1845. He early established himself as a memorable figure. A contemporary later recalled him as a "a magnificent specimen of manhood, standing over six feet, broad shouldered, deep-chested, strong and clean-limbed, with a face whose every feature denoted inflexible will and a courage that would not quail before any danger." He did not achieve much success in the way of business, however. Galveston was a bustling city where opportunities appeared widespread, but the economy in fact was dominated by a business elite. These entrepreneurs had been active in the economy of Texas when it was still part of Mexico, and they tended to stifle competition. As early as 1834 Michel B. Menard acquired a claim to the eastern end of Galveston Island and several years later joined with Thomas F. McKinney and Samuel May Williams in chartering the Galveston City Company to sell land. They subsequently established the powerful merchant firm of McKinney and Williams and would go on to join with other firms to establish a virtual monopoly over Galveston's economy when they created the Galveston Wharf & Cotton Press Company. William Davis may have seen Texas as a land of opportunity, but tax rolls and the census gave no indication that he had been successful either as a merchant or a speculator by 1850.[12]

Despite William's lack of success in Texas, his family followed him to Galveston. Edmund later remembered that they arrived some time during the Mexican-American War, but the exact date is uncertain. Young Davis did not remain in Galveston long after the family arrived, however. He read law for a time but had inherited his father's wanderlust. Edmund, who as an adult was usually known as E. J., soon left for his own land of opportunity, the frontier country in southern Texas, possibly arriving there as early as 1846. He first settled at the town of Saluria on Matagorda Island then moved to Corpus Christi, a town that like Galveston appeared to promise success to newcomers. In the late 1840s it was just emerging as a thriving community. The town had been part of what was known as the Nueces Strip in the years of the Republic. This was disputed land that both Texas and Mexico claimed. Henry L. Kinney founded Saluria in 1839, and it became a center of trade for the ranches of the Nueces Valley and some of the illegal trade between Texas and Mexico. With a permanent national boundary uncertain at the time, however, Anglo Americans had done little else to develop the area. The war changed the prospects of the town and its inhabitants. The movement of soldiers and supplies through the port of Corpus Christi caused an initial boom. That boom ended following the war and as military trade stopped, but the permanent settlement of the boundary with Mexico and the further development of the Nueces ranches promised a better future. When Davis got to the town it remained unincorporated. Its population included only 550 individuals, of whom 112 were soldiers. The town was predominantly Mexican American. It was an obvious place for new beginnings.[13]

At Corpus Christi, Davis continued to pursue a legal career. He read law and at some point he passed the local bar. In 1849, possibly at the instigation of his father, E. J. received an appointment as a clerk in the Galveston post office. It is uncertain if he ever returned to take the position, however. He appears instead to have settled down to life in South Texas, where he practiced law. He also, for the first time, became active in politics. In 1848, during the first presidential election to take place after E. J. reached voting age, he publically supported the Whig candidate, former General Zachary Taylor. A political associate later described Davis's political fire. "In the contest for the Presidency," he wrote, "there was not a more reliable friend of the President to be found in the state, nor one who entered into the contest with more zeal, or [made] greater exertions." Did his support indicate that E. J. was a Whig? That is uncertain because many Southerners backed Taylor in 1848. He was a Southerner, a war hero, and he ran on a platform that asked for the votes of men of all political creeds and philosophies. Taylor's handlers certainly had tried to make him attractive to Southerners, putting their candidate forward as a Whig who promised bipartisan government on a platform that offered the nation "Peace, Prosperity, and Union," with few specific policies. He may also have seen little choice. Taylor's opponents included the Free Soil candidate Martin Van Buren of New York and the Democrats' Lewis Cass of Michigan.[14]

E. J. did not continue his legal practice in Corpus Christi for long. In 1849, he proposed to move to the small border town of Laredo, looking for new opportunities. He intended to work as an attorney, but wanted to supplement his income with a federal job there. Still in Corpus Christi, on 12 November he applied for an opening in the customs service at Laredo, seeking the position of inspector of customs. The job only paid six hundred dollars a year, but Davis was willing to take it. The salary provided a secure income as he continued to develop his law practice. Needing a man on the job, John S. Rhea, the collector at Port Isabel, gave Davis a commission shortly after he applied. Rhea had not yet received formal approval from the Treasury Department, but Davis did not wait. He moved to Laredo in early December and did not receive his formal appointment until the middle of that month.[15]

Davis's choice of Laredo was a good one. His new job as customs inspector provided him with a steady income, and the potential legal business in the area seemed to be substantial, even though the town had a population of only about a thousand people. Laredo had remained a part of Mexico following the Texas Revolution and had not been occupied by Anglos to any great extent until American troops arrived there in 1846 during the Mexican-American War. The war's end had settled the community's legal future and imposed American and Texas laws on the region. Disputes over land ownership, issues of inheritance, stock laws, and *ejido* rights were commonplace. These land issues were particularly important because Anglo settlers who arrived in greater numbers in the late 1840s demanded that land long held in common ownership be parceled out to private owners, surveyed, and titles verified. Plenty of work existed for any attorney.[16]

Davis had intended to use the job of customs inspector to supplement the income he gained from his law practice, but he soon discovered that the job consumed a considerable amount of his time. He found that a brisk trade moved across the border, with Laredo and the neighboring town of Eagle Pass having commerce in excess of half a million dollars by the mid-1850s. In one of his earliest letters from Laredo to Collector Rhea, Davis reported the unexpected magnitude of his job. Heavy trade had developed with the movement of corn, flour, and sugar from Mexico into Texas since many of the farms that had fed the ranches along the Rio Grande were south of the river and now had to cross an international border. He also found that hides, tallow, horses, mules, fruits, wine, and lime added to the flow of border traffic. Mescal, a product Davis helpfully explained as liquor made from the maguey plant, constituted another important item of trade. Collecting duties on all of this trade was difficult. Most local merchants were not even aware that a duty now had to be paid. No one volunteered to pay the import fees and Davis's job required him not only to collect the fees but to make local merchants aware of their obligation. He urged the Treasury to print notices of the tariffs on imports in Spanish for distribution along the border.[17]

Many who were aware of the new duties besieged Davis for exceptions. Many families owned property on both sides of the river. All their lives they had moved back and forth across the river without facing any barriers. Ranchers could see no reason why the new border should prevent them from moving stock from their property on the north side of the river to the south. Townspeople who acquired much of their food from the south bank saw no reason to pay a tax on necessities that could not be acquired on the north. In handling these problems, Davis showed signs of his character that guided him later. He followed the rules closely. He conceded no special cases. On the other hand, he clearly empathized with the troubles of those who asked for his help. Davis promised those who asked for trade exemptions that he would seek the guidance of Collector Rhea, a higher authority, to request that he approve the exceptions. Rhea never overruled his decisions, but also provided him with no word as to whether or not they were right or wrong.[18]

Davis clearly tried to do a good job as a customs inspector, but he found that his superiors provided little assistance in doing it right. From the moment he took office he found that he lacked basic materials needed to do his work. In his early reports, Davis pleaded for blank documents, information on the department's regulations, and some compilation of the revenue laws, "or at any rate such of them as are absolutely necessary." He was concerned particularly to receive a copy of the Tariff Act of 1846. Without it, he did not know with any certainty which duties individuals should pay on any of the imported articles. The Treasury had not even provided a safe in which E. J. could deposit government funds, nor had they purchased furniture for his office. The job must have been an unsatisfying one for a man whose character incorporated a concern with detail and sense of duty that remained in evidence through the rest of his life.[19]

The magnitude of the border trade complicated Davis's life, but it also led ultimately to his advancement in the customs service. Following his correspondence with Davis, Collector Rhea concluded that business at Laredo warranted the appointment of a deputy collector to that city. Again, without receiving approval from Washington, in January 1850 Rhea promoted Davis from inspector to the post of acting collector, subject to the acceptance of his appointment by the Secretary of the Treasury. The permanent appointment did not come until the following May, at which time Davis became the official collector with an increase in his salary to eight hundred dollars per year. He was forced to put up a bond of three thousand dollars. Davis made the bond without difficulty, which reflected the fact that his legal career was flourishing by this time.[20]

Little is known about Davis's law practice in Laredo, although he clearly found the time to take on clients despite his Treasury job. Most attorneys in this period followed the district courts from town to town within their district. Davis practiced in the Twelfth District, which included Webb, Starr, and Cameron counties. An account of his early practice, written much later, indicated that many of his clients came to him trying to establish title to their lands. Again, he demonstrated the ability to master detail, which is an essential skill for any attorney engaged in such a business. He established a reputation for expertise in the matter of land law and reportedly attracted numerous clients.[21]

As might be expected of a successful lawyer, a federal officeholder, and a man who had been active politically in the 1848 election, Davis did not avoid involvement in the politics of his new home. His life in Laredo situated him well for success in that arena. His choice of a rooming house was particularly fortuitous for a man with any political ambitions. His landlord was Tomasa Benavides, stepmother of Santos and Refugio Benavides. Santos and Refugio came from families that had been in the area since the founding of the town. When E. J. arrived, they were prominent merchants and ranchers and also involved in area politics. They were the nephews of Basilio Benavides who had been elected *alcalde* three times while Laredo was a part of Mexico. After annexation, Benavides had been mayor and also a state representative. The nephews followed his political bent, with Refugio serving as one of the town's first aldermen in 1850 and Santos being elected mayor in 1856 and chief justice of Webb County in 1859. For anyone with political ambition, the Benavides family was an important potential ally. Davis secured their support through the antebellum years and would remain close to the family for the rest of his life.[22]

His law practice also introduced him to other political leaders in the lower Rio Grande area as he rode circuit from Laredo to Rio Grande City to Brownsville. His most important ally would be Stephen Powers, a major supporter of Davis's political ambitions during the 1850s. Powers was another relatively recent arrival on the Rio Grande border. He was a northern attorney who had pursued a career of distinction in New York; he also had political connections. He had served as the United States consul at Basel, Switzerland, during the Van Buren administration, then been named a member of the United States Military Commission for the Government of Occupied Territory during the Mexican-American War. He came to Brownsville as a part of General Zachary Taylor's staff, then remained in Brownsville after the war. There he became leader of a political faction known as the Blues and, through Powers, Davis became connected with that group.[23]

E. J.'s connection with Powers was particularly important because Powers would play a major role in local politics throughout the antebellum years. He was a Democrat, although like others he supported Taylor in 1848. The next year Taylor appointed him postmaster at Brownsville and he held that post until 1851. In the 1852 election, Powers backed the Democrat Franklin Pierce and received as his reward the very lucrative position of collector of customs for the Texas District of Brazos Santiago. As collector he controlled most of the Treasury Department patronage along the Rio Grande, a fact that gave him considerable political clout. Holding on to federal posts, Powers would continue to play a role in the area's politics throughout the 1850s, serving as mayor of Brownsville and chief justice of Cameron County.[24]

Throughout these years Powers was a leader of the Blues, and Davis was a close ally. Blues and Reds possessed no apparent ideological differences. They simply represented rival interests among the area's local economic elites. The Blues, led by Powers, included men such as William A. Neale, John Wells, and James G. Browne. The latter were Brownsville merchants engaged in trade up river and into Mexico. They also speculated in land, purchasing large tracts along the Rio Grande. The Reds were the same sort of men and included powerful locals such as Charles Stillman, Francisco Yturria, Richard King, and Mifflin Kenedy. Like their opponents, they were merchants and land speculators. At the time Davis entered politics, Stillman had financed a steamboat venture by King and Kenedy that created a monopoly over river traffic. This made an enemy of Neale, whose control of the overland trade from Brazos Santiago to Brownsville was supplanted by the new company. Exactly why E. J. joined the Blues is unclear, other than the possible political benefits he could gain from his association with Powers. He clearly held no grudges against his political opponents and would ultimately represent some of them as a lawyer.[25]

Connections such as those made with the Benavides family and Powers gave Davis a potential base of support for his entry into politics. Davis first sought political office in 1851. That year he ran for the Laredo town council and was elected alderman. Possibly, by this time Davis had already learned to speak Spanish, a skill he would use in his future political campaigns but absolutely essential in seeking office in a town whose population was almost completely Mexican or Mexican American. Davis's initial win proved an anomaly in local affairs, however. In the election, Davis was one of four non-Mexican Americans who secured a majority on the six-position board. Davis was active in his new position and sponsored numerous ordinances while serving on the council. One of the steps taken by the board during Davis's term, however, was to place restrictions on the use of the town's common grounds and put him in opposition to the will of the town's Mexican Americans. In the next election, the Mexican Americans recaptured control over the board and defeated Davis in his bid for reelection.[26]

By 1852, E. J.'s practice appeared to have grown to the point where he no longer needed his position as deputy collector. He resigned but did not abandon his search for office. In 1853, he ran for the post of district attorney in the Twelfth District. If Davis had ever seriously considered himself a Whig, that connection had disappeared by this time. Davis publicly identified himself as a Democrat in the 1853 election, although the specifics of his political ideology are unclear. As a Democrat, he was a member of a party in some disarray. Initially seven men announced as party candidates for the governorship. Even though Elisha Marshall Pease emerged as the candidate most considered the regular party nominee, four other Democrats remained in the race. In the campaign they faced William B. Ochiltree, who ran as a Whig. Davis threw his support to Pease.[27]

What attracted Davis to Pease in 1853 was the candidate's platform. In one of his earliest political letters, at least of those remaining, E. J. informed Pease that he believed the latter's platform would appeal to the people on the border and encouraged him to visit the region. That platform envisioned a more active role for the state government in a variety of areas. Like candidates before him, Pease promised to deliver on the yet unfulfilled constitutional guarantee of state supported education. For Davis and people on the border, two other promises may have been more attractive. Pease championed state support for a transcontinental railroad, one that would have tied the border country into the broader trade of the nation. He also pledged to expel Indians from all of the settled portions of the state. For a man such as Davis, now closely wedded to the future of the border country, Pease's platform offered much that was good. Indeed, Davis's own political future focused to a considerable degree on these twin goals and indicated his continuing identification with border interests.[28]

Davis's assessment of Pease's chances along the border proved accurate. Pease received only 13,091 votes state-wide, to Ochiltree's 9,178 and 13,424 votes divided among the four other Democratic candidates. But, Pease carried the counties along the Rio Grande handily. Out of 851 votes cast in Cameron, Hidalgo, Starr, and Webb counties, Ochiltree managed to secure only three votes. Davis would not hesitate to call on Pease for help in the future and among his first claims upon the governor was his appeal for assistance in handling problems with the Indians in the region. The winter of 1853–1854 witnessed particularly bold forays into the area by Lipan Apaches who were being fed by Robert S. Neighbors, a government agent, at Fort Inge on the Leona River. In early March, the raiders moved within one hundred yards of the town of Laredo to steal horses. Local leaders, fearing that the continuation of such raids would bring about the depopulation of the border towns, called a meeting at the Webb County courthouse in Laredo that met on 11 March 1854.

That meeting showed that Davis had emerged as a local leader.[29] Davis chaired the meeting, attended by state senator Hamilton P. Bee, and opened the discussion of matters. Ultimately, a committee that included Davis prepared a report requesting aid and sent it to Governor Pease. The report described the depredations that had taken place in the previous months and focused particularly on the need for the United States Army to change its tactics in dealing with the American Indian raiders. The report described the American Indian forays as "sudden, rapid and always mounted." The government's response, which included a garrison of some five hundred infantrymen at Fort McIntosh just outside of Laredo, was inadequate. The committee report argued that mounted troops were the only possible response to Indian tactics, but the only cavalry in the area were some sixty miles away and the government refused to provide any horses or equipment for the local garrison. The proceedings ultimately sounded the despair of local citizens. They asked for help but expected little. Davis had the responsibility of sending the report to the governor.[30]

As expected, Pease could offer little assistance. After receiving the proceedings from Laredo, he petitioned federal officials for assistance. In a letter to Major General Persifer F. Smith, commander of federal troops on the frontier, the governor requested that the army send any mounted men who could be "spared from other service" to Laredo and other points along the Rio Grande. A letter to Secretary of War Jefferson Davis asked for a change in the army's basic strategy along the frontier, noting that "infantry are entirely inadequate to restrain the Indians and give protection to the frontier of the state." In his letter replying to Davis, however, the governor held out little hope for government action and little was done. The Secretary of War did authorize General Smith to call up mounted rangers if he believed the Indians were engaged in a general uprising, but made it Smith's responsibility to define what Indian actions constituted a general uprising. Smith gave no indication that he was ready to act.[31]

Davis was not done with the Indian issue. On 27 July, he and a delegation of citizens from other counties west of the Nueces went to Corpus Christi to meet with General Smith to encourage him to use the authority granted him by the Secretary of War. Smith gave them no satisfaction when he told them that he did not believe conditions were dire enough to warrant calling out troops. Davis reported on the meeting to Governor Pease and in that letter fully expressed the ideas about pacifying the frontier that he would hold through the rest of his life. Davis believed that even if the government finally did commit to send mounted troops, the troops would not achieve the desired results. In the end, he thought that the problems of the frontier lay in the "present mode of treating the Indians" and offered a solution. The border settlers could not wait for the Indians to attack. They had to battle them in "their own towns and mountain fastness." The purpose of such warfare would be either the removal or the extermination of the Indians. Treaties and agencies were the "worse kind of humbugs," and "five hundred men so employed with the objection of extermination or removal, would do more good in six months, than five thousand will in as many years."[32]

Apparently, the voters of the border country liked what they saw in the young Davis. Governor Pease also saw him as an asset to the community. In 1854, the governor named E. J. the temporary judge of the Twelfth District. Davis was only twenty-seven years old at the time. It gave him a position with considerable prestige attached and a good salary as well—$1,750 per year. Initially, Davis was unsure that he could keep the judgeship in the special election called for October 1855, and he ran for the position of district attorney. He won this election. Encouraged by his success, he entered the contest for the judgeship in the special election. Again, he was victorious. He subsequently resigned and assumed his place on the court. He now held the job as the popular choice of the people of his district.[33]

The elected judiciary that existed in Texas during the 1850s made it impossible for any officer of the court to avoid continued participation in politics. A district judge had to play a role in politics at the state level. For the first time Davis's name became associated with party leadership, although he remained associated primarily with local issues. Prior to the 1855 judicial election, Davis participated in a meeting of the Democratic Party at Corpus Christi, his first known appearance in a political event outside of his home district. Davis served on the committee of address along with other prominent Democrats, including Forbes Britton, his future father-in-law, and Philip N. Luckett, a Corpus Christi physician who also would play a role in Davis's life later. E. J. drafted the address and endorsed it. For the first time he made his position known on broader political issues of importance at the time.[34]

The report of the Corpus Christi convention responded in part to the recent organization of the Know Nothing Party in Texas and appealed to Democrats and former Whigs to band together "around the banner of Democracy." The Democratic Party, it asserted, offered the most reliable party for "preserving our institutions and government in their original purity and excellence." In terms of specific goals, it endorsed cheap postage and support of freedom of the press. Relative to Texas matters, the delegates praised Governor Pease's plan to create an inexpensive "system" of education for the children of the state. In signing the document, Davis publically placed himself behind the creation of some sort of public school system for the first time. The address of the convention was not as favorable towards Pease's railroad projects and declared irreconcilable opposition to the "doctrine of internal improvements." State support for railroads or any other such enterprises were, in the words of the committee, contrary to good policy, an interference with private enterprise, and opened a door "to fraud and speculations on the treasury." While Davis had earlier praised Pease's ideas to promote a transcontinental railroad, the address reflected the concerns E. J. would have concerning railroads throughout his political career. He wanted them, but he remained suspicious of any plan for state support of such enterprises.[35]

During the next state general election, Davis continued to be active in regional Democratic politics, but he could not be counted as a state party leader. In April 1857, he attended the party's judicial district convention at Laredo. The purpose of the meeting was to decide who to support in the Congressional district nominating convention and also to select delegates to the state convention to be held at Waco. The convention selected Hamilton Bee, another antebellum friend who would play a role in Davis's future, as its nominee for Congress. The delegates chose Davis to be a delegate at the state convention, but Davis did not go to Waco. Judicial duties kept him on the circuit that spring, although he also had yet to show any real interest in participating in Democratic politics at the state level.[36]

While E. J. refrained from active engagement in politics at the state level, he nonetheless demonstrated his political skills as he successfully negotiated the electoral complexities of his border district. In 1856 he had sought reelection to the district judgeship and handily defeated his opponent, Israel B. Bigelow, a former county judge and sometime member of the Red faction. In the two counties whose returns survive,

Davis carried Webb by 350 to 36 votes and Starr by 324 to 40. Davis stood again in 1858 and 1860 and successfully defeated his challengers with overwhelming support. His political success made it possible for him to continue to pursue his career in the law, and he managed to hold on to the district court until after the outbreak of the Civil War. He seemed satisfied with that position and showed no particular ambition for higher office.

As district judge, Davis became acquainted with much of the border country and its problems. He rode circuit within his own district and occasionally sat on the bench at Corpus Christi and San Antonio. A variety of cases were tried in his court, and they show much about life on the border during the 1850s. His decisions also provide further insight into the developing character of Judge Davis. Many of the cases tried in his court involved the numerous conflicting claims to the land titles that were the legacy of the Anglo takeover of land previously held by Spain and Mexico. An example of a typical case was that of the family of Nicholas Carabajal from Goliad County. Carabajal had received a grant of one league of land from the government of the state of Coahuila in 1829. While part of the Carabajal family had occupied at least part of the land, other parts had been claimed by O. P. Hare, then settled by Robert E. Sutton in 1847. Sutton's attorney asserted that Hare had the right to the land based on the state's preemption law allowing settlers the right to settle on and develop vacant lands and his possession of a certificate to the land given by the state land commissioners to Hare. The jury, largely Anglo, found for Sutton. Davis showed his independent tendencies and also his concern with basic ideas of justice when he overruled the jury verdict. Concluding that the evidence presented in the trial did not support the jury's decision, he issued a judgment in favor of the plaintiffs.[37]

Foreclosures, contract disputes, and allegations of misrepresentation and fraud in business and estate matters were other major cases in E. J.'s court. One such case, further reflecting the conditions on the frontier and how they sometimes involved politicians, was that of *A. Glavecke, Administrator v. A. Tijirina*. The case came before the court on a petition for a writ of certiorari from Antonio Tijirina, whose mother had possessed between nine and eleven square leagues prior to her death. His mother, Feliciana, had deeded an undivided part of this property to the firm of Basse and Hord. Elisha Basse was chief justice of Cameron County and named A. Glavecke to be administrator of the Tijirina estate. Antonio charged that Basse and Glavecke had proceeded to plunder the estate, locating Basse and Hord's property in the most desirable and well-developed portion of the estate along the Rio Grande, cutting and carrying timber off the land, and incurring wasteful expenses. With Basse's court being that of first resort, Antonio charged that he had a conflicting interest and appealed to Davis to take up the case. Davis did so and ultimately removed Glavecke as administrator, replacing him with Antonio Tijirina.[38]

The Davis court also heard the usual assortment of criminal cases. Horse theft was the most prevalent complaint and the border contributed unique twists to such crimes. Davis heard one such case at Brownsville in 1857. The case involved Simon Morales, who was charged with stealing two horses in Tamaulipas, Mexico. Morales's attorney asked that the case against his client be dismissed on the grounds that the indictment against him contained no statement that horse theft was a crime in Tamaulipas. Further, he pointed out that state criminal code made no provisions for punishing a party charged with bringing stolen property into the state, knowing it to be stolen. In this case Davis showed his awareness of the complexities of international law, agreed with the defendant, and suppressed the indictment.[39]

One of the more unusual cases that came before Davis's court appeared when he sat in for the judge in the San Antonio District in 1859. In that case the local district attorney indicted the owner of a "tippling shop" for running a game of euchre in his back yard. The plaintiff's attorney asked that the case be thrown out, contending that it was not against the law to play euchre, and no claim had been made that the game involved betting. He also claimed that the district court had no jurisdiction because the indictment stated it was made by the "district" rather than "district court." Finally, he insisted that the law prohibiting any person who kept a public house from allowing a "prohibited" game was unconstitutional because it failed to meet the constitutional requirement that each law passed by the legislature should have one object and it should be stated in the title. The case was complex and presented a serious challenge to the legal knowledge of Davis. Ultimately, he overruled the claim of unconstitutionality and allowed "court" to be inserted into the indictment. The plaintiff then pled not guilty and in the subsequent trial was found guilty and assessed a $10 fine. He did not appeal the ruling.[40]

Davis's performance as district judge showed him to be attentive to the detail of the law and also a judicious interpreter of its meaning. A newspaper report on the performance of the state's judges, which evaluated them on the basis of the fate of appeals of their decisions presented to the state supreme court in its 1858 autumn term, congratulated him on his judicial skills. Of all the district judges at the time, Davis had the best record. Only three cases were appealed, but the supreme court affirmed all of them. The supreme court did not remand or reverse the three cases. The characteristics Davis demonstrated as a judge had already appeared as he carried out his duties as a Treasury agent. They remained central to his basic character, enduring through the rest of his career.[41]

As district judge, E. J. had numerous opportunities to travel across southwestern Texas and get to know its people. In the relatively small legal community of southern Texas, judges commonly continued their private practice while sitting on the bench. The terms of the court left ample time for any judge to deal with other matters as an attorney, and these circumstances produced potential conflict of interest when a judge might find that a matter he was working on came before his court. In such instances the judge stepped down, bringing in a judge from another district to hear the case. These conditions allowed Davis to extend his connections outside of his own district and may have been responsible for a major change in his personal life. In the autumn of 1857, during the November-December Nueces County term of the 14th District, Judge M. P. Morton stepped down to plead a case and Davis filled his position. As a result, Davis spent December in Corpus Christi.

That Christmas in Corpus Christi, a time of numerous social affairs, he met his future bride, the twenty-six-year-old Anne Elizabeth

Forbes Britton, a veteran of the Mexican-American War and an associate of
Sam Houston, would play an important part of Davis's life. Davis would marry
Britton's daughter Lizzie and would adopt a Unionist stance similar to his father-
in-law in the secession crisis. (David and Hariet Condon Collection).

Britton.[42] Anne Britton, or Lizzie as she was generally known, was the daughter of a prominent south Texas politician, Forbes Britton. Her father was a West Point graduate who served in Texas with the 7th Infantry. Like many other veterans, he settled in Texas and in 1850 established a residence in Corpus Christi. There he operated a freight line to Brownsville, opened a store, speculated in land, and practiced law. Among the projects he backed was the construction of the Western Railroad, intended to run from Corpus Christi to El Paso. The road was never constructed, but his ventures generally prospered and by the late 1850s he had emerged as one of the area's business leaders. He also emerged as an important member of the Democratic Party. In 1857, Britton was elected to the state Senate from his district, then reelected in 1859. Politically, he was a close ally of Sam Houston, who named him chief of staff of the state militia in 1860 and also used him in efforts to secure greater protection of the Texas frontier from the federal government.[43]

Britton's daughter reportedly was beautiful enough to turn the heads of most men. A later observer considered her a real Texas beauty, although complimenting her as "no handsomer than her father," who was considered a man of uncommonly good looks. For a young woman in this era, she received a superb education. Her strongly Roman Catholic family sent her to Grand Coteau, Louisiana, in 1854 to attend Sacred Heart Academy. At the time Sacred Heart Academy boarding school attracted young women from around the South. Little is known of Lizzie's education there, although typical women's schools of the time tended to emphasize arts, music, and other skills that would make a good wife. Lizzie may have received this type of education. A family slave recalled that she played the harp, guitar, organ, and piano. On the other hand, evidence suggests that she may have also either obtained or strengthened a personality that was assertive and willing to challenge the status quo. While in school, she and a classmate sent a petition to Congress requesting the nation's lawmakers to consider giving the franchise to women. A marriage to Lizzie Britton was not only a political alliance, it was also the establishment of a partnership with a formidable woman.[44]

Davis married Lizzie Britton on April 6, 1858, bringing to Davis the politician the support of a strong woman who would be reputed to carry great influence with him through the rest of his political career. This image was their marriage portrait. (David and Hariet Condon Collection).

Nothing is known of their relatively short courtship, but Davis clearly was attracted to Lizzie. On 6 April 1858, the couple married in a Catholic ceremony. Dr. Philip Luckett, an associate with Davis in the Democratic Party, was the best man. The groom's other attendants included Lizzie's brother Edward and Davis's own brother Waters. Among others in attendance was another political associate, Hamilton Bee, member of the House of Representatives from Laredo and Speaker of the House in the previous session. The couple set up housekeeping at two homes, one in Corpus Christi and the other in Laredo. The Corpus Christi home was a lumber house, originally built on the Britton ranch and then moved into town. Davis also purchased another home in Brownsville the month before the wedding. During the next year's court sessions, Lizzie went with E. J. to Brownsville. At Brownsville they had their first child. Britton, named after his wife's family, was born on 7 June 1860. Their second, named after E. J.'s brother Waters, was born in Corpus Christi on 15 March 1862.

In his early years Edmund J. Davis established himself as respected leader of the legal community of South Texas. He entered politics and served as a spokesman for local communities at times, but during the 1850s his chief ambition appears to have been to remain a jurist. Had other events not intervened, he may well have spent the rest of his life as a judge. His knowledge and skill may have destined him for a place on the state supreme court or the federal judiciary. Political events, however, rapidly moved in a direction that made that impossible and forced him to action in other arenas. The struggle over slavery that emerged on the national scene and the question of the future of Texas in the Union brought him face-to-face with a personal crisis and forced him to make a decision that transformed his life.

CREATION OF A TEXAS
UNIONIST, 1855–1862

*"I cannot swear to support a Constitution or a Government,
to the establishment of which, my consent, as one of the people,
has not been asked."*

—Edmund J. Davis

Edmund Davis was part of a
rapidly changing political world in the 1850s. When Texas was admitted
to the union in 1845, the nation was involved in a serious sectional crisis
that centered on slavery. The national struggle had an impact on local
politics in Texas. Issues that were in many ways irrelevant to Davis's border community became important across the state. Protection of Southern rights and the right to own slave property came to dominate political
debate. E. J. was able to remain uninvolved in such matters through
the early years of the decade. A majority of Southerners confronted this
question with an answer of secession. During the 1850s pressure grew
for all Texans to conform. This pressure stretched all the way to the
judges in the borderlands. Davis would struggle with his own decision,
reacting to a flow of events over which he had little control. He did not
arrive at the position he took easily, but given the concern for the law
he had already demonstrated, and his own family's nationalistic feelings,
his choice appeared almost inevitable. E. J. Davis chose to support the
Union rather than secession, a choice that changed the rest of his life.

When Davis won his first elective office in 1853 the growing sectional tension over slavery in the western territories was not an item of
importance in his own campaign. Local issues and favorable political connections assured his victory, and he expressed no known views on broader

national issues. As one historian of the period has noted, what mattered in elections was "personality and reputation." Avoiding taking a position was more difficult after 1854. That year a political firestorm broke out surrounding Illinois congressman Stephen Douglas's bill to organize the Kansas and Nebraska territories. Douglas attracted Southern support for this measure by setting aside the Missouri Compromise and allowing each territory to decide whether or not it would accept slavery. The bill's passage provoked strong opposition in the North. An anti-Nebraska party, soon to become the Republican Party, actively opposed Douglas's plan arguing against the extension of slavery into any new territories. The South countered with its own arguments, insisting that any citizen of a state should be allowed to take property anywhere else in the nation, that slave owners had the right to take their property into national territories.[1]

In Texas, politicians were not divided over the idea that slave owners should be able to take their property anywhere in the nation. They did disagree on how best to ensure this right and to protect the South's peculiar institution. One faction insisted that federal law and the Constitution provided ample guarantees and that working through the democratic process ultimately afforded the best assurance of slavery's survival. The alternative position held that more aggressive action was needed, that a measure such as a constitutional amendment affirming the slave holders' rights was required to safeguard slavery. Those who held the latter position were not even certain that an amendment would provide the necessary security. Many concluded that, facing an abolitionist opposition that would ultimately not let the Constitution stand in the way of their efforts to end slavery, the only viable solution to their dilemma was secession.[2]

The latter assessment of the political situation was the one that came to dominate the thinking of leading Democratic politicians in Texas after 1855 and became part of that party's basic ideology as it moved to develop a stronger organization. The party had never created a well-organized machine up to that point because it faced little opposition in Texas. The development of the Know Nothing Party in Texas changed all of that. In 1855, the Know Nothings ran their first slate of candidates for state offices and the Democratic lieutenant governor announced his intention of running for governor on their ticket. Feeling challenged, the Democrats organized. In Austin, on 16 June, Democrats met in their "Bomb Shell" convention. The delegates selected party candidates for office and also announced a platform to which Democrats were expected to subscribe. That platform indicated that the new party organization was in the hands of Democrats who believed that the North must make concessions on the slavery issue or face disunion.[3]

The 1855 state platform established a new political orthodoxy for the Texas Democratic Party and a new ideological test for anyone who considered himself to be a Democrat. The platform began with the party's traditional affirmation of the principle of democratic government, endorsed passage of the Kansas-Nebraska bill, and then went on to make a strident statement of the party's support for the idea of states' rights. The convention's assessment of the threat to the latter principle and the need to respond to that threat was ominous. The delegates maintained that Congress had no right to interfere with the affairs of either sovereign states or their citizens. Nonetheless, they claimed that Northern congressmen had repeatedly done just that. Ultimately, the convention's delegates concluded that these attacks upon the rights of the South had to be stopped. Implicit in the convention was the conclusion that if the agreement inherent in that compact was broken and the basis for the union disappeared, Texas could leave the Union.[4]

Where E. J. Davis stood on these issues cannot be known with certainty since he left no explicit statements on them. He was in essential agreement with them, however, and was an active participant in the Democratic convention at Corpus Christi in 1855 and was a member of its committee of address. The committee's resolutions embraced the new Democratic orthodoxy established at the "Bomb Shell" convention the previous June. It opposed congressional interference with slavery in any territory or state. It also endorsed Stephen Douglas's formula for settling the slavery question in the territories, concluding that the decision should be left to the people living there at the time a territory sought statehood. Indeed, the committee went on to predict that slavery would remain an integral part of the nation and declared its support for "the acquisition of Territory when it becomes necessary for the preservation or protection of our institutions." Davis signed the committee's report.[5]

The next January, Democrats moved even further towards organizing their party upon the basis of a defense of Southern rights. Party leaders met in Austin in preparation for the presidential elections to be held that year, but the platform that they drafted focused largely on defining the ways that they believed the North threatened the rights of the South. They once again asserted the right of Southerners to carry their slaves into any national territory and voiced their approval of the Kansas-Nebraska Act. They offered a catalogue of perceived threats to their rights in which they warned against any efforts to prohibit slavery in the territories, any effort at repealing the Kansas-Nebraska Act, any attempt to restore the Missouri Compromise, repeal of the Fugitive Slave Law, refusal to admit a new state on account of slavery, restriction of the slave trade, or abolition of slavery in the District of Columbia. The threat implied in the 1855 platform was made more explicit. A Northern effort at achieving any of these goals would be seen as an "attempt to trample on the Constitution and dissolve the Union." In such circumstances, the South would owe no further allegiance.[6]

The Texas Democratic Party took a final step towards establishing the defense of Southern rights as a central part of its ideology in events leading up to the 1857 state election. The party held its convention at Waco on 4 May of that year. Party leaders had finally cobbled together a party organization, and for the first time delegates chose party nominees to run for state offices. These nominees had to pledge their support for the party's platform and assure the convention that they were united "with the Democratic Party upon all the issues now existing between them and their opponents." When establishing the basis upon which the party's candidates would run, the delegates turned to the work of the Austin convention held in January 1856. Without modification, they adopted that statement as the platform for 1857 and made the defense of states' rights the test not only of party loyalty but Democratic candidacy for office. The convention also made clear, once again, that the delegates believed any violation by the federal government of this national compact, as they had defined it, would be cause for disunion. Within three years, the Texas Democratic Party had transformed itself ideologically with a platform inferring that any attack upon Southern rights could be seen as the basis for an end of the Union. As to E. J. Davis, once again no statements from him on this question have survived. The people elected Davis to the Waco convention, however, and there is no reason to question that he had changed his positions since 1855.[7]

Davis's loyalty to the Democratic Party made considerable political sense. A Democratic governor, Elisha Pease, was responsible for Davis's first appointment to a public position. His first successful race for office, other than that for city council in Laredo, was as a Democrat. If he was unhappy at all with his party, the new Know Nothing Party, with an anti-Catholic and anti-foreign national philosophy, offered little to attract support from a candidate in a district along the Rio Grande. Election results in 1855 and 1857 showed that most of his constituents considered themselves to be Democrats. Even though Know Nothing candidates polled well in the district in 1855, the Democratic Party's state candidates readily carried it, and Pease, running for reelection as governor, crushed his Know Nothing opponent with 608 votes to 187. That next year in the presidential election, the Democratic candidate was James Buchanan and he did even better than Pease. Buchanan easily defeated Millard Fillmore in Davis's Twelfth Judicial District by 1,390 votes to only 140. Then, in the hotly contested gubernatorial campaign of 1857, the regular Democratic candidate, Hardin R. Runnels, defeated Sam Houston while running as a National Democrat, by a vote of 1,582 to 305. If anything, the Democratic Party's organization appeared to be strengthening its hold in Davis's district.[8]

Davis remained a loyal Democrat at least through the 1857 election. In the years that followed, however, his support for the leadership of the party waned. Why this happened is unclear, although several factors played a role in the transition. At least one matter that concerned him was the situation along the border, where Indian raids and unrest among Mexican Americans threatened stability. The Runnels administration was reluctant to deal with Indian raids and proved incapable of settling the unrest. American Indians had been a long-standing problem, and new raids out of Mexico and by the Plains Indians began shortly after Runnels assumed office. Like his predecessors, Runnels believed that frontier defense was the job of the federal government, and he was unwilling to use state funds for that purpose. When the legislature attempted to create a permanent frontier force, Runnels blocked it. Runnels's states' rights position may have added to the worries of a man concerned with border safety, for secession would have left the frontier without the protection of a central government and in the hands of a state government that had proven reluctant to spend the money. Davis was silent on the governor's policies, but his previous position indicated that he hardly could have approved.[9]

Indians were not the only threat to peace on the border weighing on Davis's mind after 1857. An additional issue with which he became directly involved was the stability of Anglo and Mexican American relations along the border. Events there indicated the possibility of serious upheaval, and without the presence of a strong military force, should secession occur, the region's future could only be seen as uncertain. That event was the Cortina War of 1859. Relations between the Mexicans who had lived along the Rio Grande prior to Texas annexation and the Anglos who moved into the area afterwards were bad, as many Mexicans felt that the Anglos took advantage of their law to cheat them out of their land. Among the discontented was Juan Nepomuceno Cortina, part of a large landowning family in the area. In September 1859, he headed a force of forty to eighty men who rode into Brownsville, intending to seize or kill men he considered responsible for injustices visited upon the Mexican people. Cortina remained only a short time, but from his family's ranch in Cameron County he issued a proclamation on 30 September 1859, that demanded protection of the rights of Mexican Texans and the punishment of the men who violated those rights.[10]

Tensions increased following the September proclamation. After the arrest of one of his men, Cortina threatened to burn Brownsville and on 22 October a force of militia, some local volunteers, and a company of Mexican troops marched against him. By this time, Cortina was said to have nearly five hundred men, and, when the expedition encountered him on 24 October, he routed them, taking the two cannon that they had left behind on their retreat. As conditions worsened, in November state authorities sent more men to the area, ordering Captain William G. Tobin and three companies of volunteer cavalry to Brownsville. Among the men who rode in with Tobin was E. J. Davis, who would experience first-hand the chaos that could break out on the border. After arriving at Brownsville on 8 November, Davis wrote to his brother Waters in Galveston that they had found the town in "great alarm, the streets barricaded, and cannon pointed to sweep in any direction through them." Mexican troops from Matamoros were guarding part of the town and, thinking that Davis's party might be part of Cortina's force, fired upon them. Fortunately, no one was hurt. Davis indicated that the forces at Brownsville intended to "commence operations against the insurrectionaries."[11]

Davis remained in Brownsville during the rest of the month. Major Samuel Heintzelman observed that success had bred greater confidence in Cortina and his followers. He now was convinced that "he could stand his ground against the whole State of Texas." On 22 November the force that Tobin had gathered at Brownsville, including Davis, marched against Cortina again in an effort to "exterminate" him. Two days later, near Santa Rita, seven miles from Brownsville, Tobin and his men ran into entrenchments that Cortina had thrown up and began to receive cannon and small arms fire. Tobin was unable to organize his men for a successful attack, advancing, falling back, advancing again on 25 November. After a consultation, he determined that it was imprudent to attack. Heintzelman noted that the botched attack only contributed to Cortina's reputation. He now flew the Mexican flag in his camp and Mexicans of all classes believed that he would throw the hated Americans back to the Nueces, possibly even to the Sabine.[12]

The situation worsened. In early December, more rangers arrived under John Salmon (Rip) Ford and a force of regular United States troops commanded by Major Samuel P. Heintzelman. Davis played an active role in preparing for a new movement against Cortina. Davis met with the major on 7 December and offered to procure a spy to be sent into Cortina's camp. Heintzelman agreed. Five days later the two met again and Davis provided him with a map of Cortina's position. Heintzelman, accompanied by Davis, moved out of Brownsville on the morning of 16 December with about 150 infantry, two pieces of artillery, and Tobin's rangers. The rangers appeared to have lost much of their spirit as a result of their previous expedition and when the commander tried to get volunteers to reconnoiter the enemy position, he got none from among Tobin's men. Davis stepped in and volunteered to lead the party, at which point several more of the rangers agreed to go with him. When Davis returned, he reported Cortina had abandoned his works. Farther along, the advancing troops encountered Cortina's men, who made several efforts at resistance. Near the Vincente Guerra ranch they used a four-pounder artillery piece firing grape or canister down the road with good effect. Davis, riding alongside Heintzelman, had his saddle pommel taken away by one piece of shot.[13]

Following the battle on 16 December, Davis left the expedition, returning to Corpus Christi, possibly for business of the court. Cortina's uprising had yet to be put down. At Rio Grande City on 27 December a force under Major Heintzelman defeated Cortina in a pitched battle, but failed to capture Cortina. Texas rangers and United States troops remained in the field against him into the following spring. In the end, they never managed to put a complete end to his activities. The message of the Cortina war was clear to anyone on the border. Conditions there were unstable and required the presence of some sort of strong force to keep the peace. The specter of secession that appeared at this time did not promise conditions conducive to peace on the border. Davis had seen the problem first-hand and his experiences probably helped to shape his attitudes against secession in the future.[14]

His father-in-law's own shifting political ties may have influenced Davis. Forbes Britton was concerned with the increasingly radical position of the Democratic leadership. The election of Hardin Runnels as governor placed a strident states' rights advocate in power in Austin with a legislative majority in place holding similar views. They acted aggressively to assert that agenda. In his inaugural address, Runnels frankly stated his support for secession if the question of slavery in the territories was not settled to the South's satisfaction. He placed total blame for friction between the states on Northern radicals who, he concluded, intended to block all efforts at securing the South in its rights and urged the legislature to send delegates to a convention of slave states if needed.[15]

Runnels's controversial pro-Southern stand continued during the subsequent legislative session. He supported and signed into law a measure that allowed free blacks to choose a master and return into slavery, a step towards removing all free blacks from the state. He also supported a legislative resolution that called for a reopening of the slave trade. Even a body dominated by the Democratic Party balked at such a controversial measure, and it failed to pass. Opposition to the reopening of the slave trade appeared to be strong in southern Texas. In 1859, prior to the Democratic convention of that year, a convention in Victoria counseled Democrats to avoid adding such a plank to the party platform. The delegates believed that it would cause the party's defeat, creating internal divisions and distracting people from the real issues. Governor Runnels, however, did not relent in pushing the people of Texas towards a confrontation with the people of the North.[16]

The radical disunionist position of Runnels and other Democratic leaders pushed some Texans towards the position on the Nebraska bill held by Sam Houston, one of Texas's United States senators at the time. Houston believed that the South would be safe only if it remained in the Union and he blamed national and state Democratic leaders for creating friction when they abandoned the Missouri Compromise. Subsequently, he remained a strong nationalist, even praising the Know Nothings for their stand in favor of the Constitution and the Union. As the secessionist element became stronger within the Democratic leadership in Texas, Houston's support also grew. One of the men who moved into Houston's camp was Forbes Britton, Davis's father-in-law.[17]

Britton's political shift appears to have taken place because he had reached the same conclusions as Houston concerning Democratic leaders. Britton emphasized this view in a letter published in a Vermont newspaper in 1859. The editor had urged Britton to run for Congress, endorsing him as a "union-loving, cultivated and *sensible* man" who was willing to compromise and would not allow either Northern abolitionism or "Southern fire-eating and disunionism" to threaten the stability of the Union. Britton thanked the editor, confessed he had no aspiration for office, and then praised the editor for the conciliatory feelings expressed. Britton hoped that these feelings were the "true feelings entertained by the majority of the North and South, for their friends and brethren—separated by only imaginary lines, united by all the ties of feeling and interest—and awaiting but the occasion to call them forth." The threat to the Constitution Britton saw was the same as that perceived by Houston. It was the result of actions by the "sacrilegious hands of blind zealots and reckless demagogues." If these people became too powerful, they had to be stopped, and Britton promised that Texans would join with the people of Vermont to "beat back the Satanic crew, and maintain perpetually the Union, cemented by the blood and wisdom of our forefathers." E. J.'s son, Britton, believed that his father's feelings changed at this time and that Forbes Britton's stance helped to produce that shift.[18]

Dissatisfaction with the Democratic leaders of Texas began to take a new course in preparation for the general election in 1859, when opponents organized themselves to support candidates for office, calling themselves National or Independent Democrats. Davis aligned with this movement, although he refrained from any active campaigning. Their strategy centered on putting Sam Houston back in the governorship where he could resist the disunion sentiments of the regular Democrats. Through the spring of 1859, opponents of the regular Democrats had urged Houston become a candidate. One public letter urged Texans to place Houston back in office where he could "continue to stay the tide of *Disunion,* rebuke *Sectionalism,* war upon *Black Republicanism,* and, above all, fearlessly expose corruption in high places." In May, a gathering of National Democrats at Austin placed even more pressure on Houston to enter the contest and called upon "all freemen who are opposed to the opening of the *African Slave trade, Secession,* and other Disunion issues—all who are friends to the National Democracy . . . [to] unite with us in electing General Sam Houston for Governor."[19]

Houston initially appeared uninterested in running, but on 8 June he announced that he had yielded to his friends and intended to run against Runnels, who the regular Democrats re-nominated. The principles of his campaign were to be the "Constitution and Union." In the subsequent campaign, Houston did not carry out a personal campaign across the state but did circulate his only major address, given at Nacog-doches on 9 July, as a campaign document. In that speech Houston condemned Democratic leaders who proposed to reopen the slave trade and who urged secession to right perceived wrongs at the hands of the North. He also called upon Texans to "stand by the Constitution and the Union." It was time for people to think for themselves at a time "when demagogues would mislead you." In a prophecy that proved all too true, Houston warned his audience that secession would lead to civil war and with it disastrous consequences. In the campaign, Houston became the chief spokesman for those who had concluded that the regular Demo-crats had gone too far and were leading the state, as Houston warned, to a disaster. Davis's later statements indicated that he had come to see the basic political situation much as Houston did.[20]

Houston won his race in the election that followed, defeating Runnels with 36,227 votes to 27,500. It is not clear, however, if Hous-ton's platform of support for the Union was the reason. Other issues, especially local ones, appeared to be equally important in the decision making of voters. Voters possibly cast their ballots *against* Runnels as much as *for* Houston. Runnels's apparent failure to protect the frontier against Indians and Mexicans weighed heavily against him among vot-ers. The result in Davis's Twelfth District, a district much concerned with issues of frontier security, suggested the impact of that perceived failure, and the relative lack of attraction to Houston's position. In the district's four counties, Runnels received only 540 votes, less than a third of the number he had received in 1857. Houston, on the other hand, picked up a few votes and still lost the district. Of those four counties, he carried only Webb, Davis's home county.[21]

Houston won, but relations between the sections continued to deteriorate as the nation prepared for the presidential election of 1860. Events appeared to confirm the arguments of the secessionist radicals, that the North posed a serious threat to the South and its way of life and challenged the hope that people could overcome sectional differences peaceably. Sectional trust received a major blow even before Houston could celebrate his election victory. In October 1859, John Brown's raid on Harper's Ferry stunned Texans. The event seemed to prove that the radicals had been right all along. When Congress assembled that December, the development of a two-month-long struggle over the speakership added to the feeling of hopelessness. These events led to increased radical strength in the legislature and its members elected Louis T. Wigfall, one of the state's most violent secessionists, to the United States Senate. Brown's raid in particular gave the demagogues, about whom Houston had warned in the 1859 canvass, the upper hand.[22]

In the presidential election, Texas Democratic leaders joined the rest of the South in turning the vote into a test of whether or not the North would concede anything to the South. At the Democratic state convention in Galveston in April 1860, the delegates once again adopted resolutions denying the power of the central government to intervene against slavery in the existing states or to prevent its introduction into national territories. They also reasserted their belief that Texas had the right, should the central government stray from its constitutional limits, to "annul the compact, to revoke the powers she has delegated to the government of the United States, to withdraw from the confederacy, and resume her place among the powers of the earth as a sovereign and independent nation." Ominously, the delegates specifically denounced the "unnatural" efforts of the Republican party of the North to war against slavery. If that party should succeed in electing a president, they concluded, the people of Texas should meet with delegates from other Southern states to decide how to protect their rights. Among the options was that they should "secure out of the confederacy that protection of their rights which they can no longer hope for in it." The election of the Republican candidate, Abraham Lincoln, was the signal for action.[23]

Lincoln won, and the state's radical secessionists pushed for immediate withdrawal. Governor Houston managed to delay the movement, but in the end a secessionist majority in the state legislature called a state convention to consider their action. The legislature provided for a special election to choose delegates on 8 January, then for the assembling of a convention at Austin on 28 January 1861. As a judge, E. J. Davis had tried to avoid partisan political statements in the midst of the growing crisis. With the call for a state convention he took his stand and ran for the state convention from Nueces County as an opponent of secession. Davis hoped that the people would elect him to the convention so that he could oppose any radical action on its part. In correspondence with his brother Waters, still in Galveston, Davis asserted his strenuous opposition to secession and resisted his secessionist brother's efforts to convert him. The 8 January election provided for multiple members to be elected, and he faced two prominent opponents. One was Philip Luckett, a groomsman at Davis's wedding and a leading local secessionist. The other was Henry A. Maltby, editor of the *Daily Ranchero* and a strident secessionist. Only the votes for the top two candidates were reported: Luckett received 338, while Maltby secured 264. Davis's totals are not known, but he had failed to gain a seat in the convention where he could help to beat back the secessionists.[24]

When the convention convened on the appointed day, the election of its president signaled the temper of the delegates. Oran M. Roberts had been one of the leading proponents of secession in the days after Lincoln's election, and the convention's members chose him as their president. The choice foretold quick action, and on 1 February, after only three days of deliberation, the convention passed an ordinance of secession that dissolved the connection between the state and the government of the United States. In their declaration of causes that justified their action, the members pointed to developments over the past years that convinced them that the federal government was being used to "strike down the interests and prosperity of the people of Texas and her sister slave-holding States." They made clear the interests being assaulted. The North had become hostile to the South's "beneficent and patriarchal system of African slavery" and embraced the doctrine of equality, "irrespective of race or color" that violated the "experience of mankind" and "Divine Law." To ratify the convention's action, the delegates provided for a special election to be held on 23 February.[25]

However, the delegates did not wait for the 23 February election to act. Even before passing the ordinance of secession, the delegates appointed a fifteen-man Committee of Public Safety and charged it with raising an army to confront the Federal forces stationed within the state. The convention named Ben and Henry McCulloch and John S. (Rip) Ford to head three cavalry regiments and ordered them to seize all Federal installations in the name of the state of Texas. On 15 February, eight days prior to the ratification election, Ben McCulloch moved his regiment to the north of San Antonio with the intention of seizing both the arsenal and the headquarters of national forces that were located there under the command of General David E. Twiggs, a Southern sympathizer. Twiggs surrendered the national forces, even though Colonel C. A. Waite replaced him in his command. Waite, a Unionist, would resist McCulloch's demands.

Davis could do nothing to alter the course of events. Even though he did not support secession, he continued to act as district judge in the period following the convention's action. Court brought him to San Antonio in mid-February 1861, and he and Lizzie were there when McCulloch marched into the city. Davis's position by this time was clear. He believed that there was no cause for the crisis that had occurred and that secession was a mistake. Instead of celebrating Twiggs's surrender, he tried to encourage Southern officers who were in the city to remain loyal. One of these, Robert E. Lee, commander of the 2nd United States Cavalry, arrived in San Antonio and checked into the same hotel as Davis and Lizzie on the day Twiggs surrendered. Lee was on his way to Washington where he was ordered to report to General Winfield Scott. When he entered San Antonio, Lee had been made a prisoner by Texas forces and his baggage seized. Released, Lee remained in San Antonio awaiting transportation to the coast. Davis and Lee sat up night after night, according to Lizzie, to discuss the course of events and the action each individual should take, with Davis trying to convince Lee that his duty lay with the Union. Lee told Davis that he personally was much troubled by what was taking place. Davis recalled that the colonel "shed tears, saying that it [secession] was 'unnecessary, uncalled for.'" Despite his reservations and Davis's pleas, Lee appeared to remain uncertain what he would do. When his coach finally arrived to take him to Indianola, E. J. and Lizzie went downstairs to tell him goodbye. Both Lee and Davis cried as they shook hands, and as Lee departed E. J. said to Lizzie, "He has decided. He will go with his State."[26]

Davis also tried his hand at convincing Edmund Kirby Smith, a major of the 2nd United States Cavalry who had refused to surrender

Camp Colorado to Texas authorities, to remain steadfast as well. Davis had a particular concern for Smith as they had known each other as young men in St. Augustine, where each had been born. Davis felt that Smith, like Lee, was uncertain about what course he should take and Davis appealed to his patriotism, urging him to "stand to the old Flag which his family had followed for several generation." He also warned him that the results of secession would be dire. Like Lee, Smith failed to be persuaded by Davis's entreaties. Davis believed that he was convinced to go with the South by many of his West Point associates who were around him in his regiment.[27]

Davis's position and that of other state officeholders who held pro-Union sympathies became more tenuous following the successful ratification of the ordinance of secession on 23 February 1861. The convention had reassembled on 3 March, and two days later passed an ordinance that united Texas with the Confederate states. Houston had set the course of most Unionists in the early stages of the secession movement. Reluctantly, he had gone along with the convention early in its deliberations. Its action uniting Texas with the Confederacy had been a step too far. Houston informed the delegates that he believed the convention had no legal power to act other than to consider the state's relationship with the Union. In agreeing to connect itself with another confederation it had exceeded its authority. Houston even had his secretary of state inform the Confederate secretary of war that Texas was not a part of the Confederacy, insisting that the state's "pride and dignity did not sanction being annexed to a new government without the state's knowledge or consent."[28]

Delegates to the convention reacted with hostility to Houston's arguments and responded on 14 March with another ordinance that required all state officials to swear an oath of allegiance to the Confederate government. Some Unionists at this point decided that their duty was to support their state and swear the oath, but others refused. The most prominent of the latter was the governor. Called on by the convention to take the oath, Houston sat in his office and refused to answer the call. The members of the convention responded by voting him out of office and naming Lieutenant Governor Edward Clark in his place. Although

Houston gave in rather than continue to resist the secessionists, he issued a broadside explaining his actions. In his message to the state legislature in March, however, he informed the legislators that he believed the authority he had received from the people still remained in his hands.[29]

Judge Davis followed the course of Houston and refused to swear an oath of allegiance to the new Confederacy. On 3 April, he addressed the voters of his district in a document that provided insights into his thoughts at the time and provided the public reasons for his decision. The 3 April address showed how closely Davis's thoughts had come to parallel those of Governor Houston. His principal objection to swearing an oath of allegiance was that the state convention had created an unconstitutional government in the wake of its decision to secede. Further, this unconstitutional government had assumed powers that had not been granted to it when it changed the state's constitution without a vote of the people, then raised an army, began disposing of public property, created offices, and ratified the Confederate constitution (thereby annexing Texas to the Confederacy). The oath they now required was one not to Texas but to the Southern Confederacy. Responding to arguments that the public's vote for secession implied this authority, Davis asked how that could be possible. At the time the people had voted the Confederate government had not even existed. They could not imply this assumed authority, and they had certainly not expressed the authority in the "appointment" of the delegates. Under such circumstances he could not take the oath the convention required. "I cannot swear to support a Constitution or a Government," he explained, "to the establishment of which, my consent, as one of the people, has not been asked."[30]

Correspondence among other Unionists indicated that Davis's position was not one simply excusing opposition to secession. Many expressed the same concerns about the actions of the convention and what it meant for legitimate constitutional government. For a time, it appeared that indignation at the actions of the convention was widespread. Objectively, it did appear to be an unconstitutional seizure of power, and raising the issue publicly did make possible reversing the decision to join the Confederacy possible, even if it did not repudiate secession. Some actually urged Houston to hold on to office and push for the recreation of the Republic. Unionism by this time looked not so much towards reestablishing ties with the Northern states as avoiding a connection with the Southern Confederacy.[31]

Following Fort Sumter and Lincoln's call for troops in April 1861, the position of Unionists became less tenable. They could do little to alter either secession or union with the Confederacy. Instead, in late April and early May a war-like pro-Southern patriotism infected many Texans. The state's rabid Confederates began to suppress all Unionist sentiment. In San Antonio a crowd attacked the offices of the pro-Union *Alamo Express*, edited by James P. Newcomb, and burned the building to the ground. On 22 May, Ben Epperson, a prominent Unionist from Clarksville who had been hopeful that Texas might stay out of a potential conflict, concluded that there was no hope for the Union or avoiding war. Epperson found that the situation in his area changed drastically after Sumter. A military spirit took possession of the population and with it the indignation against the convention had largely died out. The situation demanded that Unionists change their course. Epperson concluded that it was now "impossible to do anything towards a reconstruction." Aware of the violence now aimed at Unionists, he also determined that it was "impolitic to make any effort in that way." Texas was at war and Texas Unionists now had to face new realities.[32]

E. J. Davis had supported the Union; now the changing circumstances forced him to make monumental personal decisions. Some Unionists, like Ben Epperson and James W. Throckmorton, decided to throw their support to their state and the Confederate cause. Others determined to remain at home and sit out the war rather than fight against the people of their state. Initially, Davis appeared ready to follow the latter course. Following his resignation as judge, he remained in Corpus Christi, apparently looking after the interests of his wife's family after her father had died the previous February. By the spring of 1862, however, the ability of men like Davis to remain uninvolved became more difficult. When the initial war spirit died, Texas and Confederate officials began to pursue more drastic measures to maintain the war effort and that involved forcing men like Davis to come to its support.

The measure with the most direct effect on Davis's life was conscription. On 30 December 1861, Governor Francis R. Lubbock took
the first step towards conscription in Texas by declaring all white males
between the ages of eighteen and thirty-five, unless exempted, liable to
military service. Texas thus prepared for a draft even before the Confederate government took that action. Conscription forced men who
did not want to fight into the Confederate army and state officials
quickly discovered that the number of men who did not want to serve
was large. Opposition to forced military service encouraged opposition
to the Confederacy, and, by early March, the commander of the military district along the Rio Grande informed army headquarters that
he perceived "a pretty considerable under-current at work through this
country against our cause." Colonel Henry E. McCulloch reported that
when hearing of Union victories, Union men publicly had said that "we"
had gained a victory. Others worked to destroy the value of Confederate currency, accepting payment in Confederate money at only half its
face value. More critically, in a subsequent letter written on 25 March,
McCulloch reported that many Union men were leaving the country
both to avoid Confederate service and to work against the Confederate
cause. He warned that if the war worsened for the Confederacy, "a considerable element of this character" would have to be "crushed out, even
if it has to be done without due course of law." McCulloch had already
concluded that martial law would be necessary to assert Confederate
authority through much of western Texas.[33]

Other military men agreed. Shortly after he took over command
of the Sub-Military District of the Rio Grande from McCulloch on
24 April, Brigadier General Hamilton Bee proclaimed martial law in the
area extending southward from San Antonio to the Gulf of Mexico and
the Rio Grande. The content of Bee's proclamation is unknown, but it
probably was similar to that made a month later, on 30 May 1862, when
Brigadier General Paul Octave Hébert, commander of the Department of
Texas, extended martial law throughout the state. Hébert ordered every
white male above the age of sixteen years and a resident of the Department of Texas to appear before the local provost-marshal and have his
name, residence, and occupation registered. The proclamation further

ordered the removal of all disloyal persons and all persons "whose presence is injurious to the interests of the country" from the district. Aliens could remain, but only if they swore an oath to abide by and maintain the laws of Texas and the Confederate states and not to act in support of the United States. Hébert's order indicated that even an attempt to "depreciate the currency of the Confederate States is an act of hostility; will be treated as such, and visited with summary punishment." Noncompliance with the proclamation would be "dealt with summarily."[34]

Under such circumstances Davis could hardly remain at peace in Texas. He already had refused to swear an oath of allegiance to the Confederacy. He would never serve in the Confederate army. He now had to determine what course he should pursue. He had remained a loyal Democrat until his party failed to secure the interests of his community. He became a Unionist in 1857 after his disillusionment with the Democratic leadership. Failing to preserve the Union, he sought to remain a loyal Texan. The course of events ensured that he could not retain his political principles and remain in Texas. Rather than change, Davis decided that he had to get away. On 3 May 1862, he left Corpus Christi for the Mexican border in the company of John L. Haynes, a pro-Union member of the Texas House of Representatives from Rio Grande City, and William Alexander, an attorney from Austin. Davis had to leave his wife and sons, Britton and Waters, behind since Waters was still an infant, only two months old. E. J. thought that he might soon return. Davis's party managed to get to Brownsville where they secured passage on a Federal blockader off the coast. Davis boarded the ship *Montgomery*, which carried him to New Orleans and new experiences.[35]

Davis's political and ideological journey took a new direction with his departure to Mexico. He now faced the question of what action he would take after opposing politicians had forced him from his home. These politicians espoused a cause that he not only could not support but that he considered unconstitutional. He could have sat out the war in Mexico or the North, waiting to see its results. Davis already had shown himself to be a man of action. He had left home at a young age to seek out new opportunities along the Mexican border. He had rapidly advanced his career through his active pursuit of a legal career and public position. He had not refrained from breaking with and criticizing the leaders of the party that had provided him his first access to office. He would not sit by and remain uninvolved in a war that he had never sought. Shortly after arriving at Matamoros he let representatives of the United States government know that he was interested in returning to Texas and bringing the state back into the Union. As a result, he would enter into a new phase of his life as a soldier of the Union Army, as one of Abraham Lincoln's fighting men.

CHAPTER 3 CIVIL WAR SERVICE

"I ask them to give me a command in the field."
—E. J. Davis, 1865

Davis left Texas for New Orleans, headquarters for Union forces under General Benjamin Butler, after the Union captured that city the previous April. He made it clear that he wanted to fight for the Union cause. In particular, he wanted to lead a Union force back into Texas. They gave him the opportunity to fight, but he would find his goal of carrying the war back to his home state thwarted. Nonetheless, from 1862 to 1865 Davis found himself fighting as a part of the Union Army. These years further molded his character, particularly strengthening his pro-Union stance. They also deepened his mistrust of the politicians in Texas who he believed had caused the war. Indeed, it is likely that he felt considerable anger, perhaps even hatred, for these men. Davis controlled his emotions and never admitted to such feelings, but his behavior during the postwar years would indicate that he did not emerge from the war without emotional scars.

Shortly after he arrived in New Orleans, Davis met with federal authorities and shared his plans to recover Texas. In early August 1862, he journeyed to Washington where he met with President Abraham Lincoln and asked that the government provide arms for the Unionists in Texas. Davis assured the president that there were enough Unionists in the state to defeat Confederate forces and that he could recruit enough of them to gain control over the Rio Grande country and possibly the area up to the Nueces River. Such a force might be able to move even as far as San Antonio and could swiftly re-inaugurate "National Authority." He asked for 2,500 to 3,000 weapons. Lincoln appeared interested in the plan but promised no help. Instead, he sent Davis to Secretary of War Edwin M. Stanton with a letter asking him to consider the proposal. Davis found Stanton had little interest, and left believing that the administration was more concerned with prosecuting the war in the East than engaging in any other movements.[1]

Stanton was not supportive of a Texas invasion, but he did encourage Davis to move forward with his plans to raise troops among refugees. In their meeting the secretary asked Davis, "And are you a southern man?" Davis replied, "Yes sir, this is my first trip north." In turn, Stanton asked, "And you say you have a regiment of Texans to muster into the service of the government?" "Yes sir," Davis replied. "How soon can you return to New Orleans?" Davis answered, "Immediately, to-day." Stanton officially authorized Davis to form the regiment, and Davis returned to New Orleans to undertake that task. Other Texas refugees, including John L. Haynes and Andrew Jack Hamilton, remained in Washington to lobby for a Texas invasion. In the end, the administration never warmed up fully to the idea and the Texans would have had to rely on help from the military to secure their end.[2]

Davis, on his return to Louisiana, immediately set about organizing Texas refugees into a fighting force. He received authorization from the local commander, General Butler, to recruit a cavalry regiment, which would become the 1st Texas Cavalry, U. S. Volunteers. He also was appointed colonel. A newspaper advertisement published in New Orleans at the time called upon all men interested in joining the Texas regiment to contact Davis at the Park Hotel on the city's Lafayette Square. He indicated that the government would provide the men of the regiment with the weapons and accoutrements necessary for a unit of mounted rifles. However, initially they would not be mounted. Instead, Davis promised that the regiment would be "supplied with horses in Texas," suggesting that he remained hopeful for a Texas invasion. Indeed, General Butler was planning an incursion into the state, despite the lack of support at Washington, and Davis would play a role.[3]

On 12 November, Butler revealed his plan to capture and occupy Galveston Island to the United States consul at Matamoros. He proposed

In November 1862 E. J. Davis's break with Confederate Texas was made final as he was commissioned colonel and authorized to raise a Union regiment composed of Texas refugees. He is shown here in his colonel's uniform as commander of the 1st Texas Cavalry. (David and Harriet Condon Collection).

taking the island, placing Texas troops there to hold it, and sending refugees from Texas there. To acquire more recruits for the Texas regiment he proposed sending Davis to Mexico to appeal to the refugees. Davis was not to enlist men at Matamoros because that would be a violation of Mexican neutrality. Instead, he was to send anyone who wanted to serve to New Orleans to be sworn in. Davis soon returned to Mexico where he spent two months gathering men for his unit. Shortly after Davis left for Mexico the plan encountered potential trouble when General Butler was replaced by General Nathaniel Banks. Banks, however, concluded that the plan was viable and ordered an expedition to take Galveston later that month.[4]

While Davis was in New Orleans and Mexico, events in Texas added to the flow of refugees and possible recruits and also provided ample reason for Davis and other refugees to harden their feelings towards Confederate authorities in Texas. Within Texas, Confederate officials had imposed conscription and that had led to resistance to the draft and a growing antiwar sentiment in the spring of 1862, with many Unionists leaving the state. Mounting pressure on Texans to proclaim their loyalty to the Confederate cause had forced Davis to leave the state in March. That insistence had only increased in the following months. On 30 May 1862, Brigadier General Paul Octave Hébert, commander of the Department of Texas, proclaimed martial law throughout the state. That proclamation required the registration of all men above the age of sixteen, the swearing of oaths of loyalty by alien residents, the removal of disloyal persons from the district, and the prosecution of those who undermined the Confederate cause. Hébert promised that those who failed to comply with the provisions of the proclamation would be "dealt with summarily."[5]

In the months that followed, Confederate authorities acted aggressively against any sign of disloyalty. In the German-populated counties of the Texas Hill Country, officials sent in troops to suppress loyalist organizations. In May, a company of Confederate troops was sent into Gillespie County, where its commander declared martial law, dismissed the local militia company led by a Unionist, and required all avowed Unionists to appear at the county seat and swear an oath of allegiance to the Confederacy. In subsequent days the command at Fredericksburg carried out numerous atrocities against the local population, including the murder of those suspected of anti-Confederate sentiments. In August, the same Confederate command pursued a party of German unionists attempting to flee to Mexico, attacking them on the morning of 10 August in their camp along the Nueces River. They left few survivors in a battle that local Germans considered a massacre. The fate of the men on the Nueces was not an uncommon one for Unionists throughout the state.[6]

Confederate officials also used the courts to intimidate and punish those with Unionist sentiments. Anyone suspected of Unionist sympathies was subjected to increased scrutiny. In the summer of 1862, Confederate authorities established military commissions authorized to arrest and try anyone accused of disloyalty. These courts did not hesitate to execute their charge and busily set about making arrests and holding trials. For example, Edward Degener, a prominent German merchant in San Antonio, was arrested and charged with having failed to give information on the existence of bands of men trying to escape to Mexico, having written exaggerated and slanderous statements designed to bring the Confederate government into disrepute, and having corresponded with armed enemies of the Confederate States. Degener was found guilty and let go, but only on the grounds that he posted five thousand dollars against his future behavior. Other Unionists were not so fortunate and found themselves forced into the Confederate army or imprisoned.[7]

Even those who left the state had not gotten beyond the reach of Confederate authorities. Many properties were confiscated under the Confederate Sequestration Law. The Confederate Court for the Western District of Texas began trying such cases during its first session, beginning on 6 January 1862. In the next three years Judge Thomas J. Divine, judge of that court, presided over 2,774 cases. All of these but twenty-four involved the seizure of the property of those who had left the state rather than support the Confederacy. While many of these cases involved the property of Northern merchants and land speculators, other cases involved the property of the Unionists who tried to keep the state from seceding. The courts disposed of both real and personal property, selling it to the highest bidder. Union loyalists saw their assets liquidated overnight.[8]

For Edmund Davis, Confederate persecution took on a particularly ominous personal tone. He had little choice but to leave his family in Texas when he escaped in May, only two months after Lizzie had given birth to their youngest son Waters. Ordinarily Confederates would not bother his family, but in those times Confederate authorities could mistreat even the families of men seen as traitors. In August, Lizzie approached an old family friend, General Hamilton Bee, commander of the sub-district of the Rio Grande, for a pass to leave the state. Bee provided the document, but when Lizzie arrived at Brownsville she met Colonel Philip Luckett, another friend. Luckett advised her that Bee had told him that Mrs. Davis had no pass, and that if she arrived at Brownsville she was to be sent back to Corpus Christi immediately. When she protested that the trip had so fatigued her that if she returned immediately, "it *would kill me*," the former groomsman at her wedding replied, "it makes no *difference* whether *you* are *killed one way or another,* and if you attempt to cross the River, you will be *shot,* and your body will float down the river, and be like so many deserters, you will never be heard of again!"[9]

Lizzie returned to Corpus after a grueling five-day-trip, in the company of a Confederate paymaster. The Confederate officer was told to keep close watch on the Davis family and not to stop at any ranches or houses on the way. At home, Lizzie received further communications from Bee, informing her that if her husband came to Texas with an army she would be sent into the interior. Later, Bee informed her of rumors that Davis did intend to return and to rob the citizens of their property and that if he did, "*I must be prepared to have my throat cut first.*" Her reply was an appropriate one for a woman of the frontier. She told the general that when her husband came she would be prepared and the general might "*come and cut it!*"[10]

Despite the blockade, messages did move back and forth through battle lines. E. J. was aware of much that transpired with his wife. Despite the failure of Lizzie and the children to escape at Brownsville, Davis worked to effect a reunion. In September another effort was made to get the family out of Texas. On 12 September 1862, the U.S.S. *Arthur* arrived at Corpus Christi and delivered a request from Admiral David G. Farragut that Mrs. Davis be allowed to board the ship and leave. The local commander refused, although he forwarded the request to General Bee. As in August, the general refused to allow Lizzie and the boys to leave. Further negotiations ended when the commander of the *Arthur*

Lizzie Davis was a woman of the frontier and her ordeal during the early years of the Civil War showed her toughness. She found herself persecuted even by family friends, yet she refused to be subjugated by them. This image of Lizzie comes from the war years. (David and Harriet Condon Collection).

attempted to land a force below Corpus Christi and was captured. At that point the *Arthur* withdrew.[11]

Lizzie made her own plans, and in December she secured a pass that allowed her to travel to Brownsville, but did not authorize her to leave the state. The family's possession of property in that town may have made the new pass possible. She was determined that on this trip she would leave, despite lacking official permission. The family arrived on the border on 23 December and spent the night at the home of a friend. Reducing her baggage to a carpetbag that contained one change of clothes for each of the children, she wrapped herself in a Mexican blanket and, with friends carrying the children, walked to the Rio Grande ferry on Christmas Eve. The guards at the ferry did not question her identity, assuming her to be a family member of the friends that accompanied her. Stepping off the ferry on the Mexican side of the river, she recalled that she "drew a long breath, and said, 'Is it possible I am free?!'" The ordeal had been a traumatic one, and Davis's family did not forget what had happened.[12]

Lizzie did not find her husband at Matamoros. The colonel was in New Orleans preparing for the occupation of Galveston. On the day that Lizzie had crossed the border into Mexico, a small Federal force had landed on the island and taken possession of that town. Only two companies of the 1st Texas were equipped and, along with Davis, these companies boarded the steamship *Cambria* bound for Galveston to reinforce the Union troops that had landed. They arrived off Galveston harbor on 2 January 1863, ready to return to Texas soil but never landed. On 1 January, Confederate troops had recaptured the island. The blockading force was unaware of the Confederate return, and on 3 January, Confederates tried to lure the *Cambria* into the harbor to capture the Texans on board. The plan was foiled when men aboard the Cambria recognized the pilot sent to guide the ship across the Galveston bar as a Confederate sympathizer. Discovering that Union forces had lost the town, the *Cambria* withdrew. Davis and his men returned to New Orleans to await another try at returning to their home state.[13] Back in New Orleans the 1st Texas joined the Union Army's Nineteenth Corps, a part of the defensive forces arrayed around New

Orleans. Davis took a quick trip to Washington, then returned to New Orleans where he renewed his efforts at recruiting a full regiment. There he found that Andrew J. Hamilton, now a brigadier general, had secured the resources needed to transport refugees and potential recruits from Matamoros to New Orleans. Davis requested permission to accompany the transports to Mexico to help bring out the refugees. He went while on leave for he had personal business to take care of there as well. On 8 March, Davis arrived at Matamoros and finally reunited with Lizzie, Britton, and Waters.[14]

We can only surmise Davis's relief at the safety of his family and the happiness of the reunion. In fact, once E. J. arrived he had little time for family matters. He found over a hundred recruits for the 1st Texas gathered in Matamoros. The Union fed, clothed, and provided these recruits a bounty of fifty dollars by the American consul there in anticipation of their joining the Union Army. Many of these men had deserted from the Confederate command at Fort Brown, a fact that reflected the growing discontent with the Confederacy among many Texans. Davis arranged for their departure and on 13 March he led them to the town of Bagdad at the mouth of the Rio Grande. They were to board a steamer for New Orleans, but rough seas delayed their embarkation. Their position, across a narrow river channel from Confederate forces, made them a tempting target.[15]

Confederate authorities were aware of Davis's arrival at Matamoros, but were not certain why he had come. Rumors circulated in Brownsville that he had brought the first contingent of an invasion force and was prepared to move into Texas. General John B. Magruder, commander of the District of Texas, had heard that Davis had brought military equipment with him for the purpose of raising the people on the border against the Confederates and occupying the frontier. Brigadier General Bee believed that Davis was the "proved originator of all the troubles on this frontier." Confederate officials were worried and wished to stop whatever Davis was doing. Their hostility towards the colonel was patent. A Brownsville correspondent of the *San Antonio Herald* summed up the extent of the anger directed at Davis when he wrote, "Judge Davis has come to a bad place for his health, for if he should fall into the hands of any of our soldiers, they would hang him to the first tree."[16]

The small Confederate force placed across the Rio Grande from Bagdad to prevent Federal troops from crossing the river could see Davis and the refugees. They were close enough that the men exchanged insults. One Confederate picket reported that the Texas refugees delivered a "series of indignities which were very provoking." The tension between the sides was high, and the Confederate commander worried that his men might try to cross the river and attack the men who had "brought so much disgrace on Texas." General Bee, aware of the diplomatic dangers of such an effort, tried to maintain calm and personally visited the picket, warning them not to communicate with the Yankees and stay on their side of the river. Bee's admonition was either not taken seriously or was never meant to be taken seriously. On morning of 15 March the men did exactly what he warned them not to do, crossed the river, and attacked the refugees on Mexican soil.[17]

At about three A.M. on Sunday, a party of what was officially described as "citizens and soldiers off duty" crossed the river and attacked Davis's camp. The Federal recruits fought back and in the ensuing melee the Confederate raiders killed or captured about a dozen Unionists. Colonel Davis was in a house with his wife, and when surrounded and ordered to surrender, he gave up rather than endanger Lizzie. The Confederate raiders made it clear that their intention was to lynch Davis. One of the participants reported that Lizzie intervened for E. J.'s life, and the leader of the attackers promised that he would ensure that E.J. was delivered alive to General Bee. Having captured Davis, the Confederates headed back for the river about six A.M. A small party of Mexican soldiers tried to stop them and a skirmish followed in which several of the Texans were wounded.[18]

Elizabeth Davis's intervention may have been all that saved Davis from a quick death, although exactly what determined the fate of the captives cannot be known. The attackers clearly had murderous intentions in marching across the Rio Grande. As soon as they returned to Texas, they separated into two parties. One took Colonel Davis and three other captives with it. The second took Captain William W. Montgomery, an officer with the 1st Texas and a refugee from Caldwell County. The party that took Montgomery lynched the captain soon after the two separated. Given the feelings toward what local newspapers called the "notorious traitors and renegades," this was not unexpected. The party that took Davis, however, hid him, apparently in an effort to prevent military authorities from taking him. Their exact plans are unknown. In the end, Davis remained alive.[19]

General Bee's prediction that an attack on Davis would have diplomatic repercussions was realized quickly. Texas officials heard that the Mexican army might even cross the border and strike in retaliation for the raid. In Matamoros, Texas refugees marched by torchlight through the city streets protesting the Confederate action. The governor of Tamaulipas sent a protest, demanding return of the captives. Albino López condemned the incident, complaining that it was not the only violation of Mexican neutrality that had taken place. Conceding that General Bee had not ordered the attack, López called for the perpetrators to be censured and punished. He also asked Bee to show his good intentions and release Davis. Confederate authorities faced a difficult situation. While they did not fear Mexican military action, they were concerned that the border might be closed to the critical cotton trade. When Bee finally located Davis he released him to Mexican authorities. The editor of the *San Antonio Herald* praised Bee for his action, even though it believed "any Texan would be justified in shooting [Davis] down like a dog, should he be found voluntarily upon our soil."[20]

Once freed, Davis rejoined Lizzie in Matamoros; then the family sailed for New Orleans. Lizzie and the boys remained with E. J. for a short time, then left for Maryland where they stayed with relatives for the rest of the war. Davis rejoined his regiment, and in May, he had his first opportunity to fight. He was given command of a raiding party consisting of five companies of the 1st Texas along with companies from the 6th Michigan and 128th New York. Their goal was Confederate facilities along the Amite River in Louisiana. Davis's command rode from New Orleans to Hammond's Station on the Jackson Railroad. There they burned a shoe factory and railroad bridge and destroyed Confederate encampments nearby. From Hammond they moved on to

In April, 1863, Lizzie Davis had escaped from Texas after a harrowing journey and E. J. had avoided a lynching at the hands of Confederate raiders along the Mexican border. They journeyed together to New Orleans from Matamoros, at which time this picture was taken. (David and Harriet Condon Collection).

Tangipahoa where they burned the depot and another bridge. Upon leaving that place, they encountered their first significant opposition. Davis sent his men against five companies of Mississippi and Louisiana cavalry and scattered them. One soldier on the expedition reported that when the Union forces moved into action, the Confederate line quickly fled. The return to New Orleans saw Davis's column destroy more railroad facilities. His commander judged the expedition a success. Davis's cavalrymen had proven themselves in their first fight, and E. J. had shown his ability to command forces larger than a regiment.[21]

Now actively engaged against his enemy, Davis still hoped that he would return home to fight. He continued to push political and military leaders for that opportunity. In July 1863, he returned to Washington. This time he went accompanying five hundred Confederate prisoners being moved to Northern prisons. His own command consisted of one hundred convalescents taken from the hospitals at New Orleans who were being sent to hospitals elsewhere. He carried out his assignment, then remained in Washington for several days to meet with friends. He lobbied for the Texas invasion, and on 15 July met with his old friend Samuel Heintzelman, now a brigadier general. He regaled the general with the story of his escape in Texas and also complained about the difficulties he encountered gaining support for a Texas campaign. Everyone listened sympathetically, but he received no promise of a Texas expedition.[22]

In fact, a Texas campaign was already in the offing. In July, unknown to Davis, officials in Washington ordered General Banks to prepare such a campaign. Their goal was to place troops between Mexico and the Confederacy, avoiding any potential complications to the war effort that might result from the establishment of a French-controlled government in Mexico. Banks did not have to be convinced of the value of moving against Texas. He believed the destruction of the Texas economy would shorten the war. He was convinced that "the rebellion in Louisiana is kept alive only by Texas." He immediately initiated planning for the expedition.[23]

Banks's second invasion involved landing troops at Sabine Pass, the entry to the Sabine River. Banks believed a force could move overland rapidly from there to Houston, approximately seventy miles to the west. When Houston fell, Galveston would also surrender and the invasion force could then move down the coast towards the Rio Grande. He named Major General William B. Franklin to lead the expedition with a force consisting primarily of men of the Nineteenth Army Corps, which included Davis and the 1st Texas Cavalry. On 4 September 1863, Davis and two squadrons of the 1st Texas boarded transports at Algiers for another trip to Texas. Escorted by five gunboats, twenty-two steamers arrived at the mouth of the Sabine on 8 September.[24]

As the Yankee fleet entered the river, they found a small earthworks fort. The gunboats moved past the transports to engage the Confederate defenses. The 6,000 Union soldiers on the troop ships soon witnessed one of the United States Navy's most embarrassing defeats. Although containing only six guns serviced by no more than forty artillerymen under a Houston barkeeper, Lieutenant Richard W. Dowling, the Confederate fort was in an excellent position to defend the river. Dowling's men proved good shots and disabled the U.S.S. *Sachem* when a shot broke a steam pipe. Unable to control the vessel, the crew surrendered. In the western channel the Federals had equally bad luck when a shot holed the boiler on the U.S.S. *Clifton,* forcing its commander to ground it and surrender. Franklin, even though far outnumbering Dowling, decided to return to Louisiana. Colonel Davis and the First Texas had sailed to Texas once again without being put ashore.[25]

Banks was not through with Texas, however, and Davis and his men had little rest before becoming part of a third campaign. This time Banks determined to take his army up Bayou Teche from the vicinity of today's Morgan City to modern Lafayette. It would then move to the Sabine River at Niblett's Bluff, near the town of Vinton. When the army moved, Davis was present but in a new capacity. In September, General Franklin had named him commander of a cavalry brigade consisting of the 1st Texas and 1st Louisiana. The brigade's first combat would take place when it encountered a superior force of Confederate cavalry near New Iberia. Sharp fighting occurred at Nelson's Bridge on 4 October, at Vermillion Bayou on 9 and 10 October, and finally at Carrion Crow Bayou on 14 and 15 October. Division returns indicated that in these fights Davis's command did well. They suffered only slight losses and captured forty prisoners. Davis had once again demonstrated his skills as a commander.[26]

The Teche campaign had just begun when Davis and the First Texas were separated from their advancing column and returned to New Orleans. Davis and the unit received orders to prepare for yet another expedition to Texas. On 24 October, General Banks informed President Lincoln of his new plan, one already in operation. While moving infantry overland towards Texas through Louisiana, he also planned a lodgment somewhere along the Texas coast. Naval forces scouting the coast had indicated such a move was possible and Banks thought the results would be significant. In fact, when he wrote to Lincoln the plan was already in motion. On 23 October about 3,500 men sailed with orders to land somewhere between the Sabine and the Rio Grande. The First Texas was the only cavalry assigned to the expedition. Davis was along, but this time he had the title of commander of cavalry.[27]

Davis and his men sailed for Texas one more time, this time in the company of General N. J. T. Dana's Thirteenth Corps. They left Carrollton, Louisiana, on 23 October and landed at Brazos Santiago on 3 November. The landing went badly because of heavy surf. The first waves of men were thrown in the water when their boats capsized, losing their equipment. Many of the horses drowned. Only 200 Texas cavalrymen reached the shore that evening. Having lost arms, horses, and equipment they remained unsupported through the night. Fortunately for them, the Confederates made no effort to attack. The infantry followed the Texans the next day, wading ashore in water up to their armpits. They walked onto the beach, according to one report, without a single dry cartridge in the entire division. A Confederate agent in Matamoros later complained that the invasion could have been repulsed if it had met any resistance. Having survived, the Federal column began moving down the coast to the rear of Brownsville.[28]

General Bee, commander of Confederate forces at Brownsville, had few troops to repel the invasion. One resident believed that the general had only one regiment of infantry in the town and their duties generally had consisted of "standing guard, eating, drinking, gambling, answering roll call, drawing their monthly stipend (specie) and chasing men who were trying to get into Mexico to keep out of the army." Bee's cavalry did harass the advancing Union columns and one Federal recalled, "They were not long in letting us know that they had the best and first right to that land." However, the Confederates were overmatched numerically and could do little but delay the Federal movement forward. Bee abandoned the town without a fight, ordering his men to push their artillery into the Rio Grande, set fire to the enormous stores of cotton gathered for export, then burn the government buildings at Fort Brown. One of the first Union soldiers into the town observed that the "Rebels had skedaddled and attempted to fire the town." The explosion of the magazine at the fort damaged almost every house in town.[29]

Unbeknownst to Colonel Davis, he played a part in creating the chaos in Brownsville. Panic spread through the civilian population when they heard that Davis was part of the landing force. Rumors quickly spread through the town that he was leading "Ten thousand drunken negro troops" towards the city. Davis was supposed to be heading for Brownsville determined that it would be "pillaged and burned and the inhabitants put to the sword in retaliation for the hanging of Colonel Montgomery." Davis, of course, was not in command of any black troops and had no plans for retaliation. Rather than riding directly for Brownsville, the Texas cavalry, at least the part still with horses, screened the Union army's march. Davis and thirty of his men rode as an escort to General Banks. The Federal column took two days to move the fifteen miles from the mouth of the river to the town, finally arriving on 5 November.[30]

One of the purposes of this expedition was the creation of some sort of loyal government. Earlier President Lincoln named former congressman and now Union Army General Andrew Jack Hamilton as the state's military governor. Hamilton had awaited the opportunity to set up a government and he arrived at Brownsville shortly after its fall. There he proclaimed restored state government, and Mexican authorities immediately recognized it. On 6 December, when Hamilton crossed to Matamoros to meet with Mexican officials, he was greeted with "a grand national Salute of 15 guns." Colonel Davis played no role in the new government, but one of its first acts was of particular importance to him.

On 18 December searchers located the body of Captain Montgomery, Davis's companion when captured on 15 March 1863. Montgomery's body was brought to Brownsville for a public funeral on the town square. Soldiers from the First and Second Texas Cavalry, a large number of soldiers from the garrisons, and the Masons of the town crowded the square. Governor Hamilton delivered a eulogy full of praise that convinced everyone that Iowan "Montgomery was a patriot." The inscription on the headboard placed on his grave probably expressed the sentiments of Davis and the other Texas Unionists well. It noted the kidnapping of Montgomery from the Mexican side of the Rio Grande and that he was "most shamfully [sic] murdered by the traitors H P Bee, Lucket, Chilton, Bowin, Dick Taylor and the miserable wretches under him."[31]

Davis had little to do with the new state government. The campaign's military goals kept him busy. Once again he would find many of his ambitions disappointed. A major objective of the invasion was cutting off the extensive trade that passed across the border between Mexico and Texas and also, if possible, initiating a movement into the interior. Governor Hamilton believed that the Confederates would quickly abandon all of Texas west of the Colorado River. He intended that Davis and his cavalry would play a major role in this effort, and Davis had already planned a movement into the interior. The colonel wanted to expand the size of his cavalry force, then carry out large scale raids to the north. Success would not be easy. He later advised his commander that the raids would require the creation of "strong, and well-equipped cavalry forces," and he believed that he would need at least 2,500 men. Part of his job was raising the needed manpower. From the beginning that task proved frustrating.[32]

Davis early encountered problems that did not promise good results. As soon as the landing had been made, Banks had asked for more cavalry. Military officials in Washington were not interested in expanding operations in Texas and those troops never came. This meant that whatever force Davis commanded would be raised, for the most part, locally. To that end, Banks had authorized the recruiting of two Texas units in addition to the 1st Cavalry. The first was the Independent Company of Partisan Rangers, which had begun mustering in men shortly after the Federals arrived at Brownsville. Their commander was a Confederate deserter, Adrian J. Vidal. The other was the 2nd Texas Cavalry, which began recruiting on 15 December. Command was given to John L. Haynes, Davis's fellow-refugee in 1862. It was left to Davis to bring these units up to combat strength. On 3 December, Major General Dana named Davis General Superintendent of Recruiting Service for the Rio Grande country. Dana's order gave Davis authority over all other recruiting officers at work in the area and allowed him a free hand at bringing in men to serve. He would achieve some success at this task, but none of the units in question ever reached their full quota of men.[33]

The extent of Davis's problem was apparent when the 1st Texas arrived at Brownsville and mustered only 260 men. A typical regiment had at least a thousand. Initially Davis recruited primarily among Union refugees in Mexico and his recruiting parties also worked up the Rio Grande. Word also was sent to refugees who had fled into the interior of Mexico, and by December parties of these men had begun to arrive. While his command's strength improved, the numbers remained inadequate for the planned campaign's needs. Davis then turned more of his efforts towards recruiting Mexicans, but they did not respond in the numbers expected. Davis discovered that word of the treatment of those who had signed up discouraged others from joining. He found that the Union promised Mexican recruits a bounty on enlistment but the bounty was not paid. As a result, they felt "badly treated." Enlistees also lacked supplies; men who had been in the army for two months had not yet received shoes. By February, Davis increased his force to only about a thousand men. Still, he remained hopeful. Anticipating a move into the interior, he urged his commander to consider converting some of his infantry regiments into cavalry.[34]

Recruiting men was only one of Davis's problems. He also had trouble equipping the men who enlisted. After three months in Texas he was not able to secure enough horses to outfit his men. Davis embarked with nearly nine hundred horses when the expedition began at New Orleans, but, because of bad management aboard the transports, the long voyage, problems in disembarking, and problems of finding forage, upon landing, many had been lost. Others were not fit for service. When his men escorted General Banks to Brownsville the horses of ten of the thirty men played out. His plan always had been to find horses in Texas, but that proved impossible. For two years the border country suffered a drought that left many of the local animals useless. When he obtained horses he could not feed them. One source of horses was in the Mexican interior, but Davis believed that because they were smaller than those used by the Confederate cavalry they would not match up and would be useless on the intended raid. By February he had only two hundred serviceable horses.[35]

Davis's men also lacked basic military equipment. The expedition had brought enough supplies to outfit a thousand men. This included saddles, bridles, weapons, and ammunition. When the landing parties encountered difficulty going ashore most of this equipment was sent back to New Orleans. Some of these supplies were lost when one of the boats sank. By December, none of this equipment had been sent to Texas—nor an additional three hundred sets of ordered equipment. As a result, Davis's soldiers armed themselves with what they could find. Davis reported his men possessed both old and new pattern Sharps carbines and also Burnside carbines. The commander of the Thirteenth Corps hardly understated the situation when he described the Texas cavalry as "destitute." Davis complained of the "strange neglect" his command experienced.[36]

Davis determined to move despite all these problems. In November, he used the few men at his disposal to probe Confederate positions along the border. His force, consisting of the 1st Texas accompanied by men of the 37th Illinois Infantry and a detachment of artillery, moved up river to Rio Grande City. Davis had heard that one of his old friends from Brownville, Santos Benavides, had a force at Ringgold Barracks and he intended testing its strength. The Texans moved overland, while the infantry went upriver on the steamer *Mustang*. The cavalry reached the old army post on 25 November, long before the infantry on the boat, which had grounded on a sandbar thirty miles down river. They found Benavides had abandoned the position. Davis did seize eighty bales of cotton found there. His men marched back to Brownsville with little else accomplished.[37]

For Davis the expedition up the Rio Grande was discouraging for more reasons than his failure to find Benavides. Davis found that the country around Rio Grande City and then south to the Mexican town of Camargo was bare of supplies. The little corn that was available was expensive. This meant that a force moving into the interior of Texas would not be able to forage along the way. It would have to carry its own supplies. This argued against quick cavalry raids and forced Davis to delay his planned attacks into Texas indefinitely. While he had managed finally to return to Texas soil after the frustrated Galveston and Sabine Pass expeditions, Davis found his personal goal of confronting the Confederacy at home frustrated once again.[38]

Facing conditions that delayed a march into Texas, Davis turned to other methods of undermining the Confederacy. His exact purposes are not known, but he shifted his efforts into developing an alliance between Juan Cortina, a man he had faced in 1859, and the Federal forces. When the Federals arrived at Brownsville they found that Cortina was once again creating trouble. At the time he was commander of the Mexican garrison at Matamoros and Confederate authorities believed he was working against them. They saw his hand in matters in late October when a company of Confederate soldiers under Captain Arian J. Vidal mutinied and "raised the standard of Cortina." The Federals believed that Cortina could help them, and General Banks, Governor Hamilton, and Colonel Davis all met with him. Davis in particular thought that Cortina's help would be useful in furthering the expedition's goals. In April, Davis procured two hundred Sharps carbines to arm Cortina's personal bodyguard, and informed General Banks that he believed by providing the weapons, "some good to our interests might result therefrom."[39]

Davis never saw any fruits of his efforts in Texas. On 18 April 1864, he left his command at Brownsville and returned to Louisiana to take over the Fourth Brigade of General Richard Arnold's cavalry division. The assignment was not an enviable one. His new command had been part of General Banks's Red River campaign and, defeated at Sabine Cross Roads and Pleasant Hills, it was now in retreat. On 20 April, Davis took over his brigade at Grand Ecore on the Cane River. The brigade included the 2nd Illinois, 3rd Massachusetts, and 2nd New

Hampshire cavalry regiments, plus the 31st Massachusetts Mounted Infantry. The brigade constantly skirmished up to the point that Davis arrived and the day after he took command it was still fighting as Banks withdrew from Grand Ecore. On 21 April, Davis's brigade faced the difficult assignment of moving through the woods and swamps on the west bank of the Cane River to clear away sharpshooters. The day ended with success, and Davis had proven himself once more as an effective commander.[40]

By 22 April, Banks's men approached a critical crossing of Cane River at Monette's Ferry about five miles south of Cloutierville. There they found that Confederate forces, including artillery, had reached the vital crossing before them and had positioned themselves on bluffs that covered the crossing. Advancing infantry encountered a strong enemy battle line and Davis's brigade moved to the left of the infantry to cover its flank. His brigade received intense artillery fire before being ordered to move back into a thick wood. Davis then moved his men down river, ordered to find another crossing that would allow Union infantry to flank the Confederates. Davis's squadrons ran into thick woods, swampy grounds, and ravines but were unable to find a crossing. Returning to the field of battle, the 4th Brigade was used to divert attention from Banks's main attack on the Confederate lines, an attack that finally allowed the Federals to get across the river.[41]

Davis's cavalry remained in the rear of Banks's infantry after it had crossed Cane River to protect it from Confederate cavalry, and Davis demonstrated continued skills as a brigade commander. On the 27 April, Davis received information that Confederate General Richard Taylor had concentrated five thousand men near Alexandria, on the Red River, to keep Banks from reaching that town. Davis ordered the colonel of the 3rd Massachusetts to hold a line seven miles north of Alexandria. That evening, a sizable Confederate force began advancing and the 3rd pulled back to Muddy Bayou. Davis joined the unit. Entrenched behind a rail fence, Davis's men strongly resisted the Confederates. After exchanging artillery and rifle fire the Confederate force withdrew. Davis's command allowed Banks to escape at Monette's Ferry; at Muddy Bayou it interfered with Confederate pursuit of the retreating Federals.[42]

At Alexandria, Banks's withdrawal stalled because of low water on Red River. Waiting to effect an escape, Banks put his cavalry into the countryside to keep the Confederates away. On 30 April Davis's brigade rode fifteen miles up the river in search of Confederates. On the second day out they were attacked near the small town of Pineville. Davis's attackers were rumored to be part of the command of William Quantrill. Davis did not hesitate to fight back. He maneuvered his regiments into line facing the attackers. Following the command to "cheer," he ordered them "Forward!" and "Charge!" One of his men described the charge as sweeping forward "like an avalanche. . . . Shots from carbines and revolvers had been heard, and now a thousand sabres flashed in the morning." The Confederates retreated and the brigade had shown that "Davis and Sargent [colonel of the 3rd Massachusetts] were not men who could be stampeded."[43]

After nearly two weeks at Alexandria, Banks finally managed to move his gunboats down Red River, and on 12 May the army departed, marching towards the Mississippi. Their escape was not guaranteed, however, because Richard Taylor had managed finally to put a sizable force of Confederate infantry and cavalry in the way. Davis's cavalry protected the rear. On 14 May some two or three hundred Confederates attacked. The 2nd Illinois and 31st Massachusetts dismounted and beat back the assault, but the pursuit continued and skirmishing continued on the following days. On 16 May General Taylor finally made a large-scale effort to keep Banks from reaching the Mississippi, advancing against him in force to Mansura. Again, Davis was in the rear and all that stood between Taylor and Banks. The 3rd Massachusetts quickly threw up a line of battle between Bayou Glace and a swamp, and Davis sent up the rest of the brigade with artillery. The exchange of fire caused Taylor's cavalry to retire. Failing to overrun Banks's rear, Taylor moved to his front but finding himself greatly outnumbered and Banks's men ready to fight, Taylor withdrew. The road to Simmesport was open and the Federals were out of danger. E. J. Davis had played a major role in effecting the Union Army's escape.[44]

Banks was on his way to safety, but Confederate cavalry continued to harass the Union column, leaving Davis's brigade with work.

On 17 May General Wharton's cavalry attacked Davis near Moreau-ville. Davis beat back the attack, and the brigade camped that evening at Yellow Bayou. The next morning Davis and his men fought one of the last engagements of the Red River expedition when Confederates attacked their camp. That morning his men moved forward to support their pickets after Confederate pickets began efforts to locate the Union lines. A serious engagement began about nine A.M. with a Confederate advance. Davis and his regimental commanders rallied their troops and counter attacked, then held through the rest of the morning. At eleven o'clock infantry and artillery under General Joseph A. Mower moved up to support them. Davis used his men to protect the flanks of Mower's line. Fighting initially as skirmishers, they remounted when ordered to charge the enemy. Davis led his men in a sabre charge that broke up the Confederate advance. In the process they captured hundreds of prisoners.[45]

Remaining in line after the battle at Yellow Bayou, Davis's brigade held off Confederates until the last infantry had boarded transports on the Mississippi. They had done exemplary service in an exhausting duty. On 18 May Davis requested permission to move his men from the front lines into camp. Davis explained, "For five days and nights my men have been almost constantly in the saddle, and during that time the horses have had but one ration of forage. Since daylight this morning we have been in the saddle and engaging the enemy, and both men and horses are exhausted and actually suffering." His commander agreed and asked headquarters to allow the brigade to pass through the infantry. As to the campaign, Arnold wrote, "His command has suffered severely, and has urgent need of recuperation."[46]

On the evening of 20 May, the brigade crossed the Atchafalaya Bayou on a bridge composed of twenty-two steamboats connected by gangplanks and rough boards. It marched back to the cavalry depot at Morganza on the Red River. Davis had no rest, however. He received word that he was to join General Arnold immediately to take part in a campaign intended to prevent Confederates from crossing the Red River and attacking the Union lines that had reestablished themselves on the east bank. Davis had, at least temporarily, a new command, for Arnold turned over the cavalry division of the Nineteenth Corps to him. Davis found himself responsible for making sure that Confederate forces did not cross to the east of the Atchafalaya Bayou to attack the Federals who had pulled back to Morganza and Baton Rouge.[47]

Little glory came with his new command. He was soon involved in a campaign involving hard riding and skirmishing in the swampy lands to the west of the Mississippi. On 29 May Davis took part in a sweep through that area, responding to information that a major force of Confederates had crossed the Atchafalaya Bayou. Moving out of Morganza at four A.M., the cavalry, accompanied by infantry, reached Fordouche Bayou, about twenty miles west, by mid-afternoon. They pushed a small party of Confederates away from the crossing, after which Davis sent one of his brigades towards Morgan's Ferry on the Atchafalaya. They found few Confederates. General Michael K. Lawler, commander of the expedition decided the rumors had been false and ordered his men to return to Morganza by an indirect route, "clearing the country thoroughly before me."[48]

The return would typify the kind of operations Davis undertook in his new command. Davis's division left Fordouche Bayou on the afternoon of the division's arrival, riding ahead of the infantry towards Livonia on the Grosse Tete. This time they encountered a large party of Rebels who resisted their advance. Davis's cavalry quickly pushed them aside, reached their destination, and camped overnight. The next morning Davis pushed down the Grosse Tete to the David Barrow plantation. There he found a large Confederate camp, attacked it, dispersed the Confederate soldiers, and destroyed the commissary stores and clothing that were left behind. At the end of the day, Davis's cavalry returned north to the infantry on the Morgan's Ferry Road. On 1 June they set out on another mission, this time destroying a saw mill near Morgan's Ferry, then taking down all the bridges between the Atchafalaya and the Fordouche. On 2 June Davis's cavalry moved towards Rosedale, skirmishing with Confederates along the way, reaching the Mississippi on 3 June. When Davis's command finally returned to Morganza on 4 June, seven days later, they had ridden about 120 miles through Louisiana's

From assuming command of the 1st Texas Cavalry, E. J. Davis had shown himself to be an excellent soldier and quickly advanced to brigade and division command. His steadily increasing responsibilities were not recognized by promotion, however, until he received a brigadier general's star in December 1864. This image of Davis was made at Baton Rouge after that promotion (David and Harriet Condon Collection).

swamps and bayous, fighting much of the time. Taking fifteen prisoners and believing they had killed or wounded up to thirty Confederates, the men suffered only one death and two men wounded.[49]

Davis had excelled as a division commander, but in October he returned to brigade command when assigned to a new brigade consisting of the First Texas, which had returned to Louisiana after Banks withdrew from Texas, the 87th Illinois, the 2nd New York Cavalry, and the Massachusetts Light Artillery. He had acted as a general officer since the beginning of the Texas expedition, but as a Southerner in the Union Army he had no political allies to urge his promotion. Finally, on 24 December 1864, he was commissioned as a brigadier general. His appointment was dated back to 10 November. The promotion meant a new assignment, and he left his newly created brigade to take over General Joseph J. Reynolds's cavalry in the Division of Western Mississippi. This turned into only a temporary assignment, and, as the war wound down, he moved to additional commands—acting commander at Morganza, commander of the District of Baton Rouge, and brigade commander of a unit charged with cleaning out Rebels in Louisiana.

The latter proved particularly onerous. The war was passing Davis by. It was being won elsewhere and he had been left the nasty job of suppressing small bands of Confederates in the Louisiana swamps. Little glory accrued from such combat. It certainly was not suited for a man who had hoped he could lead victorious Union forces back to Texas. A member of one of Davis's cavalry regiments provided a graphic description of the type of fighting involved in his efforts. The trooper recalled that Confederate guerillas often approached the Federal camps at night to capture or kill the Yankee pickets. Union forces found themselves unable to stop this strategy. At one point, desperate to stop the Confederates, the men decided to "meet this brutal practice in a like spirit." On the next occasion that Confederates attacked the picket, one company charged out and captured the men who had fired the shots. They immediately hanged the captives who were forced to stand on their own mules while ropes were put around their necks. The men were left hanging for two days before being taken down. "The example was a grewsome [sic] one," the soldier related, "but it proved effectual." Another of Davis's soldiers provided an additional picture of the Louisiana campaign. On a scouting expedition to Alabama Bayou, the 2nd New York Cavalry found Confederates camped near the plantation of their captain. The Federals drove the Confederates into the swamp, then returned to the house where they found the captain's wife. She had offered help to the Confederate forces and paid the price. The New York trooper reported, "She was ordered out of the house & it was burned to the ground."[50]

Davis left no evidence of how such combat affected him, but it could not have diminished the hard feelings he already held towards Confederates. If his men were like their commander, their hatred only deepened. A quartermaster assigned to Davis's force in the autumn of 1864 found the Texans to be "a hard set of soldiers, but men who are not afraid of the Confederates, but hate them." Davis wanted to be elsewhere, to be where the war was being won. He did not understand fully why he had been given his assignment. "I ask to be given a command for active duty in the field," he requested, "or in case I am here unemployed by way of punishment, that I be informed of the cause." By the winter of 1864–1865, however, there were no places elsewhere for a general from Texas as officers from the North readied themselves for their post-war lives by making reputations as war heroes.[51]

Davis found, however, that the nation had a final role for him. In March, he received orders to accompany Major General Lew Wallace to the Rio Grande to try to negotiate a surrender of border forces. At the time the outcome of the war was yet uncertain and officials desired to close off the border. As a result, Wallace and Davis offered magnanimous terms. They allowed Confederate cotton to be sold and the proceeds divided among the officers and soldiers; the men could retain all property except for slaves; there would be no forfeitures, "pains or penalties;" and those who wished to remain in Union lines would retain "all rights." The two waited off Brazos Santiago for a reply, but received none. Moving to Galveston they offered the same terms. This time General J. C. Walker rejected the offer, "with appearance of great indignation." Unfortunately for the Confederates, such generosity would not appear again. Only a few weeks later General Lee would surrender at Appomattox, accepting terms much less liberal.[52]

Davis returned to New Orleans, to find Confederate agents nego-tiating their own surrender with General E. R. S. Canby. By then word had arrived of Lee's surrender. Canby offered similar terms and after all had agreed, Canby sent Davis to Texas with documents for his old acquaintance, General E. Kirby Smith, to sign. Davis arrived at the bar off of Galveston on 31 May. He visited with Confederate officers who boarded his vessel, the steam tug *America.* They exchanged information, including word that President Andrew Johnson had named Andrew J. Hamilton military governor of Texas and that the federal government intended to send a large number of troops, including possibly two corps of black troops, to Texas to take possession of the Rio Grande fron-tier. Two days later he met with generals Smith and John B. Magruder aboard the *Jackson,* the flagship of the blockading squadron for a formal surrender. The final chapter of the war passed uneventfully, although Davis found both Smith and Magruder "much alarmed." Davis reas-sured them that no "severe measures" would be taken against them. He reminded Smith, however, that he had warned him of the prob-able results of secession. The document signed, Davis offered to take the Confederate officers back to New Orleans. Neither went. With this last act the Civil War came to an end for General Davis. He would remain in the service for only five more months, mustering out of the army on 5 November 1865.[53]

The war years would have a profound effect on E. J. Davis. They brought him face-to-face with experiences that helped shape his views and solidify many of the character traits that he already possessed. He had experienced persecution. Bitter feelings, a demand for retribution, and a deep distrust of his opponents were inevitable consequences. He saw the triumph of a new nationalism. Hope that his home state might be part of that new world was a natural outgrowth. He had honed the skills that made him a good lawyer, his attention to detail and organiza-tion. These would serve him well as he played a role in restoring Texas to the Union. In 1865, like so many veterans of the war, E. J. Davis moved into a new era of peace. His future, despite all that he had accomplished, was not clear.

POSTWAR UNIONIST

"The recent election ought to satisfy every loyal man North and South that the Secession party is just as well defined and just as intensely malignant against the Union and Unionists as in the palmiest days of the Confederacy."
— Edmund J. Davis, 1866

In the summer of 1865, the future was uncertain for Texas veterans, whether Confederate or Unionist. Davis returned to Texas, landing at Galveston on 7 September, unsure what reception he would receive. It turned out to be a good one. Willard Richardson, the pro-Confederate editor of the *Galveston News,* welcomed him as "an old and much respected citizen of Texas." Richardson recalled Davis's career as a judge who had obtained "an enviable reputation for the correctness and impartiality of his decision." The war had seen him differ with his fellow Texans, but the editor believed that even the most zealous secessionist conceded the "purity of his patriotism." The war had made toleration of those who opposed the state government impossible, but the war was over. Richardson believed that thousands of the state's citizens would "sincerely rejoice in the opportunity of welcoming back to Texas, an old citizen as universally respected as Gen. Davis always was."[1]

The war disrupted the lives of many Texans, and these individuals, including Davis, looked for their place in a peacetime world. He liked army life, and, for a time, tried to get a commission in the regular army. He used his political and military connections to that end. Former governor Pease was one supporter, but possibly his strongest advocate was General E. R. S. Canby. Despite their support, however, Davis did not get an appointment. In part, the rapid reduction of the size of the army made it difficult for anyone to get an appointment, but Canby informed Davis that he also had a political problem. Davis had made it known that he disagreed with President Andrew Johnson's reconstruction policy and Johnson had intervened. Canby concluded that Davis's "politics stood in the way *with that gentleman.*"[2]

Even before being turned down for a commission, Davis had returned to Corpus Christi and reestablished his law practice. He also worked to settle his family's affairs. Just before the outbreak of the war, Lizzie's father had died, leaving behind a relatively large ranch in Nueces County. Now, his widow wanted Davis to take charge. Davis assumed that job, although his law practice appeared initially to flourish. He believed the ranch would have to be sold at some time, but the low prices for land at the war's end caused him to continue operations and wait for prices to rise. Davis was uncertain how to manage the operations, but in January 1866 he proposed to his brother-in-law, Charles Worthington, that he and Worthington operate the ranch together. Worthington, an Englishman, had been in Texas before the war but had fled to the North during the fighting. He returned, hoping to remain, and Davis argued that a working arrangement concerning the ranch would make that possible. For a time the arrangement worked, but ultimately the ranch was sold. At that point Davis and his family came to rely totally on his legal work for their income.[3]

Davis had no apparent political ambitions when he came home, but events forced him to reconsider. He did have ideas about how a reconstructed Texas should look, and the direction of Reconstruction quickly diverged from those ideas. His private correspondence showed that he unquestionably returned holding harsh feelings towards former Confederates, especially to those who had been his friends. He had made this clear in war-time correspondence with Hamilton P. Bee, the officer who was in charge of troops on the Rio Grande at the time of the murder of Montgomery and Davis's capture. Davis told Bee that he considered him to be a war criminal and thought he should be tried for war crimes. He had informed Bee that he would be given the privileges of

At war's end, roughly the time this picture was made, Davis was reunited with Lizzie and his sons, Waters and Britton, and the family returned to Corpus Christi. As the father's political role grew, the two boys remained out of the spotlight, but would go on to their own successes—Waters as a businessman and Britton as a soldier and engineer. (David and Harriet Condon Collection).

a prisoner of war but would be held for trial for his role in the "death of Montgomery." Texas was full of men like Bee who had visited great harm on Unionists in the state, and Davis looked for a reconstruction that included some sort of retribution.[4]

On the issue of political reconstruction, Davis made no public statements in the months immediately following the war. In all probability his views were similar to those of Jack Hamilton, the former military governor whom President Johnson named provisional governor at the war's end. Hamilton believed that only those who acquiesced in the war's results should participate in the reconstruction. To Hamilton, acquiescence meant accepting the ideas that secession was wrong and illegal and that slavery was at end. The end of slavery also meant that former Confederates had to assent to government that secured to the freedmen equal treatment before the law, even allowing them to testify in the courts. Hamilton would not accept any legal restraints on blacks or their labor.[5]

President Johnson's plan of reconstruction ultimately provided little hope that Davis would see either of these goals achieved. Prosecution of former Confederates was not part of the reconstruction plans Johnson laid out. Instead, the president's proclamation of 29 May 1865 promised amnesty and a return of all property, except slaves, to former Confederates who swore an oath of allegiance to the United States. The president excluded some Confederate officials and wealthy Southerners from the general amnesty, but he offered even these an opportunity to apply to him for an individual pardon. Any real hope for some sort of legal action against Confederates who had used their positions to persecute Unionists diminished as Johnson pursued a liberal policy in granting individual amnesty.

On the same day as his amnesty proclamation, President Johnson set out his basic plan for the reconstruction of states by naming a provisional governor for North Carolina and giving him the task of preparing the state to restore its normal place in the Union. Johnson's North Carolina proclamation established the procedure he would use in the rest of the Southern states, including Texas, and, like his amnesty proclamation, it showed a remarkable degree of magnanimity towards the former rebels.

The provisional governor was simply to call an election for delegates to a state constitutional convention, which would then write a new constitution recognizing the war's results. The only limits that he placed on this rapid restoration of the democratic process was that only men who had taken the oath of allegiance and who qualified either for the general amnesty or had received pardon from the president could participate in the election and the convention. No other conditions and certainly no demands for the implementation of particular policies were made.

With the president apparently placing no demands on them, former Confederates appeared ready to make no concessions on secession or the freedmen. From Governor Hamilton's arrival, Davis recognized a widespread unwillingness to accept what he and other Unionists considered to be those basic results of the war. Former Confederates even appeared to hope that they could reverse abolition. One of the most hostile recorded responses came from a prewar Unionist, James W. Throckmorton. Throckmorton contended that they could implement a program of gradual emancipation while leaving a system of coercive labor in place. To a friend he observed that he would rather remain "under military rule always rather than yield anything but an acknowledgment that the negro had been freed by the act of the government." Attitudes such as Throckmorton's indicated that the reconstruction goals of E. J. Davis and his Unionists friends would not be implemented easily.[6]

Observing the position of men like Throckmorton and the former secessionists, and convinced that a proper reconstruction would not be achieved with their participation, Governor Hamilton delayed an election in Texas. His policies placed him in opposition to the president, who wanted to bring an end to reconstruction as quickly as possible. In November, submitting to pressure from Washington, Hamilton finally ordered an election for a constitutional convention to be held on 8 January 1866. By this time E. J. Davis had determined that he had to participate in any convention, and he decided to run for a seat in the district that included his home at Corpus Christi. He did not have an opponent in the election, and it appeared to attract little interest. When the secretary of state certified the results, no votes had been received from three of the four counties—Duval, Encinal, and Webb. In Nueces only seventy-six votes were cast. In the 1861 gubernatorial election, the same four counties had returned a total of 538 votes. The turnout may have been low, but Davis received all of the votes cast in Nueces County. Davis was going to the state convention. After months of silence following his return from the war, Davis would now move into the political arena where he would emerge as one of the leaders of the post-war Unionists.[7]

When the delegates finally assembled in Austin on 9 February 1866, changes had taken place in Washington that had implications for Texans. The delegates knew that opposition to the president's reconstruction program had developed in Congress. Events in the South caused moderate Republicans to join the Radicals in questioning the efficacy of the president's policy. By the spring of 1866 the Republican majority in Congress began to demand measures that would protect the freedmen. Their goals included passage of a civil rights bill that they believed would guarantee freedom for African Americans, a goal most considered to be one of the war's results. The Republicans also supported a continuation of the Freedmen's Bureau operations in the South until local authorities guaranteed protection of the freedmen. President Johnson opposed both measures. The outcome of this conflict was important for Texas. A Johnson victory ensured that those favoring minimum change could move ahead. If the president lost, the future was less certain.[8]

On 10 February, the convention received a message from Governor Hamilton that reaffirmed the steps he believed necessary for the state's restoration to the Union and reflected his own perception of the measures Congress demanded. He insisted that the laws of Texas must conform to the "spirit and principles, to the actual changes that attended the progress of the late war, and followed the overthrow of the rebellion." The governor contended that this required a clear and explicit denial of the right of secession. In addition, he maintained that any measure designed to repay any debt created in aid of the rebellion would be unsatisfactory. Relative to the freedmen, he once again insisted that the North expected Texas to accept slavery's end and to recognize the new condition of the former slaves. Recognition required guarantees of their civil rights, including their right to sue in the courts, to testify under the same rules applied to whites, to be considered equal with whites in the punishment of crimes, and to be able to acquire and hold property. As to suffrage, he observed that he believed the great mass of blacks were unqualified to vote at the time, but insisted that Texas should not exclude them from voting because of their race. Instead, he recommended universal rules governing suffrage, such as educational tests applied to all who sought to become voters in the future. Whatever the delegates decided to do, he assured them that the North would not accept any laws applicable solely to the freedmen.[9]

As a delegate, E. J. Davis aligned himself with Governor Hamilton from the beginning and linked himself to other Unionist delegates. In the context of national politics, their position paralleled that of the moderate Republican majority in Congress. From the opening day of the convention, however, the opposition press called them Radical Republicans, a mislabeling that has remained attached to them. Davis played an active role in pursuing the Radical Unionist agenda, but through most of the convention he remained a minor figure. Two prewar Texas politicians played more important roles, Albert H. Latimer and Isaiah A. Paschal. Latimer, a planter from Red River County, had been a delegate to the Convention of 1836, signer of the Texas Declaration of Independence, a member of the Congress of the Republic of Texas, a delegate to the constitutional convention in 1845, and a state senator. Paschal, a resident of San Antonio, served in the Texas Senate in 1853 and 1857. A Democrat, he voted for Douglas in 1860, opposed secession during the crisis, and then resigned from the Senate rather than take an oath of allegiance to the Confederacy in 1861.[10]

The Radical Unionists found themselves in a minority in the convention from the beginning. The first test came over measures to ensure the loyalty of the delegates. The governor pointed out that the president excluded some men in the convention from the general amnesty, and they had not received his pardon. Their presence could hardly assure Northerners of the willingness of Texans to accept the war's results. On the second day, Paschal introduced a resolution indicating that the convention was organized and its members were ready to take the "Constitutional Oath" affirming that the individual had never voluntarily supported the

Confederacy. Davis made his first speech on the floor when he spoke in favor of Paschal's motion. The resolution provoked an immediate, strident response by former secessionists. Led by Oran M. Roberts, who chaired the secession convention, they contended the oath was unnecessary. Reflecting the very spirit that Hamilton had cautioned against, Charles A. Frazier, delegate from Harrison and Panola counties, objected on the grounds that the convention was independent of the Constitution of the United States, independent of the authority and power of the United States, and independent of the laws of the United States. Taking an oath to support the United States would be against the law. Frazier went further, saying, "Some people talk about acquiescing . . . . I cannot pronounce those words. They are unworthy of my mouth." Such attitudes gave Davis and other Unionists little reason to believe that the war's results were accepted by former Confederates.[11]

Davis and other Radical Unionist delegates replied with more insistent demands that the oath be taken, asking why delegates who supposedly had already taken the oath should refuse to do it again. They did not have the votes, however, to force adoption of Paschal's motion. In the end, a combination of former secessionists, who the press called Moderate Secessionists, and Conservative Unionists, delegates who had been Unionists before the war but were unwilling to accept Governor Hamilton's policies, tabled it. At that point Radical Unionists resorted to the only real power that they had. They threatened to break up the convention by walking out. The North would see then that the convention was in the hands of the secessionists. A newspaper correspondent saw in this threat and their refusal to compromise the bitterness of the Radicals. "They hate the Secessionists," he wrote, and unless they could secure their goals "had just as lief bust up the Convention as not." The Radical Unionists unquestionably did not want to see their former enemies back in power. The Radical threat forced the majority to reconsider the Paschal resolution, and in a new vote they passed it with only eleven hard-line secessionist delegates refusing to vote for it.[12]

In the wake of their success on the question of the oath, the Radical Republicans moved against those delegates who the president had not pardoned. Davis began to emerge as a spokesman for the party when, on 12 February, he introduced a measure that demanded the removal from the convention of any person who had not been pardoned by the general amnesty or personally by the president. Again, the majority frustrated Davis and his associates when it refused immediate action. Instead, Davis's resolution was sent to the Committee on Elections, and there it languished through the rest of the convention. The convention's refusal to consider his resolution on unpardoned Confederates appears to have convinced Davis that the majority of the delegates were not loyal. On 14 February he moved to table a resolution expressing the convention's gratification at having the opportunity to amend the state constitution and resume normal relations with the federal government. Davis asked that the motion be delayed for the purpose of "ascertaining how many members were really gratified."[13]

Davis's conclusions undoubtedly were right. The majority in the convention showed little willingness to make any concessions on the measures Governor Hamilton recommended. The next confrontation between parties would take place when Latimer introduced an ordinance that would declare the act of secession and all acts and proceedings of the Secession Convention "null and void from date of adoption." It also maintained that no state had the right to withdraw from the Union. The ordinance introduced into discussion an issue that would come to be known as the *ab initio* question—a problem that remained a point of contention for the next four years. If the ordinance passed, all actions of the state convention, the Confederate legislature, and state officials would have been overturned. Implications would be far reaching, potentially allowing the reversal of everything from land grants to the actions taken against Union loyalists. It might even allow legal action against Confederate state and county authorities. As a steadily more visible party leader, Davis helped advance the ordinance when he moved its referral to a special committee. A Conservative Unionist, John Hancock countered with a substitute that avoided a clear declaration of the unconstitutional character of secession. Both were sent to the Committee on the Condition of the State rather than a special committee.[14]

The *ab initio* ordinance that finally emerged from committee and went on to passage was evasive and unacceptable to the Radicals. Davis and his colleagues voted against its passage, but once again, did not have the votes to block it. Hamilton's attorney general, William Alexander, provided the view of the Radicals when he criticized the final statement as an "equivocal" one that refused to declare the ordinance void *ab initio*. Its language allowed the convention's leaders to present it for national consumption as meaning that the ordinance was void when adopted, while explaining it to Texans to mean that the ordinance was made null and void only by the failure of the war. Alexander believed that when combined with other actions taken in the convention, their design was "manifest and unmistakable."[15]

Former Confederates ultimately wanted even more than an equivocal statement on the ordinance of secession. The majority in the convention went on to consider an ordinance specifically exempting all officials from any prosecution for acts taken during the war. On 29 March, the convention took up that measure and passed it, validating the acts of Confederate officers that were not in conflict with the Constitution and laws of the United States. The same ordinance also prohibited all suits or prosecutions against executors, administrators, trustees, agents, and bailees who surrendered the assets they controlled to Confederate authorities. It prevented anyone from suing in a civil action or prosecuting in a criminal proceeding any persons who might have sold, seized, impressed, or injured property in the name of the military and civil authority of the Confederate states. While setting aside all sales of lands for unpaid taxes during the war, the convention blocked all avenues for Unionists to take in recovering their assets seized during the war.[16]

Davis and the Radical Unionists also supported Governor Hamilton's position on the rights of the freedmen, although once again they encountered uncompromising opposition. This opposition was true especially when the delegates considered the issue of black suffrage. Davis became a floor leader in this particular fight and earned himself the possibly undeserved reputation of being a true "radical" among the Radical Unionists. He gained his notoriety when on 14 February he introduced a resolution that, according to a reporter for *The New York Times*, provided for all black males over the age of twenty-one to be enfranchised and allowed to vote after 4 July 1866. Whether or not Davis actually supported unrestricted adult male suffrage, however, is unclear. The exact wording of his resolution was not published in the convention journal, and a prominent Unionist later contended that no one in his party supported unrestricted suffrage at the time. Davis had offered a more radical position hoping to force compromises that would produce a document with provisions on suffrage more in keeping with those proposed by Hamilton.[17]

The Radical Unionists concluded, however, that some form of limited suffrage for blacks was desirable. The actions of the convention convinced them that they could not trust the existing electorate to restore loyal government, and an expansion of the suffrage to include the freedmen now seemed in order. In fact, many thought they were in line with the president's desires, since the previous August he advised the Mississippi governor to support an extension of the franchise to propertied and literate blacks. By the time the Texas convention gathered, Albert Latimer indicated he generally opposed black suffrage but was willing to accept it if educational qualifications were applied. Even Edward Degener, considered to be the most radical of the Unionist delegates, supported black enfranchisement only if voting was restricted to those "who shall be able to read and write the English or his native language *understandingly.*" The inaccuracy of the original report concerning Davis may be further inferred from the fact that in a later story the same reporter portrayed Davis as one of the men in the convention who stood in favor of suffrage, with "proper educational qualifications."[18]

Whether or not Davis offered a radical resolution intending to provoke compromise or if he actually offered a resolution calling for a restricted suffrage will never be known. The majority of the delegates, however, made it clear that whatever the exact character of his resolution, they would not support it. When a motion was made to lay his resolution on the table, only three other delegates voted against tabling it—Edward Degener of San Antonio, Hardin Hart of Hunt, and Daniel Murchison of Comal. The delegates clearly were indisposed to make such a major concession in defining the civil rights of the freedmen and thus showed their reluctance to concede much of anything regarding the end of slavery. Ultimately, the convention passed resolutions that specifically denied the right of suffrage for all time to Africans and their descendants.[19]

The question of black suffrage and Davis's action in the convention provides at least some insight into the man, but his exact thoughts in this critical period can never be known. None of his speeches in the convention were published, and little of his correspondence for this period survives. However it is clear that at the heart of his considerations were concern with creating a state governed by loyal men and a willingness to support whatever measures would guarantee that result. Such motives, in fact, appeared to be behind the actions of most of the Radical Unionists. A reporter in Austin during the convention provided some support for that idea when he tried to explain Davis and his associates. He speculated that, in part, they had come to support black suffrage because they believed it would be good for blacks and that they deserved it. On the other hand, he saw an even stronger reason for their position. He wrote that they "prefer that even negroes rather than secessionist should rule the country." Davis certainly distrusted his former enemies and postwar experience reinforced this feeling. Distrust also would play a role in fashioning Davis's opinions throughout the remainder of Reconstruction.[20]

Black suffrage failed, and over the course of the convention, none of the other measures related to the civil rights encouraged by Governor Hamilton passed. The secessionist and Conservative Unionist majority restricted the right of blacks to testify in court cases to those cases involving injury to them. The majority adopted an ordinance specifically prohibiting the marriage of whites and blacks. It also specifically excluded blacks from sharing in the state's public school fund. The state was allowed to collect a tax for black education, levied only on blacks. In all of this, E. J. Davis stood with the minority trying to secure some good for the freedmen. In the debate over schools, he showed the concern for the rights of the freedmen that he would display over and over through the rest of his career. He managed, at least, to have an amendment grafted on to the constitution's education article that future legislatures should "encourage schools among these people."[21]

The actions of the convention convinced Davis and most Union-ists that loyal men would have little to look forward to in a reconstructed Texas. As a result, Davis and other Radical Unionists became associated with a measure that had been a political issue in the past—division of the state. It appeared to be the one way that the loyal people of the state could create a state government that would protect them. Davis had never been an advocate of division in the past; in the convention he became one. The possibility of division rested on a provision of the joint resolution annexing Texas that authorized the state to divide itself into as many as five states as its population grew. Now, for Davis and other Radical Unionists, a state of western Texas was seen as one where loyal Texans could be free of the influences of the pro-slave, plantation, secessionist Democratic leaders. As a result, they introduced numerous measures to secure that end into the convention, and Davis supported them. On 2 April, he managed to push that goal forward when he made a motion that allowed a last-minute passage of an ordinance providing for the organization of a new state.[22]

The Radical Unionists clearly did not approve of the work of the convention, which amended the 1861 constitution rather than writing a new one. Numerous ordinances, which the Radical Unionists believed rewarded former rebels, also passed. Trying to defeat the measure, they attempted to force the convention to submit each of the amendments and the ordinances to a separate vote of the people. One former seces-sionist believed that they thought this would defeat the constitution and keep the state under a provisional government. In implementing this strategy, the Radicals failed once again. Before the convention adjourned on 2 April, the delegates declared the amended constitution of 1861 to be in effect immediately. The people would vote on their work, but not until the first general election. At that time they would have to vote on the constitution, amendments, and ordinances in a package. They had to accept the whole or have no government. This action left the Radical Unionists with little hope of preventing what they considered to be a disloyal government from being organized. They would hold the elec-tion on the fourth Monday in June 1866.[23]

On 31 March, Governor Hamilton appeared before the convention and chastised the delegates for their work. He believed that national politics influenced them and that they concluded that in the conflict between President Johnson and Congress, the president would win. As a result, they had done little to recognize the war's results or to protect republican government. They restricted the freedom of the former slaves and refused even to consider the possibility of black enfranchisement. They skirted the issue on the legality of secession. He warned them that they still had another chance to prove their loyalty—the June election. Hamilton cautioned them that unless they did an about-face in their policies they would deal with a new reconstruction under Congress. The June election proved that few of the delegates took the governor's warning seriously.[24]

The upcoming general election began to take shape even before the convention's delegates left Austin. The Unionists began holding caucuses to plan strategy during the convention's last days and Davis clearly emerged as one of the party's leaders. Conservative Unionist John Hancock, observing the activities of the caucus, concluded that E. J. was an active participant in developing Unionist plans, attending the caucuses with Governor Hamilton, Albert Latimer, Edward Degener, and former governor Elisha Pease. Hancock believed that Davis helped to formulate a party platform for the canvass and also played a role in selecting a ticket. By this time Davis concluded that black suffrage had to be implemented and that caused a division within the Unionist caucus. Davis must have compromised or backed down on the issue, however, for the platform that emerged from the meetings never advocated black suffrage.[25]

The results of the Unionist caucus were finally made known on 20 March. Davis and other Radical Unionists from the constitutional convention met as representatives of a new party. They called themselves Union Republicans, although they had no connection with the national Republican Party. Styling themselves delegates to a party convention, they selected candidates for the June election. They initially asked Jack Hamilton to run for governor, but Hamilton refused. Left without a candidate, the delegates adjourned and then reconvened eleven days later.

This time they announced a full slate of candidates, including Elisha Pease for governor and Ben H. Epperson, a well-known Unionist from northeastern Texas, for lieutenant governor. The Union Party's declaration of principles reflected the positions Radical Unionists took in the convention. The delegates declared their devotion to a republican form of government, recognition of the supremacy of the Constitution of the United States, support for paying the national debt, devotion to freedom of speech, and toleration of different opinions. As to secession, they held it to be null and void from the beginning. Concerning the freedmen, they offered their sincere acceptance of abolition and promised to ameliorate their condition by "treating them with justice, and by according to them, not grudgingly, but willingly, and heartily, the rights which are now, or may here after be, secured to them by the constitution and the laws." Remarkably, despite the growing evidence of a split between Congress and the president, they expressed their confidence in the "wisdom and patriotism" of both the president and the Congress.[26]

Davis returned to Corpus Christi after participating in the state convention and that of the new Union Republican Party. He left for home as a leader of his new party after having played significant roles in both. His opponents believed that he was one of the major forces responsible for the emergence of the new party. The Conservative Unionist James W. Throckmorton named four men he believed played significant roles in development of the new party: Andrew Jack Hamilton; William Alexander, Hamilton's attorney general; John L. Haynes, the prewar Unionist legislator and then associate of Davis in the Texas Cavalry; and, lastly, E. J. Davis. It is important to note, however, that while Davis now was better known, he remained to a considerable degree in the background of state political affairs.[27]

In the June election, Governor Pease and the Union Party faced James W. Throckmorton as their chief opponent. Throckmorton was president of the state convention and one of the principal creators of the alliance forged there between the moderate secessionists and Conservative Unionists. Members of that alliance approached him soon afterwards to see if he might consider running as a candidate for governor on a platform supporting the president's Reconstruction program.

Throckmorton was flattered by the offer and agreed. On the last day of the convention, Throckmorton's supporters joined together to form the Conservative Union Party and formally nominated him as their candidate for governor.[28]

Throckmorton's nomination provided further proof to Unionists of the hostile position of their opponents. Throckmorton was from Collin County and had been a Unionist before the war, but when the war began he became an officer of state troops, rising to the rank of brigadier general. At the war's end, he found that he could support none of the reforms proposed by returning refugees. In fact, he was outraged by what he considered the radicalism of the refugees on the question of black rights. Just before the convention he explained to a friend that he opposed even allowing blacks to testify in court because it would be simply the first step to their "sitting on juries, suffrage; and finally, to perfect social and political equality [sic]." The men who nominated him chose him because of what they considered to be his support of the policies of President Johnson and his basic acceptance of the avowals of loyalty of the state's former Confederates. They also saw in him a man opposed to the "radicalism of the day," black suffrage, and any "inconsiderate elevation of the negro to political equality." Throckmorton epitomized the attitude that demonstrated to Unionists the reluctance of ex-Confederates to accept the war's results.[29]

The general election campaign was to be over Reconstruction policy. Union Republicans argued that more was needed for the state to demonstrate its loyalty and to be restored to the Union, and the Conservative Unionists insisted that all that was needed had been done. Davis, home at Corpus Christi, obviously sided with the Union Republicans and determined that he wanted to continue to try to influence events. He decided that he would run for the state Senate on the Union Republican ticket. Unopposed in the convention, in the election he faced John T. Littleton from Helena in Karnes County. Littleton epitomized the men who refused to accept the full extent of changes the war had produced. Before the war he was a captain of the Knights of the Golden Circle, a group dedicated to the expansion of slavery into the Caribbean.

In 1861, he was an ardent secessionist, running successfully for the state secession convention. He later volunteered for the army and served as a captain in the Confederate cavalry fighting Indians during the war. Two more diverse candidates could not have faced each other, giving the voters in the 29th District a clear choice between an ardent loyalist and a prominent supporter of the Confederacy.[30]

Nothing is known about the campaign in the 29th District, but events at the state level demonstrated the problems Union Republicans faced in the election. There Elisha Pease tried to convince voters of the need for further concessions and the necessity of making their loyalty clear to national political leaders. In a speech at Galveston on 10 May, Pease outlined the Unionist position, telling his audience that Throckmorton's argument that the president would make it possible for them to minimize change was a false hope. Events in Washington, Pease insisted, worked in favor of Congress and the Republican majority, not the president. He warned that unless voters placed Unionists candidates into office the people of the North would be suspicious of the loyalty of the new government. Only if Texans sent known loyalists who could work with Congress to head their government would the state return to its prior relationship in the Union.[31]

Pease defined loyalty to mean acceptance of rights for the freedmen beyond those made in the convention. Responding to charges that he was radical on this issue, Pease answered that a radical was one who favored conferring unrestricted suffrage on African Americans and disfranchising former Confederates. Pease desired neither of these. Instead, he pointed to the civil rights bill then being considered in Congress as defining what he was willing to give. That bill defined national citizenship and assured all born within the United States, other than American Indians, the rights to make contracts, bring lawsuits, and enjoy full and equal benefit from all laws that secured person and property. He warned, however, that even this might not be enough. Changing circumstances in Washington might make black enfranchisement ultimately a requirement for reunion, and he assured his listeners that if the state did not respond to these demands on the part of the North then they would never readmit Texas to the Union. While he opposed black suffrage, he indicated that he would do whatever it took to restore the state to the Union, even granting the vote to those blacks able to read and write.[32]

Conservatives campaigned assuring Texans that no more compromise was needed, no more bitter pills remained to be swallowed. Events in Washington were working in favor of Texas and the rest of the South. The conservative campaign emphasized the idea that the election really was a show of support for President Johnson in his conflict with Congress and contended that the choice confronting voters was to back the president and constitutional reconstruction or risk a radical triumph and a revolution in the character of the nation's government. Throckmorton warned voters that securing state rights was the single "living issue" in the politics of the day. Voters could either "sustain the President, and in so doing sustain the Constitution, or go with the radicals." A radical triumph would see consolidation and centralization of the government, the imposition of central authority on the state, and the reduction of the states to "mere appendages to centralism, without power to protect their citizens against the encroachments of tyranny & oppression."[33]

The conservatives did not hesitate to play upon the fears of the white electorate. If the Union Republicans won in Texas, they would reinforce the Radical Republicans in Congress, and the results would be disastrous for the South. A national Republican victory meant ultimately that full social and political equality for blacks would be imposed on the South. At the same time, it also meant the disfranchisement of former Confederates. It would be the end of a white man's government. The campaign rhetoric of W. L. Robards, candidate for comptroller, was similar to that of all conservative candidates. "I do not believe that the negro is equal to the white man [*sic*]," he wrote the editor of the *Galveston News*. "I believe that it was intended by our fathers that this should be the white man's government, and am in favor of embodying that principle clearly and unequivocally in the fundamental law of the land."[34]

The campaign demonstrated the sentiment of the majority of the state's enfranchised voters on the question of Reconstruction. Voters did not appear ready to make further efforts at appeasing the North or the state's refugee loyalists and had little sympathy with those who were willing to make concessions. Davis recognized that this sentiment remained pervasive in the days leading up to the election. He also found that his opponents were ready to use the same sort of intimidation against their opponents that was used in 1861. Well aware of the adverse climate within which they would hold the election, Davis had little hope for the success either of himself or his party. His lack of faith was warranted. Davis lost the senatorial election to Littleton and the results probably were not close. No official returns exist for the Senate race, but the gubernatorial vote probably paralleled that for the Senate seat. Six of the district's nine counties reported returns, and Pease did not carry a single county. Throckmorton carried the district by a combined vote of 820 to 369. Only in Goliad County, where a sizeable ethnic population may have contributed to a better showing, and in Nueces County did Pease come close to Throckmorton. Davis probably did not do any better. This failure of the Union Republican ticket was general. In the gubernatorial contest, Throckmorton carried all but a few of the German counties in central Texas, defeating Pease by a total vote of 49,177 to 12,168.[35]

The election provided a new insight into Texas politics for Davis. In a letter written to Pease after the election, Davis admitted that he had never been very optimistic about the results. The election proved him correct. Of particular concern for him was the fact that when faced with intimidation, Union Republicans were overawed. His opponents had been successful with such methods in 1861. Now they were successful again. Prior to the election, party leaders at Austin discussed the need to organize their voters into some sort of "home-guard." What that might have been is unclear, but its purpose was to help party members to stand up against the threats that they faced. Davis bemoaned the fact that nothing had been done and the result was an election disaster. "I presume," he wrote, "you at no time during the canvass, seriously believed that we could carry the day under such adverse circumstances." Davis never took for granted again that an election that challenged the power of the antebellum Democratic leadership could be conducted without having to deal with some sort of intimidation and violence aimed at the challenger. Maintaining peace at the ballot box would become a major concern for him. He would always expect violence but also would do whatever he could to suppress it.[36]

The 1866 general election also proved significant for Davis in another way. It convinced him that loyal government in Texas could not be restored under existing circumstances. He was not willing to accept that result. "The recent election," he wrote to E. M. Pease, "ought to satisfy every loyal man North and South that the Secession party is just as well defined and just as intensely malignant against the Union and Unionists as in the palmiest days of the Confederacy." Davis's perspective left him few alternatives. He supported the efforts to reconstruct the state under President Johnson's program. The convention and the election indicated that Johnson's plan had failed. The result was that a threat remained in place, a threat both to those in Texas who had remained loyal to the Union and the very Union itself. A man who had fought to preserve the Union could hardly sit by and watch his efforts come to nothing. The problem Davis and other Unionists in Texas faced was what to do next.[37]

At least for a time, the perspectives gained in 1866 reaffirmed Davis's interest in creating a loyal state out of southwest Texas. Rather than submit to being governed by the men who had led the state into secession, Davis proposed to Pease in July that Unionists should work for division. The boundary he proposed would run up the Brazos River to a point roughly due east of Austin, then north to the Red River. Having heard a rumor that Hamilton had resigned as governor and that Pease had replaced him, Davis wrote to his political friend Pease proposing that he call a convention to establish a new state. He recognized that this was a revolutionary proposition, but deemed it necessary to establish a loyal state on the frontier. Initially he was optimistic about the chances for success of such a plan. He believed that Congress and the loyal people of the North would approve of their actions, especially if the new state government assured that "the rights of all persons would be thoroughly equalized." The sense of hopelessness that infused the interchange between Davis and Pease indicated how desperate he believed the situation to be for men of his sort. Even if creating a new state amounted to revolution, he believed that it had to be taken "unless we are prepared, quietly to let the rebels again cement their power and control over us."[38]

Ultimately, division proved to be an unrealistic immediate solution to the problem Davis and other loyalists faced. He began a search for other ways of countering the return to power of the very men he blamed for secession and the violence visited on Union men afterwards. Hope ultimately sprung anew as the division between the president and Congress reached its climax. In the months following his election defeat, Davis would become increasingly involved in encouraging that split and pushing for congressional intervention in the South. Intervention would begin the Reconstruction process anew. His involvement in this effort would change his own goals and ideals even further.

CHAPTER 5   UNIONISM TO
REPUBLICANISM

"[A] ripe scholar, a fine lawyer, an earnest and logical debater."

On the Character of Edmund J. Davis
Editor, *San Antonio Express,* 1869

Events in the months that followed the disastrous election of 1866 were critical to Davis's political development. The division between Congress and President Johnson widened as the president repeatedly blocked efforts to provide federal protection for the freedmen. On 27 March he vetoed the civil rights bill that encompassed the minimum rights Texas Union Republicans had argued needed to be recognized by the state convention. Eleven days later Congress overrode his veto, and afterwards congressional Republicans prepared an amendment to the Constitution that embraced the act. That summer the break appeared irreconcilable when the president tried to create a new centrist party position between the Radical Republicans and the radical states' rights Democrats. A Johnson victory would bring an end to Reconstruction and acceptance of the government created under his plan. A congressional victory promised a chance at a new reconstruction. For that reason, Davis and other Texas Unionists worked for a congressional victory. The struggle helped reshape E. J. Davis's views and pushed him into a political conversion. Davis would finally connect himself with the national Republican Party.

Davis was in Corpus Christi most of that summer, tied down by his law practice and family affairs. He wanted to play a role in the political struggle taking place, but the town's isolation limited what he could do. In a July letter to Governor Pease, sharing his thoughts on the late state election, Davis complained of the problems he faced. Much of the information that he received on politics was based on rumor, and little of that was accurate. Mail to Corpus Christi remained irregular, which prevented him from understanding what was happening on the national scene. Nonetheless, he offered advice on Union Republican strategy. He clearly became wedded to the idea that dividing the state was the only way to protect loyal men in Texas. Unaware of the increased alienation of President Johnson from Congress, he even hoped that the president would endorse a plan to create a loyal state in western Texas.[1]

In fact, the struggle between the president and Congress had reached the point of an open break by the time Davis made his proposal to Pease. Jack Hamilton had gone to Washington shortly after the state convention adjourned to join other Southern loyalists in trying to convince Congress that the president's policies had to be reversed. Hamilton played a leading role in pushing for that end, openly denouncing the president before the Congressional Union Caucus on 11 July. He followed that speech by joining in a call for a convention of Southern loyalists to be held at Philadelphia in September. In seeking a new basis for reconstruction, Hamilton and many other Southern loyalists now concluded that they could secure loyal government in the South only through the enfranchisement of the freedmen. In Texas, Governor Pease explained their reasoning. He initially opposed enfranchisement, but President Johnson's policies placed state governments in the South in "the possession of the rebels." Their actions "denying to the freedmen the enjoyment of those civil rights that are the legitimate consequences of emancipation" convinced him that the only means to secure loyal government was to give them the vote. Another Unionist, Colbert Caldwell, contended that the refusal of the state's secessionists to make even moderate compromise gave the Radical Union opposition no other option. The Philadelphia convention would lobby for congressional intervention in the South and enfranchisement. Loyalists found a positive reception in the nation's capital.[2]

How E. J. Davis's thoughts developed on the issue of black suffrage is uncertain, but they probably paralleled those of men like Pease.

Davis had supported some form of enfranchisement in the state convention. He believed the state government fell back into the hands of secessionists. He held real concerns about the future of Unionists in the state. He unquestionably had come to agree with Hamilton and Pease that unrestricted black suffrage was now necessary. Given his position, he was a logical choice to go to Philadelphia with the delegation from Texas. On 16 August, the Corpus Christi Loyal Union League met to make recommendations for delegates to the upcoming convention, and they included Davis among their nominees. As a result, Davis went to Philadelphia where he joined twelve other Texans. The delegation included the principal architects of the Union Republican movement—Jack Hamilton, former governor Pease, and Davis, along with other prominent Unionists such as George Paschal, Lorenzo Sherwood, Colbert Caldwell, and Jesse Stancel, a veteran of the Texas Union cavalry. At the convention the Texans played a major role, with Hamilton emerging as one of the principal spokesmen for Southern loyalists.[3]

The meeting, attended by over two thousand delegates from both the South and North, ultimately laid out the position of the Southern loyalists on the question of reconstruction in their resolutions adopted on 6 September, in response to changing events in the South. Jack Hamilton, as chair of the committee and a major author of the resolutions, presented the document to the convention. The report condemned the president's policy, which had produced "unjust, oppressive, and intolerable" effects on the loyal people of the South. As a result, they looked to Congress to secure loyal government in the South. The delegates offered their support to secure the ratification of the amendments to the Constitution proposed by Congress. They also condemned the existing governments of the South as illegitimate until recognized by Congress. Their resolution on suffrage was indirect, but they declared themselves in favor of universal liberty and believed in the "inherent right of all men to decide and control for themselves the character of the government under which they live." The report of the Committee on Non-Reconstructed States adopted the next day was more direct, declaring "there can be no safety for us or our children . . . unless the Government by national and appropriate legislation, inforced [*sic*] by national authority, shall confer on every citizen in the States we represent the American birthright of impartial suffrage and equality before the law." Davis approved of the convention's resolutions and its report.[4]

Davis did not present a high profile during the convention's proceedings, but he was asked to be on the platform at a mass meeting held at Independence Hall on the evening after the convention adjourned. Davis shared the stage with Jack Hamilton and Lorenzo Sherwood. After Sherwood presented a defense of the convention's demand for black suffrage, Davis was asked to speak. Davis had not believed that he was expected to make a speech and apologized for not being prepared. He proceeded, however, with extemporaneous remarks that vividly described the condition of affairs in Texas. The policies of Andrew Johnson allowed the return of the old secessionists to power, and he believed that they would persecute loyal men once again, just as they had during the war. All he asked of the president, he told his audience, was to be allowed to remain in Texas in peace. If the president's policies were not changed, Davis concluded, that would be impossible. If Johnson's policy triumphed, there would be "disastrous results" for the loyal men of the South.[5]

While Davis and other Unionists were in Philadelphia, the actions of the state government appeared to confirm the worst that they expected from that new state government. The new legislature chose Oran M. Roberts, president of the secession convention and wartime member of the state supreme court, to the United States Senate. Roberts could not even take the test oath. One Unionist newspaper editor concluded that he had been chosen specifically to challenge the constitutionality of that oath. At least one conservative legislator certainly chose Roberts for that reason, writing, "We do not want men to go there [Washington] who have already taken it [the test oath] or would do so." A state senator added, "it is better not to be represented at all, than to be misrepresented." The newly seated Eleventh Legislature also implemented statutes to control the freedmen, new Black Codes. A vagrancy law, one regulating labor contracts, and another allowing the apprenticing of black minors led Colonel John Haynes to conclude that the legislature was busy trying to "reenslave the negroes [sic]." Gerrymandering the state's congressional districts to make it difficult for Unionist candidates to be elected, changing judicial districts to throw out pro-Union judges, and further legislation protecting former Confederate officials provided even more evidence of their disloyal intentions.[6]

When Davis returned to Texas from Philadelphia he saw what had happened and reached the same conclusions as those Unionists who had remained at home. He had predicted these results and now determined that only extraordinary measures could reverse what was taking place. Several of the Texans who had attended the Philadelphia convention had remained in the North to campaign for congressional candidates opposed to the president. Davis urged action. In letters to former governor Pease, he insisted that the North be made aware of the situation, that life for Unionists would be difficult if not impossible unless Congress intervened and remove the state government. Immediate action by Congress was necessary. "Delay," he insisted, "will only encourage false hopes on the part of the rebel party in power."[7]

Davis was emphatic about black suffrage, indicating that he unquestionably had concluded that unrestricted black suffrage was essential for loyal reconstruction. If, indeed, he previously had desired some sorts of qualifications on black voting, that was no longer true. He urged Pease to explain to the Northern representatives that success in the South demanded they take this step and that they must not compromise. Any sorts of limits on black voting would be useless to Southern loyalists. Davis was optimistic that the congressional elections would ensure that those who favored unrestricted black suffrage would be in a majority, but he worried that events might weaken their will. He specifically feared that attempts to reconcile Congress and the president might water down suffrage provisions. On this issue, he now insisted, there could be no half measure that would be effective.[8]

In his correspondence with Pease that autumn, Davis presented some of the clearest insights into what personally motivated him in his concerns in the immediate post-war years. Above all, he believed that the state government had to act in a way that accepted the war's results. Among other things, that meant making recompense for the harm done during the war. If the state government would not do this, he wanted congressional intervention. Davis urged Pease to encourage members of

Congress to support a bill designed to help Southern loyalists regain the property that Confederate authorities confiscated during the war. Davis insisted that such matters could not be left to the civilian courts in Texas, where he believed local juries would never render a verdict in favor of a Unionist. He also wanted Congress to provide for the arrest of responsible Confederate officials and for their trials by a military commission. Davis's correspondence showed the depth of his desire to punish the Confederate officials who had harassed the state's loyal population and to secure some sort of repayment for the lost property.[9]

Davis saw a political crisis developing in 1866 and supported the efforts of Union Republicans to encourage congressional action against the Johnson government and in support of black enfranchisement. Despite his concerns, Davis was unable to devote much of his time to politics. He spent only a short time in the North when he went to the Philadelphia convention and returned to Corpus Christi immediately afterwards. His exact economic situation at the time is unknown, but his activities indicated that rebuilding his law practice and providing for his family was a priority. In December, he renewed his partnership with an old associate, Stephen Powers. In partnership with Powers, Davis worked extensively in defending the interests of Richard King & Company. The principal in the company, Richard King, was involved in the steamboat business when Davis first arrived on the border and had used the revenues from that business to buy lands in southern Texas. His wide-spread holdings by this time included the 15,500 acre Santa Gertrudis ranch along the Nueces. King's partners in the company were James Walworth, who died in April 1865, and Mifflin Kenedy. The company purchased land and managed livestock operations. The business of King & Company was substantial and any attorney working for it would have much to do.

Almost immediately after joining Powers, Davis became involved in a lawsuit that King & Company filed against Edward N. Grey. Grey claimed to be in possession of interests in the Santa Gertrudis and a large amount of company livestock that had belonged to Walworth. The parties agreed to submit the dispute to arbitration in the district court in Nueces County, but Grey and his counsel, in day-to-day meetings, prevented a decision by various delaying maneuvers. Finally, in February 1867, the arbitrator for the King interests and the umpire assigned by the court made an award in the case that favored King. Grey appealed, however, and in April 1867, the district court for Nueces County granted his petition and set aside the award. In the meantime, District Judge B. F. Neal ordered that Grey turn over 2,000 head of sheep, 900 cows, 85 horses, and the ranch. Davis and Powers responded to the unfavorable district court decision by trying to have it overturned. Cases like this consumed a considerable amount of time and clearly diverted Davis from politics through much of the winter and spring of 1866–1867.[10]

However, Davis did not just do legal work. Like his father, he looked for opportunities and did not hesitate to become involved when he considered they might improve his own economic position or benefit his community. Among the efforts that attracted him was the opportunity to build railroads. One of particular interest to him was the plan for the construction of the Galveston, Kansas, and Little Rock Railroad (GK&LR). The proposed line was intended to run from Galveston to Fort Gibson in the Indian Territory, but with a branch to Little Rock, Arkansas. It clearly was intended to tie Texas directly to the cities of the North through Little Rock. That branch would be a direct avenue for trade to the east. Davis saw the economic need for such a connection, and through the rest of his career he would support what he considered reasonable plans to build an eastern tie. In February 1867, he joined other prominent Texas Unionists in asking Congress for a charter and support for the GK&LR. His associates included Lorenzo Sherwood, a long-time railroad promoter, former governors Pease and A. J. Hamilton, and many others who would continue to play important roles in anti-Democratic politics through Reconstruction.[11]

Events relative to Reconstruction continued to move forward, despite Davis's inability to participate in the way that he wished. Ultimately, in the spring of 1867 Congress intervened in Southern affairs. The autumn elections in 1866 had gone the way Texas loyalists had hoped and strengthened the resolve of Congress to step into the reconstruction process and reverse much of what was done by the state governments created under the Johnson plan. The new program closely resembled that for which Davis and other Unionists had lobbied. Congress initiated it on 2 March with the passage, over President Johnson's veto, of the first of three Reconstruction Acts. That act declared the existing state governments of the South to be provisional and of no legal standing. Until they could establish new governments, the act divided the South into military districts, each to be commanded by a general officer of the United States Army. To establish civil government, the people, including all adult males regardless of race who were not disfranchised for their participation in the rebellion, would elect a constitutional convention. Delegates could include all adult males who were not excluded from office in the proposed fourteenth amendment. The convention then had to write a constitution in conformity with the Constitution of the United States and provide for an electoral franchise based on the same qualifications for the election of delegates. Afterwards, they would hold a general election to ratify the document and elect a new government. If a majority voted for the new constitution and the new state government approved the proposed fourteenth amendment then the state would be entitled to representation in Congress. Congress had set in motion events that ultimately would pull Davis away from his legal practice and push him back into the political arena.[12]

The passage of the congressional reconstruction measures renewed the possibility that Texas could create a truly loyal government, and Davis could not remain uninvolved. Before becoming involved, however, he would take advantage of provisions of the new law to help his clients in the King & Company versus Grey case. For Davis, Judge Neal's order favoring Grey was a legal travesty and the "last feather on the camel's back." He did not hesitate to use whatever tools he could find to reverse it. The Reconstruction Act provided that tool, throwing into doubt the legitimacy of the existing courts. In May, with the jurisdiction of local courts in uncertainty, Davis petitioned General Charles Griffin, assigned to command the District of Texas, to restrain the Nueces County judge from carrying his order in the case. He made the same request of the military commander at Corpus Christi. The local commander acted, restraining the district clerk and the sheriff from enforcing Neal's order. Griffin refused to interfere, but Davis immediately filed a plea to stop the execution of the judge's order and have the case transferred to another court. Griffin refused to act once again, but given the uncertainty of affairs the receiver refused to execute Neal's order. Davis and Powers then appealed the case to the state supreme court, which reversed Neal and found in favor of King & Company.[13]

The King case complete, Davis turned more of his attention to the implications of Congress's intervention in the South. The most obvious result of Congress's action was the prospect that they could reverse the results of the election of 1866, and Unionists would have a chance to secure control over the state government. Initially Unionist leaders were uncertain how they should organize to take advantage of the new situation. Some believed that they should now tie themselves to the national Republican Party. Doing so would link them to the party of Lincoln, emancipation, and Union victory. That connection would secure the vote of the newly enfranchised African American voters. At least some believed that local Unionists should remain independent, avoiding what many feared would be a heightened partisan conflict. In the end the more prominent leaders, including General Davis, agreed that the link with the national Republican Party was essential for success. Davis became a Republican and subsequently worked for the new party's success, although he initially found his isolation at Corpus Christi limited his role.[14]

The first step to create a Texas Republican Party was taken at Austin on 27 April. Unionists held a mass meeting there to put in motion the process of creating the new party. The group that met consisted largely of the city's Union men, who avowed their support of the "National Republican Union Party" and passed resolutions endorsing the congressional plan of reconstruction. They also announced a platform that they supported, calling for a state constitution that did not discriminate on the basis of race, guarding and increasing the school fund to provide for the education of every child without regard to race or color, extending state aid to railroads, encouraging immigration with a homestead law, and offering "cheerful" support of the military. Those attending the Austin meeting called for all men with the same goals to join in a convention at Houston on 4 July to organize a state Republican Party.[15]

Unionists gathered around the state after receiving reports of the meeting in Austin and endorsed its platform and the call for a convention. Newspapers provided details on some of the meetings and their participants. The reports indicated that support for the new party was widespread, although larger meetings were held at Prairie Lea, Lockhart County, Waco, Brenham, and San Antonio. The accounts showed that most of the men who became Republicans were old Unionists. One noteworthy participant, because of his future connections with Davis, was James P. Newcomb, an avowed Unionist who had fled the state in 1861 after his newspaper was burned at San Antonio. Davis signaled his own approval of the steps towards organizing the state Republican Party when he attended a meeting at the Nueces County courthouse in Corpus Christi on 25 May. Those attending passed resolutions giving whole-hearted support to the actions of the Austin meeting. Like the delegates at Austin, the men from Nueces County called upon men who believed in the equality of all men and loyalty to the government to join them in their move into the Republican Party.[16]

As the Texas Republicans organized, Davis did what he could to encourage the party's development. Among his efforts was the establishment of a Republican newspaper at Corpus Christi, a fact that showed his law practice may have been relatively lucrative by this time. In April he began publishing the *Union Record,* a newspaper that described itself as Union Republican in its sentiment. He hired a young journalist and former officer in the Union army from Chicago, W. A. Bartlett, to edit the paper. The content of the *Union Record* surprised the editor of the *Galveston News* who had christened Davis the orthodox leader of "Texas Radicalism" following his role in the state constitutional convention and the formation of the Union Republican party in 1866. What the editor of the *News* meant by orthodox at this point is unclear, as Davis hardly possessed unique ideas among the new Republicans and was not in a position to do much leadership. On the issue of party ideology, most of the men who joined the party by this time shared Davis's views on black suffrage and his support for congressional intervention in the Reconstruction process. The editorial policy of the *Union Record* unquestionably supported Reconstruction under the military bill, but to the surprise of the editor of the *News* nowhere called "for more victims, nor does it denounce Texans for treason that should be made odious, nor is anything said of the necessity of confiscation." The editor of the *News* welcomed the tone of reconciliation that he saw in the paper of this man "whom all Texans once delighted to honor."[17]

Davis's experience as a newspaper publisher did nothing to alleviate his fears concerning the uncompromising nature of his political opponents or their willingness to let Union men live in peace. The short history of the *Union Record* reflected the hostility that these men felt towards the Texas Unionists and Reconstruction. Some former Confederates clearly remained ready to use whatever weapons they had on hand to defeat the new Reconstruction effort. While the editor of the *News* praised the moderate tone of Davis's paper, another news item in the same paper reported that the publisher, the editor, and the paper had many opponents from the very beginning. On 25 May the newspaper's office burned to the ground. Officials found no cause for the fire, but Davis was convinced that someone started the fire on purpose. Others in the town agreed, believing that those who opposed the politics of the paper and its owner set the fire. Unsympathetic officials at Corpus Christi, men elected in the conservative landslide the previous June, made no arrests. Davis made no further effort at financing a newspaper in the city, but his efforts on behalf of the Republican Party and Congressional reconstruction intensified.[18]

Davis also found himself able to encourage Republicanism in another important way. On 19 March 1867, General Philip H. Sheridan assumed command of the Fifth Military District, encompassing Texas and Louisiana. Sheridan placed General Charles Griffin, then commander of the army's military district in Texas, in control over affairs in Texas. To facilitate the registration of voters, Griffin created fifteen registration districts and named two supervisors to oversee the process within each of these districts. The position of supervisor was a critical one, since supervisors appointed local registration boards and acted as the final authorities when an individual appealed a registration board's decision. In essence, the supervisors determined who would and who would not vote. E. J. Davis received one of these powerful positions when General Griffin appointed him as a supervisor for the district encompassing southern Texas. Exactly what Davis did as supervisor is unknown, but the position gave him the opportunity to travel around his district. As he moved around the district he would have the opportunity to encourage men who shared his views to organize and to join his party. Whether he did this or not cannot be known, but he probably did since supervisors commonly worked as political agents.[19]

Prior to the Houston convention, Republican leaders also took another major step to organize support. Sometime in late March or early April they began chartering chapters of the Union League. The league was a secret organization used to mobilize voters in the North during the war. National Republican leaders believed that they could use it with good effect to organize the freedmen in the South. Because the league was a secret organization, little is known about its initial efforts. Most believed, however, that James H. Bell, secretary of state during the Hamilton administration, was the league's leader in Texas and directed the attempt to introduce it into local communities. Through that spring organizers worked intensively in the state's black belt counties, often irritating their political opponents by insisting that unless blacks joined the league and the Republican Party their former masters would re-enslave them. Davis may or may not have worked as an organizer. He certainly approved of its work, having encouraged a similar organization to mobilize white voters prior to the previous general election.[20]

Davis was not present at Houston when the first Republican convention finally convened on 4 July. Although he was absent, the work of the gathering would have a profound impact on his future. The issues addressed and the goals advanced provided the framework of the political world within which he would live for the rest of his political career. That world was defined by the basic ideology of the new party that the delegates set forth. It included a pledge to work for the protection of all citizens and guaranteeing them equal treatment before the law. It also contained a promise to pursue policies that would secure the economic prosperity of Texans. In particular, the delegates declared their support for the creation of a system of free schools "for equal benefit of all children and youth of scholastic age, without distinction of race or color."

They also placed themselves behind passage of a law to distribute home-steads out of the state's unappropriated public domain for "those of our citizens, without distinction of race or color, who have never received any portion of the public lands." These basic goals would remain unchanged through the Reconstruction era, and E. J. Davis would be perhaps their firmest advocate.[21]

To pave the way for Republican success in any future election, the Houston delegates also took steps towards gaining control over the apparatus of state and local government before any vote was held. The convention urged military officials to remove all of the office holders in the state who had "participated in rebellion or who are hostile to Congress." This was a goal since Congress acted in March. Indeed, shortly after the creation of the Fifth Military District, Unionists at Austin sent a delegation to meet with General Sheridan at New Orleans to push for the removal of Governor Throckmorton. On their way, they met with General Griffin in Galveston and found that they had an ally. A member reported that they had a "most cheering and satisfactory interview with Genl. Griffin." In fact, on 2 April Griffin telegraphed General Sheridan at New Orleans asking for Throckmorton's removal, charging that the governor impeded the process of registration and concluding that securing a successful reconstruction could only be achieved with sweeping removals of disloyal men in office. This gave the Unionists hope. However, Sheridan did not act because he was uncertain that he had the power to make such removals. The Houston convention gave Sheridan and Griffin another push.[22]

The military commanders sympathized with the Texas Republicans, but remained unwilling to act until the end of July. The way for removals was opened on 30 July, when General Grant informed Sheridan that he had the authority to remove any civil officials considered to be impediments to Reconstruction. Sheridan did not hesitate. On the day that he received Grant's telegram he removed Throckmorton from office, declaring him to be an impediment to Reconstruction. This was the first step taken towards putting Republican officials into local offices before the election. Who those appointees should be was not initially determined. The principal candidate for the governorship was

Elisha Pease. Pease later denied that he sought the office, but his supporters forwarded his name as early as the previous June. However, some
Republicans were uncertain about Pease. In private discussions Pease's
opponents urged that General Davis be considered. Davis's supporters preferred him because they believed that he would be a "harsher
and sterner" official. Without question, Davis's career up to this point
indicated that he still looked for some sort of justice to be carried out
towards the participants in the Rebellion. Davis's duties elsewhere kept
him away from both Austin and Griffin's headquarters in Galveston, so
he was unable to put forward his own cause. In the end, Griffin named
Pease as the new governor.[23]

Republicans hoped that Throckmorton's removal was just the
beginning and were ready to put their supporters into as many public
offices as they could. General Griffin agreed with their goals and was
ready to act. However, both were frustrated when following his action
against Throckmorton, General Sheridan got cold feet and refused to
make the wholesale removals they sought. Ultimately, President Johnson, the man who tried to protect Southern governments like that of
Throckmorton, paved the way for the Texas Republicans to secure their
goals. In August, the president replaced Sheridan as commander of the
Fifth District with General Winfield S. Hancock. Hancock did not go
to New Orleans to take over his command immediately. On leaving
the South, Sheridan gave the command temporarily to Griffin and also
authorized him to replace whichever officials he deemed disloyal. Even
before formally assuming his command, Griffin acted. On 27 August
he removed the heads of the state executive departments, then followed
with the dismissal of the state supreme court and some of the district
judges. He subsequently turned his attention to county officials. Republicans appeared on the verge of taking over state and local governments
prior to the proposed convention election.[24]

As removals proceeded, Davis did what he could to ensure that
men he considered loyal were protected and the disloyal replaced.
Through the early days of Reconstruction, Governor Hamilton found
determining loyalty very difficult. Some of the men he appointed to
office turned out to be his most active opponents. When Pease moved

into the governor's office he asked for local Republicans to help him with appointments. Davis, who practiced law in southern Texas for years and whose work as registration supervisor took him across the area, was well-positioned to help. The news he shared with party leaders in Austin, however, was not optimistic. Indeed, he presented a gloomy picture of loyalty in the southern counties of the state and expressed considerable pessimism as to the Republican Party's ability to effect significant change. He believed that disloyalty was prevalent among officeholders across the region, and concluded that most public officials required removal in every county "between the Nueces & San Antonio Rivers." Davis believed, however, that wholesale removals were impractical and would leave the area without government since "it is entirely impossible to find persons who can fill the offices under the requirements of the act of Congress." When he found men who could meet the requirements for office, he did make recommendations, but the numbers were few. In the end, the problems exposed by Davis became one of the reasons that Republicans never effectively removed disloyal officeholders.[25]

Griffin's removals did present Davis with another opportunity to move to the center of political developments. Once again he found himself in a position that prevented him from taking advantage of that chance. This time, following the removal of the judges of the supreme court, General Griffin offered Davis the position of chief justice. The appointment created an awkward problem because the King case appealed to the state supreme court and was scheduled to be heard in its December term. As a result, Davis did not accept the position. Instead, Griffin named Jack Hamilton to the bench. Davis didn't get the job, but he did finish with his obligation to the King interests. When their case finally appeared before the court, Davis presented the arguments and Judge C. J. Morrill ruled in favor of the King interests, ordering that the judgment should be entered on the basis of the original award. Davis had won his case. Legal business, however, had kept him away from that of helping to build the state Republican Party.[26]

In the midst of political upheaval, Davis and other Texans faced a natural catastrophe that turned their attention, at least for a time, away from politics. The Texas coastal region was long subjected to periodic plagues of yellow fever, and in late summer 1867, the fever appeared once again. Communities along the coast were scourged. In September, one of its victims was General Griffin, who died at Galveston on the 15th. Davis's family had been in Corpus Christi through most of the summer, a location that placed them in the center of the epidemic. Davis was there with his family when the fever struck, and they decided to remain at home rather than travel inland. Davis escaped the fever, but his two sons, Britton and Waters, contracted it. The family was fortunate, however, for the children's cases were what Davis described as light, and they recovered. Lizzie, like her husband, didn't contract the fever, but the very threat to her that it presented elicited from Davis one of the few statements he ever made regarding his feelings towards his wife. The fact that she might become ill frightened him, and he worried, informing a friend, "I'll never feel secure for her as long as there is any of it here."[27]

Davis's behavior during the epidemic provided dramatic insight into the strength of character he had developed by this time, showing how his ideas of duty and responsibility provided a framework for his actions. The fever not only threatened his family but inflicted serious suffering on the people of Corpus Christi, and Davis did what he could to help. In a letter to his law partner, he estimated that by mid-August over one hundred persons had died locally. In such a situation, he did not hesitate to do what he could for the sufferers. Contemporary accounts described the general's actions as virtually heroic. He nursed the ill, providing "diligent and willing" service. In one case, he carried a dying woman to the home of her mother, who also was dying, so that they could spend their last moments together. His behavior in the crisis that summer indicated that Davis was a man who not only possessed a deep love and concern for the well-being of his family but that he also possessed a similar compassion for the people of the community in which he lived.[28]

Davis had not been able to take advantage of the opportunities afforded him to assume a greater leadership role in the developing Republican Party. As has been seen, he was not even able to attend its first state convention. He had done what he could, however, to facilitate the party's growth, and he intended to play a greater role in the future. That autumn, 1867, Davis announced that he emphatically wanted to participate in the next constitutional convention and that he would run for a seat. In a letter to his law partner, Stephen Powers, he shared his plans for the future. "*I will be a candidate* for the convention in my District," he wrote, "whenever that may be."[29]

Davis's opportunity came soon enough. General Sheridan delayed an election in Texas when he stepped down as commander of the Fifth Military District that September without calling an election and his replacement, General Winfield Scott Hancock, was delayed in reaching New Orleans to assume command. Hancock finally arrived there in late November and called the election. On 18 December, Hancock issued an election proclamation, declaring 10–14 February 1868, as the dates that the people of Texas would go to the polls to choose delegates to the new constitutional convention.[30]

In early December, Davis received the nomination for the district that included Corpus Christi. At San Antonio, the editor of the *San Antonio Express* welcomed his choice, expressing his belief that Davis possessed the qualities that made him well-suited for framing a constitution. He would bring with him to Austin a reputation as a "ripe scholar, a fine lawyer, an earnest and logical debater." That would make him a natural leader in the convention. A subsequent editorial elaborated further on the characteristics that defined Davis's identity and made him a potential leader, describing him as a man who possessed ability, integrity, and trustworthiness. In fact, Davis's candidacy would need little promotion in the campaign, for the Democratic opposition was uncertain what strategy they should use in the election. The election not only would select delegates, but it also would determine whether or not a convention would be held. A majority of registered voters had to participate at the polls for a convention to be called. Initially, Democrats considered defeating the convention by not voting, then changed their position just prior to the election. As a result of the indecision, many Democrats simply sat out the election in the hopes that not enough people would cast votes to allow the convention. As a result, Davis faced minimal opposition.[31]

Statewide, the turnout indicated the indecision among those who opposed congressional Reconstruction. The number of men who voted,

52 percent of those registered, just barely met the requirement that a majority of voters had to participate in the election for a convention to be called. Across the state most of the opposition stayed at home on election day, resulting in overwhelming approval of the convention and the selection of Republican candidates. The vote in Davis's district reflected the broader trends. He carried his district with a crushing defeat of the opposition in the counties that held an election. In Nueces County he received 114 of 119 votes, 29 of 30 in Zapata, and all the votes in Webb and Hidalgo. The turnout, however, indicated that only a small proportion of the potential voters in the district cast ballots. In Nueces County, Davis's 119 votes was only 43 percent of the total of 280 who voted only a year and a half before and just 36 percent of the 330 who participated in the 1861 gubernatorial race. Nonetheless, E. J. Davis would go to Austin and work once again to establish the loyal government that he had hoped to put in place since the war's end. The convention also would become the arena within which he would finally emerge as one of the unquestioned state leaders of his party.[32]

DAVIS AND THE REPUBLICAN SCHISM: THE CONSTITUTIONAL CONVENTION OF 1868–1869

"I would say that in my judgment the great mass of the conservatives of the State with their views and feelings towards the government of the country are not fitted to govern this State."

—Edmund J. Davis to
the Constitutional Convention, 1868

T hrough the war and then the first years of Reconstruction, Edmund J. Davis found himself relegated to secondary roles as he attempted to change the direction of events that involved him. His experiences had helped to shape his character, but Davis seldom had the opportunity to shape these events. His election to the new constitutional convention changed all that. During the sessions of the convention Davis would find himself having to make choices once again. This time the choices he faced were forced by the divergence by the associates of Governor Pease from Davis's own view of the proper course for Reconstruction. Breaking with them, Davis would find himself accepted as their leader by a large number of the state's Republicans who had similar views. The constitutional convention provided the stage upon which Davis became the chief of what contemporaries called the state's Radical Republican Party, a role that would make it possible for him to try to reshape events in the future.

Davis had been a team player within the Texas Republican Party prior to the convention. He was seen as an associate and supporter of

Governor Pease. His position as a party regular was recognized prior to the Austin convention when the party's state executive committee named him as one of the delegates to the national convention in Chicago. The appointment was an honor, although Davis was not able to attend. Military authorities made any participation at Chicago impossible when they changed the opening date of the constitutional convention from 15 June to 1 June. On the first of June, Davis was in Austin, where reporters recognized his presence, particularly noting that he was the tallest man present at six feet two and a half inches in height.[1]

That Davis would play an important role in the state convention became apparent on the first day when a majority of delegates elected him its president. His choice probably had as much to do with a dispute between Governor Pease and members of the executive department as with any particular virtues of the general. That dispute centered on the old question of *ab initio* and involved the governor and his comptroller, Jack Hamilton's brother, Morgan. Morgan Hamilton believed, as had the Unionists in the 1866 convention, that secession was illegal and that all acts of the state government afterwards were null and void. The comptroller's interpretation of *ab initio* had come to apply also to the work of the constitutional convention in 1866 and the Eleventh Legislature. Pease, on the other hand, had changed his mind on the issue. Certitude cannot determine his motives. His supporters later insisted that the governor saw that accepting Hamilton's idea would deadlock government and that he had no choice other than recognizing the legal character of past governments. His critics contended that his new position simply accommodated the state's railroad interests, particularly the Houston & Texas Central. At the war's end, the state legislature allowed several railroads to make payments on loans they had secured from the state school fund in Confederate money. Pease's stance would legitimize these payments. Morgan Hamilton's would force them to repay these debts in specie, as required by the law originally authorizing the loans. Unable to resolve the question among them, Pease, Hamilton, and their adherents would try to settle it during the convention.[2]

The selection of a convention president was the first test of strength between the rival factions of Morgan Hamilton and Governor

Pease, parties by this time labeled Radical and Conservative Republicans by the press. While the terms were the same as those used to describe divisions within the national party, in Texas they initially reflected only rivalries produced by the *ab initio* dispute. In the contest for the president, Jack Hamilton, who was a delegate and a strong supporter of the governor rather than his brother, nominated Colbert Caldwell of Bowie County. Caldwell was not an attractive choice among conservative and moderate Republican delegates. He possessed a reputation for being radical on the question of civil rights for the freedmen and also was disliked for his role in helping to organize the Union League. Morgan Hamilton's immediate associates in the convention were equally unattractive and their nomination probably would have ensured Caldwell's victory. For strategic reasons, Morgan Hamilton surprisingly nominated Davis, who up to this point had not taken a strong stand on the *ab initio* issue. Davis won, giving the comptroller a president who was at least neutral rather than one who would be hostile.[3]

Contemporaries were uncertain what Davis's victory meant, but most welcomed it and offered general approval of his choice. The editor of the *San Antonio Express,* a Republican journal not yet clearly linked to either faction within the party, believed that Davis's choice indicated that the convention would pursue a straightforward Republican course. He believed that the selection of Davis meant that the delegates would be governed by the "most ultra principles of human liberty and justice, [and] wherever principle is at stake there will be no compromise." Davis would ensure this adherence to principle, and the editor praised him as a lawyer and judge of "no mean reputation" who stood among the heads of his profession. The reporter for the *Galveston News,* a conservative journal, concluded that Davis's victory meant that moderates controlled the convention, seeing in the general the less radical of the candidates. While the maneuvering behind his nomination and victory and their significance relative to party factionalism can never be known with certainty, no one seemed to think that Morgan Hamilton had won. They did believe, however, that Governor Pease had lost.[4]

At least as president of the convention, Davis's subsequent actions showed that he ran affairs with an eye to rules, acting with fairness, and getting a constitution written. While in the president's chair he tried to run the convention without regard to faction and frequently even played the role of compromiser. He did his job with the dedication and precision that always had characterized his work. The following December one of the delegates proposed that Davis receive double the pay allotted to him for his "incessant and unremitting labors." While thanking the delegate, Davis's response was characteristic of his sense of public duty when he told the convention that he would not accept such a reward. During the convention sessions Davis would take strong stands and become an advocate for controversial positions. These would attract considerable criticism from his enemies. When he acted as president, however, little that was partisan appeared, and contemporary newspaper observers appeared to be correct in outlining the role they predicted he would play.[5]

A fair leader of the convention, Davis nonetheless had strong views on policy and worked hard to implement those he supported. Understanding the positions that he took required some grasp of his views of Texas in 1868 and what kind of constitution and government that he believed such a community needed. Without question, the characteristic that he and many others in the convention saw as dominating political life was the hostility that existed to any effort at creating a government that accepted the results of the war, which allowed Unionists any voice in government, or that acquiesced in black freedom. Further, this opposition was not expressed just in legitimate political opposition but in the use of violence and intimidation against those who favored acceptance. From the beginning, no single issue hung over the deliberations of the convention and helped to shape its course more than this view of the uncompromising and violent character of the political opposition.

Critics argued that Republicans over-dramatized the violence, but events seemed to support them in their contentions. In the governor's message to the convention, delivered on 3 June, Pease wrote that "crime was never more prevalent in Texas." All Davis and other Republicans had to do to recognize the validity of this assessment was look at the violence aimed at Republicans in the convention election. In one of the more notorious attacks, Colbert Caldwell was assaulted while campaigning at Marshall. On 31 December 1867, an effort had been made to break up a Republican rally being held in the courthouse. Local law enforcement officials not only had failed to break up the attack, but the police chief and sheriff actually participated in the assault. When the attack was pushed back, gunfire broke out and someone shot at Caldwell in an attempt to assassinate him. The attack on Caldwell dramatically illustrated the character of the political opposition at the time.[6]

That opposition began to effect a real organization as the convention sat, and it showed little desire to compromise on the issues of the day. Particularly on the question of black rights, they showed no willingness to bend. On 7 July, pre-war Democratic stalwarts such as John H. Reagan and Henry E. McCulloch joined with conservative Unionists such as James Throckmorton in a meeting at Bryan to reorganize the Democratic Party. While professing loyalty to the union, they made it clear that they not only opposed the course of congressional Reconstruction but ultimately would try to overthrow it. In their platform they proclaimed the belief that "the power to regulate the question of suffrage within the States rests exclusively with the States themselves" and their conclusion that the effort of Congress to force black suffrage on the states was unconstitutional. Black suffrage was seen as "temporary," and they believed Democratic success would ensure the repeal of black suffrage, along with "all kindred legislation." This spirit manifested itself even in the constitutional convention, where in debate on suffrage provisions for the constitution M. L. Armstrong, a Democrat from Jasper County, introduced a substitute that excluded "Africans and descendants of Africans" from the vote. Clearly, the Democrats had in no way accepted the idea of political equality.[7]

A parallel development was even more disconcerting. As Democrats held their meetings across the state to create local party organizations, meetings of the Ku Klux Klan also took place. The Klan was a secret organization with earlier origins in Tennessee. In 1868, local newspapers took notice of its sudden appearance in Texas and its activities aimed primarily at the intimidation of black communities. One particularly brazen display of their strength came at Millican in Brazos County in July. There men dressed in the costumes of the Klan and had marched through a freedmen's community. The freedmen attacked the marchers and drove them out. The Klansmen threatened to return. When fighting did break out, the Klansmen killed several blacks, including George E. Brooks, a prominent political leader and minister. Only intervention by a Freedmen's Bureau agent and United States troops prevented a potential massacre. Democrats insisted that there was no relationship between themselves and the Klan, but the fact that the Klan appeared at the same time as Democratic reorganization and the common goals of the two groups convinced Republicans that the Klan and the Democratic Party were one and the same. Republicans believed that violence would be part of any future political campaigns.[8]

Faced daily with news of violence across the countryside and the uncompromising attitude of their opponents, on 5 June the convention adopted a motion to name a special committee on lawlessness and violence. Davis appointed Colbert Caldwell, his opponent for the president's chair, to head the committee. The committee reported back to the convention on 30 June, and the picture it presented was a dark catalogue of crime, much of which was anti-Reconstruction in character. Davis had no questions about the accuracy of the committee's figures or its interpretation of the causes of crime. On 2 July he stepped down from the president's chair to give a speech that set out his views, calling the pervasive outlawry a "reign of terror." For Davis the situation had its origins among the men who took Texas into secession and then ruled through the war years. He also had no doubt that the violence was aimed at overturning Reconstruction and led by the "old secession rebel elements" and the "devoted adherents of the lost cause."[9]

Later in the convention, Davis went to the floor again to talk about violence, and once more, he blamed the unstable situation on the Democrats. "I would say," he told members of the convention, ". . . that in my judgment the great mass of the conservatives of the State with their views and feelings towards the government of the country are not fitted to govern this State." Still, they desperately wanted to regain power and were driven by a singular idea. That idea, according to Davis, was one that asserted, "We Confederates are the rightful rulers of this country, and no persons will be tolerated among us who call in question our right to govern it." Such ideas ran counter to Davis's own. He wanted to take the steps necessary to place state government in the hands of its "loyal people." To do that, given the character of the opposition, free speech, freedom of expression, and equal rights for all would have to be guaranteed and protected. Creating the conditions necessary for loyal government would be the chief aim for Davis throughout the convention.[10]

Davis went to Austin believing that the members of the Republican Party agreed, at least in general, on what they should do to guarantee that the old secessionist element did not regain power. He quickly concluded that divisions within the Republican Party threatened those goals. Not only could they not find common ground, the rival parties also refused to compromise their positions. In the end, Davis would conclude that the conservative position posed the greatest threat to restoring loyal government. That conclusion would force him to become an active leader of the radical Republicans by the end of the summer.

Davis's concern with Republican factionalism emerged first as the two groups fought over the question of *ab initio*. A resolution dealing with the legality of secession and all subsequent governmental actions first came up on the floor on 5 June, when Andrew Jackson Evans of Waco introduced a measure declaring all of these null and void from the beginning or *ab initio*. Davis had not taken a hard line on the issue before the convention, although, like most Unionists, he assuredly supported the basic idea. Debate on the convention floor, however, threatened to tear apart the old Unionist alliance. The conservatives charged that the radicals who supported *ab initio* were men wedded to an impractical theory who were willing to nullify every marriage since secession. In turn, the radicals charged the conservatives with betraying principle and doing nothing more than working for the state's railroads. Debate was passionate and often contentious.[11]

Davis did not participate in the debate during the early proceedings, but with no compromise in the offing he acted. On 1 July he introduced his own *ab initio* measure, stepping down from the president's chair to support it from the floor. His declaration attempted a practical solution that would allow the radicals to secure some sort of retribution from former Confederates and at the same time legalize some of the acts of government, as desired by the conservatives. It offered a compromise between the contending parties that recognized the theory of *ab initio* while avoiding the chaos predicted by Governor Pease. Davis's proposal declared all action by the state government between February 1861 and August 1865 null and void and the action of the convention of 1866 and that of the subsequent legislature as without legal authority and provisional in nature. At the same time, the declaration allowed the convention to name specific laws to be considered valid and with the force of law. Provisions also were made for the validation of all actions such as marriages, land agreements, and private contracts. The measure additionally recognized private legislation, such as the incorporation or chartering of companies. There was a restriction on the latter, for the declaration proposed that they considered corporate charters legal only when the company had actually commenced operations and pursued a meritorious object and was not "for the purpose of rewarding persons lately in rebellion." Davis also excluded from legalization any action that might impinge upon the right of loyal men and their heirs to commence legal proceedings against those who had taken their property, thus ensuring that loyal men would not be "prejudiced in their rights." The exclusions raised serious questions about the legality of laws that allowed the state's railroads to repay their debts to the school fund in Confederate money.[12]

Davis's declaration came to nothing. It was sent to Morgan Hamilton's Committee on General Provisions, and when it came out of that committee they stripped it of language allowing the validation of any legislation. The report expressed the committee's "repugnance to accepting as valid any law passed by those in rebellion against the government." Morgan Hamilton refused to compromise. As deliberations on the issue continued, however, the conservatives proved equally uncompromising. Jack Hamilton successfully blocked any effort at retaining language in the constitution that would challenge the legality of measures such as the wartime railroad legislation. Republican factionalism gave little hope to

Davis that anything the convention did could lead to a loyal government and reinforced his belief that only a division of the state might produce the desired result. The question of division ultimately came up in the convention, and it would become another issue over which radicals and conservatives would fight. In the mind of E. J. Davis, it also produced growing concern for the future.[13]

Davis had first concluded that division was necessary to create a haven for Texas Unionists following the 1866 election. He had not actively pursued that goal afterwards, although some Unionists did. One of the most prominent of these men was Edward Degener of San Antonio who had led efforts to get congressional intervention in favor of division. Now, Degener was a delegate to the convention, and he introduced the issue when he proposed the creation of a committee to consider a division. Davis named the committee, and it produced a report that favored division. Its supporters, however, were unable to get the convention to act favorably on it or any other pro-division measure. Once again, radicals and conservatives divided, with the radicals favoring action and the conservatives in opposition. As in the case of *ab initio,* Jack Hamilton led the conservatives.[14]

Much was at stake in the division question, a fact that made compromise more difficult. In petitioning Congress earlier for the creation of a new state, men in San Antonio made the radical case. They desired the formation of a state to the west of a line mid-way between the Colorado and Brazos rivers. The result would be a state in which the majority of the people would "prove firm supporters of the Union." In addition, citizens would be able to take care of their own interests, interests that differed from those of northern and eastern Texas. The consequences of not acting were dire. They warned that, if not protected, Union men would be "compelled to abandon the country and seek homes elsewhere." Governor Pease presented the conservative argument to keep Texas together in his message to the convention when he argued that division would simply create expensive, under-populated states. Davis believed that more was involved and that the anti-divisionists worked in support of the interests of Austin and central Texas. Division would see a relocation of the capital and the destruction of Austin. Austin's backers, Davis concluded, would do anything to keep that from happening.[15]

Given what the parties believed was at stake, the early appearance of the division question in the convention and the amount of time spent considering it is not surprising. A majority of the delegates favored creating a new state, but they faced stiff opposition in the form of Jack Hamilton, a master of the parliamentary maneuver. Hamilton took advantage of the fact that the pro-division delegates could not agree on where to draw the boundaries between the proposed states and the doubt some had that the convention had the authority to even consider division to keep the majority from working together. When they appeared to reach an agreement, Hamilton prevented a favorable vote by taking advantage of a parliamentary rule known as a call of the house. When a call was made all other business on the floor was suspended until a roll call determined all members of the convention were present. If they were not, nothing could be done until all, unless excused, were present. Orchestrating the absence of members, Hamilton would request a call when any division measure came up for a vote and successfully block votes. The maneuver stalled the other work of the convention, as well. Hamilton's use of what many in the convention considered a technicality to thwart the will of the majority generated considerable hostility towards him. Some pro-division delegates ultimately concluded that the convention had to move ahead, however, and on 17 July, Hamilton managed to get a favorable vote on a resolution that temporarily barred further discussion of division unless Congress gave the convention the authority to act.[16]

For E. J. Davis, the inability of Republican factions to reach agreement on *ab initio* and division offered little hope that when Texas returned to the Union it would not fall quickly into the hands of the men who had led Texas out of the Union. In terms of avoiding this likelihood, Davis saw an even more ominous threat when the Republicans fractured on the question of voting rights. In his address, Governor Pease called for restrictions on the voting rights of men who had participated in the rebellion, a position with which Davis agreed. An early version of the suffrage clause for the constitution reflected this intent, when it provided for a state system of voter registration. All who registered to vote were to swear an oath that they were not disfranchised by any earlier disfranchisement provisions, had not served in any office of state government and then engaged in the insurrection, had never taken an oath to support the Constitution of the United States and then rebelled, had not as a minister or newspaper editor urged secession, had not been a member of any state convention and voted in favor of the Ordinance of Secession, and were not members of any secret organizations hostile to the government of the United States. The restrictions would prevent most of the state's prewar leadership from voting or holding office and would make sure that they would realize the goal of men like Davis was to keep the men who took the state into war from ever having power again. By late June, however, the conservatives backed away from such measures. On 25 June, Jack Hamilton, in a speech at the state convention of the Union League, declared his belief that the new constitution should place no restrictions on the voting rights of former Confederates. A failure to restrict the political activities of these former Confederate leaders struck at the very heart of the loyal government E. J. Davis desired.[17]

For many Republicans and especially the radicals, Jack Hamilton's actions in the convention suggested that the Pease administration had surrendered to the rebels. Discontent first appeared outside the convention when the Union League held its state convention in Austin in late June. The state league organization had been in the hands of associates of Governor Pease since its formation the previous year, but they could not contain the protest of black delegates who charged that Pease and the Conservative Republicans in the convention had failed to protect them from the endemic violence and had done nothing to secure their civil rights. When James Bell, a friend of Pease and long-time officer in the state league, ran for the presidency, he faced opposition from George T. Ruby, a black delegate to the convention from Galveston and an organizer of local league chapters. Ruby won, sending a warning to the conservative leaders of the strength of those dissatisfied with their course.[18]

Discontent among Republican voters opened the possibility that E. J. Davis might change the course of the convention by making a case for his own plan of reconstruction to the delegates at the state Republican convention that was to be held in Austin on 12 August. Davis now aligned himself for the most part with the Radicals. He determined to bring up the issues of *ab initio* and division in the convention and have these measures written into the party platform. On the evening before the convention opened, Davis met with Morgan Hamilton, James Newcomb, and George Ruby to determine strategy for the convention. As in the constitutional convention, Davis's hopes were defeated quickly when it became clear that the Pease conservatives had the votes to control business. They elected their candidate as chairman. As a result, when Davis introduced a resolution to add *ab initio* to the platform, it failed.

Davis was convinced by its actions that the convention did not represent the will of the majority of the state's Republicans. As a result, he concluded that the only course left was to challenge the leadership of his party. Davis, along with Morgan Hamilton and many of the radicals from the convention, walked out of the convention. On 15 August they met at the capitol in the Senate chamber to discuss their course of action. The result was the creation of a second state Republican organization. The radicals had now created what the press called the Radical Republican Party. Their platform reflected its author's concern with the conservative course in the convention. It embraced the *ab initio* idea. It called for protection of the state's citizens. It also evidenced a further moving away from the conservative agenda when it insisted that the formation of public schools should take precedence over state support for either manufacturing or railroads. Morgan Hamilton became the head of the new party when he was named chairman of the state executive committee. E. J. Davis, however, had now assumed a major role in state affairs, standing in opposition to the Pease administration and assuming a major role in the creation of the new party.[19]

Shortly after the Radicals formally split with the Conservative Republicans, the struggles between the two factions that had occupied much of the time of the constitutional convention temporarily came to a halt. Radicals and conservatives combined to adjourn the convention on 31 August, with the provision that it would reassemble on the first Monday in December. At least for a time national politics had intervened. Early in July, a delegation was sent to Washington to deliver a report the convention had produced that described the problem of violence in the state. The situation in Texas concerned national Republican leaders, who concluded that Texas could not have a peaceful election in the upcoming presidential contest and that a Democratic victory would occur if one were held. Texas Republicans responded by adjourning the convention. If the constitution was not completed, then the state could not return to the Union. There would be no election giving the Democratic presidential candidate more electoral votes. Davis and the other delegates returned home, and for three months factional fighting in Texas appeared to cease. The respite would be short.[20]

On 7 December the constitutional convention reassembled. Davis returned believing that the time spent at home had been good for the delegates. In particular, he believed that some had seen the concern voters at home had with the course of conservative Republicans in the first session. This changed attitudes. He found this to be true particularly concerning the question of division, where many who had opposed division had converted to "unconditional" divisionists and were ready to support an ordinance dividing the state or to ask Congress to do so. Subsequent votes confirmed Davis's analysis. This shift gave Davis a clear majority in favor of division and promised action that would finally provide the one truly workable solution, as he saw it, to the problem of Reconstruction.[21]

Even though now a majority, the divisionists still confronted the capable parliamentarian, Jack Hamilton. Although now leading an unquestionable minority, Hamilton had tools at hand to frustrate the majority. A number of delegates had not returned for the second session of the convention and their absences were not excused. As a result, a call of the house would bring an end to business on the floor and could not be stopped since the absent delegates were not even in Austin—at least one was no longer in the state. Through December, Hamilton repeatedly used this tactic to block any effort at acting on the division question. In frustration, some delegates from western Texas essentially attempted to secede from the state, drafting a constitution for a new state and planning to ask Congress for admission. They attempted to adjourn the convention.[22]

Hamilton's tactics blocked division. Unfortunately for the process of writing a constitution, they halted that as well. Even though floor discussions during the first session and then through December had centered on *ab initio* and division, committees had been busily drafting elements of the constitution. When the convention adjourned in August, the editor of the *San Antonio Express* understood that the work of the convention was on the verge of being finished. Now the constitution sat in committee, kept off the floor by Hamilton's maneuvering. E. J. Davis faced a difficult problem as president of the convention. His job was to shepherd a new constitution through to completion, and that was not happening. In mid-January, Davis finally broke the deadlock.

On 16 January, Davis acted: when a committee asked how to stop Hamilton's delaying tactics, Davis reported a resolution that would change the rules governing a call of the house. The new rule would consider only members who had attended during the previous five days in determining if all members were present. Hamilton tried to block consideration of the amendment with another call. This time Davis responded, ruling on a procedural matter that the presence of a simple majority of delegates was what was required for action. Hamilton and his supporters tried to break the quorum by leaving the floor, but Davis moved again. Reacting with what a reporter for the *San Antonio Express* called "firm and manly bearing," he had the delegates who left the floor arrested and returned. The convention then changed the rules. The anti-division Pease administration and the Democratic press viciously attacked Davis for his rulings, charging that he had acted illegally and not followed convention rules. In fact, as he had done in the past, Davis appeared to follow common rules of parliamentary practice closely, in this case, the rule that unless otherwise stated, a simple majority always governed proceedings.[23]

Davis's determination on the question of rules and the subsequent vote allowed the convention to move forward on division and the business of writing a constitution. On 20 January delegates took up another division resolution that asked Congress to divide the state. The opposition tried to use the call of the house again. This time one of their members purposely left the floor. Davis ordered the sergeant-at-arms to find him. When he was unable to bring him back, the majority voted to expel the member and the House was announced as full. Hamilton appealed, but Davis ruled the expulsion was in order, that the rules of the convention were made to facilitate business, and that the convention had the power to protect itself by expelling members who had purposely acted to impede its business. At this point the question of division finally came to a vote, passing thirty-nine to thirty. The next day delegates chose a party to carry the resolution to Washington. Davis was to be among the members.[24]

Uncertain how Congress would respond, some divisionists determined to adjourn and let Congress either accept or reject their proposal before continuing. Believing that the convention would adjourn, some left Austin, shifting the majority in the convention back into the hands of Jack Hamilton. Hamilton was not ready for the convention to stop its work, and those supporting adjournment were to secure their goal. Davis remained in Austin and now watched as Hamilton and the conservative Republicans placed their own brand on the proposed document. The committee had already written much of its provisions in committee and secured general agreement from the delegates. Inclusion only awaited action on the floor. One issue, however, had not been settled. Hamilton wanted to replace the restrictive draft suffrage clause with another. On 3 February he offered a substitute that gave the vote to every adult male citizen not disfranchised by the United States. It did pose a potential threat to black voting, requiring voters to have lived in the state for a year and in the county for sixty days. Only fifty-six of the ninety elected delegates remained in the convention. Hamilton's supporters pushed the measure through, thirty to twenty-six.[25]

E. J. Davis had not believed the convention should stop after the division question passed, but the work it had now completed he found unacceptable. On 4 February, the Radical Republican members placed their disapproval of the proposed constitution in the *Journal.* They once again returned to *ab initio,* charging that the new constitution had failed to recognize the continuing supremacy of the United States and state constitutions during the war, and that it refused to accept that the acts of the state government during the war and presidential Reconstruction were null and void. They also condemned the new constitution because it gave the vote to men who had voluntarily become the public enemies of the United States, something the minority felt Congress never intended. Further, they charged the document removed all safeguards protecting loyal white and black voters, by removing the registration system and the oath of loyalty from the process. In particular, they contended that the provision regarding suffrage passed by the majority with a premeditated and deliberate deception and by methods of intimidation. Davis signed the protest.[26]

The feelings between members of the two Republican factions worsened, however, and the final days of the convention witnessed the two sides come to the verge of violence as each jockeyed for some advantage after the convention adjourned. On 4 February the two sides sparred over a resolution offered by Morgan Hamilton condemning Governor Pease and calling for every bill, declaration, and ordinance passed by the convention to be submitted separate from the constitution to the people. Jack Hamilton's supporters defeated it. The fighting then turned to the declaration providing for an election. Jack Hamilton wanted the returns submitted to the provisional governor. The radicals wanted them submitted to the commanding general. In this case the radicals carried the day. Through the evening of 4 February, the delegates struggled over adjournment, then a radical attempt to place some restrictions on the suffrage.[27]

On 5 February tensions between the various factions in the convention finally exploded when they took up the question of who would publish the results of the convention. The committee created to consider the issue introduced a report that would have divided the publication among various Republican newspapers, but Hamilton's supporters introduced a substitute to give the whole job to the *Austin Republican*. This would give the administration newspaper thirty thousand dollars, a significant subsidy to set the paper up for the election campaign. With many members already gone, Hamilton had enough votes to pass the measure. Then the opposition blocked him by using his own tactics. They left the floor and broke the quorum. Davis ordered the arrest of members of his own party, but ultimately adjourned the session until that evening.[28]

The evening session proved even more chaotic. Some radicals remained away, intending to stop convention business. Hamilton demanded a call of the house and dispatched the sergeant-at-arms to round up those who were gone so that the convention could take up the printing question again. In addition, he made it clear that he had no intention of adjourning the convention. During the afternoon, however, Davis had met with General E. R. S. Canby, now in command of the district, to determine how the convention might be brought to an end. Canby urged Davis to see if some sort of compromise might be reached that would allow the convention to adjourn in a "decorous manner." In addition, Canby said that he would see to printing the convention journal and the constitution. Canby effectively had stopped the *Republican* from receiving any money from the convention itself. That evening Davis announced the details of his conversation with Canby and urged the delegates to adjourn. Exactly what followed is unclear, but following Davis's announcement, W. W. Mills, the delegate from El Paso and a relative of Jack Hamilton, rose and insulted Davis. Placed under arrest for the insult to the president and ordered to apologize, Mills insulted Davis further. Confusion followed until Davis finally gaveled the session closed until the next morning. Gathering his papers and putting on his hat, Davis headed for the door. When some of Hamilton's supporters tried to stop him, the president continued down the aisle until he reached the door, where he turned and ordered the convention officials not to obey any order given by those who remained. When one of Jack Hamilton's supporters tried to prevent him from leaving, pistols were drawn and Davis exited.[29]

The convention finally came to an end the next day. On the morning of 6 February, Davis and most of the radicals remained away. Hamilton and his supporters, however, were there. The thirty-six members present did not constitute a quorum, but they proceeded to elect a new president to replace Davis. In addition, they appointed a committee to meet with General Canby. The meeting with Canby did not go well, and the general told them that since their work was finished they should adjourn and go home. They reassembled, then adjourned to meet again on the following Monday. On the afternoon of 6 February, however, Canby and Davis met again. This time Canby told him to adjourn the convention without delay and sent one of his officers with him. Davis immediately sent out a call for all members to be present in the Representatives hall at 7:30 P.M. When he arrived he found the gallery filled with men whom a reporter from the *San Antonio Express* believed would have assassinated Davis if they had a chance. When they found Davis accompanied by the officer, however, they left. Despite the fact that no quorum was present, Davis adjourned the convention and turned the convention's papers over to the officer who had accompanied him. When they left the building, the officer had the side doors of the hall nailed shut and the main door locked. The convention was over.[30]

Davis left Austin, but another role remained for him to play relative to the convention. He became an advocate for division in Washington. Following the passage of the convention's resolution recommending division, commissioners had been named to carry the resolution to Washington. He was one of the commissioners. After a short visit to his home at Corpus Christi, he sailed to New Orleans where, along with some of Jack Hamilton's supporters, he took the train to the East. He arrived at the capital on 27 February, where he found the city full of visitors who had come to town for the inauguration of Ulysses S. Grant. He also found that Jack Hamilton had beaten the division commissioners to Washington and already presented their case. He urged no new state be created and an election be ordered immediately. Newspaper reports of a 2 March meeting at the White House suggested that the president had responded favorably, indicating that he thought an election should be held and that he did not favor division. Davis and the other commissioners did not get to meet with Grant until 1 April, but made their case to congressmen before then. They argued against an election, contending that Jack Hamilton's actions in the convention branded him and his supporters as traitors, and only division would protect loyal men in Texas.[31]

Grant actually washed his hands of Texas matters when he left the question to Congress. There a decision was left to the Joint Committee on Reconstruction, and it did not begin its hearings on the Texas situation until 30 March. The acrimony that had been part of the convention's breakup reemerged in Washington, and the committee's chair had trouble controlling the proceedings. Exactly what happened is uncertain, since the only source of information on the hearings are the letters of John Haynes, chair of the conservative Republican executive committee and clearly hostile to division. Jack Hamilton was the first to testify. Then, four days later, Davis spoke for the convention delegation. Davis repeated his belief that conditions in Texas were not amenable to the creation of a loyal government and that division was the only solution. He confessed his willingness to remain under military rule otherwise. Haynes reported that when Davis spoke, Hamilton broke in on his testimony, and the hearing nearly witnessed a physical confrontation. According to Haynes, Hamilton won the argument, but Congress's lack of quick action gave no clear indication who may have won the day.[32]

The rival parties had made their presentation. Following that, they could do little other than wait. Ultimately, conditions in the North were as important for the administration's decision as anything the Texans had said. By the spring of 1869 even the most radical Republicans in Congress were ready to end the military presence in the South. No one had sympathy with Davis's plan for a continued military occupation. When Congress finally acted, the conservative Republicans got their election. On 7 April the Committee on Reconstruction reported an election bill, it passed quickly through both houses, and the newly inaugurated president signed it on 10 April. The bill gave Grant the power to call an election, but it did not set the date. Hamilton had wanted an early election, but Congress encouraged the radicals to believe it could be delayed. Before they left Washington, what the president would do remained uncertain.[33]

In the wake of the decision by Congress, Davis and the other Texans returned home to prepare for whatever eventually presented itself. Davis had opposed an election, but one would be held. His own course was unclear. His efforts in the constitutional convention, however, had marked him as a figure to be reckoned with in Texas politics. He had proven his political skills as president of what may have been Texas's most tumultuous convention. His actions as president had demonstrated that he could be fair, even when possessing a partisan agenda. At the same time, he now had a clear political agenda and shown his willingness to work for it. He was an unquestioned leader of the Radical Republicans. At the same time, he had made powerful enemies, and they began to create the negative picture of E. J. Davis that became part of the view of him held by future generations of Texans. When he finally halted Jack Hamilton's delaying tactics in the convention and brought it to an end, he faced the wrath of conservative Republican newspapers and those of the resurgent Democrats. Alfred H. Longley, editor of the *Austin Republican,* may have contributed more to Davis's future image than any other when the editor charged that at the convention's end Davis had overcome justice, that Davis had permitted himself to "lose all sense of self-respect, to forget the gravity of the assemblage over which he presided, and to ignore any decency and decorum which were due to the Convention and the cause for which they met." Another editorial sounded the same tone, when after Davis's appearance before the Reconstruction Committee Longley characterized the general as a man who was "vindictive, malignant, and revengeful." Neither portrait did justice to the reality of Davis's character, but it would not be the last time his enemies would assault his personal character rather than the programs he advanced.[34]

THE ELECTION OF 1869

"I propose, Mr. President, if possible, to be the candidate of the whole Republican party, without regard to faction of clique. . . . Let us make every reasonable effort to bring about good feeling with such Republicans as heretofore differed from us."

—Edmund J. Davis, Speech Accepting
Nomination for Governor, 1869

Edmund J. Davis returned to Corpus Christi after his journey to Washington with an unclear picture of Reconstruction and his own future. He had emerged as a leader of the Radical Republicans, but the role he would play in that party's future was uncertain. Congress provided for a campaign and election, even though President Grant had not determined when it would be held. Davis certainly would participate in the canvass in some capacity. Davis was not sure what part he would play, but events already were unfolding that would thrust him into his party's candidacy for the governor. One of Texas's most controversial elections would make him the unquestioned chief of his party and the governor of Texas.

Even before a decision was made in Washington on a Texas election, the supporters of Jack Hamilton moved to obtain the political advantage. In February, Hamilton announced that when the election was held he would run as a candidate of the people, not affiliated with any party. On 15 February he made what amounted to the first campaign speech at Brenham prior to leaving for Washington. He declared his support for the proposed constitution, indicating that, while it had shortcomings, Texans should accept it. He reiterated the stand he took on universal suffrage in the convention, insisting that it was time to allow former Confederates to return to the political process. He counseled black voters to accept the return of their former masters to the polls, arguing that not to do so would only create ill-will. Going further he also advised them to accept their place and not demand more. He met criticism of the segregated school system that the constitution required, insisting that the schools required were good precisely because they did not compel white and black children to go to the same schools, to have "our children insulted by being compelled to mix with other than their own color." That speech raised serious questions about his political identity that would plague him in the coming year.[1]

Radical Republican leaders were uncertain, however, how to proceed if the administration ordered an election. Observers believed that Morgan Hamilton had concluded that the party should run E. J. Davis for governor, but in mid-February he asked party leaders to give their opinions on the matter. Hamilton particularly wanted to know how well his brother Jack would do against Davis. The result of his queries are unknown, but Morgan Hamilton gave no indication that a choice had been made prior to his own departure for Washington. Davis provided no evidence of a decision. He showed no sign of preparing for a campaign either at Washington or after his return.[2]

Jack Hamilton and his supporters continued to campaign after the delegates returned from Washington. His backers concluded that the radicals would put Davis forward for the governorship, and in May, Hamilton's men began an assault on Davis's policies and character. Alfred Longley, who had savaged Davis at the end of the convention, continued to do so on the pages of the *Austin Republican*. Asking why Davis and the radicals took the positions that they did on *ab initio*, division, and suffrage, Longley had provided his own answers. These were not practical issues, so the radicals must possess character flaws that motivated them. They were driven, in Longley's opinion, by personal grievances. The editor of *Flake's Bulletin* continued in this vein when he maintained that "these gentlemen are political invalids—they suffer from torpid livers—they see everything through a vision clouded with bile." By discounting the motives of the radicals, they attempted to dismiss real concerns that lay behind much of the radical agenda.[3]

Simply suggesting that such issues as *ab initio,* division, and suffrage were not important was not enough to win over many new Republicans who had yet to take sides in the dispute between conservatives and radicals. After the convention adjourned, Governor Pease began to receive letters from anxious prominent party members. August Siemering, whose *San Antonio Express* generally took a very moderate tone, was one. He reported widespread opposition to the proposed constitution and Jack Hamilton's support of it. Stephen Hackworth of Brenham expressed personal concern with the constitution's franchise clause in particular, asking Pease whether he now believed that they could trust the men who tried to destroy the federal government. He thought most of the old secessionists were not reformed, and he could not see turning over the "reins of Government into the hands of men who curse and openly abuse the Government." The conclusion they both reached would have significance for both Jack Hamilton and E. J. Davis. If an election were held, given what they considered the disloyalty of the opposition, Republican Party unity was essential, and they needed to take steps to find a candidate who could bring together conservatives and radicals.[4]

The demand for some sort of party unity ultimately came to focus on calling a Republican convention to make party nominations. Siemering, who would have known well the wishes of party members in western Texas, was convinced that a convention was needed to bring about party peace. Rather than a meeting called by one of the rival executive committees, he suggested one convened by a "dozen well known and respected citizens of both wings of our Party." Such a bi-partisan gathering would pressure the contending factions to unify for the well-being of the party. The pressure for some sort of meeting reached the point that by late April, even Ferdinand Flake, whose *Bulletin* generally supported Hamilton, concluded that a convention was necessary. Attacking both executive committees, Flake wrote, "Neither of you represent anybody but your little petty factions, about which we care nothing, . . . you must now join in calling for a convention."[5]

As pressure increased for a convention, Jack Hamilton made it clear that he intended to run no matter what and that he did not want a party nomination. Hamilton explained his position in an interview with one of the editors of the *Houston Union* that May. Hamilton concluded that thousands of people who acted previously with the Democrats were ready to affiliate with the Republican Party. If the Republicans held a convention and drew party lines, it would simply "rekindle the old animosities and prejudices" among Democrats, leading them to make their own nominations and involving the state in a bitter political fight. He doubted that the people would elect him governor if he ran as the nominee of a Republican convention and expressed his resolve not to accept a nomination from any source whatsoever. As to compromise within the party, he did not believe that his opponents desired any reconciliation, that their differences were "radical and irreconcilable."[6]

Jack Hamilton's position only increased pressure for a meeting. At the same time, it made a run for the governorship by Davis even more likely. That there would be a convention became more likely when a young newspaper editor, James G. Tracy of the *Houston Union,* took up the cause. Tracy's advocacy was important, for he had the support of General Joseph Reynolds, who also believed an effort at unifying the party was critical. On 28 April, Tracy joined with Edwin M. Wheelock, editor of Siemering's *San Antonio Express,* in calling for a convention to meet at Houston on 24 May. Morgan Hamilton had also seen the necessity of a convention by this time, and he muddied the picture when he published his own invitation, as chairman of the radical executive committee, for all loyal Texans to meet in Galveston on 10 May. Hamilton went ahead with his own meeting, despite the call of Tracy and Wheelock, but did not attend. Tracy was there, however, and worked out an agreement in which he cancelled the 24 May meeting in favor of a new one in Houston on 7 June.[7]

E. J. Davis remained at Corpus Christi as efforts were made to reconcile the Republican factions. He unquestionably came to believe that whoever ran as a Republican had to have the nomination of a convention, which he personally believed they should hold in July. For Davis, a convention was the only way to bring Republicans together in the campaign and give the appearance of party regularity. In May, following Tracy's call for the 24 May meeting, he urged the editor to reconsider, asking him to let Morgan Hamilton's meeting take precedence. While accepting that many did not recognize Hamilton's committee, he believed it was the only one that could speak for "any part of the Republicans," and he considered it important to show the meeting had the backing of a party organization. At this point Davis did not appear to be seeking that nomination. However, he did think that party unity before an election was critical.[8]

On the eve of the 7 June meeting many Republicans believed that the basis for a compromise between the radicals and conservatives was reached, and E. J. Davis's name appeared at the heart of the reputed arrangement. Rumors circulated that a deal had been worked out between Jack Hamilton and the radicals, despite Hamilton's insistence that he would not run as the nominee of a convention. The editor of the *San Antonio Express* reported that the compromise efforts centered around creating a fusion ticket, naming Jack Hamilton as the gubernatorial candidate and E. J. Davis as the lieutenant governor. Private correspondence at the time suggested that the rumors had some substance. A treasury agent in the state privately informed John L. Haynes that he understood that the negotiators had agreed that Hamilton ultimately wanted to go to the United States Senate, and after the election would be sent to Washington while Davis moved up to the governorship. Davis, in turn, would abandon his canvass against the constitution for *ab initio* and division. Davis was quoted as having said that Republican success should not be "jeopardized by individual interest."[9]

When the 7 June convention finally assembled, the presence of men from all factions of the party indicated that many in the party came to believe that such a meeting was necessary. A goodly number of radicals was present, since Morgan Hamilton encouraged them to turn out so they could ensure that no compromise was made on critical issues. The convention, however, clearly was not controlled by the radicals or by the supporters of Jack Hamilton. Early on it was clear that compromise was in the air and even the men associated with the two factions proved willing to make concessions. The conciliatory spirit of the delegates became apparent when they elected James Tracy as the chairman. The platform introduced and adopted on the second day demonstrated even further the tendency to modify positions. After the usual resolutions in support of the national Republican party (passage of the fourteenth and fifteenth amendments, payment of the national debt, President Grant, and General Reynolds) the delegates broke completely with Morgan Hamilton on the proposed constitution. The platform recognized that the proposed constitution was not perfect, but concluded that it achieved the purposes of constitutional government—"The equal, civil and political rights of all persons under the law." The delegates recommended passage.[10]

The hope that the factions might be reconciled proved ill-founded. Despite the apparent conciliatory character of the delegates, when Jack Hamilton found he did not have enough votes to secure the nomination he refused to enter the convention hall. When the delegates produced their statement on the current political situation, their frustration with Hamilton was apparent. It warned that the work of Reconstruction was not yet complete and asserted that its enemies were still at work to prevent its success. In such circumstances, the delegates believed that the preservation, unity, and organization of the Republican Party was the only way to succeed. They cautioned, in a reference to Jack Hamilton, that the opposition to such a course threatened their work. It was, in fact, they charged, nothing more than an "insidious design" by their enemy that would bring about the "practical surrender of the State to the disloyal." For the organizers of the convention, Jack Hamilton's refusal to cooperate came to be seen as part of a purposeful plot.[11]

Late on 8 June the delegates finally selected a slate of nominees for state office. Once again, their choices showed the conciliatory mood of the convention. Jack Hamilton's refusal to participate in the convention took him out of consideration, and the delegates turned to E. J. Davis. Given the character of the convention, he was a good choice. Although associated with the radicals in the constitutional convention, he had never been intractable on basic issues. By this time, he was well known and generally respected by party members. Delegates also saw him as a man who possibly could unify the party. His was the first name placed in nomination, and the delegates moved immediately on the motion of George Ruby to accept his nomination by acclamation.[12]

That evening Davis addressed the convention as its nominee. He began by insisting that he had not sought the nomination, but that having received it, he did not believe that he could evade the responsibility thrust upon him. Significantly, given his long opposition to the proposed constitution, he now stated that he not only accepted the nomination, but also the platform that called for its ratification. Davis went on, indicating his intention of drawing all Republicans back into the party fold. "I propose," he told the delegates, "if possible, to be the candidate of the whole Republican party without regard to faction or clique." He promised that he personally would adopt a conciliatory course towards Republicans in general in order to renew the party's unity and harmony. He charged the delegates with making every "reasonable" effort to restore good feeling between themselves and those who opposed them, to be ready at the very least not to be the ones to "cast the first stone." Republicans faced a significant challenge of reconstructing the state on a Republican basis, a task expected of them by the nation, the Congress, and the president. He believed that Texans would do that, "if all loyal men do their duty." Charging them with the task before them, he described their job in military terms. Success was theirs only if they made sure that "all men are at their places in the ranks."[13]

The rest of the slate showed a serious effort at including men from various parts of the Republican coalition, although, in the end, the nominations offered to Jack Hamilton's supporters were turned down. The clearest indication of efforts at binding all together came with the selection of James W. Flanagan to run for lieutenant governor. Flanagan was a delegate in the constitutional convention and clearly had not been an ally of the radical faction on any issue other than division. In fact, Flanagan had done what he could to promote railroad interests and ensure a conservative course on racial issues. He even voted with Jack Hamilton on the suffrage question. Jacob Keuchler, a prominent German Unionist who had at times associated with the radical party in the convention, received the nomination for commissioner of the land office. William D. Price, an attorney from Austin who was a captain in Davis's regiment, was nominated for treasurer. James Tracy, one of the chief instigators of the Houston convention, was named chairman of a new state executive committee.[14]

Davis's acceptance of the Houston nomination and his position on the proposed constitution did not sit well with many radicals. "For God's sake," one wrote, "tell me the difference between the Jack Hamilton party & our party." Morgan Hamilton, viewing the situation similarly, refused to serve on the executive committee named by the convention. Davis never explained fully his decision, although it belies his purported inflexibility. Probably the best explanation for what happened was that circumstances had undermined his stand on most of the important issues. In his 2 January speech on division at the constitutional convention, Davis indicated that if the state was not divided he was willing to reorganize under whatever constitution the convention produced. "It would be disgraceful," he had said, "if we were to return home and say to our constituents that after spending months in deliberation and taxing the people hundreds of thousands of dollars . . . we have returned without maturing anything." Congress had not opted for division and was determined to hold an election, so little choice existed. *Ab initio* also had to a large degree become meaningless as a result of court rulings, including the United States Supreme Court's April decision in the case of *Texas v. White*. If Davis had any hopes of influencing the Reconstruction of the state, he had no choice other than the one that he made.[15]

When the delegates left Houston, the president still had not called an election. As a result, Davis did not begin his campaign. He did seek to establish his credentials as the regular Republican nominee by gaining the recognition of the Grant administration and national Republican leaders. That recognition was critical for any election campaign. Controlling the appointment of federal officials in Texas was important to any election campaign, since these men often provided financial support and the promise of office to their friends. At the time, most of these men were connected with the Jack Hamilton party. If Davis could claim the authority of the regular party nominee, he and his supporters could take over. In securing that end, Davis and his friends made quick strides. By late June, Hamilton supporters found that the Houston convention gave Davis a considerable advantage, and many in the North considered Davis to be the Republican candidate for governor. The situation was troublesome enough that on 30 June, Governor Pease left Austin for Washington to try to counter Davis's efforts.[16]

President Grant proved slow to act on the question of federal officials, but Davis personally worked at convincing Republican leaders that not only was he the representative of the regular party but that Jack Hamilton had sold out. A particular object of attack was John L. Haynes, then holding the lucrative position of collector of the customs at Galveston as well as chairing Jack Hamilton's executive committee. Davis personally acted against his former lieutenant, informing Secretary of Treasury George Boutwell that Haynes was using his patronage to destroy the Republican Party and had to be removed. These efforts began to pay off in mid-summer. On 7 July, the Republican Party's National Executive Committee recognized the Houston convention's executive committee as the legitimate representative of the Republican Party. Newspaper reports also indicated that Davis convinced Secretary Boutwell and his representatives that the Hamilton movement was dangerous. Other prominent Republicans reached the same conclusion. Republican newspapers began referring to Davis as "the regular Republican nominee for Governor," further indicating Davis's success. Pease, trying to control the damage, met with the president on 12 July and believed that he still had the president's support when Grant indicated he would not remove Hamilton appointees. That decision, however, was short lived.[17]

Davis recognized that the tide was moving against Hamilton, and one convert was particularly critical. As early as July, Morgan Hamilton believed that his brother lost the support of General Reynolds, that the general had told Pease before he left that he could not support his mission to Washington. Reynolds clearly desired some sort of compromise between the rival factions and had encouraged Tracy and the convention movement in June. Now the general's chief complaint against Jack Hamilton was that he should have cooperated with the radicals. When he did not, that had put him in the wrong. Davis realized that Reynolds's opinion was important because the president had confidence in the general's views on Texas affairs. Davis believed Reynolds was unfair to his party at times, but he advised care in dealing with him. "[W]e had better get along the best we can with him," Davis counseled. "Don't let us enter into a quarrel with him." Courting General Reynolds ultimately would prove to be one of the more important strategic moves in the subsequent campaign.[18]

Finally, on 4 September, the Davis party got Reynolds's backing. On that day Reynolds sent a letter to President Grant that endorsed Davis and his branch of the party. The general finally concluded that a coalition between Hamilton and the Democrats, a connection charged by the Davis faction, did exist. Reynolds observed that when these charges were made initially, he asked for proof but was given none. Now, he saw in the overall picture the basis for no other conclusion. The Hamilton party rebuffed all attempts at reuniting themselves to the other faction. Democratic papers now openly advocated Hamilton's election, and men called themselves Conservative Republicans and could not even take the Test Oath. This convinced him that Hamilton's success would mean the "defeat of Republicanism in Texas" and place the state back in the hands of the men who "exerted every nerve to destroy the Union."[19]

Reynolds's letter finally pushed the president into action. On 9 September Grant publically endorsed the Davis party. The president's decision was important. He had now given the stamp of authenticity to the Davis Republican Party, indicating that anyone who wished to support the Republican Party in Texas should support Davis. The decision also precipitated the very rapid removal of Hamilton supporters from federal positions and their replacement with Davis loyalists. The Davis party could now expect financial support from national Republican supporters and also these federal appointees. It also gave the party hundreds of salaried workers who could enter the campaign in Davis's behalf. The ax began to fall on Hamilton's men in mid-September, when the postmaster general replaced the pro-Hamilton department's special agent in Texas with a Davis supporter. At Houston the pro-Hamilton postmaster was removed and replaced by James G. Tracy, one of Davis's most ardent supporters.[20]

Reynolds's letter and the president's decision to throw his support to the Davis party had other political fallout as well. On 30 September, Governor Pease resigned as provisional governor. He informed Reynolds that he had become convinced that the only mode of carrying out the policy of Congress to form a government giving equal civil and political rights to all citizens and elect a government was the election of Hamilton. Pease thought Reynolds's action would undermine that end. "Under the existing circumstances," he wrote, "I am unwilling to become, in any way responsible for the course being pursued by the military commander and the administration at Washington."[21]

Davis watched events unfold in Washington and Austin from his home in Corpus Christi. He initially delayed his canvass, intending to wait until the president ordered an election. When President Grant finally issued an election proclamation on 15 July, he gave Davis no reason to hurry. The president did not provide for an election until 30 November. As a result, although Hamilton already was in the field, Davis remained at home. In part, his own uncertainty about what would happen caused his reluctance to start. On 5 September he wrote to a friend and fellow-radical, James P. Newcomb of San Antonio, that he understood that the Democrats would make their own nominations before the end of the month. Uncertain of his own strategy in the campaign, he noted that he was "anxious" to see how the political picture developed before he began his own canvass.[22]

Davis finally began an active campaign when he went to Galveston, where he delivered his first address as a candidate on 22 September. By that time Jack Hamilton and his supporters were before the public, defending the constitution and Hamilton from charges that he betrayed the Republican Party and formed a coalition with the Democrats. At the same time they developed an extensive critique of Davis and his party to which Davis had to respond. In their campaign, the Hamilton party charged that Davis and his supporters were simply malcontents, who, when failing to secure their impractical theories in the constitutional convention, disrupted the convention and the Republican Party. They did not want Texas back in the Union and hated the people of the state. Unexplainably though, those who opposed the constitution were now running for office under it. They asked Davis what kind of man would be willing to be governor under a constitution he condemned and to administer government to a people he had denounced? They provided the answer: Davis was nothing more than an ambitious man actuated more by a desire for office than the public good.[23]

Davis's Galveston speech on 22 September answered these questions and established the basic message he would repeat as he crossed the state. That speech was received by the largest political turnout since the war, as one reporter believed. Listeners gathered on the town square where a bonfire provided the light. On the candidate's arrival a U.S. Army band played "Dixie." Following his introduction by the Galveston mayor, Davis proceeded in a systematic way to address the questions raised about his candidacy by Hamilton and his supporters one by one. Although it is noteworthy that he did not talk about any programs that he might implement as governor other than to reaffirm the platform of his party, he began with the issue of who represented the Texas Republican Party. He retraced the steps leading to the Houston convention, insisting that the *ab initio* wing of the party was willing to reconcile differences, leading to a call for a May convention. Republicans representing the other side appeared willing to make concessions as well. The result was the Houston convention, but Governor Hamilton refused to participate and had even tried to break it up by encouraging delegates to leave. Nonetheless, Davis contended it was as representative a convention as had ever been held in Texas and reflected a real effort at reconciliation and compromise.

Davis then turned to what he believed now separated the two men running for the governorship. *Ab initio* was the chief difference, and Davis pointed out that most Republicans, including Governor Hamilton, had supported *ab initio* at first. Now Hamilton and others abandoned the idea and charged Davis and his supporters with hanging on to a dangerous theory. They were calling the Davis men "a bad set of fellows" whose idea would bastardize all the children born during the war, set aside all marriages, and destroy all contracts. That never was the intent of the men who remained true to *ab initio*, Davis insisted. Instead, it was a matter of "dollars and cents." There were two very practical issues at the heart of the controversy. The supporters of *ab initio* wanted to force the return of monies to the school fund that had been taken out during the war. They wanted to take away the thousands of acres of public lands that came into the possession of speculators during the war. Hamilton's men simply wanted to guarantee the railroads and the speculators in their ill-gotten gains. In the convention Davis and his supporters were willing to go over the laws passed and validate all that was just and right, but that was blocked and the issue turned against them. "They were shrewder than we and understood better how to manufacture public opinion," Davis concluded.[24]

Davis also addressed charges that he was vindictive towards the whites of the South in his efforts in the constitutional convention to disfranchise some former Confederates. Davis reminded them of the condition in the summer of 1868, of the open opposition of Democrats to the enfranchisement of blacks. Davis asked if good reason did not exist to believe that the rebellion had not died out. He had lost in the convention, and now he was willing to vote for the proposed constitution even with its unrestricted enfranchisement. He was ready to take his opponents at their word and accept their promises that they were now ready to accept the securing of black rights. Did he support disfranchisement because he hated white Southerners? Davis's answer was no. His own brothers were Confederates. He acted simply in the way he thought best for "the security and safety of all."[25]

The Galveston speech may actually have made an impact on some Republican voters. Even the editor of *Flake's Bulletin* believed that Davis raised serious questions that needed to be considered. Flake admitted that he had not believed that a convention would reconcile the differences between the Republican factions, but he urged Governor Hamilton to try. Hamilton refused to make "the proper effort." Flake also welcomed Davis's charge against Hamilton on the *ab initio* issue. "This was his first statement put into a clear and intelligible proposition. It was the foundation . . . of his address. We thank him for bringing the charge with considerable plainness." On the issue, the editor looked forward to a clear vindication of the charges by the other side, an explanation that needed to be made for the moderate Republican to "clear his skirts."

Hamilton never addressed the questions raised by Davis. Indeed, after making joint appearances with Davis initially, Hamilton refused to be at the same rallies as the canvass proceeded.[26]

After appearing at Galveston, Davis went to Houston where he appeared the next evening and once again presented a defense of his position. From there he began a canvass that took him around central Texas and then into the eastern parts of the state. On 27 September he was at Austin, then the following day at Brenham. An intended joint appearance at Houston in October failed to take place, but Davis would address an 29 October at a rally at Rusk, where Governor Hamilton was also present. In early November he was at Tyler, Marshall, Jefferson, and Paris. Even while campaigning, Davis could not afford to ignore his law practice. In the midst of the campaign he was forced to return to Corpus Christi to take care of legal business before he could resume his efforts. While violence became a central part of Texas elections, at least at the places Davis appeared things remained peaceful. At Paris an observer reported that he spoke to a crowd of nearly six hundred people, both white and black. There had been a little disruption when a few individuals in the crowd tried to interrupt him, but town leaders suppressed the questioning, declaring that Davis should have a full hearing. With no further interruption, Davis spoke for two hours in a "plain" fashion that "abounded in facts" to a crowd that listened with "marked attention."[27]

Davis worked to convince voters to support him in public appearances, but at the same time his supporters worked behind the scenes to perfect an organization that would turn out voters who would cast their votes for him. In large part this effort focused on black voters and was done with the Union League. George Ruby took the state organization out of the hands of Hamilton's supporters the previous summer, and he now used all of its resources for Davis. A circular issued in August by the Grand Council urged members to organize and support their "honored brother, the soldier, hero, and statesman, General E. J. Davis" against the "apostate, ex-military Governor A. J. Hamilton." From the countryside, reports indicated that Ruby's push to create local league chapters was successful. In a note providing a clearer picture of these efforts, a correspondent from Brazoria County indicated that Ruby himself was there and working in Davis's behalf. Ruby saw to it that black speakers were sent into the county to campaign on Davis's behalf. The organization ensured that black voters went to the polls. Especially in the black belt counties along the Colorado and Brazos rivers, the league appeared to be actively engaged in the campaign.[28]

As Davis and his party looked for votes across the state, it became clear that the one place they would not find them was among Democratic leaders and the men who supported them. Their position in the election could potentially effect its outcome; a Democratic turnout for Hamilton could possibly swamp Davis. As to the governorship, the nominal Democratic leaders made it clear that they would not support Davis. One of the more important of these individuals had stated the party's position in a letter to the *Galveston Daily News* when he concluded Democrats had no choice. General Henry E. McCulloch characterized the race as one between a man who would make blacks equal to whites (Hamilton) and another who would subordinate whites to blacks (Davis). He liked neither, but saw Hamilton as preferable. Ashbel Smith, another prewar Democratic leader, urged support for Hamilton because he had "crushed out the negro wing of the Radical party," and victory would provide the "shortest road to the ultimate triumph of the Democratic party." Whether or not they could deliver votes for Hamilton was uncertain. Some party newspapers never came in line with the position of state leaders. One contemporary estimated that, of twenty newspapers east of the Trinity River, only one favored Hamilton.[29]

It became less probable that Davis would be overwhelmed by a Democratic turnout for Hamilton when opposition to Hamilton bubbled over in a convention of Democratic editors at Brenham in early October. The exact intent of those attending the meeting is not clear, but their broad goal appears to have been to maintain a Democratic organization in an election that essentially was a Republican fight. The Brenham gathering nominated one of their own, newspaper editor Hamilton Stuart, for governor, recommended Democrats vote against the proposed constitution and the Fifteenth Amendment, and urged Democrats to organize. Two weeks later the Democratic Central Executive Committee sounded a similar call for organization, although advising party members to vote for the new constitution. The committee encouraged Democrats to hold local conventions and nominate Democrats for the legislature and local offices. If they could not secure the governorship, they could take control over the legislature and local government. Some Republicans believed all of this worked to Davis's advantage, frightening many who worried Hamilton might be simply a front for the Democrats. Reports from the countryside in late summer indicated that many were concerned and moving to Davis. One concluded that Hamilton majorities in Lavaca and Colorado counties shifted to Davis almost overnight. A report from Navasota indicated that all Republicans in eastern Texas shifted to Davis.[30]

On the other hand, Democratic efforts, often accompanied by intimidation and violence, had the potential for keeping Davis supporters from the polls. Davis encountered no open hostility as he canvassed the state, but as the election approached, reports of violence increased. Reports from Wharton County in late August indicated that blacks in that county, led by two white men, were prepared for a battle with other whites in the community. Ultimately the reporter failed to give reasons for the confrontation but concluded that the election would worsen the conflict. In early September one of the state's district judges was attacked near Greenville. Once again, reports failed to say whether the attack was politically or personally motivated, but the fact that a judge could be attacked with impunity sent a clear message concerning the safety of anyone. At Gonzales, the teacher at the freedmen's school was taken and lynched by disguised men, although the reporter concluded that the men were radicals seeking to stir up bad feelings. At Columbia a group of "cowboys" attacked an African American church, killing the minister and causing blacks to call for support from surrounding counties. In Fort Bend County, the level of violence increased, although the Democratic press attributed it to a fight over labor issues. In the end, the exact cause of each act of violence became irrelevant. All violence had a political impact, for it contributed to the sense of insecurity that would surround the polls once the voting started.[31]

Much could happen before the final vote was tallied, but Davis received further encouragement on 1 October when General Reynolds issued his election proclamation. At the time the order did not appear to have any particular relevance for the outcome at the polls; Reynolds simply set up the rules of the election, detailing an additional registration, rules applicable to the registrars, and general rules to be applied to the management of the polls. Two parts of the order, however, had later significance. First, it empowered the registrars to close the polls in the case of any disturbance that would "obstruct the free and full exercise of the privilege of voting." Once closed, they could reopen only by order of the district commander. If a poll closed, it would be virtually impossible for the votes in that county to be counted. Second, the order made it clear that military and not civil officials would determine the official count of the votes. The local election manager and clerk would count the votes, but their tally was sent to Reynolds for an official total and the ballots themselves to the local military post. Hamilton's supporters feared that the general might not count the vote fairly. On the other hand, Davis's backers were pleased since the count was taken out of the hands of local officials, many of whom had been appointed by Governor Pease and were elected along with Throckmorton in 1866.[32]

Voting finally began on 30 November. General Reynolds requested and received permission to keep the polls open for four days. The polling began with good weather, but in subsequent days rain and colder weather appeared in some parts of the state. Observers believed the change in the weather dampened turnout. Conservative newspapers initially reported that the election was going in Hamilton's favor and that blacks were voting conservative. Subsequent results suggest that this was simply wishful thinking. With military observers at many of the polling stations, few instances of violent disturbances occurred. The noteworthy exceptions took place in Milam and Navarro counties, where officials closed the polls. In Milam County, a confrontation occurred between blacks and whites. Hamilton's supporters blamed the episode on an army officer who attempted to vote a large number of blacks *en masse* and provoked local whites. Radicals countered that conservatives were compelling blacks to vote for Hamilton or leave the polls. Whatever the cause, shooting occurred, and on the second day of the voting the election board closed the polls, took the ballot boxes, and left the county for safety. In Navarro County, no election was held after the president of the registration board was threatened and halted the registration.[33]

General Davis went to Houston as soon as the polls closed, then on to Galveston where he met with friends to assess the votes as they came in to military headquarters. By mid-December, Davis was convinced that he won the election. "We are waiting for returns from Northern Counties, where Hamilton will receive his largest vote," he wrote to Newcomb from Galveston. The potential size of the turnout in those counties left the outcome of the election in some doubt, but Davis nonetheless concluded, "we can hardly be beaten as the matter looks now." The election violence in Milam and Navarro counties created further uncertainty as to the outcome, but Davis's supporters believed that because poll officials had closed down the elections there, no votes would be counted from those counties.[34]

If Davis was optimistic, many conservatives were not. As the votes came in they watched the turnout and concluded that the results would not be good. Their greatest concern was the fact that large numbers of whites did not bother to vote, while blacks did. By early December Ferdinand Flake of the *Bulletin* admitted defeat, observing that the election had shown that "in the hands of shrewd and unscrupulous managers, the negro vote is reliable; that he can be kept to the work like a machine." The Democratic *Houston Telegraph,* seeking an explanation for Davis's success, marveled at the political skills of the candidate and his party. They had begun the race in June and at the time the editor concluded "no one thought they had a ghost of chance of success." Instead, they managed to secure recognition in Washington and the North and that recognition brought in money allowing them to publish newspapers and hire speakers to canvass the state. All the while, Hamilton's supporters were "unorganized and unharmonious." Party organization and the Union League made it possible for the radicals to march their men to the poll where they voted with great unanimity. The race was likened to one in which "organization and drilled troops" triumphed over an "unorganized mass." In short, Davis had mobilized his supporters while Hamilton was unable to overcome the indifference most whites felt about him and the election.[35]

Verification of the results waited, however, for an official tally. That took weeks. As late as 28 December officials reported Davis ahead of Hamilton in the returns that had been received, but they still had not yet received a count or the ballots from twenty-five counties where elections had been held. Reynolds did not get all of the votes in until early in January, and the official returns confirmed Davis success. Davis carried the election by a thin margin, receiving 39,838 votes to Hamilton's 39,055. The Democratic candidate, Hamilton Stuart, received 445.[36]

General Reynolds announced the official returns, but that did not bring the election of 1869 to its end. Hamilton did not take his defeat well, and he and his supporters determined to challenge the results at Washington. Their challenge hinged on events in Milam and Navarro counties and the fact that General Reynolds had not counted the votes there. Contending that both counties would have voted for Hamilton, they concluded that General Reynolds gave Davis the victory when he refused to allow the counties to hold another election. Reynolds, the man who tried so hard to remain out of the middle of the rival Republican groups through much of the election struggle, now found himself not only in the middle of a fight but charged with facilitating Davis's triumph. On 28 December, former governor Pease delivered a protest to President Grant that asked him not to accept the results, charged the election had been illegal, and accused General Reynolds of not taking the precautions to ensure a fair election and inviting fraud at the polls. Grant, however, refused to intervene, thus settling the election.[37]

In Texas, General Reynolds took steps on the day that he announced the official returns of the election that would prove another complication in E. J. Davis's future. On 8 January 1870, Reynolds appointed Davis provisional governor. Had Davis simply become a military appointee to serve until he, as governor-elect, took control over a civilian government, or had he begun the term for which he had been elected? At the time no one could foresee that this would ever be the issue that it would become in 1874. Whether as a military governor or the new constitutional governor, Davis left for Austin and moved into the governor's mansion. On the evening of 22 January a crowd marched in a torchlight procession from the county courthouse to the mansion, led by a band and party of fifty African Americans to honor their new governor. Davis spoke to them from the balcony. Thanking them for their support, he declared his intention of carrying out the ideas that he had advocated in the canvass and asked for the assistance of all parties in his efforts. Following the address Davis mingled with the crowd, shaking hands with those in attendance. There was little time for celebration, however. As he took office he fielded correspondence from around the state concerning election violence. He also began receiving a steady flow of letters requesting consideration for government jobs.[38]

The question of the constitutional character of the government inaugurated in January was complicated further by the proceedings of the subsequent legislative session. When Reynolds announced the results of legislative races on 11 January, he, not Davis, ordered the men elected to the Twelfth Legislature to gather on 8 February. By implication, this action indicated that civil government remained unrestored and that the military commander possessed the only power to call the legislature into session. That Reynolds saw this as so was apparent when he declared that all members of the legislature had to take the test oath, assumed the authority to settle cases of contested seats when they involved conformity to the Reconstruction laws, and forbade action on any other legislative measures until the cases were settled. Further, Reynolds named a temporary speaker of the House of Representatives. Governor Davis recognized the legal questions regarding the character of the government when notified that the two houses were ready to receive any communications that he might wish to make. Davis replied that under the circumstances he felt it would not be "proper for me to assume to direct their deliberations by sending any formal message to the House."[39]

When assembled, the legislature completed the steps necessary for Texas to be restored to the Union. With little debate the members ratified the fourteenth and fifteenth amendments. They then turned to the business of electing United States Senators, and on 24 February chose Morgan C. Hamilton and James W. Flanagan. That day, Davis wrote to President Grant informing him that the amendments had been adopted and that he believed the legislature had shown "a disposition in good faith, and with alacrity" to follow the requirements of Congress in the matter of Reconstruction. He also pointed to the election of two United States senators, "in Sentiment fully in accord with the majority in Congress," as indicating that Texans had accepted Reconstruction. Davis recommended the "prompt admission of this State." However, Davis may not have believed fully his statement on Texas's acceptance of Reconstruction, for he also suggested that United States troops be left in the interior counties of the state, to be withdrawn gradually. The new governor obviously remained uncertain about the temper of many Texans.[40]

Despite having completed the requirements for readmission, the fate of Texas remained uncertain, at least for a time. At Washington some pressure was exerted on Congress not to accept the new constitution. Newspapers attributed the lobbying to railroad speculators who disliked its provisions prohibiting land grants to railroads. At least for a time, the bill to readmit Texas languished in the Senate Judiciary Committee, with some senators discussing territorializing the state in order to get at the public lands. Davis and his supporters, however, pressured friends in Congress and in the end were able to maneuver a bill restoring civil government through the legislative process. Even A. H. Longley of Jack Hamilton's *Austin Republican* believed that Davis, in office, had benefitted the state. "It would have been impossible for General Hamilton or any one else to have procured the admission of the State to representation in Congress any quicker than it has been done under General Davis," Longley concluded.[41]

On 30 March, President Grant signed the bills that returned Texas to its normal place in the Union. For E. J. Davis the restoration of Texas marked the beginning of new responsibilities and new opportunities. He was destined to be the fourteenth governor of his state. In his new position, he would face enormous challenges in his efforts to build a community that ensured the goals he had sought since the war's end—a state that accepted the war's results and particularly guaranteed to its people basic security, equal protection before the law, and a full share of the rights guaranteed by the Constitution of the United States.

E. J. DAVIS AND THE FUTURE OF TEXAS: THE LEGISLATIVE PROGRAM

"We have it in our hands to place our great State at once among the foremost in wealth, population and civilization, and if we can be made fully sensible of the extent of this, our opportunity and responsibility, we will not fail in the performance of our part."

—E. J. Davis, Inaugural Address, 1870

Governor-elect Edmund J. Davis was shaped by many different forces by 1870. As a young man, his work as a lawyer and a public official in the state's border country brought him face to face with the problems of a multi-ethnic community, Indian relations, and the cattle country. His Unionism, at least in part emerging from the needs of that border world, exposed him to hatred and violence, directed at him by many of his closest friends. His experiences after the Civil War's end did little to convince him that his antagonists during the war years had modified their views towards him and other loyalists. As a leader of the Republican Party he began to develop a clear view of the problems, at least as he saw them, confronting the state and a belief that something could be done to solve them. Now, as governor, Davis made clear his perception of these problems and also, for the first time, his ideas about what could be done about them. His first year as governor would be devoted largely to implementing his solutions. His answers promised to change Texas. They would radically alter the role of state government.

After the called session of the Twelfth Legislature ended and word was received that Texas was restored to the Union, Davis returned to

Corpus Christi and prepared his family to move to Austin. Local citizens took obvious pride in his victory. On 4 March over eighty men, "of all parties and shades of political belief" gathered at the town's St. James Hotel to honor him. William Headen, a prominent local merchant and chair of the proceedings, welcomed Davis as "an upright citizen, a gentleman of unblemished integrity" on behalf of citizens who wanted to show their regard for "his many virtues as shown in all the relations of life." When introduced, Davis was met with repeated cheering. After the speeches, the women joined the men for a social occasion. A local reporter noted the occasion continued until late in the evening.[1]

Davis took the opportunity at the St. James banquet to emphasize his belief that it was time for reconciliation. He told those present, political friends as well as opponents, that Texas should leave behind the issues of Reconstruction and move forward. He hoped that the time had come "when the political restraints that now separate us would be removed and leave only that which drew the line of demarcation between the good and the bad." Responding to the toast to "His Excellency E. J. Davis, Provisional Governor and civil governor elect," Davis went further. Texans were divided into Federals and Confederates; loyalists and rebels; Democrats and Republicans. Now he hoped that all would be "united in a determination to build up and improve our great State." The future would test the ability of both Davis and those who opposed him to leave behind the issues that dominated their relationship for so many years.[2]

Davis remained in Corpus Christi for over a week before starting his journey back to Austin with his family. On 13 March he arrived in San Antonio where his trip was delayed by a public celebration of his election. General James H. Carleton, commander of the post, greeted the governor-elect with a fifteen-gun salute. Davis and his family checked in to the Menger House, the same hotel where he said goodbye to General Lee and Kirby Smith nine years before. In the evening a procession headed by a brass band, including the Mexican Club and the city's Fire Company No. 1, marched to the Menger to honor Davis. Later, civic leaders honored him with their own banquet. In his public addresses at San Antonio Davis sounded once again his message of conciliation. He hoped it was time for the people of Texas to put aside past differences. It was time for all to work together for the good of the state.[3]

Davis's apparent desire to move away from partisan politics received a welcome public response across the state and indicated that a new day in politics actually might dawn. The editor of the usually hostile *Houston Telegraph* "rejoiced" to hear that Davis avowed his "determination to administer the duties of his office as the Governor of the whole people." The pro-Hamilton *State Journal* congratulated Davis for carrying out Hamilton's program of securing ratification of the new constitution and readmission to the Union and expressed its determination not to condemn in Davis what it would have approved in Hamilton. The editor believed that it might be possible that the troubles that divided kindred spirits would pass away and voiced his own intention to "earnestly labor for this consumation."[4]

Davis finally returned to Austin about 15 March. Little is known about his activities after he arrived, although later events suggest that he devoted much of his time to preparing for the legislative session, particularly putting together plans for the program he wished to put into place. He also probably finished up some of his legal work and early in April he actually left the capital city for a week to deal with important cases before the district court at Victoria. On 2 April, however, he took the first step towards restoring civil government when he issued the official proclamation calling the Twelfth Legislature for a special session to begin on 26 April. He received further authority on 16 April, when General Reynolds issued orders relinquishing his own authority over the state and local government and handing it over to the provisional civil authorities.[5]

The return of Texas to civil control finally took place on 28 April 1870, the day of Davis's inauguration as the elected governor. The weather provided an auspicious welcome to the new governor. The celebrant was welcomed that morning by what one reporter described as a bright morning with the "clear strong sunshine of Texas." For him, "nature seemed to breathe a benediction on the occasion of the glad return of our State to self-government." Davis's first appearance that day was at the Travis County Courthouse where veterans from Davis's old

On April 28, 1870, E. J. Davis assumed office as the elected governor of Texas. Although made two years later, this image indicates Davis's maturation and how he may have looked on that auspicious day in his political life. (David and Harriet Condon Collection)

unit formed the First Texas Cavalry Association and elected him its first president. In a scene that was unimaginable only a few years before, and which would be forgotten in later years, men from Texas who fought for the Union organized to bring together "comrades who shared common toils and dangers" and who took part in a struggle that "has so happily ended by the admission of our State back to its proper relations with the Union." For Davis, holding the inauguration and the formation of the First Texas Cavalry Association at the same time must have been meaningful. His military career had helped to preserve the Union; now he would lead Texas back to its regular relationship in that Union.[6]

At mid-day the actual inauguration ceremonies began. A military band and an escort of soldiers from the local post led a procession up Congress Avenue to the capitol. Davis marched behind the band, accompanied by General Reynolds and his staff. Behind them followed numerous state and local officials, veterans of the First Texas, and the uniformed members of the Austin Fire Department. A large crowd assembled at the capitol and when Davis arrived they filled the galleries and the floor of the hall of the House of Representatives. Davis stood before them and delivered his inaugural address. It was, in the words of one observer, "terse and eloquent." His audience listened in deep silence, "interrupted only by frequent and hearty applause."[7]

Davis's speech sounded again the themes of reconciliation and the governor's hopes for a new future for Texas and its citizens. New realities did exist that he thought had to be accepted. The recent troubles were over, but now he asked white Texans to acquiesce in the freedom of their slaves and asserted that they must see that "we cannot afford to be unjust to the weakest of God's creatures." If doing what was right was not enough, he warned that any reluctance to ensure security, freedom, and justice to all might provoke a response from Washington. With acceptance of black freedom and putting conflict behind them, Davis believed that Texans were able to work together to make their state stand among the foremost in wealth, population, and civilization. Their efforts would leave to future generations a world that was "industrious, prosperous, intelligent, law-abiding, and temperate." The governor hoped that men would now put behind them the divisions based on loyalty and disloyalty and judge men on a different basis. If they could, he looked to a "fresh departure in political affairs."[8]

Following the ceremony the crowd adjourned to a grove behind the home of Nat Raymond, where the Veterans Association threw a barbecue and dance. The barbeque was massive. He treated fifteen hundred ladies and gentlemen to "two fat beeves, twenty sheep, twelve [goat] kids, four hundred pounds of pork and two hundred of veal." Bread, butter, pickles, canned peaches, cakes and "two barrels of lemonade and claret punch" topped off the spread. After the barbecue, Governor Davis spoke, complimenting the many brave men who followed him into battle. Other speakers followed Davis, and then the guests adjourned to two dance halls created from canvas tents. An African American band played in one; in the other couples danced to a German band. The day was a glorious one for Edmund Davis.[9]

As Davis assumed the governorship, observers looked at his personal side, and they found a man considerably different from those who occupied the mansion before him. Above all, they saw in him a sophistication not usually associated with the state's leaders. A Northern observer was surprised to find that Davis did not have the "top-boots, sombrero, go-as-you-please style of his Southwestern surroundings." Instead, Davis possessed cultured ways, and his manners were "exceedingly quiet, impressive and aristocratic." A reporter for the *San Antonio Express* observed that at social occasions the governor presided over the mansion with a "genial and courtly manner." He also was religious, an Episcopalian who married a Catholic. His secretary of state encountered Davis's religiosity when the two traveled to the East Coast and the governor insisted that the secretary go to church with him each Sunday morning.[10]

Davis clearly possessed a taste for finer things and could mingle easily with the nation's elites. He enjoyed music and forced a traveling companion to attend the opera in Washington to hear Theodore Wachtel, a well-known German tenor of the time. What performance they attended is unknown, although on his first American trip Wachtel sang Manrico in *Il Trovatore* and the title role in *The Postillion of Lonjumeau*. That same evening, the secretary of the interior invited Davis to a reception, where he met President Grant. The next evening he was the guest of honor at a dinner given by the president of Washington's First National Bank. The guest list that evening included the secretary of war, Davis's old commander in Louisiana, Nathaniel Banks, and other notables. Three nights later he was the guest at the home of Judge Louis Dent, President Grant's brother-in-law.[11]

His marriage to Lizzie perhaps explains where Davis acquired his sophistication. She had a fine education, and her work at the mansion suggested a taste for finer things. Lizzie and the governor tried to make it a more attractive place once they moved in. They personally planted shrubbery and flowers. In 1870, the governor hired the first gardener for the mansion, and Lizzie began to landscape the grounds. The project included benches, gravel paths, small fountains, and a gazebo in the front yard. The gardeners planted petunias, narcissus, hyacinths, tea roses, and hollyhocks that Lizzie ordered from the East in the backyard flower beds, along with a vegetable garden. E. J. welcomed a gift of plants from the Department of Agriculture, and he placed them in the mansion gardens to see if they would prosper in the local climate. The

The Davises, shown here on the porch of the governor's mansion with their sons riding a mule on the side, brought with them a new life to that residence. E. J. and Lizzie planted flowers and vegetables on the grounds and entertained graciously throughout their tenure there. (David and Harriet Condon Collection).

Express's reporter noted that E. J. took the mansion and made its "barren grounds bloom."[12]

As first lady, Lizzie also showed her skills in a social setting. One reporter found her to be a "lively contrast" to the governor, who tended to be a quiet man. On Thursday evenings, especially when the legislature was in session, the governor and his wife held a levee and invited guests of all political persuasions. The levees typically consisted of a reception, a supper, and a dance. A reporter attending one on 21 July 1870, a time when partisan feelings were intense, found "[r]epresentative gentlemen, of all shades of politics" in attendance. The rancor of the legislative hall gave way to "hearty, harmonious and joyous" collegiality. The reporter found that the governor and Lizzie "exerted themselves to make everybody happy." Even when many politicians were not talking with each other at the capitol, at those evenings at the mansion they let go some of their partisan feelings and lingered late into the evening. A correspondent for the *Houston Union* found Lizzie to be one of the most "happy spirited ladies I have ever seen," noting that "Her passages at arms, retorts and sallies with our Democratic friends who attend these levees are truly delightful." At least by the end of the evening, "They all agree to subscribe to Her Republicanism." All of the social skills possible would be needed to keep the political peace in E. J. and Lizzie's next four years in Austin.[13]

Davis's inaugural address on 28 April concentrated on what Texas might be, but the message he delivered to the legislature on 29 April focused on the problems they had to overcome. It outlined the barriers that the governor saw standing in the way of peace and prosperity and called for their removal. The message provided the clearest statement up to that time of what Davis believed was taking place in Texas and does much to explain the legislation he subsequently proposed. His greatest concern was that law and order was far from established; its restoration was the most important task facing the state government. "Having peace and security for life and property," he wrote, "everything else will follow of course." He pointed specifically to the existence of mobs of lawless and disguised men who preyed upon the state's African American citizens as evidence of the validity of his view. Such mobs represented a major threat to order, and Davis saw no crimes equal in the danger that they posed to public security.[14]

The crisis of public order was extraordinary, and not surprisingly, the solutions Davis proposed were extraordinary as well. He asked the legislature when reorganizing the militia to provide for a disciplined, armed, and readily available "National Guard" that could be used against organized bodies of men who resisted the law. He also recommended a state police force that would operate throughout the state and provide protection in areas where local authorities were too weak or indisposed to enforce the law. Davis also asked for power to establish martial law where local law enforcement officials failed to maintain order. He also moved to disarm the mobs by asking for restrictions on the carrying of firearms. Although usually not considered a law enforcement measure, Davis called for the creation of public schools, arguing that preventing crime was more effective than its suppression. Davis believed this would reduce crime, as well as create the responsible electorate required for republican political institutions to flourish.

When Davis talked about lawlessness, he was not just talking about outlaws or racial violence—he saw Indian depredations as part of the problem and believed these had to end. As an old resident of the frontier, he discounted the explanations that Indian raids were savage ways of redressing wrongs previously inflicted by whites. These explanations were nonsense advanced by "[p]hilanthropic people" in parts of the nation where "Indian reminiscences exist only in romantic story." In Texas, raiders traveled hundreds of miles to murder and steal from people against whom no grievance could exist. Davis once again took the position he had taken in the 1850s, arguing that the only permanently effective solution was either the extermination or total conquest and submission of the Indians. Davis looked to the federal government to provide protection, but believing that delay would occur, he urged the legislature to arm and equip frontier companies to fight the Indians.

Davis envisioned the state playing a more active role in maintaining order; believing that the state's economic growth was set back by the war, he thought state government would have to take on a larger role in encouraging growth. Most Texans wanted to see growth in terms of a railroad system, and Davis did as well. He asked the legislature to provide a "liberal charter and the right of way," all the encouragement he believed necessary, for entrepreneurs willing to build a single road that would provide the greatest stimulus to the state's economy. He also recommended the creation of a bureau of immigration to encourage and actually aid Europeans who wanted to move to Texas. Additionally, he thought the state needed a geological survey to inform people of the state's mineral riches.

The governor's message also dealt with numerous housekeeping matters. Something had to be done to repair the state's asylums, its penitentiary, and the capitol grounds, which were all neglected during the war. The boundaries of the judicial districts had to be drawn. The rules for the constitutionally required voter registration boards had to be written. Elections had to be provided for the newly mandated county treasurer and surveyors. As to the latter elections, recognizing the need to have men in those offices immediately, the governor asked the legislature to allow him to fill them until they could organize elections.

Even a cursory glance at Davis's message makes it clear that his plans would lead to an increase in the state's expenses. He reserved the question of finance to the end of his message. He confessed that given all of the work that needed to be done he could not offer even an approximation of the amount of money needed. He warned only that the amount was large. A school system, immigration bureau, state police, and militia organization would cost nearly $1,500,000. If the legislature decided to provide aid to any work of internal improvement, the cost would be even greater. At the time the treasury contained only $368,426. Davis believed that they could raise much of the necessary revenue by creating a more efficient system of assessing and collecting taxes. Still, additional revenues needed to be raised. For Davis, the costs would need to be borne, for the needs of the state were enormous.[15]

Despite the good spirits evidenced at his inauguration, the composition of the state legislature did not guarantee an easy passage of Davis's program. Republicans controlled both houses of the legislature, but they did not have either a cohesive ideology or common goals. The differences apparent in the constitutional convention and the 1869 election persisted. The state's two United States senators reflected such diversity. Morgan Hamilton, who was associated with Davis as a radical, was a wealthy land speculator who readily accepted civil rights for African Americans, strongly supported public education, but wanted to maintain low government expenditures and low taxes. James W. Flanagan, on the other hand, was a social conservative who had little interest in the civil rights of blacks or public schools. Flanagan simply wanted state support for railroads. The Twelfth Legislature included Republicans who mirrored the positions of the two senators and possessed many other interests as well. Democrats were also present, holding eleven of twenty-nine seats. With 38 percent of the votes, they were strong enough to throw roadblocks in the way of any plans they found objectionable.

Davis obviously worked drafting bills to implement his programs prior to the legislature's meeting. As soon as its sessions began, members of the Republican caucus introduced these proposals. These bills would put all of the governor's proposals in place. In the House, a large Republican majority moved them forward quickly. In the Senate, however, the package quickly bogged down. Signs that the Senate could be trouble first appeared in a fight over Davis's appointment to the new superintendent of education position, Joseph W. Talbot, one of his associates in the constitutional convention. Underneath the confirmation process a debate was taking place concerning whether or not the government should segregate the new schools. Davis's views on race were never very clear, and he may not have objected to some form of separation. On the other hand, he saw any system that required segregation as legally and ideologically objectionable. In a first test of how far the governor might go to ensure at least legal equality in the state, Davis discovered that real limits existed. The majority in the Senate refused to confirm the Talbot nomination and signaled that the governor's program faced a serious challenge in that body.[16]

The militia bill drew the next fire. The proposed legislation looked much like earlier ones concerning the state militia, but Davis provided for two classes of military forces—the state guard and the reserve militia. The reserve militia consisted of all male citizens between the ages of eighteen and forty-five. They were liable to regular musters and could be called out in emergency by the governor. The state guard was a volunteer force, which the state would train regularly and provide arms. One part of the bill gave the governor the authority to declare martial law when he believed civilian law enforcement officials could not maintain order. The state guard appears to have been intended for use in such occasions. Opposition emerged almost at once, with critics charging that Davis intended to create a black militia to suppress white opposition. Indeed, such fears were fueled the previous January when William Alexander, then the United States District Attorney, said, "I tell you colored men now, . . . that when you are organized as a part of the militia, with U. S. arms in your hands, then will reconstruction be complete," and Davis did intend to enlist blacks. For most whites, arming blacks was not acceptable, and criticism was widespread. A crowd gathered at the Tarrant County courthouse offered a typical response when it charged that the bill's passage would "endanger the safety of the country by begetting and fostering an antagonism between the races." Even Senator Morgan Hamilton feared that recruiting black members to the state guard would "provoke a war of races."[17]

Concern for the racial component of the proposed militia system was a given, but to oppose it on racial grounds raised questions about the willingness of the opposition to guarantee the civil rights of black Texans. Instead of talking about race, the opposition in the Senate and across the state ultimately focused instead on the potential for abuse built into the organization. A. H. Longley of the *Austin Republican* and spokesman for the Hamilton faction proved one of the most outspoken critics, warning that the bill would grant to the governor power that could be used to "deprive the law-abiding citizen of the liberties guaranteed to him by the Constitution of this country." Longley especially condemned the provisions allowing the governor to declare martial law as "conferring powers upon the Governor that Gen. Reynolds never dreamed that he possessed under the military bills." The editor of the Democratic Dallas *Herald* worried not only about the governor's power but his possession of a military to enforce it, complaining that the bill provided for a "standing army, and one which makes the Governor a despot of the first water."[18]

Davis had the votes to get the militia bill through the House, but overall success was uncertain because of opposition strength in the Senate. The House passed the bill on 21 May with an overwhelming vote, but in the Senate at least five Republicans expressed concerns with the bill. Senators Webster Flanagan, Bolivar Jackson Pridgen, and E. L. Alford actually spoke against the bill on the floor. Two more, John S. Mills and Mijamin Priest, privately expressed uncertainty. The five, joining with the Democrats, blocked passage with a vote standing at sixteen against and thirteen for. The strength of those opposed began to solidify on 12 May when senators Pridgen and Alford announced that they definitely would not vote for either the militia or the police bills, which also had been introduced. As a result, Davis's men in the Senate let the bills sit in committee.[19]

While the militia and police bills remained in committee, Davis's supporters succeeded in passing a frontier defense bill, a law that made it possible for Davis to carry out his plans for protecting the frontier. That law authorized the organization of twenty companies of troops for the frontier. They would be standing units, raised when possible from men on the frontier for twelve-month enlistments. Individual soldiers were to provide their own horses, six-shooting pistols, and accoutrements. The state was to provide breech-loading cavalry arms and would replace any horses killed in action. Subsequent legislation provided immediate funding for the force by authorizing the issue of $750,000 in 7 percent state bonds. The interest and ultimately the principle on these bonds were to be paid with receipts from a special tax. Davis received the bill with the approval of both houses and signed it into law on 13 June.[20]

The frontier defense bill had wide support, but it also had opponents. No one would openly argue that the frontier did not need protection, but many did not want to pay the taxes to provide it. Davis's opponents developed a strategy, as a result, that they would use against most of his programs. They did not disagree that the state needed one of his programs, but invariably they charged that his particular plan was too expensive. The editor of the *Austin Republican* typically agreed that settlers needed protection, but he labeled the governor's measure as an "extravagant bill." Even some Republicans, including Senator Hamilton, worried about the cost. Hamilton concluded it would "sink the treasury." Ultimately, Davis's insistence on passage of the frontier bill produced a break between him and Hamilton because the senator, holding thousands of acres of land in the state, became increasingly concerned with the costs of the governor's programs.[21]

With the frontier taken care of, Davis's men in the Senate returned to the militia and police bills. Davis believed that both were essential to the success of his administration, and there could be no compromise. He could not afford to withdraw them. As early as mid-May he began to place pressure on the legislature. He showed himself adroit at political maneuvering, using his majority in the House of Representatives to effect his ends. In the House, Davis's supporters halted consideration of all private legislation and engaged in a lengthy debate on the public printing. They made it clear that they would continue this course until the governor's bills passed in the Senate. At the same time, the governor announced that he would veto any private bill received prior to the passage of the militia and police bills. By mid-June, Davis's men even threatened adjourning the legislature. This tactic posed a particular threat to various railroad and business interests that at the time were seeking charters and debt relief. As a result, railroad lobbyists pitched in to build support for the governor's bills. When the chairman of the state Democratic Committee tried to get $2,000 from the railroad lobby to bribe a Republican senator to vote against the bills, he found no one willing to put up the funds.[22]

Davis also used patronage to pressure the wavering Republican senators. Many local offices remained open at this time, and the governor had the power to fill them until the next election. Davis stopped making all appointments while the Senate debated the militia and police bills, reserving his decisions to accomplish the most good. At the end of May he made two critical appointments. On 24 May, Dr. Robert N. Mills, a "live man in the Republican party" and the brother of one of the uncertain senators, was named superintendent of the State Asylum for the Blind. Senator Mills's vote in favor of the militia bill became firm. The vote of Senator Priest was secured, apparently, with the promise of a district judgeship. The sixty-year-old Priest was seated in a contested election in a district considered strongly Democratic, and he apparently had no interest in remaining involved in politics. On 17 June Priest spoke in favor of the bill. After the legislature adjourned, Davis named Priest to one of the judgeships. Whether or not a *quid pro quo* existed can never be proven. But either way, Mills and Priest gave Davis the critical votes he needed.[23]

With Mills and Priest in hand, Davis had a fifteen to fourteen majority on the militia and police bills. The militia bill came up first, and after lengthy debate a test vote was held on 21 June. The matter under consideration was an amendment offered by Senator Flanagan that would remove the governor's power to declare martial law. As expected, they defeated the amendment, fifteen to fourteen. Supporters immediately called for a vote on the bill itself. At this point the minority attempted to break the quorum by withdrawing from the floor. Davis had plenty of experience with such tactics in the constitutional convention, and his supporters appeared prepared. The chair immediately ordered the arrest of all those who moved from the floor. The bolters were held in the back of the Senate chamber, then enough sent on to the floor to restore the quorum. That done, the militia bill passed by a vote of fifteen to five. Davis signed it on 24 June.[24]

The breakthrough in the Senate assured the success of the rest of Davis's legislative package. Reacting to reports that the opposition intended to break the quorum by resigning their seats, the president of the Senate ordered that the men who attempted to break the quorum be kept under arrest. They would remain under arrest for the next three weeks, ensuring no further attempts at breaking a quorum. This meant that when Davis's state police bill came up the opposition could do nothing to stop its passage. The bill that passed on 29 June created a police force of 257 officers and men, directed by the adjutant general who also would serve as chief of police. Men were expected to provide their own horses, arms, and equipment. In turn, they received monthly pay of sixty dollars for privates, seventy-five dollars for sergeants, one hundred dollars for lieutenants, and one hundred and twenty-five dollars for captains. The force was empowered to exercise authority throughout the state and, if necessary, independent of local police officers. A particularly controversial part of the law defined all local police officers to be members of the "state police" and ultimately subject to the supervisory control of the chief of police and governor. The opposition criticized the bill as something "unknown to our Constitution." Davis received the bill and signed it on 1 July.[25]

The critical police measures passed, the legislature moved quickly on much of the rest of the governor's program. Two days before receiving the police measure the governor signed an act that allowed him to fill numerous vacancies by appointment until the next general election. On 11 July the governor approved a bill that provided for the registration of voters. This act allowed the governor to appoint a registrar for each county to supervise the registration of voters and maintain voting lists. Critically, the law gave registrars the power of a district judge for the purpose of preserving order during registration and also made any action interfering with the business of the registrar a crime. On 12 August, he signed a bill that criminalized the carrying of arms, including a "bowie-knife, dirk or butcher-knife, or fire-arms," into any church, hall where persons were gathered for literary or scientific purpose, social gatherings where both women and gentlemen were present, and election districts on a day of election. With these last three measures Davis secured considerable control over the execution of the law and the electoral process, control he considered essential to the pacification of the state.[26]

Davis got his legislation passed, but the manner in which the bills were handled in the legislature produced widespread criticism. Davis, however, believed that these measures had to be passed, no matter what the price. The governor provided insight into his thoughts in a public statement made to a large crowd that gathered at the governor's mansion on 29 June to celebrate passage of the police bill. In his remarks, Davis touched on his motives. He was charged with desiring to use force and violence to keep the Republican Party in power, but that was not his intent. Davis was educated to obey the law, and to suppose he desired to use violence was to assume he was lawless. Lawlessness was what he aimed to stop. Charged with implementing measures he never talked about in his campaign, the governor reminded his audience that establishing law and order had always been his goal. Texas had once been relatively safe, and a man could travel from Galveston to Austin without carrying a pistol. Now, that was not so. He did not believe all violence was political, but the governor clearly believed some of it was. "I tell you," he said, "there is a slow civil war going on here and has been ever since the surrender of the Confederate armies." With the police and militia he proposed to put an end to it. "I intend," he concluded, "if Heaven helps me, to establish law and order, before my term expires, as permanently and securely in this State as it is in the State of Massachusetts. (Applause)."[27]

Davis was interested in pubic schools, but securing his police measures clearly occupied most of his time. He apparently left an education bill to others. It did not appear on the floor until late in the session, and it was not what Davis considered adequate. The constitution of 1869 required a "uniform" system of schools but the bill did nothing to produce uniformity. It gave the superintendent of public instruction supervisory control over all public free schools, but the position had little power. The bill vested real control in the local school district, where the members of the county courts sat as ex-officio boards of school directors. The enabling legislation offered little guidance for the day-to-day operations of the schools, only prescribing that the "English branches of education" were to be taught and that classes had to be held for at least four months each year. The bill passed with little opposition. Governor Davis signed the bill on 13 August 1870, but he never considered the law adequate and would move to reorganize the system in the next legislative session.[28]

Davis was able to hold together a Republican majority on much of his agenda, but that proved very difficult when the legislature turned to railroad issues. Davis counseled a conservative approach in his message, but large economic interests backed railroads, and each wanted state support for their effort. Railroad lobbyists appeared in considerable numbers in Austin at the beginning of the session. Reports indicated they were oiling the wheels in favor of their particular projects by a liberal distribution of money and favors. Davis used them effectively in gaining passage of the controversial militia and state police bills, but their concerns had been and remained getting state aid. Their power ultimately proved difficult for the governor to counter.

Davis, from the beginning, thought that the proposed International Railroad was the economically most useful project. It was to be an extension of the Cairo and Fulton railroad being constructed in Arkansas at this time. The company proposed to run its line southwestward from the Red River to Austin, then on to San Antonio and Laredo. From the border it would run to the Pacific in the vicinity of Mazatlán or San Blas. It would tie Texas to the Northeast, but also potentially would open the Mexican market. The railroad also appeared to have the best chance of being built, with economic backing from an imposing syndicate of New York bankers. It also attracted significant local support from Texans interested in the Mexican market, including Richard King, rancher and former client of Governor Davis, and George Brackenridge, president of the San Antonio National Bank and an investor in the Mexican economy. Another prominent supporter was Thomas W. House, Galveston merchant, financier, and developer of the Houston & Texas Central Railroad.[29]

A bill providing state support for the International Railroad moved through both houses with ease after Davis lifted his opposition to private legislation, and legislators appeared ready to be generous. Governor Davis thought that offering railroads right-of-way and breaks on taxes was sufficient to promote construction, but the legislature passed a charter that not only provided for right-of-way and relief from state taxes for five years, but also gave the company $10,000 in state bonds for each mile of road actually constructed along the proposed route. The state limited its liability by restricting the total grant to twelve million dollars. The charter went into effect on 5 August after Davis let the legislative session end without taking action on it. The governor was not happy about the grant of bonds, but in the end, he was not against the road and he did not veto the bill.[30]

Davis was willing to provide support for one railroad, but others were in line for handouts in Austin. The legislature was willing to be generous, but Davis proved much more conservative. Legislators provided temporary relief to several railroads threatened with seizure for failing to pay their debts to the state school fund, giving them a year to pay six months' interest and an additional 1 percent of their debt into a state sinking fund to avoid foreclosure. Davis signed this bill. Then the legislature settled the debt of the Houston & Texas Central railroad to the school fund by allowing it to pay the debt in bonds rather than specie; Davis vetoed the bill. He also balked when the legislature granted a charter to another road, the Southern Pacific. The Southern Pacific was one of Senator James Flanagan's projects, and it managed to get the legislature to provide the project land grants, claiming that it was the successor of the prewar Memphis, El Paso, and Pacific and assumed that company's right to receive land for its work. Davis, insisting that the new constitution ended land grants, vetoed the bill. Davis was able to retain the support of enough loyal Republicans to keep the legislature from overturning either of the vetoes.[31]

The veto of the Southern Pacific bill led to an immediate break with Senator Flanagan. Senator Hamilton complained that all Flanagan had done since reaching Washington was play a "long role on railroad matters and hand in disability petitions." Flanagan was not going to be stopped by the governor, and he declared war on him, criticizing him for not understanding the provision that forbade land grants. It was intended to prevent further land grants to individuals, according to Flanagan, not grants to railroad corporations. In a public letter, the senator vowed that if he had known that this was how Davis viewed the matter, he would never have allowed his name to be placed on the same ticket. He took the opportunity to criticize the recently passed police measures, placing himself now in line with Davis's opponents. "We want this State developed with railroads and accompanying blessings, not armies; white or colored," he wrote.[32]

Davis found himself the object of more and more criticism by the end of the legislative session that summer. Ironically, fellow Republicans laid the basic groundwork for opposition complaints that would persist through the rest of his administration. On 3 July 1870, *Flake's Bulletin* printed a "Declaration of Wrongs Suffered by the People of Texas" that made two accusations against the governor. The first was that he had established a tyranny and imposed an unconstitutional government upon the people of Texas. The basis for this charge was that the militia and police bills created a standing army in time of peace and made it superior to civil authority, quartered troops upon citizens, threatened suspension of *habeas corpus,* and allowed courts martial when not needed. All of this was accomplished wrongly when the governor blocked regular legislative business until his program was implemented. The second charge was that the administration imposed an enormous tax burden on Texans. This claim was based on the bonds authorized for the frontier regiments and the projected costs of the militia and state police. The potential costs of public schools and railroad bonds had yet to be calculated. The "Declaration" ended with a call upon Congress to intervene to restore republican government, the author declaring, "We . . . in the name of common honesty, declare Edmund J. Davis to be a tyrant, and his government to be oppressive, and we ask the Federal government of the United States to relieve us of the same."[33]

A subsequent conference of Hamilton Republicans and Democrats encouraged opposition to the governor and proposed ways the public could obstruct his work. At an Austin meeting on 16 July, members of this coalition urged Texans to obey the law, but suggested they hold public meetings expressing their concerns and send petitions for repeal of "obnoxious" laws to the governor and legislature. They also urged sending petitions to Congress. Afterwards, however, Jack Hamilton, now Davis's long-time nemesis, proposed what would prove to be the most effective strategy for making Davis's programs ineffectual. In a speech at Austin, Hamilton pointed out that the government could not implement any of the governor's programs if they had no money. Insisting, as he had in 1869, that Davis had not actually been elected, he held that Texans owed the administration no obedience, including the payment of taxes. Efforts at stopping the collection of taxes would subsequently hinder Davis's efforts greatly. Hamilton also helped destroy the governor's ability to raise money to cover immediate expenses by issuing bonds. The former governor declared that anyone who purchased bonds should realize that any debt created to "subjugate the people" or to "subsidize speculation railroad companies" would never be paid.[34] The full impact of this opposition was not felt immediately, but in the long run the effect would be enormous.

The called session of the Twelfth Legislature in the summer of 1870 was a tumultuous one. The first regular session of that body, which assembled only five months later, in January 1871, proved much quieter although in some ways equally troublesome. In his address to the legislature Governor Davis recognized the success of his program in the previous legislature, noting only that he believed the school system needed to be revised to bring it in line with the constitutional mandate. Much of his time was devoted to finances. After six months in office he found the state's revenue system was broken, and now he wanted it fixed. The heart of the problem was that many people simply did not render their property for taxation. The comptroller estimated the value of property in 1869 at $250,000,000. County officials reported property worth only $149,665,386, an amount less than the 1867 assessment and with no relationship to actual value. Davis further pointed out that of 90,000,000 acres of titled land in the state, they reported only 47,272,201 for taxation. Davis's message was clear: individuals were evading taxes and leaving the burden on those who are "too honest." The governor found that the situation made it impossible to realistically estimate state revenues.[35]

The legislature readily gave Davis a new revenue bill that appeared to resolve some of the problems that existed. The new code provided a clear statement to local officials what taxes were to be collected. It left assessment in the hands of local justices of the peace, but in a critical change it authorized the assessing officer to list and value property that property owners did not render. The result of the new law was immediate. The assessment of real property increased from $106,798,165 in 1870 to $138,777,347. The assessed value of livestock increased similarly, from $31,036,651 to $43,582,007. Assessed merchandise climbed from $12,009,568 to $15,277,077. Even the amount of occupation and poll taxes increased. The former rose from $148,149 to $262,406; the latter increased from $103,858 to $171,378. The tax base increased in every category from 20 to 40 percent. While that promised more revenue for state government, it did little to counter the cry of Davis's opponents that the new government was simply too expensive.[36]

The legislature would increase the cost of government even further when it modified the school law and created the first real state school system. The new law created a Board of Education, consisting of the governor, the attorney general, and a superintendent, which would adopt the rules and regulations for schools, oversee the examination of teachers, and "define the course of studies in the public schools" as well as direct what "apparatus and books" were to be used. The superintendent was given "supervisory control" over all public schools and was to be assisted by a salaried bureaucracy of educational supervisors to make sure local schools conformed to the state's educational program. Making the new system potentially even more expensive, the law allowed school districts to make "any separation of the students that the peace and success of the school and the good of the whole may require," thus allowing the creation of two sets of schools in each district. The new law effectively created a system of schools; at the same time its maintenance would be costly and another potential problem for the governor. Nonetheless, he signed the bill on 24 April 1871.[37]

Davis got his revenue and school bills, but he faced a legislature more ready than it was the previous summer to provide support for railroads. The fact was that Texans wanted railroads. For some, an expanding system of rails meant better access to markets and easier transportation. For many railroad men and railroad speculators, the roads meant personal wealth. Huge financial interests were involved, and for those legislators without a personal stake, lobbyists circulated in large numbers to convince them that their interests did lie with the railroads. The result was a run to give railroads as much support as they desired, and Governor Davis found himself unable to hold even members of his own party in line against the giveaway. As a result, the legislature readily handed out railroad charters, potentially saddling the state with a massive debt. The Southern Pacific moved through the legislature again, this time receiving the promise of $16,000 in bonds for every mile of track completed. Other roads found the legislature equally generous. Legislators also took steps towards removing the constitutional restriction on land grants, passing a bill placing an amendment to that effect on the ballot in 1872. The Southern Pacific bill assumed that the amendment would pass and provided for an exchange of state bonds for public lands when the constitution was amended. Davis used his veto against these bills, but this time he found members of his own party willing to overturn the vetoes.[38]

When the Twelfth Legislature adjourned its regular session, it unquestionably added to the financial burden of taxpayers. Davis opposed railroad giveaways, but believed most of what was created was essential. The governor's future ultimately depended on whether or not his programs produced results and whether or not voters saw the results as justifying the cost. Initially there was cause for optimism. There were positive results from most of his creations. The operations of the state police were particularly successful. Davis named James Davidson, a veteran of the United States Army, as adjutant general and police chief, and his rapid organization of the force and vigorous efforts at enforcing the law showed him to be a good choice. Davidson gathered lists of criminals at large from county sheriffs. He rapidly recruited the men and put them to work. By the end of the first six months of the state police's existence, the chief reported arrests of nearly a thousand men. In 1871, that number increased to 3,602. While subject to considerable political criticism during its existence, the state police went far towards accomplishing the governor's desire to bring an end to the criminal activity that swelled in the wake of the Civil War.[39]

The next year he could point to the new state school system as equally effective. In May 1871, he appointed another Union Army veteran, Jacob C. DeGress, as his superintendent of public instruction, and DeGress proved to be as efficient and aggressive as Davidson. By the end of the summer of 1871 DeGress appointed school supervisors and carried out a scholastic census of the state. He began the process of examining and employing prospective teachers. He also put together the rules to operate a graded school system based upon a standardized curriculum and common texts. By September 1871, the system was ready to receive its first students, and DeGress reported an initial enrollment of 63,504 students, a number equal to 28 percent of all school-aged children. The spring semester of 1872 saw even more progress, and at the end of the first year the superintendent reported that the schools had enrolled 56 percent of the school-aged population, a total of 127,672 students. Unfortunately, the larger the school system grew, the greater the costs it incurred, and rising costs made it an even bigger target of the governor's opponents.[40]

The state police and schools produced results, but the frontier force failed. The problem was not Davis's plan but his inability to raise the money necessary to put the troops on the frontier. He immediately signed up volunteers and went so far as to purchase arms and ammunition for them from the Winchester Repeating Arms Co. Threats to repudiate state bonds made by Jack Hamilton and others, however, made marketing the frontier bonds impossible. Few financiers would take the risk. In December, Davis sent Secretary of State Newcomb to New York City to find an agent for the frontier bonds, but Newcomb found

Davis's opponents at work undermining the market, and the bonds were never sold. By the end of 1870, no troops were put into the field. In the summer of 1871 the governor discharged all of the volunteers.[41]

The state police arrested criminals across the state. Public schools attracted thousands of young scholars. Even though Davis did not approve of their support, railroads advanced across the Texas countryside bringing economic change in their path. He carried out his promise to put measures into place that, at last, would lead the state to the place in the nation he believed it should occupy. The long-term effect of all this, however, remained to be seen. Violence continued on the frontier, undermined race relations, threatened the political process, and subverted the society Davis hoped to create. It is not surprising that suppressing this violence remained one of the governor's top priorities. From the summer of 1870 onward, he would spend much of his time in efforts to bring an end to the upheaval that plagued the state.

CHAPTER 9 THE FIGHT AGAINST LAWLESSNESS AND VIOLENCE

"Having peace and security for life and property, everything else will follow of course."

—Edmund J. Davis, Message to
the Twelfth Legislature, 1870

As governor of Texas, Edmund Davis spent what his contemporaries would have considered an enormous amount of time performing his duties. A San Antonio reporter expressed amazement at the hours Davis devoted to his work, noting that he arrived at the governor's office at eight in the morning and often stayed there until ten or eleven o'clock in the evening. Through the years of his administration, many different concerns demanded his attention. Passage of his legislative program, political matters, and the day-to-day paperwork of office all required his consideration However, he appears to have spent more of his time on efforts to bring an end to the violence wracking the state than on efforts to accomplish any other single goal. Davis believed that Texas could only achieve prosperity and happiness when its citizens could go about their daily business and perform their civic duties without fear. When he took office, this was not possible. If the future of Texas he desired and his own political future were to be secured, he had to bring the violence to an end.[1]

Davis saw the solution to the problem of violence as focusing attention on its major sources. The first source consisted of individuals and groups who robbed and murdered because they recognized no social constraints upon their behavior. The government created the state police to suppress such behavior, and Chief Davidson had done much to further that goal. The origins of other types of violence could be dealt with less easily. To Davis, these other sources included the warring and thieving behavior of Indians against frontier settlers and the hatred towards blacks and Unionists born of the war and underlying much of the political violence of the day. His daily correspondence showed the intractability of these two problems, and his efforts at dealing with them help to account for the fact that he often left the capitol only for his meals and to sleep.

Indian raiding actually was nothing new—Indian attacks had troubled white settlers since they moved into what was now Texas. In the post-war years, members of the Kiowa and Comanche tribes appeared to be primarily responsible for the raids along the state's northwestern and central frontier. Kickapoo and Lipan Apache, accompanied often by Mexican nationals, marauded along the Rio Grande border. Exact numbers cannot be known, but whites believed that the attacks exacted a large price in lost property and human lives. Whites considered the loss of property as nothing more than theft; the loss of lives, graphically portrayed in the contemporary press, was seen as evidence of savagery. Edmund Davis became an adult dealing with Indians on the frontier, and he saw the problem from the white man's perspective. The Indians had to be suppressed. In a letter written to President Grant in February 1870, Davis showed the lengths to which he was willing to go when he concluded that ultimately a "war of extermination seems necessary to secure permanent peace here."[2]

Davis was willing for the state to use its own military force to settle Indian affairs, but when his political opponents undermined the sale of the frontier bonds, he did not have the funding he needed to put his companies in the field. Volunteer ranger companies were mobilized, but they could hardly solve the problem since Indian raiders could retreat into the Indian Territory or Mexico where the rangers could not follow. The only real answer was to pressure the United States government into acting. Davis spent the rest of his time in the governor's office working for that goal. He harassed agents in the Indian Territory for not turning Indians charged with theft in Texas back over to state authority, complaining that it was "difficult to make our frontier people understand that the treatment of murderous and rascally Indians should be different from that allotted to a similar class of white men." He pushed the president to send more troops and to remove Indians from the frontier. He forwarded legislative petitions, endorsing their requests for relief.[3]

For all his efforts, Davis was able to get little help from Washington. His response to the defeat of a bill to fund minute companies along the frontier in the spring of 1871 expressed his deep frustration and his concern with what he perceived as the wrong-headed attitude of men in Congress. Congressman Degener introduced the bill, and when it failed, Davis responded with a bitter letter to Secretary of War William Belknap. Davis lamented that "members of Congress did not seem to believe that our complaints were well founded." Pushing Belknap to support his and the legislature's request for a congressional committee to be sent to Texas to investigate Indian affairs, he insisted that if Congress discovered the number of lives lost on the frontier "the philanthropists in that Body may come to the conclusion, that . . . these white men, women, and children were entitled to at least the same consideration as the savages whose lives may be taken in an effort to make them behave themselves." Congress did not provide for such a committee until 7 May 1872.[4]

After a year in office the Indian problem continued to plague the governor, but in the spring of 1871 events occurred that appeared to give him some leverage in dealing with the raiders out of Indian Territory. On 18 May 1871, a Kiowa party headed by Satanta, Big Tree, and Santank attacked a wagon train near Fort Richardson. Nine days later the three chiefs were arrested at Fort Sill, where Satanta admitted he participated in the affair. Officials in Indian Territory subsequently sent the three to Jack County for trial in the state courts. On the trip back to Texas, Santank died trying to escape, but the other two were tried, found guilty, and condemned to death. The death sentence produced objections from a variety of sources. Enoch Hoag, superintendent of Indian Affairs for the Central Superintendency at Lawrence, Kansas, advised President Grant to set aside the verdict, warning that he believed their execution would produce "fearful consequences to the people living on the frontier." Members of the national Committee of Friends on Indian Affairs also asked the president to intervene, calling the surrender of the chiefs to state authority of "questionable propriety." Like Hoag, they warned the chiefs' deaths could produce retaliation, but made clear that the principal reason they opposed executing the chiefs was because of the "antecedent history of their race."[5]

Attention turned quickly to Governor Davis. President Grant initially appeared disposed towards some sort of intervention in the affair, although military officials opposed such a course. General William T. Sherman, who was present when the chiefs were arrested, argued that the frontier would be a safer place once they were dead. The president went ahead anyway and asked the attorney general what power he had in the case. He found that he had no power since the trial took place in the state courts. The advocates for clemency then turned to the governor. Davis found himself the recipient of pleas from the acting secretary of the interior and the acting commissioner of Indian Affairs. He even received a letter from Alfred E. Love, president of the Universal Peace Union. One of the most surprising requests came from Charles Soward, district judge at Weatherford. In an earlier letter to President Grant, Soward complained about the federal government's failure to protect the frontier, asking, "What kind of Philosophy or Ethics is it, that teaches, that if our People are murdered by the scores, by savage beasts, it must be endured, and the savage beasts fed and cared for by the Government whose citizens are murdered thus." In his correspondence with Davis, he urged commutation of the death sentences, contending that he feared it would only increase violence. Soward's argument appeared to be similar to Davis's own thoughts on the matter. In the end, Davis concluded the death penalty would not produce good results, and in August he changed their sentence to life imprisonment.[6]

At some point, Davis came to see the fate of Satanta and Big Tree as an opportunity to push the federal government towards a solution to what he considered to be the Indian problem. When he went to New York and Washington in January 1872, Davis took that opportunity to meet with Charles Delano, Grant's secretary of the interior, to discuss a plan for settling matters on the frontier. Delano stated that his intention was to bring all of the tribes onto reservations, but no effective measures were put into place to keep them there. Davis suggested that when

Indians arrived at the reservation, the government should immediately take away their horses and arms. Subsequently, the government would only give them rations for a day at a time, handed out at a daily roll call. Davis also proposed that all of the inhabitants should be either persuaded or "compelled" to work at some employment; the money made would help pay for their maintenance. Davis clearly believed that only a system that destroyed the mobility of the Indians would stop the frontier raids. Without such an arrangement, he believed the reservations would not help to protect the frontier. Davis concluded that Delano agreed with him on the need for such a plan.[7]

The next step in the evolution of Davis's efforts at influencing federal policy came after he was informed that Satanta offered to bring all of the members of his tribe back to the reservation in return for a gubernatorial pardon. If the federal government did create the controls over the reservation that Davis and Delano discussed, the Indians on the reservation would no longer pose a threat. Davis visited the two chiefs at Huntsville in March 1872 to discuss their proposal, and he informed them that if they could convince all tribal members to go to the reservations and surrender their horses and arms, he would pardon them. In April, the governor contacted the commander of the District of Texas, Brigadier General Christopher C. Augur, and asked his views on such a plan. Davis noted that he would not pardon the chiefs unless the "whole Tribe is brought under subjection," and the military agreed to act in concert. General Augur did not endorse Davis's plan, but Davis believed that he had enough support from Secretary Delano to proceed.[8]

The governor should not have put as much faith as he did in what he considered to be the consensus he reached with Delano the previous January. In fact federal authorities already gave him reason to doubt that Delano would carry out his plan fully. In his meeting with Delano, Davis believed that the two had concluded that force might be needed to make sure that all of the Kiowa moved to the reservation. The governor offered to raise a force that would remain in the field through the summer of 1872 and into the winter campaigning against the Indians. He would place these companies under the command of the United States Army and paid for by the federal government.

In late May, the governor was certain that the national government was ready to carry out his plan, although there were delays. He sent James Newcomb to Washington to impress upon Delano the need for immediate action. But, as would be too often the case for Davis regarding relations with Washington, his perceptions of the administration's intentions and willingness to act proved overly optimistic. No money was provided, and Davis was unable to undertake a campaign.[9]

Even though Washington failed to provide the money that would allow Davis to move against the Indians, he continued to negotiate over the future of the Kiowa chiefs. Davis was still optimistic that they could make some sort of arrangement in which the chiefs would surrender to federal authorities in return for the settling of the Kiowa on the reservations. Throughout the negotiations, the governor insisted that he would free the chiefs only if the federal government took steps to end the raiding. Repeatedly he stressed the idea that they must be put on foot, disarmed, and put under close surveillance. In September, Davis agreed to a proposal to allow Satanta and Big Tree to go to Fort Sill to discuss a possible deal. The council achieved no immediate results, although subsequent events indicated that Indian agents promised that the chiefs would go free. They returned to the state prison at Huntsville, and then no further movement on the matter took place until the next spring.[10]

Davis returned Washington the next June, taking time off from a trip to New York where he discussed state finances with bankers, hoping to meet with officials from the Department of the Interior and bring an end to the negotiations regarding the Kiowa chieftains. When he arrived, he found no one in authority in town to discuss the matter and was forced to wait until July to have his meetings. On 7 July he finally managed to see the secretary of the interior. Once again, Delano pressured him to surrender the chiefs, but Davis responded with a restatement of his own demands. He also explained that he did not feel obligated to respect any promises that government agents might have made to the tribes unless the government guaranteed peace on the frontier. If the government held to its promises to abide by his terms, he would turn the chiefs over to federal authorities, who would then have the responsibility of dealing with them. The two reached an agreement, although a reporter suggested Davis differed from Delano in the "degree of confidence they respectively place in the assurances of future good behavior on the part of the Indians." As a result of the meeting, a council would be held with the Kiowa and Comanches at Fort Sill later in the year.[11]

The Fort Sill conference was held at a critical time for Davis. He was in the middle of a campaign for reelection to the governorship that fall, and the outcome of the meeting could potentially influence that election. The chiefs were transferred to Fort Sill under a military escort in September so that they could consult with their people prior to the meeting. In October, Davis went to the fort for the final negotiations. There he received a pledge from Commissioner Edward P. Smith that the governor's conditions were met, and Davis returned Satanta and Big Tree to their tribes. Smith reported that the Indians were delighted with the return of the chiefs and that they hugged Governor Davis, "whom they now look upon as among their best friends." One of the principal chiefs of the Kiowa was so pleased that, according to a story later related by Davis's son, he presented the governor with a red flannel lined wolfskin robe with an ornamental border. The ornaments were scalps. Perceiving that Davis was uncomfortable with the gift, the chief assured him that the scalps were taken only from Mexicans and Indians and not from any women or whites. Davis took the robe, but insisted that the chief keep the scalps, since the governor did not wish to deprive him of the proof of his greatness. The chief agreed to remove them, and Davis left with a new robe and the promise of peace.[12]

If the peace held, Davis could take credit for it in the last days before Texans went to the polls. The prospects for peace, however, were limited. A reporter at the conference found that despite Commissioner Smith's positive view of the council, the interaction between Satanta and Big Tree and members of the tribe evidenced dissatisfaction with what had taken place among some men. Both chiefs told members of the tribe that the white men were too numerous and had too many guns for the Indians to fight, but some members of the tribe were not ready to give up their raiding. One critic charged that the words of Satanta and Big Tree were bought by the whites. "For his part," the protestor said, "there was nothing like fighting; for if they never fought they never got anything for keeping at peace." Satanta discounted the response, indicating that while he learned the pointlessness of fighting, his people were "like children. . . . I shall have to be very careful what I tell them."[13]

Skeptics turned out to be reasonable in their doubts. Less than a month after the release of the chiefs, the Kiowa raided into Texas once again. At the time of the election as many as one hundred Indians were at work raiding ranches along the Little Wichita River and the West Fork of the Brazos, and the Democratic press was certain to publish the news. For Davis the renewed attacks were particularly disappointing. None of his work had borne fruit. In fact, Big Tree was one of the participants in the raids. Further, Davis discovered that the government had done nothing to carry out the measures to which it agreed on at Fort Sill. Since that conference, Davis concluded the raids along the northwestern frontier "have not sensibly abated" and if anything they were "more frequent than they were before."[14]

Davis found his efforts to deal with Indian problems along the Rio Grande frontier even more frustrating. From his own life on the border he believed that conditions there were more complicated than on the northwestern frontier. Kickapoo and Mescalero Apaches were the primary raiders, but the Mexican citizens joined in. Davis did not see the same motivation behind these raids as those of the Kiowa and Comanches. He recognized that in some cases Americans provoked the Mexicans and Indians by buying property stolen in Mexico; the Mexicans retaliated in turn. He also thought that some of the trouble was stirred up by Americans who were interested in provoking a war with Mexico, motivated by their desire for excitement or revenge against Mexico for its position during the Civil War. Here raiders could not be pursued to their bases, since that would require crossing an international boundary. Any solution ultimately required dealings with the Mexican government. Davis could not do that, and as a result, he was forced to do what he could to pressure the United States government to act. His efforts here proved as unsatisfactory as those to solve the problem of raiders from the Indian Territory.[15]

When Davis took office, Congress had already moved towards a solution to the border problem; in 1869 it had appropriated money to remove the Kickapoos from Mexico to the Indian Territory. After assuming the governorship, Davis found little progress towards that goal. As with incidents along the northwestern frontier, Davis responded by pressuring both the president and Congress to act. In a typical letter, he pushed Congressman Degener to move Congress towards action. "Surely the general Government, which keeps our hands tied as I may say, will not longer strain the credit of the U. S. by tolerating such outrages." If any other foreign nationals perpetrated such crimes on another peoples it would be a good cause for war. The Grant administration and the Congress were slow to act. In May of 1872 Congress finally appointed a commission to investigate matters, but it had not made its appearance in Texas by the following autumn.[16]

The federal government finally acted to deal with affairs along the Mexican border in February 1873. That month Grant ordered a regiment of cavalry to the Rio Grande and instructed his secretary of state to ask the Mexican government to be more active in preventing marauding across the border. The president went further, indicating that unless the Mexican government responded he might, out of necessity, have to order troops to pursue marauders into Mexico. In response, the Mexican government actually invited American action, making it known that it would ignore any such incursions. At the same time, the government finally reached an accord with the Kickapoos and began removing them from Mexico to Indian Territory. Davis's pressure encouraged the federal government to action, but it moved at its own pace and with small concern for the governor's complaints. In the end, these actions produced little positive results. The raids out of Mexico would continue at least into the middle of the 1870s.[17]

As troublesome as the Indian problems along the frontier were, a more dangerous threat, in Davis's view, was the pervasive mob violence that posed a direct threat to the survival of the Republican Party and, indeed, to constitutional government. Since the war's end, whites had assaulted blacks with impunity. Motives for such attacks varied. Some attacks were retaliatory, directed at a people many whites considered instrumental in their defeat. At times they were for economic purposes, helping landowners to take away the economic gains of the freedmen. After 1867 many were to achieve political ends, keeping blacks from organizing and voting. Some whites also directed their hostility towards white Unionists, then to those who joined the Republican Party, and finally against any authority created by the Republican regime. Conservatives and afterwards Democrats usually denied such politically motivated violence existed. Davis believed that it did and subsequent scholarship generally confirmed his view. If it could not be suppressed, little real chance existed for the survival of a party based on a biracial coalition or committed to even the most moderate conception of racial equality. Davis had to end violence, yet at the same time he faced the challenge of convincing most white Texans that the threat was real and the measures he employed to meet it were justified.[18]

Davis intended the state police to operate against individual or small groups of thieves and murderers who roamed the state, but the organization was never intended to cope with larger groups, mobs, and secret organizations such as the Ku Klux Klan that interfered with the Reconstruction process. Such bodies were a major reason that Davis asked the legislature for the power to declare martial law and for the creation of the state guard, a readily mobilized force that Davis could use to intervene in situations where local law enforcement officials failed. He believed that simply possessing the power might stop some violence, observing that "The mere knowledge of the fact that such power is given the Executive, and he will not hesitate to exercise it when the case warrants will go far towards obviating the necessity for its exercise." He soon found that mere possession of such power did not achieve his goal and that increased problems would force him to intervene in local affairs.[19]

During the three years of his administration Davis used his authority to declare martial law and utilized the state guard on only three occasions, in four different counties. They ultimately provided a test of his intentions. In 1870 his opponents argued that conditions in the state did not justify giving him the power to declare martial law or the need for what they called a "standing army." When Davis did declare martial law, they asserted that intervention was unnecessary. If not needed, the opposition claimed, the only explanation for his actions was his tyrannical purposes and his stubborn and inflexible character. Many contemporaries and later scholars accepted these charges as the truth, and it did much to damage his reputation. In fact, each case was complicated and usually came in places where local authorities historically had difficulty keeping order. Davis always was reluctant to intervene, gathering information before acting. While each side would read the evidence differently, it invariably proved the existence of mobs and the failure of local authorities to maintain control. Under the law, Davis had every justification in acting.[20]

Davis's first declaration of martial law would come in Hill County in January 1871. He was made aware of problems with law enforcement there shortly after he took office. The local district judge, William Chambers, alerted the governor in June 1870 that a black farmer was murdered and that others, fearing violence, had fled to Waco. Chambers concluded that local law officers showed little inclination to track down the murderers. Later that summer another murder took place, and once again, local officials were reluctant to seek out the murder. The county sheriff confirmed Chambers's assessment, indicating that since the county became filled with fugitives he was reluctant to act. In his letter, the sheriff made two points that helped create the context within which Davis would view later events. First, he indicated that the people of Hill County could not be counted on to provide aid in arresting outlaws and often appeared actually to be working with them. Second, he observed that without assistance, local law enforcement officials would find it impossible to arrest any member of the outlaw bands. The lawless character of the community became obvious that August when unknown parties attacked an officer of the state police.[21]

Conditions continued to deteriorate. In September, Adjutant General James Davidson ordered a state police detachment to Hillsboro to arrest the men responsible for the August incident. When the state police arrived they were unable to get help making arrests and were themselves attacked. The commander of the detachment concluded that the area was experiencing a "reign of terror." On 3 October, the governor informed the sheriff that he blamed local citizens for allowing the situation to continue and, based on reports he received, charged them with assisting the outlaws. Davis informed the sheriff that citizens must help suppress the lawless elements, and he imposed a deadline for their help. If the outlaws responsible for the attack on the state police were not arrested in thirty days, the governor would declare martial law and send in the state guard to pacify the region. Davis backed off when he received petitions from the county pledging support for his efforts. In his letter to the county's citizens, the governor indicated that he did not wish to declare martial law. All he desired was a restoration of order.[22]

Events in the following months indicated that despite the promises of local citizens, little changed. Continued violence, including an escape from the county jail and the murder of a black couple in nearby Bosque County by men from Hill County showed how little respect existed for the law. Davis watched, but did nothing until provoked by a confrontation between state police officers operating in the county and a prominent local family. The police discovered that the men supposed to be responsible for the murder of the couple in Bosque County were the son and a ward of James J. Gathings, one of Hill County's founders and a wealthy rancher. The police went to Gathings's home to search for the two. The elder Gathings helped the two escape, but the police searched his home anyway. Gathings was outraged that the police would enter his house and found a local justice of the peace who issued a warrant for the arrest of the officers. Gathering a party of men, Gathings went after the policemen, stopped them, and took them to Hillsboro where he held them on the basis of the warrant. Based on the commander of the police detachments report, the officers feared that local law enforcement officers could not protect them, managed to get out of the town jail, and left the county.[23]

With neither local authorities nor the state police able to restore order in Hill County, on 10 January 1871, Davis signed a proclamation of martial law but refrained from putting it into effect. Instead, he sent his adjutant general to Hillsboro to gather more information and gave him the authority to impose martial law if he thought it warranted. Davidson arrived and was joined by a company of fifty men from the state guard. He found the situation to be much as described by the state police and in his report to the governor described a chaotic situation with "officers intimidated, authority resisted, and a spirit of defiance to law extant." Davidson announced the declaration of martial law and immediately began making arrests of the seven men involved in the Gathings affair, including four members of the Gathings family. Davidson never fully explained what happened after the arrests. Instead of trying the men, who he claimed admitted their guilt, he fined them and used those monies to pay the expenses of the state guard. Two days after his arrival the adjutant general lifted martial law, contending that the civil authorities were now able to enforce the law.[24]

State troops had only left Hill County when serious troubles developed in Walker County. Local law enforcement officials there had earned a reputation for ineffectiveness, just as in Hill County, and Davis was made aware of conditions in Walker County immediately after he took office. In December 1870, he wrote to the district judge expressing his concerns with the local sheriff. Davis questioned if the accusations against him, if he had murdered prisoners and made no effort to arrest the killers of a freedmen, were true. The judge confirmed the charges and proposed that Davis remove the sheriff. Davis agreed with him that it was necessary, writing that even if all charges were not true, "I must have men in that office beyond suspicion or I cannot enforce the laws." Before he could remove the sheriff a riot broke up a pre-trial hearing in the county courthouse on 11 January 1871. The hearing involved four white men arrested by the state policemen, and also involved the sheriff when he refused to act for the murder of a freedman. The days prior to the hearing were tense, and the judge received numerous warnings of trouble. At the hearing, after the judge ordered the men held without bail, shooting broke out when their friends smuggled weapons to the defendants. When they broke for the door, Captain L. H. McNelly and his state police officers tried to block their escape, but outside the courthouse the escapees were joined by a heavily armed crowd that prevented the policemen from stopping them. When the sheriff tried to organize a posse, only two men volunteered. Emotions did not settle down and the next evening someone attempted to assassinate the presiding judge.[25]

The state police kept Davis informed of events, but as in Hill County he did not act rashly. On 12 January the district judge finally asked for help, reporting that in the wake of the courtroom escape civil authorities were "still unable to cope with the lawless men in our midst." Davis responded to the requests within the strict legal boundaries of the existing law. Davis responded that he intended to sustain the judge and his authority. "I am preparing to regulate affairs in the County of Walker," he wrote, and authorized the judge to inform local citizens that the outrage would lead to "severe expense and retribution." On 20 January, he declared martial law. General Davidson did not arrive in Walker County until 15 February and immediately determined that the civil courts could not be protected. He then set up military courts to try anyone charged in the courthouse affair. Backed by a company of the state guard, state policemen quickly arrested over twenty men and charged them with crimes ranging from murder to failure to assist an officer of the law. The military court convicted some of the men, including Nat Outlaw, one of the men being held for the freedman's murder. Before leaving, the adjutant general imposed a fine upon the county to pay for the expenses of the state troops and military courts. Davis justified the fine on the basis that local citizens failed to assist local officials. "While doubtless many of the citizens of that county deprecate the act," he informed a Senate committee, "they all stood by supinely, or actively aided the attack upon the judge and officers of the law while engaged in the exercise of their legitimate authority and sworn duty."[26]

In the cases of Hill and Walker counties Governor Davis showed little desire to intervene. He watched events unfold in both for months before acting, and he moved only when he found resistance to legal authority that county officials were unable to cope with. The opposition press, however, paid no attention to the broader set of events leading up to the governor's actions. They poured out invective, charging that Davis acted unconstitutionally and denied the basic rights guaranteed by both national and state constitutions. His use of martial law and the state troops proved, in their view, a part of his tyrannical designs. The San Antonio *Daily Herald* likened him to a "modern Caligula." In making their charges, the Democratic papers turned men like James

Gathings and Nat Outlaw into heroes, despite the fact that each broke laws that justified their arrest and punishment. Insisting that the Davis government's efforts at suppressing lawlessness were themselves unlawful, the Democrats excused all resistance to the law. They thus created a climate that encouraged further violent opposition to Davis and his administration. If at some point Davis could have ended such lawlessness, the charges against him might have been forgotten. However, subsequent events would show that neither the threat of martial law nor its application could produce that result.[27]

Davis could do little but continue to pursue the course he had laid out. In following that course he continued to avoid state action in any but the most outrageous cases, and he repeatedly passed up chances to act. One such case occurred only a month after the state guard marched out of Walker County. In March, he received a request from the district judge in Van Zandt County reporting a jail break and asking for the governor to send troops. As he had done in the past, the governor showed no desire to act impulsively. Davis replied to the judge, writing that he did not propose to "act hastily in declaring martial Law at any time." He intended to wait and see how the county sheriff responded to the situation. If local authorities manifested a disposition to sustain civil authorities he would "leave the matter in their hands." In the end, Davis sent no troops to Van Zandt. Similarly, he did not declare martial law in Bastrop County despite the fact that through the summer of 1871 bands that Davis believed were part of a growing Ku Klux Klan movement terrorized blacks, burning their schools and kidnapping their teachers. The state police found that the community protected the perpetrators of the outrages, but local officials never asked for help and Davis refrained from acting.[28]

Davis was pressed to use force one more time, as violence increased in the months leading up to an election in the autumn of 1871. This time he focused on Limestone and Freestone counties, neighbors of the turbulent Hill County. As in the case of the latter, unrest had prevailed in Limestone and Freestone throughout the postwar period. Shortly after taking office, Davis received reports from the county clerk in Freestone that the Ku Klux Klan appeared and was murdering politically active blacks. The clerk believed that only the army could restore order. Davis continued receiving reports of local problems and in December the district judge, Frank P. Wood, informed the governor that he believed the public possessed little sentiment in favor of maintaining law and order. Partly because of the warnings, state police and local citizens recruited into the State Special Police were sent into both counties prior to the fall election. Four days before polls opened, on 30 September, a black policeman and locals became involved in a shooting affray in the town of Groesbeck. The shootout quickly escalated into a full-scale confrontation between whites and blacks. The confrontation began when whites tried to seize the policeman and his associates. In turn, the police received reinforcements, and whites came to believe that blacks were arming and intended to burn Groesbeck. Whites responded by organizing a resistance that included a local white company of the state guard. As in previous cases, what happened exactly cannot be known, as each side produced its own story of events. The heart of the matter, however, was that local citizens resisted the authority of the state police. In the process, they disrupted the election and drove black voters from the polls.[29]

On 1 October, the county sheriff, district clerk, and a local justice of the peace informed the governor that the county was in a "state of riot and insubordination" and insisted that only martial law could restore order. Davis responded on 9 October with the necessary proclamation. He justified his action as necessary to suppress a "combination of lawless men, claiming themselves to consist of several thousand persons organized as an insurrectionary force" who had committed murders, participated in violence, and "intimidated and controlled the civil officers." They also prevented a fair election. Adjutant General Davidson was sent once again. Bringing in units of the state guard, he quickly pacified the community, although he did not restore civil law until 9 November. The affair in Limestone and Freestone counties showed that state troops could bring order, but clearly past declarations of martial law had not worked to prevent it. In fact, events in Limestone and Freestone suggest that many whites had grown even more willing to resist state authority. Davis's power and his use of it clearly did not bring about the results he desired.[30]

The inability of the state police and the state guard to bring an end to domestic violence offers at least one explanation for Davis's great concern with federal appointments in Texas. He needed active men in those offices to help maintain order. When Davis took office the state had two judicial districts, each with a judge, a district attorney, and a United States marshal. On 31 May 1870, Congress passed what became known as the First Force Bill and gave its officers the power to prosecute as federal crimes the use of force, bribery, or intimidation against voters. A second bill followed on 28 February 1871, broadening the power of the federal courts and giving them police power to keep the peace and protect the polls. A third, passed on 20 April 1871, empowered the president to suspend *habeas corpus* in order to suppress secret organizations such as the Ku Klux Klan that interfered with elections. If federal officers actually carried out the laws implemented by Congress, Davis would have strong allies in restoring order, especially in the critical business of maintaining peace at the polls. If his programs had any chance for success, voting rights had to be secured.[31]

Unfortunately for the governor, when he took office he found officers of the federal courts of little help. The worst situation was in the western judicial district, where they not only provided no help but stood in the way of his efforts. In that district the United States marshal was Thomas F. Purnell, a Union army veteran from the 54th Indiana Infantry who received the appointment in large part because of the support of Oliver P. Morton, United States senator from Indiana. Purnell appeared content to hold office with as little activity as possible. The district attorney was C. T. Garland, a man Davis considered "wholly unqualified and incompetent for the position." Davis and his supporters were concerned with that district's officers as early as 1870 but had done little to get them removed until after the congressional election of 1871. In that election, Davis believed widespread violence and intimidation took place, and he expected some sort of action against the perpetrators. Davis used the state police to gather information on the Ku Klux Klan and hoped to prosecute them in the federal courts. He found that neither Garland nor Purnell were willing to help in his efforts. As a result, the governor rushed to have them replaced.[32]

On his trip to New York and Washington in January 1872, Davis had not only discussed finances and Indian affairs but also met with officials in the justice department and attacked Purnell and Garland. The governor wanted to replace Purnell with Thomas P. Ochiltree, a young man who had been a Confederate soldier and who had joined the Republican Party, and Garland with Andrew J. Evans, an old Unionist and former judge. Davis made the case that quick action was needed, pointing to his own effort at having men charged with being part of the Ku Klux Klan and tried in the district court's April session. With Purnell and Garland in place, Davis believed the jury would be filled with Klan sympathizers. Despite the urgency of the situation, neither President Grant nor Attorney General George H. Williams were ready to act and the governor returned to Texas with little hope for new men in these critical offices.[33]

On his return to Austin, Davis found that an attack on federal officials was not wise. The usually inactive Purnell and Garland struck back. Purnell assembled a grand jury that Davis believed was packed with his own assistant marshals and anti-administration men, including the man fired as mayor of Austin by Davis. Garland, assisted by the chairman of the Democratic executive committee and Jack Hamilton, then secured from that grand jury an indictment of the governor for committing fraud. The basis for the charge was that Davis had issued an election certificate to an 1871 congressional candidate, whose victory was being contested, and also that he advised Secretary Newcomb to reject the vote in some counties. The grand jury further showed its partisan spirit when it also indicted state senator Andrew J. Fountain for forgery. Politics clearly lay behind the effort, for Fountain's conviction and removal from the state Senate gave Democrats control over the body. In addition, Davis's backers believed that Purnell and Garland proceeded with the indictments to divert attention from the charges against themselves. While the charges turned out to be baseless, the federal officials tied up Davis and his administration by having to deal with them and added fuel to charges being made by Democrats of Davis's tyrannical character.[34]

President Grant not only refused to remove Purnell, he also reappointed him in March 1873. Thus the marshal remained a thorn in Davis's side for the rest of his years as governor. Grant did remove Garland, however, and replaced him with Evans just before Davis's trial. Evans moved forward with the prosecution, but the jury failed to convict the governor. Democrats charged that Evans purposefully mishandled the case; Republicans insisted no viable case ever existed. Davis did get more action from the new district attorney, even if he could not count on Purnell. Evans proved particularly aggressive in enforcing the Force Acts. The governor turned over a list of names gathered by the state police—men alleged to be members of the Klan—and Evans ordered their arrests and initiated trials. In February 1873, Evans secured further indictments and trials. Little is known about what happened in these trials, although information in one case shows the character of the district attorney's feelings towards the Klan. In the case of David Boaz of Tarrant County, the president asked him for his opinion on whether or not he should be pardoned. Evans replied that Boaz led a band of men in Tarrant County in 1870 and 1871 who committed "high handed lawless acts." Evans insisted that "no clemency" be shown toward Boaz. Unfortunately for Governor Davis, Evans's efforts came too late to do much to help preserve his administration.[35]

Davis generally liked the officers in the Eastern Judicial District, but there any effective actions under the Force Acts were made impossible because of constant turnover. Finding and keeping a federal district judge proved particularly troublesome after Benjamin O. Watrous resigned the position in the spring of 1870. President Grant initially offered the job to Colonel John Appleton, a Union Army veteran from Maine. He named Appleton without consulting any member of the Texas congressional delegation, demonstrating what would be his increasing tendency to ignore local Republicans in making appointments. The congressmen protested the appointment of any non-Texan to such a position and, with Governor Davis's support, asked the president to nominate Chauncey B. Sabin, a Houston attorney and Republican. Appleton ultimately did not want to move to Texas and turned down the president's appointment.

Before Grant sent another name to the Senate, Sabin became the victim of the breakdown of relations between Senator James W. Flanagan and Governor Davis. Sabin sided with Davis against Flanagan's railroad schemes, and Flanagan withdrew his endorsement of him. As a result, the infirm and inactive Watrous remained in office.[36]

Grant finally made another nomination that December, sending up the name of Joel C. C. Winch, who had been recommended by Flanagan. Winch, however, was a former Confederate officer who had not had his disabilities removed, and the Senate rejected him the following February. Grant then sent the name of another Union Army veteran, John Bruce, for consideration, but the Senate tabled the nomination. Judge Watrous, barely able to carry out his duties, remained in office. Later in December the president made another nomination, then withdrew it in January. The president followed by sending to the Senate the name of Amos Morrill, a Texas attorney who served on the Texas supreme court during Reconstruction. This time Senator Morgan Hamilton and Governor Davis opposed the appointment, alleging that Morrill was too closely connected to the Galveston railroad interests. On the other hand, Flanagan backed Morrill, producing a confrontation with the governor and his backers. The Senate approved Morrill, putting into place a political enemy of Governor Davis as federal judge in the Eastern District.[37]

Dealing with the president proved equally frustrating for Davis regarding the district attorney and the United States marshal. Davis would have liked to see district attorney David J. Baldwin removed, but found the president unwilling to move against him. On the other hand, the governor liked William E. Parker, the marshal. Parker was a Texas Unionist who fled to California during the war, then joined a Massachusetts cavalry regiment and rose to the rank of captain. He returned to Texas after the war, become an active Republican, and received the marshalship from Grant in 1869. Parker was active against lawbreakers, but in April 1873 the president removed him and nominated Thomas Ochiltree, Davis's candidate to replace Purnell in the Western District. Davis tried to get the president to change his mind, arguing that he did not oppose Ochiltree but could not see why an official who was "reliable and honest" and a man of "action and fidelity" would be replaced. Grant withdrew Ochiltree's nomination, although for reasons unrelated to Davis's protest, then finally nominated a man backed by the governor, Lemuel D. Evans. Evans was not confirmed, however, until March 1874. This meant that this critical office was left unfilled during the critical state election in the fall of 1873.[38]

Governor Davis promised an end to upheaval when he took office in the spring of 1870. In the autumn of 1873, he faced a general election that would test whether or not his efforts accomplished that goal. Needing federal officers in place to help achieve that end, in the summer of that year, he made one last push against the men he considered impediments. His quest took him to Washington one more time, a trip that he hoped would bring a new district attorney to the Western District and perhaps a new judge and district attorney to the Eastern. As on all of his other trips he would attend to other business as well, including settling the fate of Satanta and Big Tree. Lobbying for strong and active federal courts was his principal goal, and he made appointments to see the attorney general, the postmaster general, and the secretary of the treasury. However, Davis found by this time little desire on the part of administration officials to be of help. He managed to secure no changes prior to the election.[39]

Edmund Davis became governor of Texas possessing a commitment to a program that promised significant changes for the state and its people. That program's success ultimately hinged on Davis's ability to protect the people of the state, including its black citizens, from the lawlessness that was pervasive. In particular, success required protection of voters in the exercise of their rights. His efforts to both ends proved less than effective. His use of force proved ineffectual when confronting lawbreakers who found themselves supported by the governor's political opponents. His attempts at securing the support of the federal government and its officers in Texas were frustrated by the byzantine politics of federal patronage. His failure and its ultimate political implication would be demonstrated in state elections. At the polls he would find himself undermined by the growing power of his opponents and their ability to take apart the coalition that elected Davis in 1869.

EDMUND DAVIS,
TEXAS POLITICS, AND
THE DESTINY OF
REPUBLICANISM

"Of course if you live in a hut and sleep under Mexican blankets it will cost you less than if you fabricate an elegant building. . . . If you have public schools, and law and order you must pay for it."
—Edmund J. Davis. On the Stump in the 1870 Elections

Governor Davis recognized that if any of the measures that he promoted or the efforts that he made were to have a long-term impact upon the state, he had to establish the Republican Party as a viable political institution. At the time of his inauguration it appeared that his opposition might be ready to accept Republicans as representatives of legitimate political interests and that traditional political life would return. Davis discovered quickly that these appearances were deceiving. His opponents proved unwilling to accept either equal rights, free labor for blacks, or Republican power. As previously seen, the violence continued and even intensified. Success ultimately depended on whether or not he or his programs could attract enough voters to maintain the majority in the face of this violent opposition. Inevitably, this situation required Davis to devote much time to trying to convince voters to support him and to win elections in the face of pervasive violence and intimidation.

The first test of the drawing power of Davis's administration came in the autumn of 1870. Texans would select congressmen and also vote in a special election to fill vacancies in the state legislature. Jack Hamilton early on let it be known that he intended to run for Congress. Democrats saw a chance to take control of the state Senate in the legislative elections. Hamilton's supporters and the Democrats moved once again to effect a coalition, and they made the Davis administration the basis for their campaigns. The first move came in mid-June, when Hamilton's *Austin Republican* proposed a consultation of what he called the "liberal Republicans . . . who love civil government, law and order." The call implied that Davis Republicans did not stand for these things, and indicated that some new political movement might be in order. By early July, *Flake's Bulletin,* another Hamilton paper, suggested these Republicans might fuse with Democrats who had accepted the war's results. This proposal was well-received in some Democratic circles. The editor of the *Galveston News* believed that Democrats might well consider "Co-operation in opposition to Radicalism."[1]

At Austin, an initial meeting to work out some sort of basis for cooperation led to another on 16 July. Then, a group of Democrats met with representatives of Jack Hamilton, several Democratic legislators, Republican senators who had bolted their party caucus in the struggles over the police and militia bills, the executive secretary of the state Democratic Party, and John L. Haynes, head of the executive committee that supported Jack Hamilton in 1869. This consultation issued an address to the people of Texas that condemned the Davis administration, presenting a catalogue of grievances worked out by Hamilton's supporters. They called for men of all parties to cooperate in a movement against the governor. The fusionists in Austin recommended obeying the laws, supporting law enforcement officials, and enrolling in the militia until they could overturn such measures. In particular, they urged Texans not to join secret organizations to seek redress of their perceived wrongs. Ironically, their appeal indicated the very existence of things that they denied existed—violence and the Ku Klux Klan.[2]

Jack Hamilton was in the field soon after a basis for cooperation was reached. He kept the focus of his campaign speeches on the Davis administration. In Austin, at one of his first speeches, he criticized the governor for the police and militia bills, declaring that they were unconstitutional and reflected Davis's personal desire for power. If elected, Hamilton promised his audience that he would find a remedy for the governor's abuses and bring an end to the evil that Davis had perpetrated. Hamilton openly welcomed support from Democrats, concluding that "Whoever is willing to combat tyranny and corruption and to assist in hurling from power the usurpers who are ruining our State I hold as my brother, whatever his political antecedents or predilections may be."[3]

Uniting with Hamilton, whose supporters now called themselves Liberal Republicans, made good newspaper copy for Democrats and showed an apparent willingness to accept the results of Reconstruction. Some Democratic leaders publicly supported the move, but even during the meetings in Austin most party leaders worked to reorganize the Democrats on a straight-out basis at the local level. Many Democrats were reluctant to surrender their identity in any cooperative movement and insisted on maintaining their party organization. The editor of the Houston *Telegraph* gave little reason to believe that he had accepted the war's results when he demanded that Democrats stand on the party's traditional basis of states' rights. The *Brenham Banner*'s editor offered similar advice, urging Democrats to stay away from any new political movement unless its platform expressed fidelity to the principle of states' rights.[4]

The plans of Davis's opponents to seize power were partially thwarted almost as soon as they began campaigning. Congress, seeking to establish a uniform time for congressional elections, delayed the vote on congressmen until 1871. The editor of Davis's *State Journal* welcomed congressional action, indicating that he hated to kill the rising joy of the "old political wire pullers" and "blind haters of the government" who had hoped to "overthrow or cripple reconstruction." He hoped that the delay would give Texans time to focus on peace, good order, immigration, and prosperity rather than politics. In fact, the delay applied only to the congressional elections. Texans would still have to go to the polls to fill local offices, and some voters would have to make decisions in critical legislative contests. Three seats in the Senate and eight in the House were vacant. The senate elections were critical for the Davis administration because they would determine who controlled that body. One of those seats was that of E. L. Alford, who had voted against the administration on the police and militia bills. A second was that of

Mijamin Priest, a Davis supporter. The third was held by Abner K. Foster, a Democrat who died during the session. Much was at stake. Davis had to hold on to two of these seats to retain control in the senate. If the Democrats could pick up these two seats, they would be in power.[5]

Too much was at stake for Davis not to become intensively involved in the subsequent campaign. In September, Davis took over the work of both Adjutant General Davidson and Secretary of State Newcomb so that they could work for the Republican candidate for the seat for Colorado and Lavaca counties left vacant by Foster. Davis made clear how important carrying the election there was before Newcomb left Austin, writing, "The carrying of the vacant senatorial districts is of such importance that I willingly spare you both. Only do your work *thoroughly*." Davis even offered advice on how to deal with Democratic charges against his administration, instructing Newcomb to emphasize how the Democrats were willing supporters of the "rascally 'chicken pie' schemes" of the railroad interests. Davis wanted Newcomb and Davidson to ensure that Republican candidates would back him in opposing the railroad schemes and also opposing those who openly supported payment of all the state bonds contracted to fund frontier protection and law enforcement.[6]

The months leading up to the autumn election provided unmistakable evidence to Davis of the lengths his opponents would go to defeat him. Davis's correspondence indicated that violence intensified in every district with a contested seat, and even the existence of the state police and the threat of martial law failed to suppress it. The sheriff of Leon County, where a House seat was open, reported that threats were made against his life, and he found it impossible to protect voters. "If a freed man talks about working with a Union man," he wrote, "his life is threatened at once." Further, whites were threatening to drive all blacks who did not vote with them off of their land. An agent for the Internal Revenue Service who organized Union League councils in the same district confided, "Times are exciting and squally here. A loyal man is not very safe if he is not quiet." In Anderson County, the same correspondent reported that a group of whites disrupted a procession of blacks on 4 July and drove the participants from town. An attempted assassination of the sheriff followed. In nearby Henderson County, a prominent black member of the Loyal League was murdered. In Bastrop County, where Senator Alford's seat was being filled, fifty men wearing Ku Klux Klan masks rode into the county seat to let blacks know their organization was present.[7]

Democrats claimed that none of the violence in the months before the election was politically motivated, but its timing and the subsequent problems during the election itself indicate that it had little other purpose. In the wake of the election, Davis received reports from around the state of efforts to keep Republicans from voting. Conditions in eastern Texas were bad enough that the governor sent Captain Thomas Sheriff of the state police to investigate. Sheriff determined that in Houston and Cherokee counties Union men were thoroughly cowed by the threat of violence. In Rusk County he found that the freedmen "in a mass seem terror stricken from the manner in which the election was conducted outside & around the polls." White Republicans found themselves "insulted & abused." In nearby Leon County, Democrats used another tool, trying to indict state policemen for keeping order at the polls. Davis asked Sheriff to judge whether or not he should send in state troops, but the captain concluded that in most cases Democrats had only threatened violence. However, that was enough to keep people from the polls. He found that intimidation was carried out "in such ways that the law has no chance to get hold of the parties."[8]

A close look at the results indicated that Davis had every reason to fear for his political future. On the surface the governor had reason to be thankful. Two of the three Senate seats were carried by Republicans. In every case, however, there was a fall off in Republican votes. The Democratic candidate easily defeated his Republican opponent in the Cherokee-Houston district, but the results showed a broader trend when Republican support in the heavily African American Houston County dropped from 790 in the 1869 election to 676. A Davis loyalist carried the seat for Bastrop and Fayette counties that was held by the Republican, Alford, but the party vote sank precipitously from 1,955 in 1869 to 1,051. In Colorado and Lavaca counties Republicans won the previously Democratic seat, yet Republican voters declined from 1,557 to 1,283.

The fact that two of the districts had large African American populations worked in Davis's favor, but the actual returns showed that the governor's efforts at mobilizing voters and protecting the polls and the rights of voters was not working.[9]

Davis managed to hold on to the senate, but he had little time to enjoy that victory. At a time when local, state, and national elections did not coincide, one election season gave way to another with little time for respite. Davis and his party faced another challenge almost immediately as they were forced to ready themselves for the congressional elections to take place in the autumn of 1871. In 1869, Republicans carried three of the state's four congressional districts. Holding on to these seats was essential. Only if Texas Republicans could deliver votes supporting the administration and national party's agenda could they count on having a voice in national affairs, a say in the distribution of federal patronage, or any other favors that might come from the Grant administration. Holding on to these seats would be difficult, however, because Davis's opponents indicated that they intended to mount a serious challenge. This time the real threat would come from the re-emergent Democratic Party. Democrats held their first postwar convention in Austin on 23 January, and their actions indicated Davis would have a hard fight on his hands. Much of the party platform was an attack on the Davis administration, repeating the charges they made against it the previous summer. It also indicated that as a party, Texas Democrats had not accepted the work of Reconstruction fully. The platform insisted that the regulation of elections and suffrage were within the powers of the state, suggesting that they did not see black suffrage as permanent.[10]

The reorganization of the Democratic Party did produce some positive results for Davis. It pushed some of the Liberal Republicans of 1870 back into the ranks of the regular party. The most noteworthy returnee was John L. Haynes. In a letter to the editor of the *Austin Republican,* Haynes indicated that he was ready to accept the party organization supporting Governor Davis as the sole representative of the Republican Party in Texas. He explained that the Democratic convention had provoked his decision. He found himself, after the publication of their platform, unable to "sacrifice those principles of government to sustain which I took up arms during the late war." He pointed in particular to the Democratic statement concerning suffrage as a refusal to accept the war's results and an interpretation of the relationship between state and general governments not unlike that which Democrats embraced in 1861. How many men gave up on the possibility of fusion with the Democrats is unknown, but the administration's newspaper concluded many were like Haynes, unable to stomach a union with states' rights Democrats.[11]

As the congressional campaign took shape during the summer of 1871, Republican opponents once again focused primarily on the Davis administration. A qualitative change in tactics did take place as Democrats and those Liberal Republicans like former governors Pease and Hamilton shifted the direction of their criticism. Showing less concern with the charges of tyranny leveled in 1870, they now fastened onto the question of taxation, charging that the Davis government had imposed onerous taxes on the people. This move reflected a trend across the South, where Republican opponents hoped to gain public approval in the North for their efforts at removing Republican regimes. In August, Pease, Hamilton, and prominent Democrats called for a convention of men from all parties to discuss high taxes. While the men who proposed the conference insisted it was nonpartisan and Pease addressed it, Democrats were the dominant group in attendance. Assembled on the eve of the congressional election, its intent was political, and it changed the dialogue in the campaign.[12]

The principal result of the convention was the publication of a report that became a major campaign document, furnishing opposition candidates with the bases for their canvass against supporters of Governor Davis. The widely circulated report asserted that taxes under Davis rose from $0.15 on the $100 valuation in 1866 to $2.175 by 1871. In fact, the charge was only half true, since the larger figure reflected the highest possible rate of taxation allowed, rather than the actual rate. The document went on to recommend that taxpayers challenge the constitutionality of many of the taxes and withhold tax payments until the constitutional issue was resolved. The latter suggestion was of great significance for the state government, for even if the courts ruled in favor of the taxes, when people refused to pay their taxes it starved the state of immediate revenues and forced the governor to struggle to maintain funding for everything from the public schools to the state police.[13]

His policies having become the central issue in the campaign, Davis defended himself against what he called the "tax howlers." On 27 July in Austin, then in Galveston on 16 August, and in Houston the next evening he addressed large and enthusiastic crowds and provided one of the clearest views of his understanding of the existing situation. The reporter of the *Houston Union* estimated that nearly twelve hundred people attended the Galveston meeting and included six hundred Democrats. Many who wanted to attend had to be turned away. Pointing out the national flag within the hall in Galveston, he began with remarks that indicated the turmoil of politics at that time and perhaps questioned the purpose of Democrats in being there. "That flag means free speech," he told the audience. "It means," he said, "that everybody has the right to speak. I intend to have free speech while I am Governor of this State." Davis subsequently gave his speech with only a few interruptions.[14]

Part of Davis's defense was an attack upon the Democratic Party and its congressional candidates. He showed the fighting spirit he always displayed and a readiness to confront his opponents head on. The Democratic Party was one of "false pretense," he charged. In Austin he called Democrats the "fraudulent Democracy." They attempted to destroy the Union, claiming that their liberty was threatened, but actually they feared liberty given to black men. They pretended to be the party of liberty of opinion, but anyone who opposed them before the war would have forfeited their life. After the war they tried to fool everyone again, making the freedmen slaves even though leaving them nominally free. Davis contended that the Democrats running for Congress still ran on false pretense, hiding their real plans to reverse Reconstruction with attacks upon his administration. These were false issues.[15]

Addressing the charges made against him, he turned first to the question of taxation. He did not deny taxes had risen, although he argued that they still remained less than those in any other state in the Union. Explaining why tax increases were necessary, he pointed to state finance prior to the war. Then, taxes were only twelve-and-a-half cents on the dollar, but whenever there was a deficit the state simply sold some of the bonds acquired from the United States as part of its annexation. The tax base also was larger then, including three hundred million dollars in slave property. Taxes had been low, but Democrats had offered little, "not a school, nor a bridge, not a road nor a decent public building, or public work of any kind." Now the government had to pay for this neglect. Debts had to be paid off, and that included amounts of "which the Democrats left considerable." The Democrats also had added to the burden of financing the schools mandated by the new constitution since they had plundered the school fund to support railroads.

Davis urged his listeners to see that the taxes they were paying provided necessary services that, in the long run, would improve the state's economy and their lives. He pointed to the Immigration Bureau, the Geological Survey, the state police, and particularly to the public schools as worthwhile investments. The schools constituted the largest single expenditure for the states, accounting for over eleven dollars out of every twenty raised. He trusted that the small farmer and the men of moderate means would come to understand that their interests lay with the creation of the public schools. The schools were essential for the progress of the state. "Of course if you live in a hut and sleep under Mexican blankets," he admonished his audience, "it will cost you less than if you fabricate an elegant building. If you have public schools, and law and order," he went on, "you must pay for it." He believed most Texans understood this. Who opposed the school taxes? Davis thought that "Most of the fuss made about the school tax comes from the most wealth." It came from men like Democratic congressional candidate John Hancock, "worth a quarter of a million," or land speculators such as Senator Morgan Hamilton, who Davis, in a thinly veiled reference, referred to as an "old miser, too stingy to get married and have children of his own to send to school, or too illiberal to have any of his hoarded doubloons for the education of his poorer neighbors."

Davis defended with particular vigor the state police force. Government had to protect the lives and property of its people and the state police was doing that. In its first two years policemen arrested 2,244 individuals, persons charged with horse stealing, cattle theft, and murder.

As a result, the penitentiary had twice the number of inmates than it had at any previous time. Davis also attributed the flight of thousands of criminals from the state to the new force. The police brought an end to what was "almost a warfare," and he doubted that the people of the state wanted to return to such conditions. There was less crime and Davis warned it would continue to be reduced "until the Democrats get into power."

Davis also responded to charges that members of his administration and Republicans in the Twelfth Legislature had taken bribes to help the railroads. He advised his audience to judge officials by their votes. It was not Republicans, Davis suggested, but the Democrats who were "the most corrupt set of scoundrels I ever knew." They might possess constitutional scruples about the creation of a state police, but he believed that they "saw merit whenever money was to be given away." In the end, only one Democrat voted to sustain his votes against the money grab going on in the legislature. Not the Republicans, but the Democrats "went solid for all the rascalities which came up in the Legislature."

In the course of his remarks, Davis touched upon a criticism that had arisen because of an election circular he had issued in anticipation of the upcoming election. Davis had ordered the state police and the special state police to prevent men from congregating near polls or interfering with voting. He was accused of "arbitrary conduct," but what did his opponents expect? Davis clearly expected Democrats to use force to win the election. They had urged supporters to camp around the polls. Had they not meant them to go armed and be ready to break up the election if the polls went against them? Every Democratic speech "hinted at violence," and Davis was determined that would not happen. "If you carry the election you shall have the benefit," he warned, "but you must submit to a free election."[16]

As he campaigned, Davis pushed for party solidarity and in his major speeches criticized any person who claimed to be Republican but failed to support his administration as either a "knave or a fool," but Republican unity proved elusive. In particular, the governor found himself having to deal with an internal revolt in the Third Congressional District against the sitting congressman, William T. Clark. A former

Freedmen's Bureau agent and Union League organizer, Louis W. Stevenson, mobilized African American voters to challenge Clark's nomination, charging that Clark had worked for Galveston's business interests but did little to help his black constituents. The First District included a large black minority and offered the party the greatest possibility for a victory, but only if Republican voters could come together behind one candidate. On the other hand, a successful candidate had to attract white voters, and administration officials did not believe that Stevenson could do so. As a result, when he tried to secure the support of the state Union League by taking over the state council, the chairman managed to block the move. At the district nominating convention Secretary of State Newcomb and party chairman James G. Tracy managed Clark's renomination. Stevenson, however, refused to withdraw from the race and continued to campaign.[17]

Davis remained publicly neutral as the fight took shape, but too much was at stake to allow Stevenson to divide the black vote. In August, while on his trip to Galveston for a campaign speech, reporters thought that the governor had met with the antagonists and tried to get both to drop out of the race and to run a new candidate. Whether the meeting actually took place is unknown, but if it did no agreement was reached. Both candidates remained in the field. Later, Davis did meet with some of Stevenson's supporters, asking them to pressure him to withdraw. Stevenson remained intransigent. In the end, Republicans went to the polls that fall with two Republican candidates in the field. The governor, the regular Republican Party, and the Union League did what they could for Clark, but Stevenson had strong support from the black voters he had helped politicize in the league. As a result, even in a district that offered great promise for a Republican candidate, the chances for victory were bleak.[18]

As the election approached, Davis did what he could for Republican candidates, especially for Congressman Edward Degener campaigning for reelection in the Fourth District. The governor attended a typical rally at Buaas Garden in Austin on the evening of 30 September. A Mexican band marched through the city's streets and led a large crowd to the hall. Davis, along with Senator George Ruby, Attorney

General Alexander and members of the legislature, delivered speeches in favor of Degener. When the meeting ended all joined singing campaign songs, including "Rally Round the Flag" and "The Battle Hymn of the Republic." Three nights later, he participated in another rally, marching in a torchlight procession to the capitol where he appeared with other members of the legislature and delivered another campaign speech, first in English and then in Spanish. At least in the Fourth District, local Republicans appeared hopeful, despite the adverse conditions.[19]

In fact, the governor and Republicans had little reason to be hopeful. Davis tried to respond to criticism of his party and his administration with reason. His opponents responded by using force to determine the election's outcome. A Republican correspondent from Houston County provided a detailed account of Democratic efforts there and in the surrounding efforts. They organized Democratic clubs and demanded that all whites join the club or be denounced as "Radicals." If insistent on remaining outside of the club, Democrats would exclude them from the business of the community. The game, according to the report, was "social ostracism." Further, while the governor provided reasoned defenses of his administration, the Democrats refused to accept his argument and were "mad & blind," only the threat of the militia and police prevented "open war" and caused Democratic leaders to "keep their followers in check, to prevent an outbreak." Similar tactics were used elsewhere. A correspondent from Anderson County informed the governor that, at the Democrat's county meeting, former Confederate postmaster general John H. Reagan advised visits with voters to determine how they would vote. If not a Democrat, they would be "put down as a *sneaking thieving Radical.*"[20]

Secretary of State Newcomb, in charge of the Union League, received a heavy volume of correspondence in the time before the election, none of it optimistic. Local Republicans noted Democratic efforts and predicted bad results for their party. In Navasota, the local Democratic paper carried out a campaign of abuse and slander against public officials, which made it difficult for Republican officials to carry out their duties and led to a situation where the "feeling toward Republicans is worse here now than it ever has been since the war and is growing worse all the time." Reports from Republicans in the north central parts of the state to the west of the Trinity River predicted defeat in the elections. One official likened the situation for Democratic opponents to that for the men who had opposed secession and the Confederacy. As a result of Democratic intimidation the opposition was "as completely subjugated as they were in 1862." Republicans, knowing that they could not depend on protection at all times, probably would not vote. The correspondent noted that "especially is this the case with the colored people."[21]

Such information led to Davis's controversial election order that he defended at Galveston. He expected violence and intimidation at the polls. On 9 August, Adjutant General Davidson issued orders that officers of the local police, the state police, and the special state police, plus members of the state guard were to be present during voter registration and at the polls to ensure peace. The order provided another basis for Democratic condemnation of the governor, but it also kept Democratic efforts to keep Republicans from the polls in check. Democrats continued their efforts at intimidation but avoided open violence in most cases. Generally, Republican candidates received more votes than Davis had in 1869. In Hill County, where the governor had declared martial law the previous February, a local judge reported that as a result of intimidation only fifty blacks out of two hundred registered actually appeared at the polls. Even so, Congressman Clark received 455 to Davis's 1869 vote of 322. Only in Limestone County, where election judges closed the polls, was there an obvious reduction in Republican support. In that county only twenty-eight voters cast their ballots for Clark, compared to 297 votes for Davis in the previous election.[22]

Still, the election was a massive defeat for Republican candidates, including Congressman Clark. From every part of the state correspondents indicated the same forces were at work to produce defeat. Blacks continued to vote Republican, but threats had driven whites from the party, and they almost universally voted for Democrats. Whites were more easily moved away from the Republican Party than blacks, having at least the option of voting Democratic to avoid the disapproval of other whites and the potential boycott of their businesses. The

Democratic campaign may also have served to mobilize those white voters who would traditionally vote Democratic, giving them a sense of urgency by presenting the contest as one between tyranny and freedom. For whatever reason, whites turned out in larger numbers than at any time since before the war. In 1869, Jack Hamilton received 9,798 votes in the Third Congressional District. In 1871 the Democratic candidate for Congress, Dewitt C. Giddings, received 21,844 votes in the unofficial poll. These statistics were ominous for Republicans. More whites than blacks lived in Texas. The white population was growing. Unless Republicans could pry some whites away from the Democrats, little chance existed for Republican survival in the future.[23]

The loss of the congressional seats was troublesome, but an even greater disaster faced Davis and his party if they were unable to regroup, and they had little time. Texans would return to the polls in the autumn of 1872, this time to vote for president, select congressmen once again, and elect members for the Thirteenth Legislature. For Governor Davis the legislative contests probably were the more critical. His majorities in both houses could be lost, and the situation did not look good. The Republican Party continued to be divided, with the state's Liberal Republicans remaining detached and critical of the governor. The Democrats emerged from the 1871 elections confident that population trends would give them a victory in 1872. They demonstrated this conviction when they rejected another Liberal Republican effort to promote fusion. Democratic newspapers responded that the only basis for fusion was for the liberals to become Democrats. At the local level, Democrats intended to run straight tickets and the Davis government would be their target.[24]

Davis and his party forged ahead anyway. At the party's convention in Houston during May, the delegates endorsed President Grant's bid for renomination and condemned the Liberal Republican movement. Even though Davis was not running in the election, the convention's platform endorsed all of the programs that he implemented, plus a new promise to increase the fiscal efficiency of state government and reduce taxes. Republican candidates were expected to endorse the platform, thus ensuring that any Republicans elected would be in the

Davis camp. Davis realized the importance of the election, and when the campaign actually began that autumn he went back on the campaign trail. Davis took advantage of the Houston & Texas Central's new line from Houston northward to visit some of the more populated counties. Everywhere he visited, he defended his party and administration. The Republican government pursued a course beneficial to the common men of the state. Law and order, schools, and even railroads were the result, and the party deserved their support. To blacks, Davis argued that their only choice for a party was the Republican Party because they had crushed the rebellion, ensured their liberation and now protected them. Poor whites had no other home either, for the Democratic Party offered no voice for those not part of the state's landed elites.[25]

Davis's appeals made no impact. Voting trends continued to run against him and his party. Horace Greeley, the Liberal Republican endorsed by the national Democratic Party, carried the state in the presidential contest, even though overall President Grant did better than Republican candidates for Congress the previous year. Despite Grant's showing, in some counties Republicans faced what one Republican observer called "threats of violence and various classes of intimidation." In counties where this did not happen, Republican turnout remained strong and helped explain Grant's vote. Where pressure was placed on Republicans, however, Republican voting declined. The nine counties in the northern end of the tumultuous Third District, which included Hill, Navarro, and Limestone counties, the Republican congressional candidate received 23 percent fewer votes than the party's candidate had only the year before. This decline in local Republican voting helps to explain Democratic victories in all five congressional races. Worse for Republicans, the party lost a majority in both the House and Senate of the legislature, a fact that gave the Democrats the power to reverse much of what Governor Davis had managed to accomplish up to this point.[26]

Davis realized the implications for his own political future of the Democratic surge to power in the 1872 election. In the months that followed, Davis appeared to realize that he could not be reelected, but he did try to preserve his programs. When the Thirteenth Legislature met in Austin during January, the governor appealed to the Democratic majority to look at what was accomplished. The state police and the militia act helped to produce a new level of peace. The public schools, only underway for two years, had enrolled over half of the school-aged children in the state. Davis admitted that these institutions were unpopular and could be improved, but he asked the legislators to consider modest changes rather than dismantling the systems completely. He acknowledged that the programs had cost money, but believed taxation was acceptable if the burden was equitably distributed and, in particular, corporations paid their fare share. The opposition *Galveston News* called it the best message he had ever issued, free from "partisan asperity," and intended to "promote the welfare of the state," but Democrats in the legislature showed little interest in keeping the Republican programs in place.[27]

The governor, nonetheless, cultivated legislators to protect his legacy. In late February, he accompanied a legislative excursion from Austin to Galveston for that city's celebration of Mardi Gras. The correspondent accompanying the party found Davis's behavior ingratiating. Rather than the "cold and taciturn" figure that the correspondent believed the governor had shown over the preceding three years, Davis appeared to enjoy himself as he moved from car to car talking with various legislators and even made a few jokes at the expense of one of the railroad executives. The bitterness of partisan conflict that typified the relationship between Davis and the Democrats appeared to have disappeared, and the reporter found the "display of good feeling . . . between Governor Davis and the leading Democrats of the legislature" remarkable.[28]

Good feelings may have existed at the personal level, but as the legislative session progressed Democrats dismantled the governor's programs. They almost immediately repealed the police law, abolishing the state police. They left the militia law intact, although they stripped out the governor's power to declare martial law. A new school law returned operations of the schools to local school districts, thus eliminating the state direction that had made it a true system. While the state provided some money for the schools, it cut support significantly and forced school funding on local communities. Ironically, despite their repeated criticism of Davis and his administration for its extravagance, while cutting state programs, the Democrats freely gave away the public lands, authorizing grants of sixteen sections for each mile of completed railroad to sixteen different companies. Davis tried to block legislative action on the police, the schools, and the massive giveaways to the railroad with vetoes, but even some Republicans abandoned him in his efforts. Enough Republicans joined with Democrats to override all of the governor's vetoes.[29]

When the legislature adjourned, Davis began preparing for an election campaign few thought he could win. A contest for the governorship would be part of the elections planned for the fall of 1873. As he set out his plans, Davis found himself disagreeing with some of his closest associates over the best way to approach the election. When the party's executive committee met in Austin on 28 May, the chairman, James G. Tracy, urged that the party run no candidates for office. He believed that the party feeling against Republicans was so intense that no one running as a Republican could win office. Davis, on the other hand, had not given up hope that Republicans could win. Even if defeat was inevitable, however, he thought the party's ship should go down flying its own flags. The committee reached no decision on how to proceed but did decide to hold a party convention in Dallas on 19 August.[30]

At the convention the debate over how to proceed continued. Tracy still resisted making party nominations and argued for the convention's adjournment without naming candidates. Democratic newspapers noted that several federal officeholders supported Tracy, a not surprising fact since Davis probably would get the nomination and the governor worked hard to have many of them removed. The governor was prepared to deal with Tracy and the federal officials. He had determined to run again for governor and as a Republican. Senator George Ruby had helped pave the way among black delegates, sponsoring a convention of African Americans at Brenham on 3 July that had endorsed Davis. Ruby even brought one of the governor's most vocal black critics, Matthew Gaines, back in line.[31]

Davis addressed the convention on the first day and told the delegates that they could choose anyone they wished for their nominee; all he asked was that they nominate a "good man who would not steal nor go back on his record." From the beginning, however, it was clear that the delegates favored Davis and the running of Republican candidates. Davis received the nomination. A correspondent of the *Galveston News* observed that Davis was unmistakably "the honest and unmanipulated choice of the rank and file of the party." The delegates demonstrated such unity that none of the disputes predicted by Democrats took place. Senator William A. Saylor, one of the men who opposed making any nominations, shook hands with Davis after the nomination and promised his support. The delegation from the district of Senator Flanagan, another opponent, unanimously voted for Davis. The *News* reporter concluded that there was "little question that the dissensions in the party have been healed and that the Republicans will fight like men who believe victory possible."[32]

To a large degree the platform adopted was a defense of the record of the Davis administration, and it would provide the text for the upcoming campaign. The platform endorsed the school law that was stricken by the Thirteenth Legislature and recommended its restoration. It backed state aid to railroad projects but insisted that it be done systematically with a "judicious" plan. It also insisted again that the state pass laws providing full protection for the civil rights of all citizens. It opposed repudiation of the debt created to support the International Railroad. The delegates used the platform to attack their opponents. It condemned outright the activities of the Thirteenth Legislature, its squandering of the public domain on speculative and worthless corporations, its efforts at making homesteads subject to sale, and its landlord and tenant bill, which gave landlords greater power over their tenants. All were acts that discriminated against the poor in favor of the rich.[33]

In September the Democratic convention named Richard Coke as Davis's opponent. Coke indicated the direction that the Democratic campaign would take in the acceptance speech. The four years of the Davis administration would be the focal point of the campaign, particularly the governor's declarations of martial law and the increase in taxes. Coke appealed for support, asserting, "You have been living under a government given over to tyranny, usurpation, and violence to vested rights—to the rights of person and of property." In addition, Coke resurrected an issue raised in the wake of the 1869 election and challenged the very legitimacy of the Davis government by claiming that his administration "does not pretend to represent the people of Texas, to help the people of Texas, or to take any note of the wants of the people of Texas." They could show no apathy in ridding themselves of that government.[34]

Occupied through much of the summer and then in October with Indian matters, Davis devoted as much time as he could to the campaign that fall. He did not avoid confrontation and invited his opponent to meet him during the canvass to discuss the public issues involved in the state election. Politicians already understood the increasing importance of railroads and telegraph in spreading their message, and because of Galveston's place as the center of the state's information network, Davis began his run for reelection with two important speeches in that city on 16 and 17 September. On the first day he spoke for an hour and a half to a large audience gathered at the city's Turner Hall. The next day he met with a large number of Galveston's leading merchants at the Cotton Exchange. The two speeches were similar in their content, offering a defense of his administration and predicting dire consequences for the state's future should the Democrats win.[35]

The Democrats represented the elite interests of the state, Davis contended. The Democratic convention was composed of "titled gentlemen" who held themselves above the poor. "Present were 20 captains, 60 colonels, 300 brigadier generals and the rest of them were judges," Where were the privates? Davis concluded, "perhaps they had all been killed during the war." What had these gentlemen done? The Thirteenth Legislature had killed free public schools. They tried to pass a landlord and tenant bill. They attacked the Immigration Bureau and indicated they did not want any more "d—d Dutch and Irish!" Legislators had tied his hands in all of his efforts at suppressing violence. They were responsible for the unrestrained gifts made to the railroads. His own administration, Davis insisted, had led to a period of happy prosperity and the Democrats would bring that to end. If reelected, Davis promised he would educate children, protect life and property, hold corporations to accountability, oppose the revolutionary schemes of the Democrats, and "maintain the honor and integrity of the state."[36]

In his address at the Cotton Exchange the governor devoted additional time to a discussion of the state's credit and also its relationship to the national government. He noted that most of the businessmen attending probably opposed him politically, but he asked them to consider what might happen if the Democrats secured power. The possibility that they might repudiate the railroad bonds promised by the Twelfth Legislature and their suggestions that a constitutional convention might change the existing Bill of Rights in the state already ruined the credibility and the credit of the state in the North. A Democratic administration meant little chance for federal funds for internal improvements and no chance for a flow of capital into the state.[37]

Davis had to leave the campaign trail to attend the Indian council considering the fate of Satanta and Big Tree in October, but returned quickly and traveled to speaking engagements across the state. At times he and Coke appeared together to debate the issues. At Crockett, on 8 November, more than a thousand persons, with the audience segregated and blacks standing on one side while whites were on the other, attended to hear the two speak at a grove near the local Baptist church. Davis spoke for more than two hours, making many of the same points that he made in his earlier speech in Galveston and defending his administration. Coke, on the other hand, replied with an attack on Davis's character, rhetoric typical of the Democratic campaign. The Radical Party was villainous in its management of state affairs, and Governor Davis was their leader. The Democratic Party stood for "home rule and direct accountability of officers to the people." That was the chief difference between the parties according to Coke. Coke also made an appeal Davis could not, playing on wartime sympathies. Coke expressed his happiness that he was a secessionist and that he had remained loyal to the people "among whom he had been born and bred." Davis clearly had not.[38]

On 14 November, Davis used a particularly innovative approach to campaigning. On that day the Republican Party published a full page advertisement on the front page of the *Galveston News* addressed to the state's farmers, mechanics, laboring men, and taxpayers. The advertisement again sounded the class appeal that the governor had first made in his September speeches. The Democrats represented the monied interests of the state, and the Republicans offered the only protection against the corruption of these interests. Beginning with Davis's own cautionary statement regarding internal improvements made to the legislature in 1870, the advertisement catalogued the swindles that the Democrats attempted or actually fastened on the people of Texas in giving away vast quantities of the state's resources to private corporations. Davis successfully stopped some with his veto, but was unable to block all. In the end, the governor was all that stood between the people and the monopolists and deserved reelection for his record of "statesmanship and services to the people."[39]

In the pages of the *San Antonio Express,* a paper circulated widely on the western frontier, the Davis campaign took aim at the Democrat's Indian policies. In mid-November the editor of the *Express* criticized the Democrats as "whited sepulcres" who denounced Davis as an enemy of the frontier and shed "crocodile tears" for the people of the west. Their hypocrisy was apparent everywhere, with the editor pointing out that John Hancock, a Democrat, went north to prevent Davis from selling the bonds needed to raise the frontier regiments and succeeded in blocking the governor's plans to protect the frontier. Even when a Democrat attempted to raise a ranger regiment for the frontier through congressional legislation, Democrat John Ireland persuaded members of Congress to vote against it.[40]

Davis ran aggressively in 1873 and may have been hopeful, but he had little chance for success. Democrats hated him and many Texans disliked his taxes. In addition, the Thirteenth Legislature passed a new election law that threatened to reduce black voting. That law ended the practice of holding elections at the county seat and placed ballot boxes in each precinct. The new practice made protecting voters more difficult. The *Houston Union* called the legislation "a bill to annihilate the Republican Party." Whether it was because of the new legislation or the absence of the state police at the polls cannot be known, but blacks failed to turn out in the same numbers as in previous elections. In Galveston an attorney found attendance at the polls to be light and believed that, in particular, "the colored people did not fully turn out." For whatever reason, Coke soundly defeated Davis, and Democrats carried elections almost everywhere.[41]

Davis accepted the results and prepared to leave office, but his administration's end would not be a peaceful one. On 4 January 1874 the state supreme court ruled the election unconstitutional in the case of *ex parte Rodriguez*. The reasoning behind the court's decision was debated, but once it was settled Davis believed that he had no alternative but to enforce the decision. Ignoring the court would not have been in keeping with his legal background and his lifelong dedication to the rule of law. Davis's decision to sustain the court put him on a collision course with Democratic leaders who had decided to ignore the ruling, convene the Fourteenth Legislature, and inaugurate Coke. Determined to keep that from happening, Davis asked the military commander in San Antonio to send United States troops to prevent the meeting of the legislature and the inauguration.[42]

Davis still might have called out the state guard to enforce the court's decision, and some companies were brought to Austin. He did not want, however, a violent confrontation. Democrats might have fought the guard, especially black guardsmen, but they would not have risked violence against United States troops. The army was ready to act, but the troops could not be sent without orders from President Grant. On 11 January, Davis informed Grant that the legislature's organization was imminent and required action. The next day, the president responded, but his telegram informed the governor that federal troops would not be sent because the conflict did not fall within the guidelines for intervention outlined in federal law. That evening the Democrats, no longer fearful of federal action, decided to organize the legislature. The next morning the Fourteenth Legislature assembled and began its session.[43]

The crisis was not over. Davis made up his mind not to use force to prevent the organization of the legislature, but he still contended that the election was unconstitutional. However, legislators needed his recognition to legitimize their existence and asked for it. Davis refused. Given his response, members of the legislature took the ballots from the election, counted those for governor and on the evening of 15 January inaugurated Richard Coke as governor. Texas now had two governors, at least according to Davis. In fact, the governor contended that he should hold office until four years from the date of his inauguration, 28 April 1870. Democratic attorneys argued that his term actually began when General Reynolds named him governor that January, and his term was over. When asked to vacate the executive offices, Davis refused and again called for federal help. Grant refused once more, and Edmund Davis abandoned his effort to hold on to the governorship.

On 19 January, Davis turned over the keys to the executive office to a representative of Governor Coke. He asked for time to move his furniture out of the governor's mansion, and the Democrats agreed to let him do that. As he left, two incidents occurred reflecting the momentous character of what was taking place. On leaving, Lizzie Davis, knowing of President Grant's refusal to intervene on behalf of her husband, took down a portrait of the president that had hung in the executive mansion through Davis's years as governor. She then "put her shapely foot right through the middle of it." Indeed, Davis was a victim of Grant and the North's abandonment of the achievement of Reconstruction. Davis's departure also meant a return to power of a less progressive party. That seemed clear, when newly elected Governor Coke arrived at the mansion and trampled the flowers that E. J. and Lizzie planted. The new governor detested bouquets, a reporter for the *San Antonio Express* noted, and now turned the mansion into a "dwelling whose cheerful lights have been extinguished." The two stories may be true or not, but they said much about what had happened. Coke's victory crushed out the seeds that Davis had sown in his efforts to create a different Texas.[44]

THE STRUGGLE FOR POLITICAL SURVIVAL: SEARCHING FOR NEW POLITICAL STRATEGY AND NATIONAL RECOGNITION

"We have no standing at Washington, but can at least maintain our self respect, by not importuning for favors which are never granted. We are beneath contempt now."
—Edmund J. Davis, 1880

Edmund Davis's political future appeared uncertain after he left the governor's office; however, two factors ensured that he would continue to play an important role in Texas politics. The first was the fact that throughout the nineteenth century, while party leadership came largely from among its white members, the vast majority of Republican voters were black. The second, tied inextricably to the first in determining his role, was Davis's commitment to this black constituency. He never abandoned them, and they, in the end, never abandoned him. As a result, he successfully maintained control over the Texas Republican Party through the rest of his life and continued trying to change the dynamics of life within the state. The factionalism of his own party and the unceasing opposition of his Democratic opponents stood in the way of his achieving that goal. These barriers forced Davis to experiment with new strategies to regain power. This experimentation would last into the 1880s.

In the months that followed his January departure, Davis remained politically active, although usually behind the scenes. E. J., Lizzie, and the two boys remained in Austin, initially moving to a rooming house, then purchasing a home in March. Providing for his family was the former governor's primary concern, and he worked at reestablishing his law practice. Success as a lawyer was difficult, for many were reluctant to use a man who was so unpopular politically. At times both E. J. and Lizzie wished that they had moved elsewhere. Nonetheless, Davis secured enough legal business keep him busy, even if he never became financially comfortable.

Through it all, Davis continued to have a say in his party's affairs. His voice usually was heard through his closest associates from the days of his administration, who pushed for a restructuring of the party in the spring of 1874. Davis's close ally, George Ruby, initiated the effort and called for a Republican consultation in Austin held on 27 May. Those attending that meeting agreed that harmonizing the factions within the party was essential for success. To that end, they agreed that naming new men to head the party would signal a willingness to break with the past and move in a new direction. James Tracy, who had held the position of party chairman since 1869 and was seen as violently opposed to the so-called Liberal Republicans, agreed to step down and Boulds Baker, a young merchant and editor from Brenham, took his place. Initially it appeared that this move might work for it was welcomed by Davis's opponents. August Siemering's *San Antonio Express,* a convert to the liberal cause, welcomed Tracy's removal as a measure that would give the leadership of the regular Republican Party "something like respectability."[1]

A new party chairman did not mean that Davis had lost control. Davis attended the Austin meeting and most of the men chosen to important positions were connected to him. Baker was a new face, but he had ties to strong Davis allies, including James Tracy and George Ruby. Appointments to the executive committees for each of the congressional districts also indicated Davis's continuing strength. None of them had been an opponent of Davis during the days of his administration. Typical of committee chairs were William Chambers, a Davis appointee as district court judge who survived efforts by the legislature to impeach him, and Samuel G. Newton, an active San Antonio Republican who was a former Confederate soldier, a Bexar County attorney, San Antonio mayor, and chair of the 1873 state convention that renominated Davis for governor. No revolution actually took place.[2]

Still, the overtures made to the liberals appeared to work. In the congressional district conventions that summer, many Davis opponents rejoined the regular party organization. The convention in the Fifth District, held in Austin, reflected the movement. Davis men ran the convention, but George W. Honey, who as secretary of the treasury had engaged in a bitter dispute with Davis, was also there. Jack Hamilton came as well. Some Republicans refused to move. Senator James Flanagan, who was under attack by the regular party organization, condemned Baker and his committee as "sore-headed Republicans and a lot of Greeleyites." In October, the editor of the *Galveston News* observed with some amazement that Baker managed to reconstruct the Republican Party, with ex-governors Pease and Hamilton, the Paschal family, and even Senator Morgan Hamilton working with Davis in a unified party.[3]

The May consultation was not just about internal party politics. Party leaders also embraced a new strategy. Any approach to elections had to take into account the incredible hostility that was directed towards the Republican Party and the Davis administration by his opponents. In a speech in October 1874, Davis pointed to the problem of coping with Democratic rhetoric that equated all Republicans with radicals, thieves, rogues, and godless characters. This message was pounded home in their newspapers, in political campaigns, from the pulpit, and in the schools. Davis observed that Republicans faced a "Niagara torrent, unceasing, of abuse and villification [*sic*]" that ultimately made the "Republicans more hateful even than the despised abolitionist." While the charges they made against Davis and his administration were untrue, Democrats continued to drive them home "to keep alive the hate of Republicans by their party here and to make political capital at the North." The question for Republican leaders was how to attract voters in such an ideologically charged situation.[4]

Davis and the Republican consultation turned to the solution proposed by James Tracy just before the 1873 election. Tracy recommended that the party not run candidates for office, contending that the hostility toward their party doomed any such candidate to failure. In the wake of the electoral failure, Tracy's approach appeared more relevant. Tracy laid out the framework for the party's new departure in an interview with the editor of the *Galveston News* on his return from the May caucus. Tracy believed that the national parties were reorienting themselves and moving away from Reconstruction issues. Tracy thought that what he called the "advanced" elements of the Democratic Party possessed ideas little different from those of Republicans and that it would be possible to create a coalition of Republicans and such Democrats. The editor of the *San Antonio Express* agreed with Tracy and supported his efforts to move beyond the partisan divisions of the Reconstruction era and to forge alliances based on new issues. What were the "advanced" elements of the Democratic Party and what were the new issues? Siemering of the *Express* provided the clearest definition of the type of men he believed might be attracted into a revitalized Texas Republican Party. These included Democrats who were "liberal, national Union Whig[s]." Such men were progressive on railroad issues and saw a wider role for the national government in the life of Texans. He concluded that such men were ready to abandon Governor Richard Coke, the "old Bourbon secessionists, and the anti-railroad ox-cart demagogues." Davis did not publicly say anything about the change in course, but his presence at the consultation suggests that he, at the very least, acceded to it.[5]

The new departure governed how Republicans approached the congressional elections to be held in the autumn of 1874. They waited for the Democratic conventions, then put no candidates up in districts where the Democrats nominated candidates of the "advanced" sort. If Democrats selected men considered unacceptable, Republicans determined to support independent candidates. When the Democrats held their conventions it appeared that they also might be ready for realignments based on new issues. In all but one of the six districts they chose men openly hostile to Governor Coke and not part of what Republicans considered to be the non-progressive element of the Democratic Party. That one district was the First, where former Confederate Postmaster General John H. Reagan defeated the incumbent William S. Herndon, the very sort of man Republicans hoped they could work with. Republicans subsequently held their own convention, criticized Reagan's nomination, then made no party nomination to run against him. Instead, William Chambers, who was previously chairman of the Republican district executive committee, announced himself as an independent candidate, assuring voters that he would not run as a Republican. The editor of the *Tyler Index* was not convinced that Chambers was not a Republican, concluding that his candidacy was simply a Republican effort to set "their nets for disaffected Democrats." In fact, he was right.[6]

Davis's hand was seen in the new tactics of Texas Republicans. It was even more apparent through his efforts to keep men in place within the federal district courts to protect the polls in autumn. Getting the Grant administration to cooperate in this remained elusive. In the Eastern District, Grant removed an effective marshal and replaced him with Tom Ochiltree. Davis liked Ochiltree, but a struggle over his confirmation left the marshal's office virtually unfilled for the election. In the Western District, Thomas Purnell remained marshal, having survived Davis's effort in 1872 to have him removed. He was not only an embarrassment, but a hindrance to Republican efforts. James Tracy called him a "positive obstacle to the success of our party in this State," and Davis contended that he not only failed to aid in a reconstruction of the state but used the federal court "to oppress the Republicans." Davis renewed his attack on Purnell that summer. Boulds Baker met with the president as a representative of Davis and urged action against Purnell. Davis wrote to the prospective attorney general, Benjamin H. Bristow, for help in "cleaning such [disreputable officials] out of our state."[7]

Boulds Baker returned from his visit to the president believing that something might be done. President Grant promised changes, and Baker reported that the president "now understands and properly appreciates Gov. Davis" and was ready to "back us in an effort to reform" in order to "raise the standard of Government officials in the state." The president made his promises easily while at his vacation residence in Long Branch. Baker wanted a change in the justice department that included placing a more receptive attorney general in place. This did not happen, and George H. Williams, who held the office, showed no disposition to change. When the president asked him about removing officers there, Williams replied that the removals Davis sought would "kill Republicanism in Texas." Instead of change, the Grant administration left men in place who would do nothing to secure the polls.[8]

Davis finally reemerged in the public eye in the fall of 1874. That October, just prior to the congressional elections, he attended the Southern Republican Convention in Chattanooga, Tennessee. The convention's stated purpose was to inform the nation of the "true" condition of the South, but its timing clearly was intended to influence the congressional elections. Davis initially was uncertain if he could afford to go, but finally he left Houston on the International Railroad on 10 October. A Texas delegation that included many former adversaries—Tracy; liberals such as George Honey and George W. Paschal, Jr.; and Lemuel D. Evans, a Republican who switched alliances often during the preceding years—accompanied him. As Davis departed, he indicated that he had no "fixed purpose" in going. Indeed, he had no major leadership role assigned to him. Still, he hoped to see a plan devised to "keep from cutting each others throats, and keeping or making peace down here."[9]

Davis insisted that he was unprepared to speak, but the delegates called him to the podium to discuss the Southern question, and Davis responded with what a hostile observer of *The New York Times* considered one of the best, most remarkable responses because it was "moderate in tone, and so clear in its facts." In that address Davis shared his ideas about what was happening in Texas and elsewhere in the South and provided one of the clearest statements of what he believed to be the only solution to the region's problems. His picture of the political situation in Texas showed that he believed little had changed between 1861 and 1874. The Democratic Party had returned to power and worked for goals that set it outside the mainstream of modern politics. Davis did not believe any sentiment for secession existed in the state, but Texas Democrats would be happy still if Texans could elect a national government that would provide some sort of restitution for the loss of their slaves and leave them to "regulate their local concerns" regarding relations between whites and blacks. By self-regulation, Davis believed, the Democrats meant being allowed to use whatever laws they might fashion to impose some sort of controlled labor system for the freedmen.

Davis did not think all Texans wanted such a world, but he believed that the men who controlled the Democratic Party did and that they perverted the political process in order to secure power. Democrats could not win elections based on real issues, but worked, as in 1860, to consolidate the white masses into a single party through intimidation and the suppression of debate. Few could resist such pressure. They misrepresented reality, portraying themselves as decent and honest, while tarring their opponents with outrageous lies, unfounded charges of corruption, and assertions of character deficiencies. To prove his point, Davis cited the case of General James Longstreet, whose conversion to Republicanism changed him from being an honest, faithful man, "the bravest of the brave," into the South's "Benedict Arnold." To ensure such beliefs persisted and no one challenged them, the Democrats worked to suppress education and an open exchange of ideas.

His analysis of possible solutions was astute. Territorialization and military occupation might have been the answer in 1865, but that opportunity was gone, and in Davis's view, would never have been acceptable to the country anyway. The state had fallen into the hands of the Democrats, so they offered no help. Ultimately, Davis argued only action by the national government would answer, and he advocated a course of action much like that taken by his own administration. Congress had to create a national public school system and pass enforceable national laws protecting civil and political rights. It also had to develop the will to enforce these laws. "I would rather trust the preservation of my rights to the caprice of the whole nation," he explained, "rather than to that of a small section." Of these programs the creation of a public school system was essential. Without it, he feared a quarter of a million Texans would be reared in ignorance that would fit them either to "fill white leagues or Ku klux klans" or if black, "be driven to the fields under labor and contract laws." Education would, he believed, produce a world which would undermine the ideas that divided people and bring an end to "false pretences [sic]."[10]

Davis returned from Chattanooga, spoken of as a Southern Republican leader by the national press, but none of his solutions would be implemented. There was virtually no discussion of a national system of schools up to this time, and they would never implement such a system. As was seen, Washington offered little help in placing active men in the critical district court positions needed to protect the polls. The Republican new departure had to proceed with little help from Washington. Such a situation made the outcome of the congressional elections predictable. If a less contentious campaign was supposed to make Democrats accept black voters more readily, the experiment failed. The only real contest where Republicans backed an alternative to the Democrat was in the First District. There Chambers challenged Reagan, but Democrats were no more willing to let blacks vote for an Independent than a Republican, and they continued efforts at removing them from the polls. Reporters for the *Galveston News* told the story clearly—nowhere was the voter turnout large, and the black vote was virtually nonexistent. In Mineola, within Wood County, only two blacks came to the polls, and elsewhere in the First District black participation declined as well. Further, Chambers attracted few of the whites sought by the new Republican strategy. Reagan went to Congress. Elsewhere, where no Republicans ran, black participation was low as well. Reports from Harrisburg, near Houston, indicated that no blacks came to the polls.[11]

Davis never had much faith that even moderate Democrats would be allies with a party that advocated the sort of change supported by Republicans. On the other hand, he realized that his party was demonized to such an extent that anyone running for office with the party label would face an uphill battle. As a result, Davis became even more involved in the development of party strategy, and he continued to flirt with the idea of independent candidates. The next challenge appeared almost immediately, when Democrats decided to hold a constitutional convention. Whether or not to hold a convention had been an issue since Davis was removed from office. In part, their actions in January of 1874 raised questions about the legitimacy of government that could be solved by a new constitution. Concerns also existed with the character of the constitution of 1869. The Democratic legislature finally decided to hold an election on the convention question, and Republicans had to decide what role to play. By the spring of 1875, Adolph Zadek, the Corsicana postmaster, was acting head of the Republican executive committee. Zadek asked Davis how the party should approach the election, and Davis responded that Republicans should not vote for the convention, that no good would be done in a convention "while the present partisan spirit prevails." Still, an election was held for delegates at the same time voters decided if they should have a convention, and Davis recommended that Republicans support local candidates who reflected party goals whenever possible and not run party candidates. Davis's letter indicated the lack of optimism that he possessed at the time. He feared that the Democrats would carry the convention election, send a majority of delegates to the convention, and then do what they could to reverse the results of the war and Reconstruction. Given free reign, the Democratic Party's anti-Republican principles would emerge. He had a slim hope that without Republican opposition the internal divisions within the Democratic Party might come to the fore, splintering their ranks.[12]

Davis's advice made sense, but he found his position challenged by a number of federal office-holders. Their criticism of Davis also made sense, for their jobs hinged on their ability to claim that they represented a viable Republican Party in Texas. Davis's approach might suggest that one no longer existed. Further, few of these men had any connection with Davis, for President Grant's appointments in Texas reflected little of the needs of the state party. Purnell hung on to the marshalship in Austin. The president named Amos Morrill, Jack Hamilton's old law partner, judge in the Eastern District in 1872, and put Lemuel D. Evans, another Liberal Republican, in the marshalship. To the critical positions of collector of customs and postmaster in Galveston he appointed two liberals, Benjamin G. Shields and Chauncey B. Sabin. These two controlled hundreds of patronage positions, and none went to Davis supporters. A Washington correspondent of the *San Antonio Express* claimed that Shields and Sabin also were connected to Democratic senator Samuel B. Maxey and in return for his support they placed Democrats in these government jobs. Grant's policy does not appear to reflect any real loss of faith in the regular Republican party, in the state, or in Davis but the president's failure to develop any viable strategy for helping the state's party. Grant's secretary of the treasury would later describe the president's policy as "unsteady and uncertain" and destined for a "disastrous failure" in building viable Republican parties in the South."[13]

After he recommended that the party not hold a convention, federal officers began their attack on Davis. It was led by Marshal Purnell and the Austin postmaster, Henry B. Kinney. They distributed a circular in traditionally Republican counties that called on Collector Shields in Galveston to assume the position of chairman of the Republican Executive Committee. They argued that it was their duty to act, since the party's existing executive committee refused to prepare for the election. Davis counterattacked through the editorial pages of the *San Antonio Express,* charging that the federal officers were simply trying to take over the party organization and insisting that the existing executive committee was the only legitimate one. Davis pointed out that the men behind the movement were Purnell and Kinney, and let his readers know that he thought they were not real Republicans and that he had done his best to get rid of them. This was just one more attempt on their part to hold on to their offices. Whether or not Davis's public defense made any impact cannot be known, but the revolt came to a rapid end when Shields announced that he did not have time to serve as head of the state party.[14]

The effort by the office holders, however, did force Davis to respond to the convention more actively. On 20 April, Zadek called for a party convention to meet in Hempstead on 25 May and to plan a Republican response to the upcoming election. Boulds Baker, still nominal head of the party, endorsed the plan from Washington. For the state Republican Party, the Hempstead convention had a more important purpose than planning for the election: it would determine who controlled the party. Baker was out of state and could no longer head the party, so they needed to choose a new chairman. Davis determined to take the job. His opponents opposed his choice but had trouble determining how to challenge him. Davis and his friends, on the other hand, busied themselves ensuring that the delegates who went to Hempstead would support him. Prior to the convention, he appeared in Galveston where he worked with Tracy and Baker to ensure that the large and important Galveston delegation was pro-Davis.[15]

W. KURTZ   872 B'WAY
N.Y.

After leaving the governor's office, Davis continued his efforts to implement a Republican program in Texas, heading the party and trying to influence federal appointments. This image, made sometime in the late 1870s, shows the man who managed to maintain control of his party despite efforts to wrest it away from him as in the Hempstead convention of 1875. (Harriet and David Condon Collection).

When the convention met, Davis's friends had done their jobs well. The former governor's supporters possessed a clear majority. African American delegates caucused the evening before the convention opened, and the caucus showed that black Republicans would support Davis on the floor. When the delegates turned to the election of the chairman of the state executive committee on the second day, Davis was nominated to take over from Baker. Only two men were nominated to oppose him—Anthony B. Norton, then serving as postmaster in Dallas, and General Andrew Neill. Marshal Lemuel Evans nominated Norton, then spoke at length on the need to end Davis's control over the party, arguing that the governor was out of step with the national administration. Davis spoke on his own behalf, criticizing the federal officials who opposed him as not representing the Texans who made up the party. Before the secretary of the convention finished the roll-call, both Norton and Neill withdrew their names from consideration, giving Davis the victory. His control over the party was made even more secure when N. Wright Cuney, a black delegate from Galveston and the protégé of George Ruby, overwhelmed his opponents in the vote for party secretary.[16]

Davis thanked the delegates after his election, then spoke on the question of the constitutional convention. Once again, he counseled party members to take no partisan stand. Saying that he saw a disposition among Democrats to drop party lines on the drafting of a new constitution, he proposed to meet "half way" with those who would agree to work for a non-partisan constitution. He urged party members to look for "nonpartisans" who could attract broad support in the election and who would work for the good of all Texans. Davis believed that some coalitions might develop. In control of the convention, Davis saw his recommendations incorporated into the party platform. It left it to the individual whether to vote for or against holding a convention, but urged voters to look for men as possible delegates who would support the creation of a government that would elevate the masses and restore the free public schools. The convention ended with an attack upon the Democratic party, charging that it burdened the state with an enormous debt because of the grants that its legislators had distributed to the railroads, it had destroyed the public schools, and its leaders still hoped to nullify the results of the Thirteenth, Fourteenth, and Fifteenth amendments.[17]

Davis seized control of the party machinery at the Hempstead convention, but afterwards he renewed his efforts to restore some party harmony. He achieved a degree of accord and even attracted the support of some of the old Liberal Republicans who came to see the federal officials as part of the party's problem. In a letter to former governor Pease, John Haynes observed that Davis's election was the "best that could be done," and that at least it put into power a man who was "thoroughly honest." Haynes recognized that Davis was ready to bring an end to divisions, noting that they talked at great length when they met in Galveston and then in Hempstead. Haynes found that the ex-governor clearly desired to unify Republican ranks and to get the best men in the party out front and wanted men like ex-governor Pease to join him in a "radical reorganization upon the basis of honesty and purity." Haynes encouraged Pease to listen to Davis and "if possible, let us all get together again."[18]

The hope that Republicans could establish some sort of non-partisan alliance with moderate Democrats proved as elusive in the campaign for delegates to the constitutional convention as it had in the congressional elections the previous autumn. In the 2 August election, voters approved the convention and elected an overwhelming Democratic majority of what historian Alwyn Barr has called "agriculture- and law-oriented" delegates. Davis, interviewed at the office of his brother Waters Davis in Galveston shortly after the election, expressed little hope that the convention would represent a Republican position on any issue. He believed that no more than twenty Republicans were elected, and they would be able to do little to stop what he believed was a majority "full of impracticable and illiberal notions." Indeed, Davis found that many of the men who he hoped might be allies on issues such as the judicial system and public education were disappointments. Judge Charles S. West of Austin, who Davis had believed was a Democrat with whom Republicans could work, turned out actually to want to eliminate the salaries of judges and abolish the public schools.[19]

Davis's assessment was correct for the most part. When the convention assembled in Austin on 6 September, only fifteen of the seventy-five members present were Republicans, an even smaller number than Davis had supposed. Of the provisions of the constitution of 1868–1869 that Republicans set out to protect, none were saved. Non-partisan politics proved a failure. Factions within the Democratic Party that had the greatest affinity for Republican goals were not in control of the convention. Rather, the majority wanted to impose severe restrictions on state government that would undermine all of the positive programs advocated by Republicans. Public education was the cornerstone of Republican policy, and the new constitution essentially made the creation of an effective system of public schools impossible. While containing traditional rhetorical support for such schools, the document left the organization and support of schools in the hands of local school boards who were mandated to provide segregated schools. Public schools did receive a share of the public lands for their support, but the income from this gift provided little immediate help in creating schools. The majority also defeated Republican efforts at keeping the existing election system that required polls to be in county seats, replacing it with precinct voting with little centralized supervision, and making fraud and intimidation more difficult to suppress. About the only cause that Republicans and the majority were able to agree upon was opposition to a poll tax. That was defeated.[20]

The constitutional convention set 15 February 1876 as the date for an election to ratify the proposed document and to choose men to fill the positions created under the new constitution. On 12 January, responding to a call by Davis as head of the state executive committee, Republicans met in Houston to decide a course to recommend to party members in the upcoming election, to determine whether or not to run party candidates for office, and also to select delegates to the national Republican convention that year. The national convention was important, for it would select the party's nominee for president in the autumn election. Davis welcomed all Republicans, but he clearly controlled the majority of delegates. The delegates were unanimous on the issues before them. The proposed constitution was the principal issue that they had to deal with, and they urged Republicans to vote against ratification, cataloging its shortcomings. They condemned its failure to ensure a public school system, its creation of a poor judiciary system, its lack of support for internal improvements and immigration, and its awkward system of land taxes. A more threatening challenge, implying possible federal intervention, was made when the delegates protested that the new document failed to ensure civil rights. That and the failure since 1874 by the state government to protect its citizens from violence meant, they charged, that the Democrats failed to live up to the provisions of the acts readmitting Texas to the Union in 1870. The only solution they saw as viable was that the federal government should intervene to force the state to deliver on those guarantees. Of course, such an intervention by this time was unlikely.[21]

The question of running party candidates for office was complicated this time by the upcoming presidential election. That election made it important to maintain party organization so that votes could be delivered to the national candidate. To do this, running Republicans in local elections was important, so the delegates agreed to make nominations. The delegates wanted to nominate Davis for governor, but he refused, aware of his limited chances for victory. Davis supported William M. Chambers instead, and Chambers received the nomination. The platform, however, was Davis's and reflected his perspective on the Democratic leadership and his criticism of the administration of Governor Richard Coke. That Davis would continue to play a major role in the party was assured before the convention adjourned when the delegates named him once again to the chair of the state central committee, and named him and a pro-Davis majority as delegates to the party's national convention.[22]

Davis encouraged party unity at the Houston convention, but the maneuvering that took place indicated that the tension between Davis and the federal appointees in the state had not diminished. Shortly before the convention, Davis had appealed to Chauncey Sabin at the Galveston post office for help in financing the convention and the subsequent campaign. Typically officeholders contributed part of their salary to party work, and Davis asked Sabin to give an amount equal to 1 percent of his annual salary and that he ask his employees to do the same. Sabin refused and attacked Davis for even asking for help. Davis responded by using the convention to condemn the failure of federal officials to help the party. In the speech Sabin was mentioned, but Davis showed particular contempt for Marshal Purnell, who he denounced as a "scoundrel, a robber, and a depredator [*sic*] on the public." For Davis, Purnell was the worst of the "dead-beats and imbeciles" holding the federal posts in Texas. In response, the delegates censured Purnell for his failure to protect blacks in an outbreak of violence in Limestone County. They also censured Postmaster Sabin for his refusal to provide support for the convention.[23]

Davis's public denunciation of Purnell proved too much for the marshal and his family this time. When Davis returned to Austin, he ran into Purnell's son in front of the federal courts building. The son attacked Davis, striking him with a cane. Supporters of both parties rushed to the street, and only the intervention of the police prevented a full-scale riot. The confrontation intensified the ill-feeling between the parties, and Davis renewed his efforts at having Purnell removed. In a letter sent to associates in Washington, Davis pointed to the marshal's repeated failure to protect blacks. Black schools were burned, black school teachers shot, and people committed outrages against anyone who befriended blacks. Purnell and President Grant had done nothing. Purnell remained as a continuing reminder to Davis of the Grant administration's failure to support the state's regular Republican party.[24]

The election on 15 February 1876 saw what had become the usual intimidation. In Houston the county sheriff arrested a black man for voting twice, producing a confrontation with other blacks who attempted to free the man. Local authorities called out the militia, effectively reducing black voting. In Huntsville a black voter was killed, allegedly for voting Democratic, although no unbiased sources verified the reported motive. Such activities ensured Chambers had no chance to be elected governor. Richard Coke ran for a second term and won by a vote of 150,581 to 47,719. The constitution also passed easily, 136,606 to 56,652. In counties with black majorities, even local elections reflected the decline in black voting. In Grimes County, the heart of the state's black belt, Democrats regained control of county government. The only bright spot was the election of a few Republicans running as Independents.

They secured a county judgeship in Washington County and the district judgeship for Austin. The greatest success occurred in the San Antonio area, where Independents successfully carried several district attorney and judicial races. The most hopeful sign was Galveston County, where an Independent slate was victorious for most county offices.[25]

The state election over, Davis turned to national politics. Given his problems with federal appointees, Davis had concern for his party's presidential nominee. As a result he traveled to Cincinnati for the Republicans' 14 June convention so that he could work to get a nominee favorable to the regular party organization in Texas. Davis wanted the nominee to be Benjamin Bristow, whom Davis had gotten to know in his negotiations over Satanta and Big Tree and who had indicated that he supported Davis's efforts at cleaning out the existing officeholders. On the other hand, Davis was not committed irrevocably to any of the potential candidates. His votes and those of the other Texas delegates changed in a remarkably fluid nominating process. In the end, he threw his support to Rutherford B. Hayes of Ohio, the ultimate victor.[26]

Hayes initially appeared to be a good choice for Davis. He seemed ready to confront the Southern Democracy and its apparent repudiation of Reconstruction. In his campaign, he used the traditional Republican tactic of "waving the bloody shirt" to secure Northern votes, and as a candidate, warned that a Democratic victory would lead to renewed rebellion and the undoing of all that was accomplished by the Civil War and Reconstruction. Nonetheless, all of this was designed to secure Northern voters. By this time, few in the North were willing to take any decisive action on the Reconstruction issues. When Davis turned to the national campaign organizations for help in running party candidates in Texas he found no support. After the convention Davis lobbied for help, but in July he wrote to Newcomb that he had concluded Washington politicians "don't care for the wishes of Republicans here, and don't care much whether we have any Republican party at all, or not." He showed further disillusionment in a later letter, concluding, "They seem entirely indifferent to the well-being of Texas Republicans and disregard our local organization." By August, Davis became so disappointed that he confessed, "I am sure that if Tilden were elected president affairs here could not be much worse for us." In a letter to Zadek, written about the same time, Davis confided that he could see little reason for the Texas party to even try to exert any influence on the national government. "Nobody cares for us, or what becomes of Texas Republicans," he wrote. "The Republicans of the North seem content to let the Democracy do with us as they please."[27]

The fall election season found Davis deeply disillusioned with the national Republican Party and almost hopeless about the prospects of the state party. A letter sent to the delegates of the Fifth District congressional convention showed the extent of his feelings. There the question was whether to continue the policy of allying with Independents and refraining from party nominations. George "Wash" Jones had received Republican support in the past, and he announced that he would run against the Democratic incumbent, Dewitt Clinton Giddings. Davis noted that the policy of supporting independent candidates had not produced the results he wanted, and looking at a choice between Jones and Giddings, he did not believe either offered Republicans anything in return for their support. As a result, he found he could offer his support to neither. As to running a Republican candidate, he saw no point. A campaign would be expensive, the party had little to invest, and the national party offered no support. Even if funds were available, there was little chance for success, and he believed running a candidate would simply unite Democrats behind Giddings. Davis reached the lowest point on the political prospects of changing Texas when he wrote a letter to Newcomb that said, "I am considerable disheartened and sometimes think it scarcely worth while making an effort [*sic*]." Despite the fact that Giddings was associated with various nefarious schemes, including charging excessive fees when assigned to recover state bonds in Europe and another concerning the school fund, the public still supported him. "It looks as far as these people are concerned that nothing the democracy does will open their eyes."[28]

Republicans did put forward candidates in numerous local elections that fall, but Republican voters would face the same climate of intimidation confronted in previous elections. On 9 September, Davis wrote to Attorney General Alonzo Taft to request that the justice department look into what he described as a "raid" on the African American people in Wharton County that August. The result had been the death of twenty-four blacks and the murder of Captain J. N. Baughman, who was the Republican sheriff of the county. The sheriff had asked state authorities for protection, but he had received none. When Baughman returned home his house was surrounded, his door broken down, and thirty men opened fire. Davis reported that murders still continued, and local authorities made no efforts to stop them. Davis took the opportunity to complain, once again, about the refusal of federal officials to act. However, the district attorney responded that there was no legal basis for action since he could not find anyone who would speak the facts, "because of the possible fatal result." From Fort Bend County, the *Galveston News* reported violence as well, although alleging much of it resulted from a misunderstanding in which three blacks were killed. At the same time, the report indicated that the blacks' speeches caused the murders. They talked about "abusing whites and abusing law and order." The local correspondent ultimately suggested politics was involved, predicting there would be "a more quiet time after the election." Whatever the real cause of these incidents, the public nature of the violence showed blacks that the existing government offered them little protection.[29]

Black participation in the 1876 election showed a continuing downward spiral in black voter participation and consequent problems for Texas Republicans. On election day, poll watchers reported to the editors of the *Galveston News* that the election went off quietly. The same reporter noted, however, that few people voted. Black turnout strongly suggested that intimidation had taken its toll. In the city of Houston and in Harris County, observers described the black vote as "very very small." In Walker County, with a population that was 56 percent black and where Grant received 979 votes in 1872, only one black person voted, giving Hayes the one vote he received there. In Wharton County, where the sheriff was murdered, Republican turnout dropped from 728 in the previous presidential election to 404. The editor of the *News* seemed unable to explain why black voters remained away from the polls, concluding only that they were "holding back and seem to be confused." While Hayes would carry some of the black belt counties, the overall result was disastrous. The Democratic presidential candidate swept the state with 104,755 votes to Hayes's 44,800.[30]

Despite another Republican debacle in Texas and a contested election, Rutherford B. Hayes became president of the United States. What Hayes's victory would mean for Texas Republicans was uncertain. Shortly after his election, he told a Southern newspaper that he believed Republican parties in the South needed change. He believed many federal officials there were corrupt outsiders, and he wanted to build a new coalition based on traditional black voters with native white Southerners and recruits from among Democrats. He thought the leadership would come from among the whites. When he talked about new leadership, his meaning relative to former governor Davis was unclear, and Davis tended to believe that the president-elect was ready to abandon the existing party organizations. Davis's own efforts at building a party on a similar basis had not proved successful, so he saw little chance that the president's approach would succeed, and he shared these insights with Hayes.[31]

In March, the state executive committee encouraged Davis to go to Washington to discuss Texas appointments with the president, but he was unable to go. He was in some financial straits, but in addition, his son Britton was graduating from Jacob Bickler's Texas German and English Academy in Austin. Britton was on his way to achieving a goal that his father failed to secure; he would enter West Point the next fall in the plebe class of 1877. Since Davis could not go, J. R. Burns, assistant district attorney for the Eastern District, carried a letter from Davis that expressed his serious concerns with the president's supposed policy. Burns wrote back trying to reassure Davis, insisting that rumors saying that Hayes would abandon the Republican South were "preposterous," and that the president realized to do so would be "suicidal." Hayes did not want to intervene in Southern affairs, but the South had to acquiesce in the equal rights of African Americans and maintain law, order, justice, protection of all, and good government. Davis had heard similar sentiments in the past. The test of Hayes's feelings towards the South would be in his actions.[32]

In 1877 Davis's son Britton realized a goal that his father had never achieved. That autumn he entered the United States Military Academy at West Point. Britton would afterwards engage in military campaigns in the American West and be involved in the capture of Geronimo. Here he is shown in his cadet uniform. (Harriet and David Condon Collection).

Hayes did little to overcome Davis's pessimism. Following the inauguration, Davis, Frank Britton, his former adjutant general and cousin of his wife, and other party leaders went to Washington to meet with the members of Hayes's administration. One of his stops was a meeting with the newly appointed postmaster general, David M. Key, to talk about having James Newcomb appointed postmaster in San Antonio. The meeting did not go well. Davis concluded that the president intended to use patronage to tempt moderate Democrats into the Republican Party and that Republican regulars had little chance of getting appointments. Davis told Newcomb that the only way he would get the postmaster's position was if the state's Democratic congressmen endorsed him. "The Democracy is to have things all their own way," he complained. Davis found Republican leaders divided on the president's Southern policy, meaning it could not be stopped. "It looks *now*," he wrote, "as if the unity of the Party has been destroyed and that the Democracy will have an easy time in seizing the Government [*sic*]."[33]

Davis had correctly assessed the president's policy and its impact on his influence in the new administration. The men he tried to remove would remain in office. Symbolic of Davis's impotence was Thomas Purnell, who held on to the marshalship despite all the efforts to remove him. In fact, while in Washington, Davis made one more try at getting the marshal removed. Meeting with Attorney General Charles Devins, Davis repeated the charges that he had leveled against Purnell, a catalogue that by this time included issuing false vouchers, tampering with petit juries, fraud and robbery, theft, cowardice, and being offensive to the people of Texas. Local attorneys would not complain because they realized they had to do business with him and stay on his good side. Davis later heard that Purnell might be removed, although he figured local Republicans would not be consulted on a replacement. Davis's dislike of Purnell reached a point that he would take anyone just to get him out of office, writing to Newcomb that "*any* other dead beat or rascal might be an improvement on Purnell." Despite the moment of hope, Purnell held on.[34]

That summer showed that Davis had become determined to get rid of the marshal. Davis was told by the president that he would make no removals except for cause, so Davis put together a case against Purnell. His efforts only intensified bad feelings between his family and Purnell's. The matter had become personal. On 9 August Frank Britton, Lizzie's cousin, ran into Purnell on Congress Avenue in Austin. The two exchanged words, Britton saying that the marshal had accused him of making false accusations. Purnell pulled his pistol and came at Britton. Britton responded by drawing his own weapon, the two exchanged gunfire, and Purnell went down. Purnell's wife, who had gone to Washington to counter Davis's charges, reported to President Hayes that, "not satisfied with trying to deprive him of his character they have I fear killed him." For his own part, Davis informed Newcomb that someone named "Frank" had shot Purnell, but that the marshal was not seriously wounded. Davis found that disappointing.[35]

For a time, Davis turned his attention away from politics. His law practice continued to find clients, although he frequently had to leave home to attend to cases in the state's various courts. Through much of the spring of 1878 he was engaged in lengthy litigation on behalf of the city of San Antonio, which sought to cancel bonds issued for an unrealized railroad project. That case ultimately went to the United States Supreme Court, where it ruled against San Antonio and Davis. In February, he had an opportunity to renew his partnership in Brownsville with Stephen Powers. That fell through when Davis decided that he did not want to leave Austin, despite the problems he had there. That summer, friends tried to get him appointed collector of customs in Galveston, but Davis insisted that they not push him for a job. He did not want anyone in Washington thinking he was asking for a favor. They continued their efforts, however, and the local district attorney informed the secretary of the treasury that Davis, having been "wrongfully overlooked for so long . . . he is standing upon an extreme dignity and would probably be displeased to know his friends were still urging his claims to recognition." For whatever reason, Davis did not get the job.[36]

Although uncertain what could be done to ensure the future of the Texas Republican Party or to protect what survived of Reconstruction accomplishments, Davis renewed his efforts at influencing state politics during the summer of 1878. More than ever, he looked for a strategy that could break the Democratic Party's control over the state. This time he considered a possible coalition with members of the newly formed Greenback Party. The Greenbackers had first appeared in Texas in 1877. They took their name from the National Greenback Party that was created in the Midwest earlier in the decade. The central issue of the Greenbackers was opposition to the Resumption Act passed by Congress in 1875, an act that would have redeemed all paper money remaining in circulation. The measure was deflationary in its effect and would have had a profound impact on most debtors. The Greenbackers wanted the federal government to continue issuing paper money. In Texas, the new party showed considerable strength in the 1877 local elections and in 1878 its members considered itself ready for a state contest, holding a convention in Waco on 7 August and nominating William H. Hamman for governor.[37]

The Greenback platform adopted at the party's Waco convention set goals that meshed, to some degree, with those of the Texas Republicans. It called for a system of public schools and frontier protection, measures long advocated by Republicans. Its attack on the Democratic Party for fiscal irresponsibility, increased taxes, and expanding government costs sounded very similar to those charges Republicans had leveled at the Coke administration since 1874. Some elements of the platform were out of line with Republican ideas. It expressed a tinge of anti-corporate feelings in calling for a national income tax, criticized national banks, and opposed giving land to railroads. Its very reason for existing, its monetary policy, was not attractive at all to Davis. Nonetheless, Davis saw the Greenbackers as a potential wedge that could break the Democratic Party's hold on the state, and he moved forward trying to effect some sort of alliance with them.[38]

In mid-summer of 1878, Davis suggested that some sort of coalition might be possible with the Greenbackers. He personally offered his support for Hamman and said that he would do all that he could to mobilize Republicans behind his candidacy. Davis met with the Republican executive committee after Hamman's nomination, and they determined not to hold a convention and refrain from nominating Republican candidates for any of the state offices. As usual, federal officeholders responded by criticizing Davis. This time Anthony B. Norton, postmaster at Dallas, called for a convention at Dallas on 2 October. That meeting, composed primarily of other federal officials, nominated Norton for governor. An observer for the *San Antonio Express* concluded that it was nothing more than an effort to keep up party organization with the hope of laying claim upon "federal loaves and fishes in the future." Davis himself called the meeting a "fraud," and even charged that Norton was put up to his course by Democrats, who, wary of potential Greenback success, wanted to unify whites by frightening them with a Republican ticket. Norton would run, but no formal party organization came into being that threatened Davis's control over the regular Republican organization.[39]

In the campaign, Davis's strategy for the first time appeared capable of producing good results. Republicans and Greenbackers actually cooperated. In the First Congressional District, Republicans supported George "Wash" Jones, a former Democrat who they thought was willing to work with them and run against a regular Democrat. This new cooperation was even more apparent at the local level where Greenback clubs and Republicans met and drew up tickets that included candidates drawn from both parties. One Democratic legislative candidate complained that his opponents had forced him into a "laborious canvass," his hands kept full by "green-backers & the black militia of E. J. Davis." As this union grew in strength, however, Democrats attacked with a new fury, leveling at the Greenbackers the same sort of charges that they used against the Republicans in the past. In fact, Democratic candidates usually equated the Greenbackers with Republicans. In critical districts, where the Greenback-Republican alliance had the greatest chance of success, Democrats finally resorted to the usual violence and intimidation when presented with the possibility of defeat.[40]

Despite Democratic efforts in 1878, the Greenback-Republican fusion made some inroads against the Democrats. George "Wash" Jones won his election. District Attorney J. R. Burns attributed his success "entirely to Gov. Davis who, though not a Greenbacker, took the stump for Jones and secured his election." However, such successes were limited. Overall the Democrats remained dominant. That party's gubernatorial candidate, Oran M. Roberts, former president of the secession convention, defeated Hamman with 158,302 votes to 55,002. Norton received only 23,712. As in the past, not running Republican candidates did not reduce efforts at driving blacks from the polls, and the downward trend in their participation continued. Republicans held their own in most black majority counties, but elsewhere, Republican votes continued to decline. In some cases the results were drastic. In Harrison County, for example, the black vote was crushed or, in contemporary terms, bulldozed. There, Chambers received 2,664 votes in the 1876 gubernatorial race. In 1878 the combined vote of Norton and Hamman was only 1,494. Davis's strategy in the election was successful enough to tempt him to use it again, although it held little promise for throwing the Democrats out of office statewide.[41]

Exclusion from the councils of the national government, then mixed electoral results, left Davis with little hope. His views on the national administration were made clear in a letter to Newcomb after hearing his former secretary of state finally was nominated for the San Antonio postmastership. Davis told Newcomb not to get his hopes up, since he probably would not be confirmed by this "'mealy mouthed' administration." Davis would be surprised by nothing the Hayes administration would do and expressed a profound disillusionment with the national Republican Party. "What is the use of our keeping up this war in favour of the Republican party? . . . . Our very faithfullness is turned against us." Ultimately, Davis believed, no Republican could secure support from the Northern members of the party unless he was a "nincumpoop enough to curry favor with the Democracy and get their endorsement." Hayes's track record on appointments was not good, and Davis had only to point to the marshalship in the western district. There, Purnell finally stepped down, but Hayes replaced him with someone Davis found equally objectionable, Stillwell H. Russell.[42]

Ironically, at this nadir in Davis's political career, and the Texas Republican Party, the president determined to place Davis in one of the most lucrative positions at his disposal. In 1888, he named Governor Pease collector of customs in Galveston. Pease's family, however, refused to move to Galveston, and after two years he decided to step down. To fill the place, he recommended Davis. Hayes explored the possibility of appointing the former governor, but by this time Davis felt deeply aggrieved at his treatment by the president and was unwilling to ask anything of him. Davis advised Pease to go ahead and recommend him to Hayes but insisted that he make it clear that he had not sought the position. "With this administration," he wrote, "I have especial reasons for wishing it understood that I ask for no favors." When he learned Hayes would make the nomination, Davis asked that his name be withdrawn. In the end, he stood on his pride. In a letter to his friend Newcomb, Davis wrote, "We have no standing at Washington, but can at least maintain our self respect, by not importuning for favors which are never granted. We are beneath contempt now."[43]

The years from 1878 to 1880 had not been good ones for E. J. Davis. He sought new alliances, looking to moderate Democrats and Greenbackers. He pushed for an end to partisan politics and backed independent candidates for office in his efforts to assure that at least some of the goals he tried to achieve during his administration remained intact. His success in all these efforts was limited. His lack of optimism about the South's ability to change itself was manifest in Nashville during 1874. Little happened that changed his views. He believed the national government must protect the legacy of the Civil War and Reconstruction, but its leadership and those of his own party refused not only to act, but even to listen to his ideas. His anger with President Hayes and national Republicans, by 1880, grew palpable. These years represented possibly the darkest moments in Davis's career.

A NEW POLITICAL DIRECTION

"My candidacy is without regard to party in any way, and when elected I propose, as congressman, to be bound by no party caucus, but to support those measures only which may best service the interest of the people of this district, of Texas, and of the country at large."
—Edmund J. Davis, Congressional Campaign of 1882.

Edmund Davis said in his inaugural address that Texans could not afford to be "unjust to the weakest of God's creatures." His subsequent career was an effort at ensuring that justice was provided for all people, working to protect the political and civil rights of all Texans, attempting to open up opportunities for them as well through public schools and economic development. Although the years leading up to 1880 were frustrating and disillusioning, he did not give up. He continued his search for some means of achieving that basic goal of justice for all. His persistence may be one of his most defining personal characteristics, and it also reflected the deep commitment that he had developed to securing his goal. The decade of the 1880s would see Davis continue his efforts; it would see him continue to experiment with new political strategies; it would witness a resurgence, to some degree, of his reputation. These years also would mark his last fight for what he considered to be a better future for Texas.

As the new decade of the 1880s began, Edmund Davis had given up his belief that the changes he sought could be accomplished within the state's traditional Republican Party. Another election would take place in 1880, and Davis initially responded by moving away from his own party. He laid out his views in an interview that January with a reporter for the *Galveston News*. Davis qualified his remarks by saying that they were his personal opinion and that he was not speaking as chairman of the state's Republican executive committee, but in either capacity they reflected his concerns with his party. He indicated that he had come to believe that Texas Republicans should send no delegates to the national party convention to be held in Chicago that summer. They and the other Republicans of the South would have no hearing there, and received nothing for their support in the past. In a private letter to another party member he provided insight into what led him to such a drastic view. "My experience of the last [convention]," he wrote, "was that they [Southern Republicans] were merely *tolerated.*" In the state election he proposed to follow the course he adopted in the past, urging fellow Republicans not to make party nominations for offices and to vote instead for men, without regard for party, who would "rectify what is amiss in the affairs of Texas." Davis hoped that without Republicans in the field the better elements of the Democratic Party might split away from those Davis considered the reactionaries who had ruined the state.[1]

Shortly after giving this interview, Davis called for a meeting of state Republicans to be held in Austin on 24 March to determine the party's course in the election. In the Austin meeting, Davis welcomed the delegates as chair of the party's executive committee, and in his address he personally gave them the advice he shared with the Galveston reporter. He urged them to stay out of national political affairs and refrain from sending delegates to the national convention. He pressed them to consider a new course in the general elections as well. The delegates, however, while not revolting against his leadership, showed no interest in taking his advice. Too many Republican leaders held federal appointments or wanted them, and providing support to a successful presidential candidate was critical to their political health. In the end, Davis was forced to give in on the question of a delegation and obliged to participate in the wrangling over whom that delegation would support.[2]

Supporters for all of the Republican front-runners were at the convention, including men for Secretary of the Treasury John Sherman, Congressman James G. Blaine, and former president Ulysses S. Grant. The majority of the delegates appeared to be in favor of sending a Grant delegation to the convention. Davis was not among Grant's supporters, and in his opposition he found himself allied with former governor Elisha Pease. Pease took the lead in working against Grant, insisting in a speech on the nomination that the former president was not the man to help the South. It was Grant, he charged, who had lost the South for the Republican Party, managing the Southern states unsuccessfully, and Grant had done nothing to sustain Southern Republicans. Davis was not supposed to speak on the matter because he was elected permanent chairman. A Democratic observer believed that this honor was bestowed on him purposefully to keep him from using his influence against the former president. Davis stood down from the chair, however, and spoke anyway supporting Pease's arguments on the matter. Ultimately, Davis managed to rally his supporters to back a compromise introduced by Newcomb that recognized that the convention's sense as being for Grant, but not issuing instructions to the delegates as to which candidate to support.[3]

The delegates did not follow Davis's advice on the national convention, but they did agree with his recommendations for the local elections. Rather than make party nominations, they decided to wait until the Democrats and Greenbackers had met, and Republicans could determine whether any of their or any independent candidates merited their support. Davis already decided to endorse George "Wash" Jones, the independent and Greenbacker he backed in 1878, in his bid for reelection to Congress, saying that Jones had been "reasonable, fair, and just toward the Republicans" in his first term. It was uncertain, however, whether any sort of alliances could be made as in the previous election. As a result, the delegates authorized the chairman of the executive committee to call them back together if circumstances changed.[4]

The fact that Republicans decided to send a delegation to their national convention clearly did not reflect a loss of faith in Davis. The platform that they adopted showed the ex-governor's continuing influence, restating the party's commitment to the basic ideas that Davis advocated since running for governor in 1869. The state must protect its citizens in the use and enjoyment of their guaranteed rights; it must suppress and punish all who committed violence or participated in mob action. Convinced that would not happen, they urged the national government to act. The platform also reflected Davis's criticism of the Democratic opposition, condemning Governor Oran M. Roberts's administration for its failure to create a real system of public schools, its blue laws restricting many social activities on Sunday, its increased occupation taxes, and the "bell punch," a tax on alcoholic drinks. The platform characterized the whole administration as reckless, extravagant, and expensive. Davis's views were everywhere in the platform. The delegates also showed their continuing support by reelecting him chairman of the party's executive committee.[5]

Davis was chosen as a delegate to the Republican national convention, and despite his belief that Texans should not go, he decided to attend. At the time, observers believed that he wanted to be there to block Grant. It is more likely that he simply considered it his duty to go. Complaining to his friend James Newcomb that he did not have the money to make the trip, and that he definitely should have said he would not, he conceded that his attendance was necessary for the future of the party. On the other hand, he was uncertain about what could be accomplished. "I do not expect any good result from the trip and expense," he informed Newcomb.[6]

Despite Davis's pessimism, prior to the convention it appeared that he might gain some good. Republican newspapers believed that any incoming Republican administration would abandon the Hayes administration's Southern policy and try to revive the Republican Party in the South by rewarding loyal party members with positions in a new administration. Davis might be one to receive such rewards. Indeed, the delegates at the convention urged his consideration as a vice presidential nominee. Showing uncharacteristic unity, the delegates, some of Davis's opponents among them, called upon Republicans across the nation to recognize the "moral heroism" that had caused men to "imperil home, ties of blood, friendships, reputation, property, and life" to stand by their country in the crisis of 1861, to "desectionalize" the party and "nationalize the scope and influence of the party efforts." This could be done by recognizing Davis, who they considered a "representative man of the south" who was a "gallant union soldier" and a "stalwart republican." Above all, they held him up to the nation as a man pure "in his private and public life, firm, courageous and judicious in action, experienced in public affairs, heroic in his devotion to truth, justice, liberty and his country."[7]

A Davis candidacy even gained a little traction, and the ex-governor's name began to appear in Southern and Northern newspapers as possible second on the Republican ticket. Responding to a pro-Davis editorial that appeared in the *St. Paul Dispatch* that March, a former military aide to Davis replied to the editor that a "fitter and better man" for the position does not exist. Praising Davis as an honest man, "so self-sacrificing, so utterly oblivious to self-interest," he went on to urge, "there is no place in the gift of the American people to which the judgment, honesty, and integrity of Edmund J. Davis would be inadequate." Davis responded to the hype by saying that it was so much "poppycock," but the fact that his name was even mentioned suggested a new administration might be open to major changes in its approach towards the South.[8]

Davis was in Chicago when the convention began on 5 June, but it was uncertain whom he would support. Of the three front-runners, only Grant appeared to offer anything to Southern Republicans. During his second term, Blaine had been part of the Half-Breed opposition to Grant, a Republican faction that favored an abandonment of the spoils system and civil service reform, which, if realized, would not allow Southern Republicans to build their party on appointments to public office. Sherman had been in Hayes's cabinet. The convention deadlocked, and James A. Garfield, a man who might be more sympathetic to the plight of Southern loyalists, emerged as the party's nominee. At least on paper, he appeared to be someone who would reverse the Hayes administration's abandonment of Southern Republicans and African Americans. In his letter accepting the party's nomination, Garfield called for the "faithful performance of every promise that the Nation has made to its citizen" and promised a policy that would ensure that "every citizen, rich or poor, white or black, is secure in the free and equal enjoyment of every civil and political right guaranteed by the Constitution." If Garfield delivered on any of these promises, a chance existed that he might change the course of politics in Texas.[9]

When the convention turned to the second place on the ticket, Davis's dismissal of his own prospects proved accurate. His candidacy never attracted much support, and when Chester A. Arthur, a New Yorker who could help carry that state, emerged as a clear favorite, Davis's chances of becoming some sort of compromise candidate disappeared. The Texas delegation went ahead and nominated their former governor in what a reporter for *The New York Times* called a demonstration of their great esteem for him. By the time of his nomination, however, the fight for the vice presidency was over.[10]

Davis returned to Texas not intending to become involved actively in the state campaign that year. In fact, he hoped to visit the North and work for the Garfield ticket. When he arrived at home, however, he found that circumstances did not favor his strategy of making no Republican nominations and supporting independently minded candidates. The Greenback convention in Austin on 23 June rejected Republican support. Their platform was the same as in 1878, and one that Republicans could support. They nominated William Hamman again. This time, however, they went out of their way to distance themselves from Republicans, perhaps having learned of the danger of being associated with that party in a campaign against the powerful Democrats. Their platform stated that if any Republicans wanted their support or they wanted to back any Greenback candidate, they could join the Greenback Party. In the past the open rejection of some sort of alliance masked behind-the-scenes negotiations, and even early in August, Davis informed the Republican Central Campaign Club in New York that Texas Republicans were still trying to "effect a combination of all elements opposed to the Bourbon Democracy, which, if we succeed, will brake the hold of that party in this State." The combination never developed.[11]

Davis had also hoped that better elements of the Democratic Party might seize control of that party, but that did not happen. Davis liked the young Democratic lieutenant governor, Joseph D. Sayers, a member of a group calling themselves the "Young Democracy." The Young Democracy was, like Davis, critical of the policies of Governor Oran M. Roberts. Sayers favored increasing support for education and other public services, arguing as much as Davis did that the investment would pay off with economic growth and increased wealth. When the Democrats met on 10 August, Roberts controlled the convention. The delegates rejected Sayers's proposals and renominated Roberts on the first ballot. Roberts was not a man that Davis could ask Republicans to support.[12]

Such developments led to a decision for Republicans to run their own candidates. In July, Republican newspapermen in Galveston urged Davis to run for Congress in the Fifth District. That district included many of the state's black belt counties, where Davis had already done very well, and the editors believed that the people would elect him there. That district was the one that had an incumbent who was the sort of independent minded politician Davis could support. In fact, Davis backed "Wash" Jones in 1878 and at the time told him that he could count on his continued support if he pursued a "reasonable, fair, and just" course towards Republicans. Davis believed that Jones had fulfilled his end of the bargain. Davis was a man who stood by his word, and he determined not to run. "I could not forgive myself if I were now to oppose him," Davis told party leaders. He was unwilling to secure personal advantage at the expense of his honor.[13]

The course of Greenbackers and Democrats left Republicans with little choice of strategies. The rejection of an alliance by the Greenback Party irked them particularly, and members of the Republican executive committee responded to the demand that they join the other party with the terse response that they were "averse to continuing to furnish the dog for the greenback tail to wag." At a party convention at Hearne on 25 August, members of the committee pressed Davis to run for governor. Davis was reluctant, and indicated that he intended to spend time in the North campaigning for Garfield and Arthur. He gave in, however, after a delegate from Grimes County challenged him to stick with the party in an appeal that the reporter for the *Galveston News* characterized as "very feeling." He followed Davis into alliances with the Greenbackers in the past, the delegate noted. That would not be possible this year. Now Davis had to lead the party, not abandon it. Davis never indicated whether this plea or other issues motivated him, but he was in the field once again.[14]

Davis did go to the North for a time. In September he joined with others to call for meeting of the Union Veterans' Union or the "Boys in Blue" to meet at Indianapolis to consider the situation of veterans. The "Boys in Blue" would play a major role in the Garfield campaign as well as pushing for pensions for old soldiers afterwards, but Davis did not stay for the convention. By late September he was back in Texas and working for Republican success. On 4 October he made a major campaign speech in Austin. It sounded the central themes of his campaign and was published as a broadside and circulated across the state. The speech echoed the platform that Republicans adopted the previous March, although it did little to address what Davis might do if elected. Much of it was an attack upon the Roberts administration for its failures to work for the public good, with Davis coming down hard on the cuts in funding for schools and the failure to develop a viable immigration policy. Borrowing from Democratic strategy against him in 1873, he emphasized government financing, charging that the Democrats had cut services while, at the same time, increasing the state debt, and covering the mess up by refusing to publish annual reports by the state comptroller.[15]

At least one Republican newspaper believed that Davis might win, although he never showed much optimism for his chances. Observers reckoned that Davis still retained the solid support of his own party and particularly of the blacks who provided its core constituency and that he might attract some whites dissatisfied with Governor Roberts. An article in the *Galveston Spectator* assessed the hold that he still had on African Americans. "To the colored race of Texas," the editor observed, "his name is like that of Lincoln and Grant to the whole colored race in America—a strong, brave friend." The same newspaper also recognized that some Texans had grown tired of the Democratic Party's administration of state affairs, opening the possibility that some Democrats might cross over in the election. The editor believed that some of these voters began to look with nostalgia on the Davis years. "I never did like Davis," the paper quoted one Democrat as saying, "but we had a better state government and paid less tax under his administration than we have since, and I am going to vote for him."[16]

The election showed that Republicans were overly optimistic. Roberts, whose power base was rooted firmly in the state's landowning farmers, promised to reduce taxes, cut spending, and generate additional revenue from sale of the public lands. These promises were overwhelmingly popular. By this time the Democratic Party was in firm control of the electoral process and readily used it to the advantage of party candidates. Republicans reported widespread fraud at the polls, with Democratic poll officials either telling voters that Davis was not running, or contending that Republican ballots had not arrived, or just not counting Republican ballots for what Republican poll watchers called "flimsy and purely technical" reasons. Democrats carried the state-wide elections, and Davis and the Greenbacker Hamman lost to Roberts by a combined vote of 98,103 to 166,101. If the result gave any reason for hope to Davis, it was only in that the 64,382 ballots he received indicated that he still held drawing power among Republicans. That total far outpaced Norton's 23,402 in 1878. The vote also showed that Davis may have had some attraction beyond traditional Republican voters as well, since he polled over seven thousand more votes than his party's presidential candidate. In the end, it was not enough. The only success for the anti-Democratic groups was "Wash" Jones's defeat of Seth Shepard for Congress.[17]

Despite the Republican failure in Texas, James Garfield carried the national election. Davis was uncertain whether or not the new president would fulfill any of the promises to help the Republicans in the South that he voiced in his campaign. Immediately after Garfield's inauguration, Jacob DeGress, Davis's former superintendent of public instruction, went North on behalf of Davis, seeking to influence federal appointments. Davis wanted members of the regular party organization to have the jobs at the president's disposal. Garfield appeared to favor Davis's proposals, and DeGress thought that he certainly would remove all men appointed by Hayes who were out-and-out Democrats. DeGress thought that Garfield's administration, at least on Southern issues, would be a Stalwart one, that is, associated with national Republicans who pushed for a more partisan policy regarding the South. "He," DeGress wrote, "certainly talks that way."[18]

Davis was not as confident as DeGress. In March, Davis assessed the men who were named to the cabinet and concluded that "Southern Republicans need expect nothing." No Southerners were appointed to the cabinet. The new secretary of state, Garfield's opponent in the Republican convention, was the Half-Breed James G. Blaine. Expressing the despair that had come to typify his view of national politics, Davis admitted that he believed that continuing the political struggles was pointless. "We are wasting our lives in a contest where our portion (no matter how it results) is only mortification and slight." A letter written sometime later expressed his continuing dour outlook. "The Northern Republicans only have contempt for us . . . and the southern Democracy laugh at us and say 'served you right.'" Blaine, he believed, would dominate the new administration, and Southern Republicans had secured nothing. Encouraged to go to Washington to discuss federal appointments, Davis could not decide whether to bother. His position had become painfully humiliating.[19]

Texas Republicans, anxious for office, implored Davis to make an effort at influencing appointments, so in May, despite his reservations, Davis decided to go to Washington one more time. He informed Newcomb that he would make the trip if for no other reason than he could give the administration "some plain English before I quit for good." In fact, Davis was heading east anyway, and Lizzie accompanied him. On 10 June, they attended their son Britton's graduation from West Point. There, they heard addresses by General Christopher C. Augur, the secretary of war Robert Todd Lincoln, and General William T. Sherman as Britton received the degree that sent him to the Third Cavalry and a distinguished career on the frontier. Afterwards Davis spent several days in Washington, but found that neither the president nor members of his cabinet were ready to take immediate action on the federal appointees in Texas.[20]

Garfield's plans for the South were never revealed. On 2 July an assassin killed Garfield at Washington's Baltimore and Potomac Railroad station as he prepared to leave the city. The president lingered on for seventy-nine days, finally dying from his wound on 19 September. Vice President Chester A. Arthur stepped into the presidency the next day, bringing new uncertainty to those concerned with the policy of the national administration towards the South. Arthur was a Stalwart and undoubtedly would use the federal patronage to achieve party goals. What those goals would be were uncertain, although observers believed he would continue Garfield's policy of removing Democrats. Senator Samuel B. Maxey, a Texas Democrat, writing in November, believed that because of this Davis had a good chance, for the first time, of controlling Texas appointments, even though others from the state sought the new president's ear.[21]

Maxey thought Davis's power over state politics might be increased by the new administration. At the same time, speculation developed that suggested the former governor might receive further recognition with a cabinet appointment. In December 1881, a Mississippi delegation meeting with President Arthur encouraged the president to name a few Southerners to his cabinet and to important federal jobs in recognition of their loyalty to the party. Davis's name came up as one who would be acceptable, recognized across the South as a loyalist. John B. Brownlow, son of the prominent Tennessee Republican Parson Brownlow, also backed Davis, contending he was a man "supported by the entire South." The likelihood of such an appointment became serious enough that DeGress, who had remained in Washington through the summer of 1881, urged Davis to come to the city to support his own case. Davis did go, and Texas Republicans lent their support for him. The editor of the *San Antonio Light* wanted the president to know that Davis was the "loved and trusted leader of the republicans of Texas," while Jeremiah Hamilton of the *Austin Citizen* urged his consideration as a man devoted "to the party, to principle, and to patriotism." Even an out-of-state Democratic paper endorsed Davis, contending that of the Southern Republicans "no better or abler man can be found than E. J. Davis" and praising him as a "thorough Southerner."[22]

Davis was disappointed initially. Despite the speculation and assurances from friends that he was being considered for office, the president made no direct overtures to him. A meeting between Davis and the president on 27 October, however, gave Davis some reason to believe the president might actually consider him for a cabinet appointment. He informed the president that if a nomination was imminent he would remain in Washington, but Arthur apparently indicated that nothing would be done until December. Davis, still hopeful, decided to return to Texas. Despite her husband's positive outlook, Lizzie was less positive after so much disappointment in the past. "I am one of the doubting ones," she wrote to Newcomb, "'seeing is believing' in my case." Still, correspondents in Washington contended Davis was under consideration. In November, Senator Don Cameron of Pennsylvania, a close associate of the president, informed Newcomb that while he did not know if Arthur would name a Southerner to his administration, Davis's chances would "be equal, if not better, than almost any other man that has been presented from that section of the country."[23]

Unfortunately for Davis's chances, he still had political enemies, even within his own party, and the president's delay worked to his disadvantage. In mid-November he indicated to Newcomb that he had heard that some of the state's federal office-holders urged the president not to appoint Davis to any position. Davis complained that they purported to be speaking for the Republicans of Texas, even though they were not leaders of the regular party, and he feared that they were having an impact. By late December, Davis's hope for a cabinet appointment was fading. The problem, however, was not just the opposition of his local adversaries. Davis concluded that Arthur simply decided that he would not give a cabinet position to a Southerner. Even though Davis's friends continued pressing the president to name a Southerner and give the job to Davis, he did not believe that would happen. Arthur did not name a Southerner, and Davis's hopes were dashed once again.[24]

Davis's disappointment was not just personal, for Arthur proved equally frustrating when he started naming federal officials in the South. In April 1882, Davis journeyed back to Washington, hoping to influence the naming of a new U. S. marshal in the western district. When he got there, Davis found that getting anyone in Arthur's cabinet to listen to his appeals was no easier than it was under Hayes. Once again, he concluded that the interests of Texans or Texas Republicans were not considered. He believed Northern influences would weigh more heavily on the decision than anything that he or other Texans could say. Jobs were given to reward the loyalty of Northern Republicans, not to encourage those of the South. "We are a kind of 'Botany Bay' here for Northern Politicians to put off their dead beats and bummers upon," he concluded. Arthur's appointment as collector of customs in Corpus Christi confirmed that opinion. For the man was one, Davis believed, who could "not be surpassed in the penitentiary for confirmed dead beat bummer swindler and scamp generally."[25]

After being ignored by the Hayes administration and then by President Arthur, Davis had no real reason to continue his political efforts other than his commitment to the goals that he had pursued for so long. The idea that some of those goals might yet be implemented appeared to give him renewed vigor and hope even when most disappointed. He would be up and ready for another fight as Texans prepared for another state election to be held in the autumn of 1882. His approach to that election would be set up in December 1881, when Congressman "Wash" Jones told a reporter for *The Washington Post* that he did not intend to run again for Congress but would run for governor in the next election. In what amounted to a practical invitation to Davis for an alliance, he stated that he wanted to run on "new and living issues," and he considered "the old issues had been settled." He believed the old political concerns were dying; few feared a return of radical rule. In fact, he contended, "it is becoming a matter of general remark that the Administration of Gov. E. J. Davis, the only Republican one, was the best Texas has had since the war. It has been ranked by leading Democrats with that of J. Pinckney Henderson, one of the best Governors in the entire history of Texas [*sic*]." Jones indicated that he thought most of his support would come from Greenbackers, but he also invited Republicans to give him support. Davis saw in Jones and the new independent movement a new opportunity to push the Democrats from power and joined in the effort with a vigor that he no longer seemed to possess in 1880.[26]

On 28 June 1882, Davis called for a state convention to meet in Austin on 23 August. In that call, Davis made the case that Texas Republicans should support independent candidates and distance themselves from the national Republican Party. The national party looked only to the interests of voters in the North and did not take the needs of Southern Republicans into account. It was time, he suggested, for a new movement with new alliances based on new issues. That could be done, he thought, only when party lines disappeared and men of like mind joined together. While he did not suggest that the Republican Party organization be disbanded, he did propose that the party not nominate a state ticket and recommended it endorse no individual, leaving the decision to the individual voter. This led, as usual, to complaints from federal officeholders that he was abandoning the party, but Davis was determined to pursue an independent policy this time, and he worked to ensure that the delegates who came to Austin agreed.[27]

To ensure his control in Austin, Davis worked hard pressuring the party's county conventions to elect the right men as delegates. Davis carried out a large correspondence, most of which no longer exists, with local party leaders, but his letters probably presented the same case as those he sent to James Newcomb, who often worked as his representative in the conventions held around San Antonio. Everything, he insisted, must be done to control the county conventions. Prior to a meeting in Corpus Christi, Davis sent Newcomb extensive instructions. He wanted Newcomb on the site and watching over the proceedings to make sure that no party nominations were made so that "the canvass may not be handicapped by any foolishness." Concerned with potential opposition to a non-partisan course, he also instructed Newcomb to be sure that his San Antonio newspaper took little notice of any differences, and that it emphasize Republican harmony on the question. Davis was taking no chances.[28]

Davis actually appeared hopeful that the non-partisan approach might work this time. He showed little interest in running for public office since leaving the governorship. Davis had accepted the Republican nomination for governor only reluctantly in 1880. Now he actually seemed ready to be a candidate. In May he informed Newcomb that he was considering a run for Congress. Friends suggested that if he ran for the Galveston district with its large black population he had a good chance for success. Davis, however, was not interested in running as a Republican. If he ran, it should be as an "independent." Everyone knew his political identity, and he did not need the endorsement of a Republican convention. Party support, he believed, would only create problems and even an endorsement would only "drive off some who would otherwise vote that way." Davis did not make up his mind immediately, although he had determined how to run his campaign and suggested that Newcomb might organize a group of men, without regard to party, to call on him to run for office. Still, he delayed an announcement, unsure what he should do.[29]

Davis finally ended the uncertainty and on 1 August announced that he would run for a seat in Congress. The announcement was something of a surprise, since he decided to run in the Tenth District, the one including Austin, rather than the Galveston district, with a larger black population. Davis declared that he was running as a candidate "without regard to party, in anyway," and promised that he would be bound by no party caucus. If elected, he proposed to work only for those measures that "may best serve the interest of the people of this district, of Texas, and of the country at large." Davis admitted that victory would be difficult. The previous legislature had gerrymandered the district to make sure that Democrats could control it, stringing together a diverse population that possessed conflicting interests and spread over a huge geographic area. Davis stated, however, that he intended to visit every county before the election, despite the district's size, so that he could "address you in person." His hat was in the ring once again. The warhorse would give it another try.[30]

When the Republicans finally met near the end of August, the delegates followed Davis's plan and concluded they would make no

By 1882 E. J. Davis had recaptured some of the hope for change that had been lost in 1874, a renewal that led him run for Congress in that year's election. This picture, made sometime after 1880, shows Davis as he would have appeared as he canvassed his district in what ended in an unsuccessful bid for the congressional seat. (Harriet and David Condon Collection).

party nominations. Davis had done his work in setting up the convention. Some of his opponents were in Austin, and when the convention opened a struggle took place over the its organization that one reporter referred to as "bitter." Davis's opponents blasted him in their speeches from the floor, but Davis had the votes in hand. On the second day the delegates elected James Tracy as permanent chair, thus ensuring Davis's agenda would be carried out. The convention produced a platform that restated what had by now become decades-old Republican goals for Texas and provided a catalogue of Democratic misgovernment. They did not however, make party nominations, nor did they endorse any of the candidates who had announced. One act more than any other reflected this effort at ending partisanship—Davis stepped down as the party's chairman to be replaced by a new man, C. C. Binkley.[31]

Davis, as chairman of the party, traditionally offered the opening address, and he took that opportunity to give what practically amounted to his personal valedictory. He had tried to bring Texas into line with what he called the "liberal ideas" of the nineteenth century. What were these ideas? Davis elaborated. They included securing equal rights for everyone in the country, providing equal education for the whole of the nation's people, protecting the right to vote and a fair count, and establishing law and order. For Davis, these basic goals were more important than party. Looking back at the history of Texas Republicanism, he observed that goals were always more important than party, that in 1867 some Unionists actually argued that they not become Republicans. However, practical politics demanded that they join that party. Now, the national Republican Party had abandoned the South and failed to consider the issues important to its loyal citizens, and he condemned them for that failure. Implicitly, Davis suggested that Texas Republicans owed no allegiance to a party that had failed to protect them and their interests. Now Republicans should support anyone dedicated to basic justice and opportunity. Would we not all gain, he asked, "if our State Government can pass into the hands of men sincerely in favor of these measures, even though they be not Republicans and do not agree with us in our opinions touching national politics and were on the other side during the war?"[32]

Following the convention, Davis appeared hopeful that independent candidates could be successful. Greenbackers appeared to be coming in line behind an alliance and a non-partisan campaign. In June that had not appeared possible, when at their 29 June convention they adopted a highly partisan platform that had criticized Republicans. In fact, the platform declared that the Republican Party was not "republican" and no more worthy of support in 1882 than when driven from power by the righteous wrath of the people. However, things changed after the Republican meeting at Austin. The Greenbackers reassembled at Corsicana on 31 August and agreed to support independent candidates, essentially ignoring a candidate's party background. This made cooperation possible. Davis looked at the campaign in the end of the summer and concluded that Jones was doing far better that his opponents believed in his race against the Democratic nominee, John Ireland. Davis thought Jones might actually carry the state, and he pushed his political associates to ensure that Republicans did everything they could to make the possibility come true. A strong turnout for Jones, in turn, promised to benefit Davis's own chances.[33]

Showing his renewed hope, Davis campaigned across his district, something he had not done in 1880. In a speech in San Antonio he seemed to have regained much of his old spirit. Announcing that he was an independent candidate and running with the backing of no party, he assured his listeners that he remained a Republican in his commitment to the equality of all men without regard to color or nationality, the protection of the rights of all men, encouragement of immigration, and the spread of education. He then turned to local issues, upon which he insisted he based his campaign. He favored a tariff to protect the wool trade and the developing manufacturers of his district. He then pitched into the Democrats, asking where they had created a free school outside of Austin or San Antonio, and questioning where the money appropriated for such schools had gone. As to the newly created agricultural college, he concluded it was a humbug with only thirty out of the two hundred students enrolled actually engaged in agriculture and the rest "walking around with a stiff back indulging in military exercises." Insisting that he was bound by no party caucus and that he would work for a reduction in party spirit, Davis received a warm reception and his speech provoked repeated cheers.[34]

Davis's optimism proved unfounded. The November elections showed, once again, that the possibility for an anti-Democratic candidate to secure victory in a Texas election in the years following the end of Reconstruction was a difficult task. He did not win. With the full vote not yet known, Davis informed Newcomb that he had no hope for success. Much had gone wrong. In Travis County he noted widespread corruption, with at least two hundred black voters, who ordinarily would have voted for him, either cheated out of their votes or paid to vote for his Democratic opponents. The Greenbackers also proved to be fickle supporters. Davis believed that in his district they not only had not cast their votes for him, but had tried to get Democrats to trade votes by means of Greenbackers voting for the Democrat in the congressional race in return for Democrats voting for Wash Jones in the gubernatorial contest. Analyzing returns, Davis felt that he had received as many votes from straight-out Democrats as he had from Greenbackers. In the end, however, he saw his defeat as based in his past. "Well," he wrote, "there is no doubt the old rebel hostility to me had a great deal to do with it."[35]

The defeat in 1882 greatly disappointed Davis. It deepened his disillusionment with Texas politics, and it also convinced him that it was time for personal change. In late November, Lizzie wrote to their friend Newcomb that she wanted to sell the house, "Riverside," in Austin and move to San Antonio. Rather than forgetting the past, she found that the people of Austin shut out her family more than ever before. "There is no society for us here, & it is getting worse & worse all the time." Once the new Democratic governor took office, she feared, "we will not be allowed to walk the street at all." Davis shared Lizzie's view, and he was not even convinced that the family should remain in Texas. "The hatred and malice of the democracy will follow us as long as we live here, and no matter what business we may go into," he predicted to Newcomb. Politics continued to hinder the success of his law practice. When he went to court he confronted hostile judges and juries, a fact that made it unreasonable for anyone to employ him. The election defeat and all of the anger leveled at him appeared finally to have broken his spirit.[36]

In the months after his defeat, possibilities actually developed that might have allowed Davis to leave Austin. His friends had always tried to have him recognized by Republican administrations with a federal position, and in February 1883 Newcomb, who was in Washington lobbying for an appointment as postmaster at San Antonio, met with President Arthur to discuss federal patronage in Texas. He, along with Congressman Tom Ochiltree, urged the president to consider naming Davis the nation's minister to Mexico, a position to which he was recommended in the past. Newcomb informed Davis that the president had expressed his admiration for the governor, and asked, although the Mexican position was not possible, if the governor would accept an appointment as the territorial governor of either Wyoming or Washington. Neither Newcomb or Ochiltree could speak for Davis, but for the first time it appeared that Davis might receive an actual reward from a Republican administration for his loyalty and service through the years.[37]

Ironically, that reward, had it been bestowed, would have come too late. On 8 February, Newcomb came down from his room at the Willard Hotel and encountered former president Grant near the front desk. Grant gave him a morning paper and became the first to inform Newcomb that Davis had died. The telegraph carried the news to Washington that Governor Davis had died the previous day. Newcomb was not completely surprised. Before leaving for Washington, Newcomb had gone to Austin and visited with the Davis family. He found the ex-governor sick. Davis had just returned from Louisiana, where he had been engaged in legal business, with what his doctors concluded was pneumonia. The problem did not appear serious, but he did not get better. After Newcomb left for Washington, Davis's situation worsened when, on 6 February he suffered what the newspapers called an "embolism of the brain," most likely a stroke. He lingered for almost a day, dying late on the afternoon of 7 February in the company of Lizzie. Two days later, his funeral was held at the state capitol, his body lying in state and viewed

Davis was buried in the State Cemetery in Austin with full public honors. What would become the tallest monument in that cemetery would be erected over his grave by his brother Waters, a man who had become a loyal Confederate but who supported his brother through the Reconstruction years and bestowed this last honor on him. (Scott Smith).

by surprisingly large crowds of people from all walks of life who came to pay their respects for this unusual Texan.[38]

Following his death, an unidentified newspaper writer predicted that the former governor would come to be recognized by Texans as one of the heroic figures of their state. "In after years, on the brightest page of the history of that great state will be written the name of Edmund J. Davis," he wrote. "He led her patriotic sons in defense of the life of the republic; he led the state safely over the perilous bridge of reconstruction, and now that he is dead, even his political opponents will tread softly about his bier."[39] This writer, like others at the time, recognized in Davis a nobility of purpose and a dedication to duty that in most men deserved respect. What more could be asked of an individual than that he defend his country and stand up for a society based on law and order and that discriminated against none? Davis lived, however, in a society where men with power did not see value in any of these things. They had actually fought to destroy their nation. They had little interest in a society in which all, especially blacks, were equal. Their values dominated the history of the state as it was told. There was no place for a man so different from themselves, and the political rhetoric of the era came to characterize him for later generations of Texans. In a different world, with different values, however, the prediction of that unidentified editor would come to fruition and allow the name of Edmund J. Davis to be written on the "brightest page" of Texas history.

NOTES

Chapter one: A Southern Born Man

¹ Various newspaper clippings in Mrs. E. J. Davis scrapbook, David and Harriett Condon Collection.

² Oran M. Roberts, "The Political, Legislative, and Judicial History of Texas for its Fifty Years of Statehood, 1845–1895," in *A Comprehensive History of Texas, 1685–1897,* ed. Dudley G. Wooten (Dallas, William G. Scarff, 1898), 197–98; Charles W. Ramsdell, *Reconstruction in Texas* (New York: Columbia University Press, 1910), 317.

³ Davis Family Bible, David and Harriet Condon Collection.

⁴ "Commissioner of Land Titles in East Florida," 18th Cong. 1st Sess., Public Land, No. 413, 89; U. S. Congress, *House Reports,* 17th Cong., 1st sess. no. 47, 31.

⁵ Blank, *Key Biscayne: A History of Miami's Tropical Island and the Cape Florida Lighthouse* (Sarasota: Pineapple Press, Inc., 1996), 23–27, 46, 52–57.

⁶ Ibid., 23. "St. Augustine Minute Book," http//www.rootsweb.ancestry.com/~flsags/1821–1823staugustineminutebook.htm.

⁷ Davis Family Bible, David and Harriet Condon Collection; Statement of Edward A. DeCottes, March 13, 1843, in E. J. Davis file, United States Military Academy Cadet Applications 1805–1866, National Archives, Microfilm Publication Number 688.

⁸ Brig. Genl. W. J. Worth and others to J. M. Porter, Secretary of War, January 20, 1844, in E. J. Davis file, United States Military Academy Cadet Applications 1805–1866, National Archives, Microfilm Publication Number 688.

⁹ William G. Davis to Joseph G. Totten, [undated], E. J. Davis file, United States Military Academy Cadet Applications 1805–1866, National Archives, Microfilm Publication Number 688. David Levy (Yulee) was born in St. Thomas, the West Indies, in 1810. He was sent to Norfolk, Virginia, to school in 1819, then moved to St. Augustine where he studied law and was admitted to the bar in 1836. He served as a delegate to the constitutional convention of 1838, the Territorial legislature, and was elected Territorial Delegate to the 27th Congress in 1842, then reelected in 1844. Later a prominent secessionist Democrat, Levy went to Congress as a "Whig-Democrat," suggesting that Davis may have been a Democrat at the time. Levy also was Jewish, another factor that may have played a part in Davis's views of him. *Biographical Directory of the United States Congress, 1774–2005* (Washington, D.C.: Government Printing Office, 2005), 2215.

¹⁰ Brig. Genl. W. J. Watt and others to J. M. Porter, Secretary of War, January 20, 1844, and Wm. G. Davis to Jos. G. Totten, Feb. 5, 1844, E. J. Davis file,

United States Military Academy Cadet Applications 1805–1866, National Archives, Micofilm Publication Number 688.

[11] Blank, *Key Biscayne: A History of Miami's Tropical Island and the Cape Florida Lighthouse,* 46, 52–57.

[12] Charles W. Hayes, *Galveston: History of the Island and the City,* 2 vols. (Austin: Jenkins Garrett Press, 1974), I, (quotation) 434; Earl W. Fornell, *The Galveston Era: The Texas Crescent on the Eve of Secession* (Austin: University of Texas Press, 1961), 14, 16; 1850, 1860, 1870 Manuscript Census, Galveston County; "Important letters from Gov. Davis," *The New York Times,* Oct. 17, 1874.

[13] Bruce S. Cheesman, ed. and anno., *Maria von Blücher's Corpus Christi: Letters from the South Texas Frontier, 1849–1879* (College Station: Texas A&M University Press, 2002), 19. The exact date of Davis's arrival cannot be determined, but a letter written in 1849 supporting Davis's application for a post in the Treasury service indicated that the author had known Davis for several years. John S. Rhea to William M. Meredith, Nov. 14, 1849, Records of the Division of Appointments, Registers Relating to customs Service Appointments, Records Relating to "Customhouse Nominations" ("K" Series), RG56, NA.

[14] *Register of All Officers and Agents—Civil, Military and Naval in the Service of the United States on September 13, 1849;* John S. Rhea to William M. Meredith, Nov. 14, 1849, Records of the Division of Appointments, Registers Relating to Customs Service Appointments, Records Relating to "Customhouse Nominations" ("K" Series), RG56, NA; K. Jack Bauer, *Zachary Taylor: Soldier, Planter, Statesman of the Old Southwest* (Baton Rouge: Louisiana State University Press, 1985), 223–45.

[15] Edmund J. Davis to John S. Rhea, Nov. 12, 1849, John S. Rhea to William M. Meredith, Nov. 14, 1849 (quotation), Records of the Division of Appointments, Registers Relating to Customs Service Appointments, Records Relating to "Customhouse Nominations" ("K" Series), RG56.

[16] Gilberto Miguel Hinojosa, *A Borderlands Town in Transition, Laredo, 1755–1870* (College Station: Texas A&M University Press, 1983), 58, 59, 66, 74, 79.

[17] E. J. Davis to John S. Rhea, Jan. 29, 1850, (doc. 140), in "Letters Received by the Secretary of the Treasury from Collectors of Customs, 1833–1869, Series G, Letters from All Ports Except Baltimore, Boston and Charleston, 1851 (A-M), Treasury Department, Record Group 56, Microfilm Number 174, Roll 45.

[18] E. J. Davis to J. S. Rhea, Feb. 27, 1850, (doc. 139), "Letters Received by the Secretary of the Treasury from Collectors of Customs, 1833–1869, Series G, Letters from All Ports Except Baltimore, Boston and Charleston, 1851 (A–M)," Treasury Department, Record Group 56, Microfilm Number 174, Roll 45.

[19] E. J. Davis to John S. Rhea, Jan. 29, 1850, (doc. 140), in "Letters Received by the Secretary of the Treasury from Collectors of Customs, 1833–1869, Series G,

Letters from All Ports Except Baltimore, Boston and Charleston, 1851 (A–M)," Treasury Department, Record Group 56, Microfilm Number 174, Roll 45.

[20] John S. Rhea to William M. Meredith, Mar. 13, 1850, (doc. 138), E. J. Davis to John S. Rhea, Jan. 29, 1850, in "Letters Received by the Secretary of the Treasury from Collectors of Customs, 1833–1869, Series G, Letters from All Ports Except Baltimore, Boston and Charleston, 1851 (A–M)," Treasury Department, Record Group 56, Microfilm Number 174, Roll 45; William M. Meredith to John S. Rhea, May 16, 1850, Letters Sent by the Secretary of the Treasury to Collectors of Customs at all Ports (1789–1847) and at small Ports (1847)-78), National Archives, RG, 56, Microcopy 175, Roll 10.

[21] Corpus Christi *Caller-Times,* Aug. 27, 1939.

[22] 8th Census, Webb County, NA; "Refugio Benavides" and "Santos Benavides," in *The Handbook of Texas,* vol. I (Austin: Texas State Historical Association, 1996), 484–85; see also Jerry D. Thompson, *Warm Weather & Bad Whiskey: The 1886 Laredo Election Riot* (El Paso: Texas Western Press, 1991), 16.

[23] "Stephen Powers," in *Handbook of Texas,* vol. V, (Austin: The Texas State Historical Association, 1996), 307; E. J. Davis to Stephen Powers, Feb. 10, 1876, James B. Wells Papers, CAH, UTA.

[24] "Stephen Powers," *Handbook of Texas,* vol. V, 307.

[25] Milo Kearney and Anthony Knopp, *Boom and Bust: The Historical Cycles of Matamoros and Brownsville* (Austin: Eakin Press, 1991), 81–82; "Richard King," in *Handbook of Texas,* vol. III, 1107–08; "Mifflin Kenedy," in *Handbook of Texas,* vol. III, 1064–65; Francisco Yturria, *Handbook of Texas,* "Charles Stillman," *Handbook of Texas,* vol. V, 102; "William Neal," *Handbook of Texas,* vol. V, 963–64; "Life and Background of William Alfred Neale," *Southwestern Historical Quarterly,* 47, (1943) 64–66.

[26] Thompson, *Warm Weather & Bad Whiskey: The 1886 Laredo Election Riot,* 16, 18; Hinojosa, *A Borderlands Town in Transition,* 72; see *Annals of Travis County,* 52, for his ability to speak Spanish.

[27] Election Returns, 12th Judicial District–Reports of the Secretary of State, TSAL; Thompson, *Warm Weather & Bad Whiskey,* 18; Ernest Winkler, *Platforms of Political parties in Texas,* 54–56; Patsy McDonald Spaw, ed., *The Texas Senate: Volume I: Republic to Civi War, 1836–1861* (College Station: Texas A&M University Press, 1990), 238–39; E. J. Davis to E. M. Pease, June 2, 1853, Graham-Pease Collection, Center for Austin History, Austin Public Library.

[28] Winkler, *Platforms of Political Parties in Texas,* 54–56.

[29] Mike Kingston, et al., *The Texas Almanac's Political History of Texas* (Austin: Eakin Press, 1992), 54–57; E. J. Davis to E. M. Pease, Mar. 13, 1854; H. P. Bee to E. M. Pease, Mar. 13, 1854; E. M. Pease to Robert S. Neighbors, Mar. 24, 1854 in Governors' Papers, TSLA.

[30] E. J. Davis to E. M. Pease, Mar. 13, 1854, Governors Papers, TSLA.

[31] E. M. Pease to Persifer F. Smith, Mar. 24, 1854, E. M. Pease to Jefferson Davis, Mar. 24, 1854, E. M. Pease to E. J. Davis, Mar. 24, 1854, E. J. Davis to E. M. Pease, July 27, 1854, Governors Papers, TSLA.

[32] E. J. Davis and others to E. M. Pease, July 27, 1854, Governors Papers, TSLA.

[33] Thompson, *Warm Weather & Bad Whiskey: The 1886 Laredo Election Riot*, 18; Gammel, *The Laws of Texas*, III, 1531.

[34] *State Gazette*, Sept. 8, 1855. Other named delegates were H. W. Berry, H. A. Maltby, T. A. Dwyer, John Dix, and Richard Power.

[35] *State Gazette*, Sept. 8, 1855.

[36] *State Gazette*, April 25, May 9, May 16, 1857.

[37] *Robert E. Sutton and another v. Louisa Carabajal and others*, 26 Tex. 497; 1863 Tex. Lexis 10. Davis's decision in this case was one of the few that the state supreme court reversed. In this case, the court decided that while his decision may have been the correct one, he should have ordered a new trial; for other cases involving land disputes see *Joseph F. Smith v. John Ryan and Others*, 20 Tex. 661; 1858 Tex. LEXIS 4; *Thomas Nicholson v. A. T. Horton and* Others, 23 Tex. 47; 1859 Tex. LEXIS 27; John *Martin and others v. E. A. Weyman and others*, 26 Tex.460; 1863, Tex. LEXIS 4.

[38] *A. Glavecke, Administrator, v. A. Tijirina.* 24 Tex. 663; 1860 Tex. LEXIS 16. This was another case in which Davis's judgment was overruled. In this case the state supreme court ruled that the conflict of interest was not apparent and that Tijirina had to initiate the case in Basse's court, although suggesting that he could bring charges of fraud against Basse. Other such cases that came before the supreme court were *Bierne & Burnside v. John P. Kelsey.* 21 Tex. 190; 1858 Tex. LEXIS 59; *W. H. Mayfield v. C. C. Cotton.* 21 Tex. 1; 1858 Tex. LEXIS 37; *James H. Phelps v. Emily W. Brackett.* 24 Tex. 236; 1859 Tex. LEXIS 185; *Emily W. Brackett v. George P. Devine.* 25 Tex. 194; 1860 Tex. LEXIS 56; *Philip C. Tucker, Administrator, v. Emily W. Brackett,* 25 Tex. 199; 1860 Tex. LEXIS 58; *John C. Brightman v. John Reeves, Ex'or.* 21 Tex. 70; 1858 Tex. LEXIS 44; *Pyron & Mitchell v George Butler,* 27 Tex. 271; 1863 Tex. LEXIS 113; *Henry Sheldon v. The City of San Antonio.* 25 Tex. 1877; 1860 Tex. LEXIS 53.

[39] *The State v. Simon Morales. 21 Tex.298; 1858 Tex. LEXIS 81.* The state appealed Davis's decision to the state supreme court in 1858, but Justice Wheeler affirmed his actions. For other criminal cases see *Theodosio Lopez v. The State. 20 Tex. 780; 1858 Tex. LEXIS 26; Robert F. Grier v. The State. Supreme Court of Texas, 29 Tex.95; 1867 Tex. LEXIS 17.*

[40] *J. N. Bosshard v. The State of Texas. Supreme Court of Texas. 25 Tex. 207; 1860 Tex. LEXIS 61.* Bosshard appealed his conviction to the state supreme court on

the basis that Davis had erred in not quashing the indictment, but the court affirmed the judgment.

[41] *Northern Standard,* April 9, 1859; this was only the beginning of Davis' judicial career, however, and he did not always fare as well with that body, especially after it had been taken over by political enemies during the Civil War. For his entire career, sixteen decisions were appealed and eight reversed. This was hardly surprising given the fact that most of the appeals were heard after he left the state to join the Union Army during the Civil War or during the period of Reconstruction. Most were overturned on technicalities. Typical was that of Thomas Grier, charged with horse stealing in Karnes County. In the Grier case Davis declared the bond issued by a relative when Grier failed to appear before the court. The relative appealed the decision on the grounds that the recognizance was faulty and had failed to bind the accused as well as the surety. This oversight, by judge or clerk, a very technical one, led the Supreme Court to reverse the judgment and dismiss the case in its January 1867 term. *Robert F. Grier v. The State,* 29 Tex.95; 1867 Tex. LEXIS 17

[42] *Nueces Valley,* Nov. 21, Dec. 5, 1857.

[43] *State Gazette,* Sept. 8, 1855; "Forbes N. Britton," in *Handbook of Texas,* vol. I, 744.

[44] *State Gazette* Mar. 12, 1860, Thompson, *Fifty Miles and a Fight,* 211; Annie Moore Schwien, *When Corpus Christi Was Young* (Corpus Christi: La Retama Public Library, n.d.), 4.

CHAPTER TWO: CREATION OF A TEXAS UNIONIST, 1855–1862

[1] Walter L. Buenger, *Secession and the Union in Texas* (Austin: University of Texas Press, 1984), 26 (quote).

[2] Anna Irene Sanbo, "Beginnings of the Secession Movement in Texas," *SWHQ,* 18 (July 1914), 48; Although seriously dated, Sanbo's article remains essentially the only scholarly effort at examining Texas political history in the early 1850s.

[3] Buenger, *Secession and the Union in Texas,* 26; Sanbo, "Beginnings of the Secession Movement in Texas," 50; *Galveston News,* June 23, 1855.

[4] *Galveston News,* June 23, 1855.

[5] *State Gazette,* Sept. 8, 1855.

[6] Ernest William Winkler, ed., *Platforms of Political Parties in Texas, University of Texas Bulletin No. 53* (Austin: University of Texas, 1916), 64–68, 65 (quote).

[7] Llerena Friend, *Sam Houston: The Great Designer* (Austin: University of Texas Press, 1954), 248; Sanbo, "The Beginnings of the Secession Movement in Texas," fn. 180, 57 (quote), 59; Winkler, ed., *Platforms of Political Parties in Texas,* 71–74.

[8] Mike Kingston, et al., *The Texas Almanac's Political History of Texas* (Austin: Eakin Press, 1992), 54–57, 72–75.

[9] "Hardin R. Runnels," *Handbook of Texas,* vol. V, 715–16.

[10] "Juan Nepomuceno Cortina," *The Handbook of Texas,* vol. II, 343–44; for the most recent scholarly study of Cortina and assessment of the Cart War see Jerry Thompson, *Cortina: Defending the Mexican Name in Texas* (College Station: Texas A&M University Press, 2007).

[11] E.J. Davis to Waters Davis, Nov. 16, 1859, *Triweekly Dallas Herald,* Nov. 30, 1859.

[12] "Troubles on Texas Frontier," 39th Cong., 1st sess., *House Executive Documents,* no. 81, 5.

[13] Dec. 7, 9, 12, 16, 1859, Jerry Thompson, ed., *Fifty Miles and a Fight: Major Samuel Peter Heintzelman's Journal of Texas and the Cortina War* (Austin: Texas State Historical Association, 1998), 132, 134, 137, 139–40.

[14] Thompson, ed., *Fifty Miles and a Fight,* 142–43.

[15] Sanbo, "Beginnings of the Secession Movement in Texas," 59; "Hardin R. Runnels," *Handbook of Texas,* vol. V, 715–16.

[16] "Hardin R. Runnels," *Handbook of Texas,* vol. V, 715–16.

[17] *Congressional Globe,* 33rd Cong., 1st sess, 1853–54, Appendix, 338–42; Amelia W. Williams and Eugene C. Barker, *The Writings of Sam Houston, 1813–1863,* v. 6 (Austin: University of Texas Press, 1938–1943), 98, 184, 192–204; Sanbo, "Beginnings of the Secession Movement in Texas," 41–73.

[18] F. Britton to Editor, Jan. 7, 1859, *Daily Times* [place and date of publication unknown], clipping in Lizzie Davis Civil War Scrapbook, David and Harriet Condon Collection; Britton Davis to *Reader's Digest,* in David and Harriet Condon Collection.

[19] *Harrison Flag,* Apr. 8, 1859 (first quote), and *Southern Intelligencer,* May 25, 1859 (second quote), in Friend, *Sam Houston: The Great Designer,* 322.

[20] Speech at Nacogdoches, July 9, 1859, *Writings,* VII, 343–67; Friend, *Sam Houston: The Great Designer,* 324–25.

[21] Kingston, et al. *The Texas Almanac's Political History of Texas,* 54–57; Dale Baum, *The Shattering of Texas Unionism: Politics in the Lone Star State During the Civil War Era* (Baton Rouge: Louisiana State University Press, 1998), 38.

[22] Friend, *Sam Houston: The Great Designer,* 311, 326; Baum, *The Shattering of Texas Unionism,* 229–30.

[23] Winkler, ed., *Platforms of Political Parties in Texas,* 81–85, 82 (first quote), 83 (second quote).

[24] *New York Tribune,* July 1, 1869, contains biographical information on Davis; "Henry Alonzo Maltby," *Handbook of Texas,* vol. IV, 477; "Philip Noland Lucket," *Handbook of Texas,* vol. IV, 329–30; Election Returns, Nueces County, TSAL.; Waters S. Davis to Editor, *Galveston Daily News,* Oct. 13, 1873.

²⁵ Ernest W. Winkler, ed., *Journal of the Secession Convention of Texas,* (Austin: Austin Printing Co., 1912), 47–49.

²⁶ E. J. Davis to Wm. P. Doran, Aug. 7, 1876, E. J. Davis Letters, Rosenberg Library; Britton Davis to Reader's Digest, Oct. 24, 1939, David and Harriet Condon Collection; Unpublished Biography of E. J. Davis, James P. Newcomb Collection, Center for American History, University of Texas at Austin. (There is a discrepancy in the date of the meeting with Lee between Newcomb's biography and Davis's later memory. The details of the meeting provided by Davis make his own recollection the more likely date.)

²⁷ E. J. Davis to Wm. P. Doran, Aug. 7, 1876, E. J. Davis Letters, Rosenberg Library.

²⁸ Friend, *Sam Houston: The Great Designer,* 338.

²⁹ Winkler, *Journal of the Secession Convention,* 178–79; Friend, *Sam Houston: The Great Designer,* 338–39.

³⁰ "To the Citizens and Voters of the 12th District, April 3, 1861," circular in David and Harriet Condon Collection.

³¹ Friend, *Sam Houston: The Great Designer,* 339–40.

³² B. H. Epperson to E. M. Pease, May 22, 1861, Pease-Graham-Niles Papers, Center for Austin History, Austin Public Library, hereinafter cited as CAH, APL.

³³ H. E. McCulloch to S. B. Davis, Mar. 3 and Mar. 25, 1862, *The War of the Rebellion: A Compilation of the Official Records of the Union and Confederate* Armies, 128 vols., ser. I, vol. 9 (Washington: Government Printing Office, 1880–1901), 701–02, 704–05, hereinafter cited as *OR;* G.O. No. 1, December 30, 1861, in San Antonio *Herald,* Jan. 25, 1862.

³⁴ Quotation from General Orders, No. 45, May 30, 1862, in *OR,* ser. I, vol. 9, 716; G. O. No. 3, April 24, 1862, *OR,* ser. I, vol. 9, 709, announced Bee's assumption of command; P. O. Hébert to S. Cooper, Oct. 11, 1862, *OR,* ser. I, vol. 53, 892, indicates that Bee declared martial law shortly after assuming command; see also Hamilton Bee to S. B. Davis, Oct. 21, 1862, *OR,* ser. I, vol. 53, 454–55.

³⁵ Anne E. Davis, Sept. 14, 1861, letter quoted in *San Antonio Express,* Oct. 7, 1871; *Official Records of the War of the Rebellion,* vol. XV, 522; "John L. Haynes," *Handbook of Texas,* vol. III, 517; "William Alexander," *Handbook of Texas,* vol. I, 101–02.

CHAPTER THREE: CIVIL WAR SERVICE

¹ Edmund J. Davis to Heintzelman, Aug. 8, 1862, Samuel P. Heintzelman Papers, Library of Congress; Abraham Lincoln to E. M. Stanton, Aug. 4, 1862, Roy F. Basler ed., *Collected Works of Abraham Lincoln,* vol. V, 357.

[2] *New York Tribune,* Oct. 8, 1862; meeting with Stanton recalled in San Antonio *Evening Light,* Feb. 18, 1881.

[3] E. J. Davis Service Record, National Archives; *New York Times,* Nov. 28, 1862; *OR,* vol. IX, 624; *OR* Navy, vol. XIX, 202.

[4] B. Butler to Leonard Pierce, Jr., in *OR,* ser. I, vol. 15, 592; ibid., v. 15, 205

[5] Quotation from General Orders, No. 45, May 30, 1862, in *OR,* ser. I, vol. 9, 716.

[6] Robert W. Shook, "The Battle of the Nueces, August 10, 1862," *SWHQ,* vol. 66 (July 1962), 31–42; Claude Elliott, "Union Sentiment in Texas, 1861–1865," *SWHQ,* vol. 50 (Apr. 1947), 449–77.

[7] Alwyn Barr, "Records of the Confederate Military Commission in San Antonio, July 2, October 10, 1862," *SWHQ,* 73 (October, 1969), 247–48, See also "George W. Paschal," *Handbook of Texas,* vol. V, 1180.

[8] T. R. Havins, "Administration of the Sequestration Act in the Confederate District Court of the Western District of Texas, 1862–1865," *SWHQ,* 43 (Jan. 1940), 296–322.

[9] Lizzie Davis to Dear Friend, Sept. 14, 1871, in clippings, Lizzie Davis Civil War Scrapbook, David and Harriet Condon Family Collection.

[10] Lizzie Davis to Dear Friend, Sept. 14, 1871, clipping, Lizzie Davis Civil War Scrapbook, David and Harriet Condon Family Collection.

[11] H. P. Bee to P. O. Hébert, Sept. 24, 1862, *OR,* ser. I, vol. 9, 624.

[12] Lizzie Davis to Dear Friend, Sept. 14, 1871, clipping, Lizzie Davis Civil War Scrapbook, David and Harriet Condon Family Collection.

[13] *OR,* ser. I, vol. 15, 205.

[14] Samuel Heintzelman Diary, Feb. 3, 1863, Heintzelman Papers, LC; A. J. Hamilton to N. P. Banks, Jan. 19, 1863, *OR,* ser. I, vol. XV, 658; H. P. Bee to A. G. Dickinson, Mar. 11, Mar. 15, 1863, *OR,* ser. I, vol. XV, 1013–14, 1016–17; E. J. Davis Service Record, National Archives.

[15] H. P. Bee to A. G. Dickson, Mar. 15, 1863, *OR,* ser. I, vol. 15, 1017; John B. Magruder to S. Cooper, Mar. 31, 1863, *OR,* ser. I, vol. XV, 1030–31.

[16] H. P. Bee to A. G. Dickinson, Mar 11, 1863, in *OR,* ser. I, vol. 15, 1014–1015; Bee to Dickinson, Mar. 15, 1863 (first quotation), ibid., 1016–1017; John B. Magruder to S. Cooper, Mar. 31, 1863, ibid., 1030–1031; *San Antonio Herald,* Mar. 28, 1863 (second quotation).

[17] H. P. Bee to A. G. Dickson, Mar. 15, 1863, *OR,* ser. I, vol. 15, 1017; H. P. Bee to J. A. Quinterro, Mar. 16, ibid., vol. 26, pt. 2, 42–43; "Unknown" to Mr. Hamilton, Mar. 18, 1863, in *Tyler Reporter,* Apr. 16, 1863 [quotation].

[18] "Unknown" to Mr. Hamilton, Mar. 18, 1863, in *Tyler Reporter,* Apr. 16, 1863; "Private Letter" to Editor, Mar. 17, 1863, in *San Antonio Herald,* Mar. 28, 1863; H. P. Bee to A. G. Dickinson, Mar. 15, 1863, *OR,* ser. I, vol. XV, 1016–17.

[19] "Private Letter" Mar. 17, 1863 (quotation), in *San Antonio Herald,* Mar. 17, 1863; *Brownsville Flag* in *San Antonio Herald,* Apr. 4, 1863; *New Orleans Bee,* Mar. 31, Apr. 2, 1863; H. P. Bee to Governor Albino Lopez, Mar. 16, 1863, *OR,* ser. I, vol. 26, pt. 2, 70–71.

[20] Albino Lopez to H. P. Bee, Mar. 15, 1863, *OR,* ser I, vol. XV, 1128–29; "Private Letter" Mar. 17, 1863, in *San Antonio Herald,* Mar. 28, 1863; *Brownsville Flag,* in *San Antonio Herald,* Apr. 4, 1863; "Giving Up Davis," *San Antonio Herald,* Apr. 11, 1863.

[21] T. W. Sherman to, May 18, 1863, in *OR,* ser. 1, vol. XV, 21; "Radijah" to Sister, May 12, 1863, in Nov. 2007 Catalogue, Stuart Lutz Historic Documents, Inc., Short Hills, New Jersey, 07078–2698.

[22] W. H. Emory to Dix, June 30, 1863, *OR,* ser. I, vol. XXVI, pt. 1, 608–609; Heintzelman Journal, July 13, 15, 1863, Heintzelman Papers, LC.

[23] H.W. Halleck to N. P. Banks, Aug. 10, 1863, *OR,* vol. XXVI, pt. 1, 16; N. P. Banks to H. Halleck, Aug. 26, 1863, *OR,* ser. I, vol. XXIV, pt. 1, 697 (quotation).

[24] N. P. Banks to W. B. Franklin, Aug. 31, 1863, *OR,* ser. I, vol. XXVI, pt. 1, 287–88; N. P. Banks to H. Halleck, Aug. 16, 1863, *OR,* ser. I, vol. XXVI, pt. 1, 695–96; Nathaniel P. Banks to Abraham Lincoln, Sept. 5, 1863, Abraham Lincoln Papers, Library of Congress.

[25] J. B. Magruder to S. Cooper, Sept. 27, 1863, *OR,* ser. I, vol. XXVI, pt. 1, 305–306.

[26] Edmund J. Davis Service Record, National Archives; Division Returns, *OR,* ser. 1, vol. XXVI, no. 1, p. 377–79.

[27] N. P. Banks to H. Halleck, Sept. 13, 1863, *OR,* ser. I, vol. XXVI, pt. 1, 288–90; Dyer's *Compendium,* pt. 3 (Regimental Histories), 1647; N. P. Banks to A. Lincoln, Oct. 22, 1863, *OR,* ser. I, vol. XXVI, pt. 1, 290–92; N. P. Banks to Carleton, Nov. 5, 1863, *OR,* ser. I, vol. XXVI, pt. 1, 788.

[28] R. Fitzpatrick to Judah P. Benjamin, Mar. 8, 1864, *OR,* ser. I, vol. XXXIV, pt. 2, 1031; Hamilton statement in Milo Kearny, ed., "The Fall of Brownsville, 1863, by John Warren Hunter," in *More Studies in Brownsville History* (Brownsville: American University at Brownsville, 1989), 224.

[29] Milo Kearny, ed., "The Fall of Brownsville, 1863, by John Warren Hunter," in *More Studies in Brownsville History,* 219 (first quotation), 221, 219–27; James M. Beverly, *A History of the Ninety-First Regiment, Illinois Volunteer Infantry, 1862–1865* (White Hall: Pearce Printing Company, 1913?), 11 (second quotation); Nannie M. Tilley, ed., *Federals on the Frontier, The Diary of Benjamin F. McIntyre, 1862–1864* (Austin: University of Texas Press, 1963), 255–56 (third quotation), 273.

[30] Milo Kearny, ed., "The Fall of Brownsville, 1863, by John Warren Hunter," in *More Studies in Brownsville History* (Brownsville: American University at Brownsville, 1989), 221 (first quotation), 219–27; E. J. Davis to My Dearest Wife, Nov. 7,

1863, E. J. Davis Letter, TSLA; E. J. Davis to Maj. Gen. Ord, Feb. 10, 1864, in *OR*, ser. I, vol. 34, pt. 2, 287.

[31] Nannie M. Tilley, ed., *Federals on the Frontier, The Diary of Benjamin F. McIntyre, 1862–1864* (Austin: University of Texas Press, 1963), 278.

[32] N. J. T. Dana to Charles P. Stone, Dec. 2, 1863, *OR*, ser. I, vol. XXVI, pt. 1, 830–31; E. J. Davis to Maj. Gen. Ord, Feb. 10, 1864, in ibid., pt. 2, 288; A. J. Hamilton to E. M. Stanton, Dec. 19, 1863, ibid., pt. 1, 865–67.

[33] General Order No. 74, Dec. 4, 1863, in E. J. Davis File, National Archives; *Dyer's Compendium*, pt. 3, 1647.

[34] N. J. T. Dana to Charles P. Stone, Dec. 2, 1863, *OR*, ser. I, vol. XXVI, pt. 1, 830–31; E. J. Davis to Maj. Gen. Ord, Feb. 10, 1864, ibid., pt. 2, 288 (quotation); Davis Service Record, National Archives.

[35] E. J. Davis to E. O. C. Ord, Feb. 10, 1864, *OR*, ser. I, vol. XXXIV, pt. 2, 287.

[36] N. J. T. Dana to Charles P. Stone, Dec. 27, 1863 (first quotation), *OR*, ser. I, vol. XXVI, pt. 1, 885; E. J. Davis to Maj. Gen. Ord, Feb. 10, 1864 (second quotation), ibid., pt. 2, 288.

[37] October, 1863, Henry Ketzle Diary, http://www.ketzle.com/diary/; N. J. T. Dana to M. M. Kimmey, Nov. 27, 1863, *OR*, ser. I, vol. XXVI, pt. 1, 824–25; Dana to Charles P. Stone, Dec. 2, 1863, *OR*, ser. I, vol. XXVI, pt. 1, 830–31.

[38] N. J. T. Dana to M. M. Kimmey, Nov. 27, 1863, *OR*, ser. I, vol. XXVI, pt. 1, 824–25; Dana to Charles P. Stone, Dec. 2, 1863, *OR*, ser. I, vol. XXVI, pt. 1, 830–31.

[39] E. R. Tarver to Commanding Officer, Ringgold Barracks, October 28, 1863, *OR*, ser. I, vol. 26, pt. 1, 447; "Report of Captain James Duff," Nov. 11, 1863, ibid., 439–40; N. J. T. Dana to N. Banks, Dec. 24, 1863, ibid., 876; J. A. Quinterro to Judah Benjamin, Nov. 26, 1863, *OR*, ser. I, vol. 34, pt. 2, 890; John Magruder to John Slidell, Apr. 27, 1864, ibid., ser. vol. 34, pt. 3, 796; E. J. Davis to Nathaniel Banks, Apr. 29, 1864, Nathaniel P. Banks Papers, Library of Congress.

[40] Davis Service Record, National Archives; Field Orders No. 23, April 18, 1863, *OR*, ser. I, vol. XXXIV, pt. 3, 211; Field Orders No. 31, April 30, 1863, *OR*, ser. I, pt. 3, 358; Special Orders No. 52, June 29, 1864, *OR*, ser. I, vol. XXXIV, pt. 4, 586; James K. Ewer, *The Third Massachusetts Cavalry in the War for the Union* (Maplewood, Mass: Perry Press, 1903), 163–64; Report of Maj. Gen. William B. Franklin, Apr. 29, 1864, *OR*, ser. I, vol. XXXIV, pt. 1, 262.

[41] Report of Brig. Gen. William H. Emory, Apr. 28, 1864, *OR*, ser. I, vol. XXXIV, pt. 1, 394–97; Report of Brig. Gen. Richard Arnold, May 5, 1864, *OR*, ser. I, vol. XXXIV, pt. 1, 460–61.

[42] Ewer, *Third Massachusetts Cavalry*, 167–8.

[43] Ibid., 172–73.

[44] Report of Capt. Elbert H. Fordham, May 22, 1864, *OR,* ser. I, vol. XXXIV, pt. 1, 465–67; John D. Winters, *The Civil War in Louisiana* (Baton Rouge: Louisiana State University Press, 1963), 374–76; Ewer, *Third Massachusetts Cavalry,* 80–81.

[45] Report of Capt. Elbert H. Fordham, May 22, 1864, *OR,* ser. I, vol. XXXIV, pt. 1, 465–67; Ewer, *Third Massachusetts Cavalry,* 182–83; Winters, *The Civil War in Louisiana,* 376–77.

[46] Davis quoted by Richard Arnold to G. B. Drake, May 8, 1864, *OR,* ser. I, vol. XXXIV, pt. 4, 647 (Davis quotation) (Arnold quotation).

[47] G. B. Drake to R. Arnold, May 18, 1864, *OR,* ser. I, pt. 3, 649; Davis Service Record, National Archives; Ewer, *Third Massachusetts Cavalry,* 185.

[48] Edmund J. Davis to Frederick Speed, May 31, June 1, 5, 1864, *OR,* ser. I, vol. XXXIV, pt. 1, 962–65; M. K. Lawler to Frederick Speed, June 3, 1864, *OR,* ser. I, vol. XXXIV, pt. 1, 961 (quotation).

[49] M. H. Chrysler to E. J. Davis, May 29, 1864, *OR,* ser. I, vol. XXXIV, pt. 1, 956; W. H. Emory to W. Dwight, May 19, 1864, *OR,* ser. I, vol. XXXIV, pt. 1, 956; E. J. Davis to Frederick Speed, May 31, June 1, 5, 7, 1864, *OR,* ser. I, vol. XXXIV, pt. 1, 962–65; M. K. Lawler to Frederick Speed, *OR,* ser. I, vol. XXXIV, pt. 1, 961–62.

[50] Samuel H. Fletcher, *The History of Company A, Second Illinois Cavalry,* (n. p. 1912), 144–45 (first and second quotations); Joseph Hayes to My Dear Mary, Sept. 23, 1864 (second quotation), *http://www.geocities.com/* Heartland/2101/hayes-letter.html?200618 (accessed April 18, 2006).

[51] Letter of Patterson to George, Morganza, Louisiana, advertised by AntiQ-Book, *http://www.antiqbook.com/books/bookinfo.phtml?o'cum&bnr'211569* accessed on March 22, 2006; E. J. Davis to J. Schuyler Crosby, Apr. 29, 1865, General's Papers, RG 94, NA.

[52] E. J. Davis to Wm. P. Doran, Aug 3, 1876, E. J. Davis Letters, The Rosenberg Library.

[53] E. J. Davis to William P. Doran, Aug. 3, 7, 26, 1876, E. J. Davis Letters, Rosenberg Library; *Galveston Daily News,* June 2, 1865; E. J. Davis Service Record, National Archives.

CHAPTER FOUR: POSTWAR UNIONIST

[1] *Galveston Daily News,* Sept. 8, 1865.

[2] E. J. Davis to E. M. Pease, Nov. 24, 1866, Pease-Graham-Niles Papers, AHC, APL.

[3] E. J. Davis to Charles Worthington, Jan. 27, 1867, J. B. Wells Papers, CAH, UTA; see also Samuel Heintzelman Diary, June 23, 1862, Heintzelman Papers, LC.

[4] H. P. Bee to A. J. Hamilton, Nov. 6, 1865, Hamilton Papers, Governors Papers, TSAL.

[5] *Galveston Daily News,* July 25, Supplement of Aug. 6, Sept. 20, 1865.

[6] J. W. Throckmorton to Ben Epperson, Aug. 6, 1865, Ben Epperson Papers, CAH.

[7] Election Returns, TSLA.

[8] Foner, *Reconstructon, 1863–1877,* 241–45 for a discussion of the growing division.

[9] *Journal of the Constitutional Convention of 1866,* 16–27, 21 (quotation).

[10] "Albert Hamilton Latimer," *Handbook of Texas,* vol. IV, 102; "Isaiah Addison Paschal," *Handbook of Texas,* vol. V, 80; *New York Times,* Apr. 1, 1866, p. 1.

[11] Benjamin Truman to *Times,* February 10, 1863, *New York Times,* Mar. 5, 1865, p. 1; *Journal of the Constitutional Convention of 1866,* 11, 12.

[12] Benjamin Truman to *Times,* February 10, 1866, *New York Times,* Mar. 5, 1865, p. 1 and Truman to *Times,* Feb. 14, 1863, *New York Times,* Mar. 11, 1866, p. 1 (quotation); *Journal of the Constitutional Convention of 1866,* 13.

[13] Truman to *Times,* Feb. 12, 14, 1863, *New York Times,* Mar. 5, 11, 1866, p. 1; Feb. 12 letter, Austin, *New York Times,* Mar. 5, 1866, p. 1; *Journal of the Constitutional Convention of 1866,* 29.

[14] Truman to *Times,* Feb. 14, 1863, *New York Times,* Mar. 11, 1866, p. 1 (quotation); *Journal of the Constitutional Convention of 1866,* 35.

[15] William Alexander to _____, Mar. 7, 1866, quoted in *Galveston Daily News,* May 3, 1866. C. C. Herbert to editor, June 3, 1866, in *Galveston Daily News,* June 8, 1866; Throckmorton to Eperson, Apr. 17, 1866, B. H. Epperson Papers, CAH.

[16] "Making Valid the Laws and Acts of Officers Therein Mentioned and for Other Purposes," Ordinance No. 11, *The Constitution as Amended and the Ordinances of the Convention of 1866* (Austin: Printed at Gazette Office by Jo. Walker, State Printer, 1866), 41–44.

[17] Benjamin C. Truman to *Times,* Feb. 14, in *New York Times,* Mar. 11, 1866, p. 1 (quotation); Truman to Times, Mar. 24, 1866, *New York Times,* Apr. 1, 1866, p. 1; *Journal of the Constitutional Convention of 1866,* 38; C. Caldwell to Editor, Mar. 29, 1867, in *Galveston Daily News,* Apr. 1, 1867.

[18] C. Caldwell to Editor, Mar. 29, 1867, quoted in *Galveston Daily News,* Apr. 1, 1867; *Journal of the Constitutional Convention of 1866,* 81 (quotation); Mention of Latimer in February 10 Letter from Austin, in *New York Times,* Mar. 5, 1866, p. 1; Davis's position defined in Mar. 24, 1866, letter from Houston in *New York Times,* Mar. 25, 1866, p. 1 (second quotation).

[19] Benjamin C. Truman to *Times,* Feb. 14, in *New York Times,* Mar. 11, 1866, p. 1 (quotation); Truman to Times, Mar. 24, 1866, *New York Times,* Apr. 1, 1866, p. 1; *Journal of the Constitutional Convention of 1866,* 38.

20 Benjamin C. Truman to *Times,* Feb. 14, in *New York Times,* Mar. 11, 1866, p. 1 (quotation); Truman to Times, Mar. 24, 1866, *New York Times,* Apr. 1, 1866, p. 1.

21 *Journal of the Constitutional Convention of 1866,* 52, 98–100, 119, 215; see Gamel, *Laws of Texas,* p. for prohibition on intermarriage; *Texas Constitution of 1866,* Art. X, Sec. VII.

22 *Journal of the Texas State Convention, 1866,* 357–59; "Ordinance 13," *The Constitution as Amended,* 45–46.

23 *Speeches of Colonel John Burke of Harrison County, in the State Convention, Assembled At Austin, February and March, 1866* (Austin: State Gazette Book and Job Office, 1866), 5; *State Convention Journal,* 297–300.

24 *Galveston Daily News,* April 11, 1865.

25 John Hancock to W. B. Knox, Apr. 4, 1866, quoted in *Galveston Daily News,* Apr. 19, 1866.

26 *Flake's Daily Bulletin,* Apr. 11, 1866; (Austin) *Southern Intelligencer,* April 12, 19, 30, 1866; Winkler, ed., *Platforms of Political Parties in Texas,* 95.

27 J. W. Throckmorton to Ben Epperson, Apr. 17, 1866, Epperson Papers, Center for American History.

28 Winkler, ed., *Platforms of Political Parties in Texas,* 95–97; James W. Throckmorton to Benjamin H. Epperson, Apr. 25, 1866, Epperson Papers, CAH, UTA.

29 J. W. Throckmorton to B. Epperson, Jan. 21, 1866, Epperson Papers, CAH, UTA; *Galveston Daily News,* Apr. 15, 1866.

30 Patsy McDonald Spaw, ed., *The Texas Senate, Volume II: Civil War to the Eve of Reform, 1861–1889* (College Station: Texas A&M University Press, 1999), 61–62; "John Littleton," in *The Handbook of Texas,* vol. IV, 238.

31 *Galveston Daily News,* May 11, 1866; *FB,* May 11, 1866.

32 *Galveston Daily News,* May 11, 1866; *Flake's Daily Bulletin,* Apr. 4, May 11, 1866.

33 J. W. Throckmorton to B. Epperson, May 30, 1866, B. H. Epperson Papers, CAH, UTA; *Galveston Daily News,* May 25, (quotation), see also June 2, 1866; John Hancock, et al. to J. W. Throckmorton and G. W. Jones, in *Galveston News,* Apr. 15, 1866.

34 *Galveston Daily News,* April 7, (first quotation) *Galveston Daily News,* May 25, (first quotation), Apr. 7, 1866 (second quotation); W. L. Robards to Editor, Apr. 17, 1866, in GDN, Apr. 21, 1866; J. W. Throckmorton to B. Epperson, May 30, 1866, B. H. Epperson Papers, CAH, UTA; John Hancock, et al. To J. W. Throckmorton and G. W. Jones, in *Galveston News,* Apr. 15, 1866.

35 Kingston, et al., *The Texas Almanac's Political History of Texas,* 72–75; E. J. Davis to E. M. Pease, July 14, 1866, Pease-Graham-Niles Collection, Austin History Center, Austin Public Library. Ramsdell, *Reconstruction in Texas,* 111–12; Moneyhon, *Republicanism in Reconstruction Texas,* 45–47, 49.

[36] E. J. Davis to E. M. Pease, July 14, 1866, Pease-Graham-Niles Collection, Austin History Center, Austin Public Library.

[37] E. J. Davis to E. M. Pease, July 14, 1866, Pease-Graham-Niles Collection, AHC, APL.

[38] E. J. Davis to E. M. Pease, July 14, 1866, Pease-Graham-Niles Collection, AHC, APL.

Chapter Five: Unionism to Republicanism

[1] E. J. Davis to E. M. Pease, July 14, 1866, Pease-Graham-Niles Collection, AHC, APL.

[2] E. J. Pease to J. H. Bell and others quotation in *Galveston Daily News,* Sept. 18, 1867; C. Caldwell to Editor, Mar. 29, 1867, in *Galveston Daily News,* Apr. 1, 1867; *Galveston Daily News,* June 2, 1866; *Southern Intelligencer,* June 7, 1866; Circular Letter of Andrew J. Hamilton, Andrew J. Hamilton Papers, CAH, UTA; *New York Herald* in *Galveston Daily News,* July 5, 1866; *New York Times,* June 22, July 11, 1866; *New York Herald,* June 6, 1866, quoted in *Flake's Daily Bulletin,* July 4, 1866; "Address of Southern Loyalists," in *New York Tribune,* July 12, 1866; *Pittsburg Gazette,* in *Flake's Daily Bulletin,* June 29, 1866; *Philadelphia Inquirer,* Sept. 1, 1866.

[3] *Flake's Daily Bulletin,* Aug. 16, 1866; *New York Times,* Sept. 1–6, 8, 11, 12, 15, 20, 24, 26, 1866.

[4] *Philadelphia Inquirer,* Sept. 7 (first quotation), Sept. 8 (second quotation), 1866.

[5] *Philadelphia Inquirer,* Sept. 8, 1866.

[6] *Flake's Daily Bulletin,* Aug. 23, 1866; R. K. Gaston to O. M. Roberts, Aug. 24, 1866 (first quotation), see also W. M. Neyland to O. M. Roberts, Sept. 29, 1866, O. M. Roberts Correspondence, CAH; J. L. Haynes to E. M. Pease, Oct. 4, (second quotation), Nov. 12, 1866; Wm. Alexander to E. M. Pease, Aug. 17, 1866, Pease-Graham Niles Collection, AHC, APL; Act approved Oct. 27, 1866, ch. 35, Act approved Nov. 1, 1866, ch. 80, Act approved Nov. 1, 1866, ch. 82, *11th Leg., Reg. S., 1866 Tex. Gen. Laws,* 61–63, 76–79, 80–81, reprinted in 5 H.P.N. Gammel, *The Laws of Texas, 1822–1897,* at 61–63, 76–79, 80–81; Act approved Nov. 12, 1866, chapter 145. *11th Leg., Reg. S., 1866 Tex. Gen. Laws,* 169–70.

[7] E. J. Davis to E. M. Pease, Nov. 24, Dec. 21 (quotation), 1866, Pease-Graham-Niles Papers, AHC, APL.

[8] E. J. Davis to E. M. Pease, Nov. 24, 1866, Pease-Graham-Niles Collection, AHC, APL.

[9] Davis to Pease, Dec. 21, 1866, Pease-Graham-Niles Collection, CAH, APL.

[10] E. J. Davis to S. Powers, May 12, 1867, J. B. Wells Papers, CAH, UTA; R. King & Co. v. Edward N. Grey, *Supreme Court of Texas,* 31 Tex. 22; 1868 Tex. LEXIS 37.

[11] *Flake's Daily Bulletin,* Feb. 5, 1867.

[12] James M. McPherson, *Ordeal by Fire: The Civil War and Reconstruction,* (New York: McGraw-Hill, Inc., 1992), 518–20.

[13] E. J. Davis to Stephen Powers, May 12, June 4, 1867, J. B. Wells Papers, CAH, UTA; R. King & Co. v. Edward N. Grey, *Supreme Court of Texas* 31 Tex. 22; 1868 Tex. LEXIS 37.

[14] *Flake's Daily Bulletin,* May 8, 16, June 30, 1867.

[15] *Flake's Daily Bulletin,* May 5, 1867.

[16] *Flake's Daily Bulletin,* June 9, 1867.

[17] *Galveston Daily News,* Apr. 26, 1867.

[18] E. J. Davis to S. Powers, June 4, 1867, J. B. Wells Papers, CAH, UTA.; Maria von Blucher to Beloved Parents, May 26, 1867, in Cheeseman, ed. *Maria von Blücher's Corpus Christi,* 175.

[19] Richter, *The Army in Texas During Reconstruction,* 105.

[20] Unk. to A. J. Hamilton, Nov. 29, 1867, A. J. Hamilton Papers, CAH, UTA; *Galveston Daily News,* May 1, 1867.

[21] *Flake's Daily Bulletin,* July 6, 1867.

[22] Wm. Alexander to E. M. Pease, Apr. 12, 1867, Pease-Graham-Niles Collection, AHC, APL; see also Thomas C. Duval to P. Sheridan, Apr. 3, 1867, Letters Received, Vol. 60, Records of the Fifth Military District, RG 393, NA; Griffin to Sheridan, Apr. 16, 1867, ibid.; Charles Griffin to George H. Forsyth, June 10, 1867, Griffin to Philip Sheridan, Jul 15, 1867, Philip Sheridan Papers, LC; Philip Sheridan to U. S. Grant, Apr. 2, 1867, and U. S. Grant to P. Sheridan, Apr. 3, 1867, Telegrams Collected (Bound), Records of the Headquarters of the Army, RG 108, NA; *Flake's Daily Bulletin,* July 6, 1867.

[23] U. S. Grant to P. Sheridan, July 30, 1867, Telegrams Collected (Bound), Records of the Headquarters of the Army, RG107, NA; T. H. Duval to John Hamilton, Aug. 9, 1867, A. J. Hamilton Collection, CAH, UTA; a reporter for the *San Antonio Express* later indicated that Judge Thomas Stribling, M. C. Hamilton, and John T. Allen had visited New Orleans to urge Pease's appointment, *San Antonio Daily Express,* Jan. 27, 1869.

[24] See Special Order 160, Aug. 27, 1867, Special Order 169, September 10, 1867, Special Orders 170 and 171, September 11, 1867, in Records of the Fifth Mili-

tary District, RG 94, NA; P. H. Sheridan to Charles Griffin, Aug. 27, 1867, Records of Third Term. Texas. Governor Elisha M. Pease. Archives and Information Services Division, Texas State Library and Archives Commission, hereinafter cited as Records of the Third Term, Governor Elisha M. Pease, TSLA

[25] E. J. Davis to J. T. Kirkman, Aug. 16, 1867, Records of Third Term. Texas. Governor Elisha M. Pease, TSLA

[26] E. J. Davis to Stephen Powers, May 12, June 4, 1867, J. B. Wells Papers, CAH, UTA; R. King & Co. v. Edward N. Grey, *Supreme Court of Texas* 31 Tex. 22; 1868 Tex. LEXIS 37; *San Antonio Express,* Oct. 19, 1867.

[27] E. J. Davis to S. Powers, Aug. 18, Sept. 14 (quotation), 1867, J. B. Wells Papers, CAH, UTA.

[28] *Corpus Christi Caller Times,* Jan. 18, 1959 (quotation); E. J. Davis to S. Powers, Aug. 18, 1867, J. B. Wells Papers, CAH, UTA.

[29] E. J. Davis to S. Powers, Nov. 24, 1867, J. B. Wells Papers, CAH, UTA.

[30] Election Order, Dec. 18, 1867, Annual Report of the Secretary of War for 1868," 40th Cong., 3rd Sess., *House Exec. Doc.* no. 1, 215.

[31] *San Antonio Express,* Feb. 6 (quotation), 7, 1868; see John H. Reagan et al., Address to the People of Texas, January 23, 1868," in John H. Reagan Papers, CAH, UTA.

[32] Special Order No. 78, Apr. 16, 1868, in *Galveston Daily News,* Apr. 21, 1868; Secretary of State, Election Returns, 1868, TSAL; Kingston, et al. *The Texas Almanac's Political History of Texas,* 56, 60.

CHAPTER SIX: DAVIS AND THE REPUBLICAN SCHISM: THE CONSTITUTIONAL CONVENTION OF 1868–1869

[1] *Galveston Daily News,* May 23, 1868; *Flake's Daily Bulletin,* May 16, 22, 1868; *Weekly Austin Republican,* June 3, 1868.

[2] *Statement and Memorial in Relation to Political Affairs in Texas, by Members of the Late Convention and Other Citizens of that State, Addressed to the Hon. B. F. Butler* (Washington, D. C.: McGill & Witherow, Printers and Stereotypers, 1869), 6–8; William Alexander to J. J. Reynolds, Oct. 27, 1867, *San Antonio Daily Express,* Nov. 5, 1867; Morgan C. Hamilton to George Mower, Oct. 29, 1867, *Weekly Austin Republican,* Nov. 13, 1867; *Weekly Austin Republican,* Dec. 18, 1867; *Flake's Daily Bulletin,* Dec. 19, 1867

[3] *San Antonio Daily Express,* June 3, 1868; *Galveston Daily News,* June 3, 5, 1868; *Flake's Daily Bulletin,* June 5, 1868; *Weekly Free Man's Press,* July 25, 1868, in E. J. Davis Biographical File, CAH, UTA.

[4] *San Antonio Daily Express,* June 3, 1868; *Galveston Daily News,* June 3, 5, 1868; *Flake's Daily Bulletin,* June 5, 1868.

[5] *Daily Austin Republican,* Dec. 18, 1868.

[6] *Journal of the Reconstruction Convention Which met at Austin, Texas, June 1, A.D., 1868.* Austin: Tracy, Siemering & Co., Printers, 1870, 2, 30–34, hereinafter cited as *Journal of the Reconstruction Convention. First Session; Austin Republican,* Jan. 8, 15, 1868; C. Caldwell to A. H. Longley, Jan. 2, 1868, Records of Third Term. Texas. Governor Elisha M. Pease. Archives and Information Services Division, Texas State Library and Archives Commission, hereinafter cited as Records of the Third Term, Governor Elisha M. Pease, TSLA.

[7] *Flake's Daily Bulletin,* July 12, 1868; *Journal of the Reconstruction Convention, State of Texas. Second Session,* (Austin: Tracy, Siemering & Co., 1870), 408–409, 412–15, hereinafter cited as *Journal of the Reconstruction Convention. Second Session.*

[8] N. H. Randlett to Charles A. Vernon, A.A.G., July 23, 1868, *Flake's Daily Bulletin,* Aug. 4, 1868; see *Flake's Daily Bulletin,* Aug. 4, 1868, for description of a mob attack on Republican political leaders at Jefferson on July 9.

[9] *Flake's Semi-Weekly Bulletin,* July 15, 1868.

[10] *San Antonio Daily Express,* Jan. 31, 1869.

[11] For a discussion of the *ab initio* controversy in the convention see Betty Jeffus Sandlin, "The Texas Reconstruction Constitutional Convention of 1868–1869" (Unpublished Ph.D. dissertation, Texas Tech University, 1970), 43–64,

[12] *Daily Austin Republican,* July 2, 1868; *Journal of the Reconstruction Convention. First Session,* 188–189.

[13] *Journal of the Reconstruction Convention. First Session,* 234 (quotation), 241–42.

[14] E. Degener to John Sherman, Mar. 22, 1867, John Sherman Papers, LC; E. Degener to C. Griffin, Mar. 22, 1867, Letters Received Fifth Military District, Vol. 60, RG 393, U. S. Congress, 40th Cong., 3rd sess., "House Executive Documents," No. 97, 3–4; NA.

[15] U.S. Cong., *Memorial on Behalf of the Citizens of Western Texas,* 39th Cong., 2nd sess., H. Misc Docs., no. 35 , 3 (first quotation); E. J. Davis to U. S. Grant, Jan. 28, 1869, in U.S. Cong., *Constitutional Convention of Texas. Letter from the Secretary of War,* 40th Con., 3rd sess., H. Exec. Docs, no. 97, 4 (second quotation); *Convention Journal of the Reconstruction Convention. First Session,* 15–16.

[16] Wallace, *The Howling of the Coyotes,* (College Station: Texas A&M University Press, 1979), 52–63.

[17] *Journal of the Reconstruction Convention, First Session,* 560–570; Observer to Editor, June 26, 1868, *Flake's Daily Bulletin,* July 3, 1868.

[18] *Flake's Daily Bulletin,* June 28, 1868; *Galveston Daily News,* June 23, July 1, 1868.

[19] *Flake's Daily Bulletin,* Aug. 13, 15, 16, 19, 1868; *Daily Austin Republican,* Aug. 13, 14, 15, 22, 1868; *Galveston Daily News,* Aug. 15, 1868; *San Antonio Express,* Aug. 21, 1868; Republican State Executive Committee, *Proceedings of the Republican State Convention Assembled at Austin, August 12, 1868* (Austin: Daily Republican Book & Job Office, 1868).

[20] *Daily Austin Republican,* July 31, Aug. 31, 1868; *Galveston Daily News,* July 16, 1868; *Journal of the Reconstruction Convention, First Session,* 222–24, 851–53; Wallace, *The Howling of the Coyotes,* 63.

[21] For Davis, see *San Antonio Daily Express,* Jan. 31, 1868. For the shift in voting patterns compare the vote on the Thomas Resolution to end discussion of division in the first session with the final passage of the Committee of the Whole's report favoring division in the second session, *Journal of the Reconstruction Convention, First Session,* 410; *Journal of the Reconstruction Convention, Second Session,* 327.

[22] *San Antonio Daily Express,* Dec. 17, 19, 31, 1868, Jan. 1, 1869.

[23] *San Antonio Daily Express,* August 31, Jan. 20, Feb. 2, 1869; *Journal of the Reconstruction Convention, Second Session,* 38–39, 287, 291–93, 300–303.

[24] *San Antonio Daily Express,* Jan. 21, 27, 30, 1869; *Journal of the Reconstruction Convention, Second Session,* 267–68, 301–303, 323–26.

[25] *San Antonio Daily Express,* Dec. 8, 16, 1868, Jan. 30, Feb. 2, 3, 1869; *Journal of the Reconstruction Convention, Second Session,* 408–409, 412–15, 481–86 (quotation).

[26] *San Antonio Daily Express,* Feb. 10, 1869; *Journal of the Reconstruction Convention, Second Session,* 518.

[27] *Journal of the Reconstruction Convention, Second Session,* 502–15

[28] *San Antonio Daily Express,* Feb. 10, 11, 1869; *Flake's Daily Bulletin,* Feb. 7, 1869.

[29] *San Antonio Daily Express,* Feb. 11, 1869; Ed. R. S. Canby to John Rawlings, Feb. 11, 1869, in *House Executive Documents,* 40th Cong., 3rd sess., no. 97, 2.

[30] *Flake's Daily Bulletin,* Feb. 14, 1869; *San Antonio Daily Express,* Feb. 11, 1869; Ed. R. S. Canby to John A. Rawlings, Feb. 11, 1869, in *House Executive Documents,* 40th Cong., 3rd sess., no. 97, 2.

[31] James R. Burnett to Mark Miller, Mar. 12, 1869, Governor's Papers, TSLA; *Galveston Daily News,* Mar. 3, 4, 118, 27, Apr. 9, 1869; *Baltimore Gazette,* Apr. 7, 1869, in *Galveston Daily News,* Apr. 15, 1869; *Flake's Daily News,* Apr. 10, 1869.

[32] See Haynes to Longley, Apr. 4, 1869, in *Daily Austin Republican,* Apr. 4, 1869; *Flake's Daily Bulletin,* Apr. 7, 13, 1869; Wallace, *The Howling of the Coyotes,* 122–23.

[33] *Galveston Daily News,* Mar. 20, 27, 1869; "Minutes for Meeting on Tuesday, March 30, 1869," "Select Committee on Reconstruction," Legislative Records, R.G. 233, NA.

[34] *Daily Austin Republican,* Feb. 8, 1869 (first quotation); Wallace, *The Howling of the Coyotes,* 123 (second quotation).

CHAPTER SEVEN: THE ELECTION OF 1869

[1] *Daily Austin Republican,* Feb. 23 (first quotation), 1869; *Galveston Daily News,* Feb. 12, 18, 19 (second quotation), 1869; *Flake's Daily Bulletin,* Feb. 12, 17, Apr. 10, 1869 and John L. Haynes to Editor, *Flake's Daily Bulletin,* Mar. 30, 1869.

[2] *Galveston Daily News,* Feb. 24, 1869; *Gonzales Inquirer* referenced in *Galveston Daily News,* Mar. 11, 1869.

[3] *Flake's Daily Bulletin,* Mar. 11, 1869.

[4] William Phillips to Pease, Feb. 23, 1869, A. Siemering to E. M. Pease, Mar. 8, 1869, C. T. Garland to Pease, May 21, 1869, Stephen Hackworth to E. M. Pease, May 28, 1869 (quotation), Records of Third Term. Texas. Governor Elisha M. Pease. Archives and Information Services Division, Texas State Library and Archives Commission, hereinafter cited as Records of the Third Term, Governor Elisha M. Pease, TSLA.

[5] William Phillips to Pease, Feb. 23, 1869, A. Siemering to E. M. Pease, Mar. 8, 1869, James R. Butler to E. M. Pease, Mar. 23, 1869, E. M. Wheelock to Pease, Apr. 11, 1869, Stephen Hackworth to E. M. Pease, May 28, 1869, Records of the Third Term, Governor Elisha M. Pease, TSLA; *Flake's Daily Bulletin,* Apr. 20 (quotation), 1869.

[6] A. J. Hamilton to F. Flake, Mar 18, 1869, *Galveston Daily News,* Mar. 19, see ibid., Mar. 23, May 2, 9, 1869; *Daily Austin Republican,* Apr. 21, 1869; A. J. Hamilton to Editor of *San Antonio Express,* May 16, 1869, in *Daily Austin Republican,* May 22, 1869.

[7] James G. Tracy to E. M. Pease, Apr. 8, 1869, Pease-Graham-Niles Papers, AHC, APL; Joseph J. Reynolds to U. S. Grant, Sept. 4, 1869, in *Flake's Daily Bulletin,* Oct. 5, 1869, see also Apr. 29, 1869; M. C. Hamilton to J. P. Newcomb, Apr. 30, May 14, 1869, Newcomb Papers, CAH, UTA; *Galveston Daily News,* May 11, 12, 1869; *Austin Daily Republican,* May 31, 1869.

[8] E. J. Davis to *Houston Union,* May 3, 1869, in *Flake's Daily Bulletin,* May 8, 1869.

[9] M. C. Hamilton to J. P. Newcomb, Apr. 30, May 14, 23, 1869, N. Patton to Newcomb, May 17, 1869, Newcomb Papers, CAH, UTA; Thomas H. Stribling to E. M. Pease, May, 1869; J. P. Kean to E. M. Pease, May 28, 1869, W. M. Wheelock

to Pease, June 11, 1869, Pease-Graham-Niles Papers, AHC, APL; Jas. Kean to J. L. Haynes, May 28, 1869, in *Daily Austin Republican,* June 12, 1869; *San Antonio Express* quoted in *Flake's Daily Bulletin,* June 10, 1869; E. J. Davis to Editor, June 24, 1869, draft in J. P. Newcomb Papers, CAH, UTA; "To Editor," *Flake's Daily Bulletin,* July 9, 1869 (quotation).

[10] M. C. Hamilton to J. P. Newcomb, May 23, 1869, Newcomb Papers, CAH, UTA; *Flake's Daily Bulletin,* June 10, 1869.

[11] *Flake's Daily Bulletin,* June 10, 1869.

[12] Ibid.

[13] Ibid.

[14] Ibid.

[15] Morgan C. Hamilton to J. P. Newcomb, June 19, July 25, 1869, Newcomb Papers, CAH, UTA; see Davis speech before the convention in *San Antonio Daily Express,* Jan. 31, 1869; Galveston *Daily News,* Apr. 13, 1869; see report of case of *George W. Whitmore v. R. T. P. Allen et al.* in *Galveston Daily News,* June 23, 1869, for another example. Whitmore had sued for damages against Allen and subordinate officers and court ultimately ruled Allen and others were not personally liable for their action as Confederate officers.

[16] George W. Paschal to John L. Haynes, June 20 (first quotation), 1869, J. L. Haynes to E. M. Pease, June 29, 1869 (second quotation), C. Caldwell to Pease, July 3, 1869, Pease-Graham-Niles Papers, AHC, APL; *Galveston Daily News,* July 6, 1869.

[17] *New York Tribune,* July 10, 12 (second quotation), 13, 14, 15 (first quotation), 1869; *Galveston Daily News,* July 11, 13, 1869; E. M. Pease to J. L. Haynes, July 12, 1869, in *Daily Austin Republican,* July 30, 1869; see also Charles W. Goddard to G. S. Boutwell, July 23, 1869, Thomas G. Baker to G. S. Boutwell, July 28, 1869, in Appointment Papers, Treasury Department, R.G. 56, NA; Wm. E. Chandler to B. F. Butler, Aug. 10, 1869, Butler Papers, LC; C. Schurz to Boutwell, Aug. 14, 1869, Carl Schurz Papers, LC; W. B. Moore to N. Banks, July 7, 1869, Nathaniel P. Banks Papers, LC.

[18] M. C. Hamilton to J. P. Newcomb, July 25, Aug. 17, 1869, E. J. Davis to J. P. Newcomb, Aug. 1, 1869, James P. Newcomb Papers, CAH, UTA; *Galveston Daily News,* Aug. 4, 12, 1869; *Daily Austin Republican,* Aug. 20, 1869.

[19] Joseph J. Reynolds to U. S. Grant, Sept. 4, 1869, M. C. Hamilton to J. P. Newcomb, July 25, 1869, Newcomb Papers, CAH, UTA; *Flake's Bulletin,* Oct. 5, 1869; *New York Tribune,* Sept. 10, 1869.

[20] *Galveston Daily News,* Sept. 21, Oct. 6, 1869; *Flake's Daily Bulletin,* Sept. 25, 26, 1869; *New York Tribune,* Sept. 10, 1869.

[21] E. M. Pease to J. J. Reynolds, Sept. 30, 1868, Records of the Third Term, Governor Elisha M. Pease, TSLA; Pease to Reynolds, Sept. 30, 1869, Letters Received, Civil Bureau, Fifth Military District, RG 393, NA.

22 "Proclamation by the President of the United States of America, July 15, 1869," John Y. Simon, ed., *The Papers of Ulysses S. Grant,* vol. 29 (Carbondale: Southern Illinois University Press, 1967-), 214; Davis to J. P. Newcomb, Sept. 5, 1869, Newcomb Papers, CAH, UTA.

23 John L. Haynes to Editor, July 3, 1869, in *Flake's Daily Bulletin,* July 4, 1869, see also May 30, June 18, July 4, 1869; *Galveston Daily News,* May 18, 24, June 9, 18, 27, July 6, 1869; *Daily Austin Republican,* June 12, 1869.

24 *Flake's Daily Bulletin,* Sept. 23 (quotation), 1869; *Daily Austin Republican,* Sept. 29, 1869.

25 *Flake's Daily Bulletin,* Sept. 23, 1869.

26 *Flake's Daily Bulletin,* Sept. 24, 1869.

27 *Flake's Daily Bulletin,* Oct. 1, 1869; *Galveston Daily News,* September 30, Nov. 10, 1869; *Jefferson Radical,* Nov. 13, 27 (quotations), 1869.

28 "To the Subordinate Councils, U.L.A., May 6, 1869," in G. T. Ruby to J. P. Newcomb, May 6, 1869, "To the Subordinate Councils, U.L.A., Aug. 11, 1869," James P. Newcomb Papers, CAH, UTA; G. T. Ruby to T. Baker, July 15, 1869, William Chandler Papers, LC; Chas. W. Goddard to George S. Boutwell, July 23, 1869, "Letters Received," Treasury Department, RG 56; *Galveston Daily News,* Aug. 1, Sept. 21, 26, 29, Oct. 17, 26, 1869.

29 Henry E. McCulloch to Editor, *Galveston Daily News,* Oct. 22, 1869; Ashbel Smith and others to Oran M. Roberts, Feb. 12, 1869, Oran M. Roberts Papers, CAH, UTA; see also John H. Reagan to Ashbel smith, Feb. 23, 1869, Ashbel Smith Papers, CAH, UTA: J. W. Throckmorton to [unknown], Mar. 9, 1869, in *Galveston Daily News,* Mar. 31, 1869; *McKinney Enquirer* quoted in *Galveston Daily News,* Mar. 5, 1869; *Corpus Christi Advertiser,* cited in *Galveston Daily News,* mar. 12, 1869; *Houston Telegraph,* June 13, 1869, clipping in Benjamin F. Butler Papers, LC; see *Galveston Daily News,* Mar. 13, 17, 19, 20, June 10, 1869.

30 *Flake's Dailly Bulletin,* Sept. 30, Oct. 1, 2, 3, Nov. 17, 21, 1869; *Galveston Daily News,* Sept. 30, Oct. 18, 20, 27, 31, Nov. 4, 19, 20, 24, 1869; "Address of the Democratic Central Executive Committee, Oct. 15, 1869," in *Galveston Daily News,* Oct. 21, 1869; H. B. Andrews to E. J. Davis, Aug. 20, 1870, Records. Governor Edmund J. Davis (1870–1874), TSLA; C. Caldwell to E. M. Pease, Sept. 7, 1869, Pease-Graham-Niles Papers, AHC, APL.

31 *Galveston Daily News,* Aug. 3, Sept. 1, 2, 17, 18, 22, 1869.

32 General Orders, No. 174, Oct. 1, 1869, in *Daily Austin Republican,* Oct. 4, 1869.

33 *Galveston Daily News,* Dec. 1, 2, 3, 5, 1869; *Flake's Daily Bulletin,* Dec. 9, 14, 1869; James G. Tracy to J. J. Reynolds, Dec. 11, 1869, Letters Received, Civil Bureau, Fifth Military District, RG 393, NA; Charles E. Morse to J. J. Reynolds, Dec. 7, 1869, Letters Sent, Civil Bureau, Fifth Military District, RG 393, NA; E. J.

Davis and J. G. Tracy to J. J. Reynolds, Dec. 11, 1869, Letters Received, Civil Bureau, Fifth Military District, RG 393, NA; for a discussion of election violence see Dale Baum, *The Shattering of Texas Unionism: Politics in the Lone Star State During the Civil War Era* (Baton Rouge: Louisiana State University Press, 1998), 189, 192.

[34] E. J. Davis to J. P. Newcomb, Dec. 12, 1869, James P. Newcomb Papers, San Antonio Public Library; E. J. Davis and J. G. Tracy to Joseph J. Reynolds, Dec. 11, 1869, E. J. Davis to J. J. Reynolds, Dec. 12, 1869, Letters Received, Civil Bureau, Fifth Military District, RG 393, NA.

[35] *Houston Telegraph* in *Galveston Daily News,* Dec. 17, 1869; *Galveston Daily News,* Dec. 4, 7, 1869; *Flake's Daily Bulletin,* Dec. 4, 8 (quotation), 9, 1869. Modern scholarship has shown that Republicans did have good turnouts among blacks and that whites stayed away from the poll. Historian Dale Baum has concluded that if even half of the number of men who had voted for Throckmorton in 1866 had gone to the polls Hamilton would have won handily. See Baum, *The Shattering of Texas Unionism,* 188–97.

[36] *General Order No. 19, Tabular Statement, Showing the Number of Votes Cast in Each County For and Against the Constitution, and for State Officers. Tabular Statement, Showing Number of Votes Cast in Each County for Members of Congress. Tabular Statement, Showing the Votes Cast in Each District for Senators and Representatives. Statement, Showing Vote by Counties for Clerks of District Courts, Sheriffs, Justices of the* Peace (Austin, 1870); *New York Tribune,* Dec. 29, 1869; Mike Kingston et al., *The Texas Almanac's Political History of Texas,* 61.

[37] *New York Tribune,* Dec. 24, 29, 1869; *Flake's Daily Bulletin,* Jan. 4, 1870; *Galveston Daily News,* Dec. 30, 1869. Historian Dale Baum has hypothesized that if the election in Milam and Navarro counties had continued Jack Hamilton would probably have carried them but that he could not have received enough votes to change the statewide outcome. Baum, *The Shattering of Texas Unionism,* 204.

[38] Special Orders, No. 6, Jan. 8, 1870, in *Daily Austin Republican,* Jan. 10, 1870; General Orders, No. 5, Jan. 11, 1870, mentioned in ibid., Jan. 15, 1870; *Daily Austin Republican,* Jan. 24, 1870; Elias Bonner to E. J. Davis, Jan. 18, 1870, G. A. Kelly to E. J. Davis, Feb. 16, 1870, Fred W. Sumner to E. J. Davis, Feb. 21, 1870, John A. Bagley to Davis, Mar. 6, 1870, Records of the Governor Edmund Jackson Davis, 301–61, TSLA.

[39] General Orders, No. 5, Jan. 11, 1870, mentioned in *Daily Austin Republican,* Jan. 15, 1870; *Daily Austin Republican,* Feb. 4, 14, 1870.

[40] E. J. Davis to U. S. Grant, Feb. 24, 1870, in John Y. Simon, ed., *The Papers of Ulysses S. Grant,* vol. 20, 132.

[41] *Daily Austin Republican,* Feb. 19, 25, Mar. 29, 30, Apr. 4 (quotation), 1870.

CHAPTER EIGHT: E.J. DAVIS AND THE FUTURE OF TEXAS:
THE LEGISLATIVE PROGRAM

[1] *Daily State Journal,* Mar. 15 (first quotation), 1870."Complimentary Dinner to the Governor," (second quotation) unidentified, undated newspaper clipping,
David and Harriet Condon Collection.

[2] "Complimentary Dinner to the Governor," (first quotation) unidentified,
undated newspaper clipping, David and Harriet Condon Collection; *Daily State Journal,* Mar. 15, 1870 (second quotation).

[3] *Galveston Daily News,* Mar. 18, 1870; *Goliad Guard,* in *Daily State Journal,* Mar. 13, 1870; *San Antonio Herald* in *Daily State Journal,* Mar. 19, 1870; *Daily
State Journal,* Mar. 19, 1870.

[4] *Houston Telegraph* quoted in *Daily State Journal,* Mar. 6, 1870; *Daily Austin Republican,* Apr. 6, 1870.

[5] *Daily Austin Republican,* Mar. 30 (quotation), 1870; *Galveston Daily News,*
Mar. 18, Apr. 9, 1870. "Proclamation of the Governor of the State of Texas, April 2,
1870," in *Daily Austin Republican,* Apr. 2, 1870; General Orders, No. 74, Apr. 16,
1870, in *Daily State Journal,* Apr. 19, 1870.

[6] *Houston Telegraph* quoted in *Daily State Journal,* Mar. 6, 1870; *Daily Austin Republican,* Apr. 30, 1870; *Flake's Daily Bulletin,* May 4, 1870.

[7] *Daily State Journal,* Apr. 29, 1870.

[8] Twelfth Legislatures, 1st sess., *House Journal,* 14–15.

[9] *Daily State Journal,* Apr. 19, 1870.

[10] *Washington Capital* [undated clipping] (first quotation) in Elizabeth Davis
Civil War Scrapbook. David and Harriet Condon Collection; *San Antonio Weekly
Express,* Aug. 20 (second quotation), 1874, "Clippings Scrapbook," and J. P. Newcomb
to "My Dear Nettie," Jan. 21, 1871, Apr. 28, 1872, Newcomb Papers, CAH, UTA.

[11] J. P. Newcomb to Dear Nettie, Jan. 21, 23, 1871, Newcomb Papers, CAH,
UTA.

[12] *San Antonio Weekly Express,* Aug. 20 (quotation), 1874, "Clippings Scrap-
book," Newcomb Papers, CAH, UTA; E. J. Davis to Horace Capron, Department of
Agriculture, Mar. 11, 1871, Letter Book, Records of the Governor, Edmund Jackson
Davis, TSLA; http://www.ci.austin.tx.us/library/ahc/green/public3.htm, 1/22/2008.

[13] *Washington Capital* (first quotation), undated clipping in David and Harriet Condon Collection; *Daily State Journal; Tri-Weekly Houston Union,* July 27,
1871 (second quotation), clipping in Andrew J. Hamilton file, Appointment Papers,
Treasury Department, NA, RG 90.

[14] *Daily Austin Republican,* May 2, 1870 (quotation); the entire speech is
presented in *ibid.,* May 2–5, 1870.

[15] *Daily Austin Republican,* May 2–5, 1870.

[16] *Galveston Daily News,* May 1, 15, 1870; *Flake's Daily Bulletin,* May 7, 14, 1870

[17] Gammel, VI, 185–90; *Daily Austin Republican,* Jan. 24, 1870 (first quotation); Dallas *Weekly Herald,* June 25, 1870 (second quotation); Morgan C. Hamilton to J. P. Newcomb, July 2, 1870 (third quotation), Newcomb Papers, CAH, UTA.

[18] Dallas *Weekly Herald,* June 4 (third quotation), 1870; *Daily Austin Republican,* May 23 (first quotation), 24 (second quotation), June 4, 1870.

[19] *Daily Austin Republican,* June 18, 1870; *Flake's Daily Bulletin,* May 14, 18, 1870.

[20] Gammel, *Laws of Texas,* VI, 179–82, 219–220

[21] *Daily Austin Republican,* June 9, 1870; *State Journal Appendix* (Austin: Tracy, Siemering & Co., 1870), 24, 45; M. C. Hamilton to J. P. Newcomb, June 13 (quotation), 1870, Newcomb Papers, CAH, UTA; M. C. Hamilton to *State Journal,* Nov. 10, 1870, in *Galveston Daily News,* Nov. 25, 1870.

[22] *Daily State Journal,* May 4, 16, 18, June 10, 11, 1870; *Flake's Daily Bulletin,* May 24, July 2, 1870; *Galveston Daily News,* May 4, 6, 18, 29, June 16, 23, 1870; M. C. Hamilton to J. P. Newcomb, June 26, 1870, Newcomb Papers, CAH, UTA.

[23] *Daily State Journal,* May 25 (quotation), 1870; *Flake's Daily Bulletin,* May 13, 22, June 7, 8, July 3, 1870; *Galveston Daily News,* May 22, 24, June 7, 10, 1870.

[24] *Daily State Journal,* June 18, 1870; *Daily Austin Republican,* June 22, 23, 1870.

[25] *Daily Austin Republican,* June 10 (quotation), 1870; *Daily State Journal,* July 2, 1870; See *Daily Austin Republican,* June 27, 1870 for mention of the administration's reasons for continuing the arrest of the senators; Gammel, *Laws of Texas,* VI, 193–95.

[26] *Laws of the State of Texas,* VI, 191–92, 198–205, 237 (quotation).

[27] *Flake's Daily Bulletin,* July 1, 1870; *Galveston Daily News,* June 30, 1870; *Daily State Journal,* June 30, 1870.

[28] VI, 113–18, 117 (quotation); *Constitution of the State of Texas,* Article IX.

[29] John Mason Hart, *Empire and Revolution: The Americans in Mexico Since the Civil War* (Berkeley: University of California Press, 2002), 49–51.

[30] *Special Laws of the Twelfth Legislature of the State of Texas. Called Session,* 104–10.

[31] Gammel, *Laws of Texas,* VI, 260; *Special Laws of the Twelfth Legislature of the State of Texas. Called Session,* 85–86; Texas Legislature, *Senate Journal of the Twelfth Legislature, Called Session,* 381–84, 391–94.

[32] Morgan C. Hamilton to J. P. Newcomb, June 13, 1870, Newcomb Papers, CAH, UTA; J. W. Flanagan to E. J. Davis, July 21 (second quotation), 1870, in *Galveston Daily News,* Aug. 6, 1870.

³³ *Flake's Daily Bulletin,* July 3, 1870.

³⁴ *Flake's Daily Bulletin,* July 29 (first quotation), 30, 1870; *Galveston Daily News,* July 26, 30 (second quotation), Aug. 3, 1870.

³⁵ *Senate Journal of the Twelfth Legislature. Regular Session,* 24 (quotation).

³⁶ "An Act to Give Effect to the Several provisions of the Constitution Concerning Taxes," Gammel, VI, 946–58; Edmund Thornton Miller, "A Financial History of Texas," *Bulletin of the University of Texas,* (July 1916), No. 37, See Table 11, 409, Table 13, 413.

³⁷ VI. 57–60.

³⁸ Gammel, VI, 1623–28.

³⁹ Moneyhon, *Texas After the Civil War,* 139–40.

⁴⁰ Moneyhon, *Texas After the Civil War,* 149.

⁴¹ M. C. Hamilton to *State Journal,* Nov. 10, 1870, in *Galveston Daily News,* Nov. 25, 1870. E. Davis to J. P. Newcomb, Dec. 6, 1870, Feb. 25, Mar. 1, 1871, E. J. Davis to Schuyler Colfax, Nov. 24, 1871, Davis to R. G. Ralston, Dec. 12, 1871, E. J. Davis to W. M. H. McConnell, July 10, 1871, Letter Book, Records of the Governor, Edmund Jackson Davis, TSLA; Marshall O. Roberts to W. T. Clark, Jan. 26, Mar. 7, 1871, J. P. Newcomb Papers, CAH, UTA; *Galveston Daily News,* Mar. 22, 1871.

CHAPTER NINE: THE FIGHT AGAINST LAWLESSNESS AND VIOLENCE

¹ *San Antonio Daily Express,* May 18, 1871.

² E. J. Davis to U. S. Grant, Feb. 24, 1870, in Simon, ed., *the Papers of Ulysses S. Grant,* vol. 20, 132; *Daily State Journal,* Aug. 20, 24, 1870; *Daily Austin Republican,* Dec. 14, 1870; E. J. Davis to E. Degener, Dec. 14, 1870, E. J. Davis to Edward P. Smith, Dec. 9, 1873, Letter Book, Records of the Governor, Edmund Jackson Davis, TSLA.

For the best recent scholarly overview of Indian relations up to and during the Davis years see Gary Clayton Anderson, *The Conquest of Texas: Ethnic Cleansing in the Promised Land, 1820–1875* (Norman: University of Oklahoma press, 2005).

³ E. J. Davis to Lawrie Tatum, Dec. 8, 1870 (quotation), in Letter Book, Records of the Governor. Edmund J. Davis, TSLA; E. J. Davis to U. S. Grant, Feb. 24, 1870, Simon, ed., *The Papers of Ulysses S. Grant,* vol. 20, 132; Davis to Grant, Mar. 22, 1871, ibid., vol. 21, 461.

⁴ Proclamation, May 21, 1872, in John Y. Simon, ed., *The Papers of Ulysses S. Grant,* vol. 23, 123; E. J. Davis to U. S. Grant, May 16, 1871, in ibid., 123; E. J. Davis to William Belknap, Mar. 17, 1871 (quotation), Letter Book, Records of the Governor, Edmund J. Davis, TSAL.

⁵ Carl Coke Rister, *The Southwestern Frontier* (Cleveland: Arthur H. Clark, 1928), 128–33; J. W. Wilbarger, *Indian Depredations in Texas* (Austin: Eakin Press,

1985), 554–68; *Daily State Journal,* July 18, 1871; Enoch Hoag to U. S. Grant, July 19, 1871, Simon, ed., *The Papers of Ulysses S. Grant,* vol. 22, 388 (first quotation); Lawrie Tatum to E. Hoag, Aug. 12, 1871, ibid., 389; Thomas Wistar, *et al.,* to U. S. Grant, July 28, 1871, ibid., 82 (second quotation).

[6] Charles Soward to U. S. Grant, July 15, 1872, in Simon, ed., *Papers of Ulysses S. Grant,* vol. 23, 351; see also James Dickey to U. S. Grant, Feb. 18, 1872, Franklin Moore to U. S. Grant, June 17, 1872, in ibid., 349–50; Sherman endorsement of letter of Lawrie Tatum to Enoch Hoag, Aug. 12, 1871, ibid., vol. 23, 390; Sherman endorsement of letter to William Lang to U. S. Grant, Aug. 13, 1871, ibid., p. 390; E. J. Davis to Charles Soward, Aug. 2, 1871, E. J. Davis to W. H. Smith, Sept. 7, 1871, E. J. Davis to Alfred E. Love, Sept. 7, 1871, Letter Book, Records of the Governor, Edmund Jackson Davis, TSLA.

[7] E. J. Davis to C. Delano, May 10, 1872, Letter Book, Records of the Governor, Edmund Jackson Davis, TSLA.

[8] E. J. Davis to Brig. Gen. Christopher C. Augur, Apr. 11, 1872, Davis to C. Delano, May 10, 1872, E. J. Davis to Committee for Indian Affairs, Sept. 18, 1872, Letter Book, Records of the Governor, Edmund Jackson Davis, TSLA.

[9] E. J. Davis to J. P. Newcomb, May 23, 1872, Letter Book, Records of the Governor, Edmund Jackson Davis, TSLA.

[10] E. J. Davis to Committee for Indian Affairs, Sept. 18, 1872, E. J. Davis to C. Delano, May 13, 1873, in *Galveston Daily News,* Sept. 14, 1873; E. J. Davis to C. Delano, June 4 (quotation), 1873, Letter Book, Records of the Governor, Edmund Jackson Davis, TSLA.

[11] *New York Times,* July 1, 2, 8 (quotation), 9, 1873.

[12] Sherman endorsement of Aug. 2 on letter of Benjamin R. Cowan to W. T. Sherman, July 31, 1873, forwarded William W. Belknap, in Simon, ed., *Papers of Ulysses S. Grant,* vol. 24, 439; see also W. T. Sherman to Philip H. Sheridan, Aug. 11, 1873, in ibid.; *New York Times,* Aug 5, Sept. 9, 1873; *New York Times,* Oct. 11, 12, 14, 23 (quotation), 1873; Britton Davis, *The Truth About Geronimo* (New Haven: Yale University Press, 1929), 121–22. The family apparently retained the coat until recent years.

[13] *New York Times,* Nov. 1, 1873.

[14] *New York Times,* Nov. 9, 1873; E. J. Davis to Edward P. Smith, Dec. 9, 1873, Letter Book, Records of the Governor, Edmund Jackson Davis, TSLA.

[15] Frank E. McManus to U. S. Grant, Oct. 2, 1871 (quotation), in Simon, ed., *The Papers of Ulysses S. Grant,* vol. 23, 124; E. J. Davis to U. S. Grant, Nov. 13, 1872, ibid., 130; see also P. H. Sheridan to E. G. Townsend, Apr. 16, 1872, W. H. Russell to U. S. Grant, Apr. 17, 1872, George G. Davis to U. S. Grant, Aug. 28, 1872, in ibid., 124.

[16] E. J. Davis to E. Degener, Dec. 15, 1870, Letterbook, Records of the Governor, Edmund J. Davis, TSLA; see also E. J. Davis to U. S. Grant, Nov. 13, 1872, in Simon, ed., *The Papers of Ulysses S. Grant,* vol. 23, 130.

[17] Hamilton Fish Diary, Feb. 11, 13, 14, 15, 1873, Jan. 15, 1874, in Simon, ed., *The Papers of Ulysses S. Grant,* vol. 23, 126.

[18] The extent of violence in postwar Texas has been documented amply. The only real disagreement has been over whether or not it justified the measures taken by Governor Davis. Scholars who have emphasized the extent of Reconstruction violence includes Barry Crouch, who has explored this phenomenon in numerous works, including, "A Spirit of Lawlessness: White Violence, Texas Blacks, 1865–1868," *Journal of Social History* 18 (Winter, 1984) 217–32. Crouch's work on the Freedmen's Bureau also touches on this violence and includes his *The Freedmen's Bureau and Black Texans* (Austin: University of Texas Press, 1992) plus numerous articles cited in that work. James M. Smallwood has also stressed the violent character of the period in his *Time of Hope, Time of Despair: Black Texans during Reconstruction* (Port Washington, N.Y.: National University Publications, 1981), "When the Klan Rode: White Terror in Reconstruction Texas," *Journal of the West* 25 (October 1986) 4–13. Significant effort at statistically correlated violence with political events may be seen in Gregg Cantrell, "Racial Violence and Politics in Reconstruction Texas, 1867–1868," *Southwestern Historical Quarterly* 93 (January 1990) 333–55, and Dale Baum, "Chicanery and Intimidation in the 1869 Texas Gubernatorial Race," 1867–1870," *Southwestern Historical Quarterly* 38 (July 1993) 37–54. At least one earlier study saw reports of violence to be overstated. W. C. Nunn, *Texas Under the Carpetbaggers* (Austin: University of Texas Press, 1962). William Richter, while agreeing that the period witnessed significant violence, has concluded that it did not rise to the level to justify Davis in the measures he used to suppress it.

[19] *Daily Austin Republican,* May 2, 1870.

[20] Nunn concluded that except in the case of Hill County the evidence indicated that Davis's declaration of martial law were unnecessary. W. C. Nunn, *Texas Under the Carpetbaggers* (Austin: University of Texas Press, 1962), 76.

[21] William Chambers to E. J. Davis, June 20, 1870, E. Beachamp and M. J. Morrow to E. J. Davis, Aug. 2, 1870, Letters Received, Records of the Governor, Edmund J. Davis, TSLA; *Daily State Journal,* July 29, 1870.

[22] *Weekly Austin Republican,* Oct. 5 (quotation), 1870; see also *Waco Register* in *Daily State Journal,* Oct. 7, 1870; E. J. Davis to Beauchamp, Oct. 3, 1870, and Davis to W. B. Turner *et al.,* Nov. 3, 1870, in *Message of Gov. Edmund J. Davis, with Documents in Relation to Lawlessness and Crime in Hill and Walker Counties* (Austin: J. G. Tracy, State Printer, 1871), 12–13, 14–15.

[23] See James Davidson to E. J. Davis, Feb. 1, 1871, in *Message of Gov. E. J. Davis,* 5–6 for a full description of these events; *Daily State Journal,* Feb. 10, 1871.

[24] J. Davidson to E. J. Davis, Feb. 1, 1871, "Proclamation," Jan. 10, 1871, in *Message of Gov. E. J. Davis*, 6–7, 18; *Daily State Journal*, Feb. 10, 1871.

[25] E. J. Davis to J. D. Burnett, Dec. 12, 1870 (quotation), Letter Book, Records of the Governor, Edmund Jackson Davis, TSLA; *Daily State Journal*, Feb. 10, 1871.

[26] Burnett to E. J. Davis, Jan. 12, 1871, in *Message of Gov. E. J. Davis*, 24; S. M. Jones, W. B. Bonner, and S. P. Young to E. J. Davis, Oct. 1, 1871, printed in *Journal of the House of Representatives of the Twelfth Legislature, Adjourned Session–1871* (Austin: J. G. Tracy, State Printer, 1871), 192; E. J. Davis to J. R. Burnet, Jan. 20, 1871 (first quotation), Letter Press, Texas Governors Papers of Edmund J. Davis, TSLA; E. J. Davis to Don Campbell, Feb. 8, 1871, *Message of Gov. Edmund J. Davis, with Documents in Relation to Lawlessness and Crime in Hill and Walker Counties* (Austin: J. G. Tracy, State Printer, 1871), 5 (second quotation). Davis later remitted the sentence of Outlaw. In a letter to the district judge the governor indicated that he had read the evidence of the court martial and had concluded that the man was guilty of cold-blooded murder. He saw no excuses for the crime and indicated that if the court martial had sentenced him to death, the sentence would have been carried out immediately. When the court failed to so act, Davis saw no reason to enforce the penalty that had been imposed. Outlaw, in turn, later sued the governor and Chief Davidson for wrongful arrest.---E. J. Davis to J. R. Burnett, Mar. 17, 1871, Letter Book, Texas Governors Papers of Edmund J. Davis, TSLA; *Daily State Journal*, Apr. 9, 1872.

[27] See San Antonio *Daily Herald*, Mar. 10, 1871.

[28] E. J. Davis to John A. Scott, Mar, 1871, Davis to Thomas Williams, July 19, 1871, Davis to J. B. McFarland, July 31, 1871, Davis to J. B. Cope, Sept. 6, 1871, Letter Press Book, E. J. Davis Governors Papers, TSLA; *Daily State Journal*, June 6, July 8, 1871.

[29] James King to E. J. Davis, Apr. 10, 1870, F. P. Wood to E. J. Davis, Dec. 6, 1870, Governor's Papers, TSAL; *Journal of the House of Representatives of the Twelfth Legislature, Adjourned Session–1871*, 179–223.

[30] *Journal of the House of Representatives of the Twelfth Legislature, Adjourned Session–1871*, 179.

[31] *United States Statutes at Large*, 16: 140–46, 433–40, 17: 13–15.

[32] Morgan C. Hamilton to J. P. Newcomb, June 26, 1870, J. P. Newcomb Papers, CAH, UTA; E. J. Davis to U. S. Grant, Feb. 1, 1872, in John Y. Simon, ed., *The Papers of Ulysses S. Grant*, (Carbondale and Edwardsville: Southern Illinois University Press, 1998), vol. 23, 169; E. J. Davis to George H. Williams, Feb. 13 (quotation), 1872, Letter Book, Records of the Governor. Edmund J. Davis, TSLA.

[33] E. J. Davis to U. S. Grant, Feb. 1, 1872, in Simon, ed., *The Papers of Ulysses S. Grant*, vol. 23, 169; E. J. Davis to George H. Williams, Feb. 13 (quotation), 1872, Davis to Williams, Feb. 13, 1873, Letter Book, Records of the Governor,

Edmund J. Davis, TSAL; E. J. Davis to W. T. Clark, Mar. 13, 1872, Appointments, Justice Department, RG 90, NA.

[34] *Galveston Daily News,* Jan. 18, 24, 28, Feb. 2, 10, 27, 29, Mar. 1, 8, June 13, 1872; Austin *Democratic Statesman,* Feb. 6, June 15, 1872; *Daily State Journal,* Feb. 20, 1872.

[35] A. J. Evans to George H. Williams, Apr. 10, 1873 (quotation), David Boaz to U. S. Grant, Feb. 8, 1873, in Simon, ed., *Papers of Ulysses S. Grant,* vol. 24, 336 (quotation), 335–36; *Galveston Daily News,* Mar. 9, 1873.

[36] Appleton Nomination, April 26, 1870, J. W. Flanagan to U. S. Grant, Apr. 28, 1870, C. B. Sabin to U. S. Grant, Mar. 21, Apr. 22, Aug. 18, 1870, C. C. Gillespie to U. S. Grant, June 21, 1870, in Simon, ed., *Papers of Ulysses S. Grant,* vol. 22, 290–92.

[37] Winch Nomination, Dec. 15, 1870, Samuel F. Miller to U. S. Grant, Sept. 11, 1870, A. Morrill to U. S. Grant, Oct. 11, 1870, E. J. Davis to Grant, Dec. 10, 1871, J. W. Flanagan to Grant, Dec. 19, 1871, ibid., 293–94.

[38] E. J. Davis *et al.* to U. S. Grant, April 29, 1873, ibid., vol. 23, 169–70; *Galveston Daily News,* May 13, 1873.

[39] E. J. Davis to U. S. Grant, July 7, 1873, in Simon, ed., *Papers of Ulysses S. Grant,* vol. 24, 90; *New York Times,* July 7, 9, 10, 12, 1873; *Galveston Daily News,* Aug. 2, 1873.

CHAPTER TEN: EDMUND DAVIS, TEXAS POLITICS, AND
THE DESTINY OF REPUBLICANISM

[1] *Daily Austin Republican,* June 28 (first quotation), July 2, 4, 1870; *Flake's Daily Bulletin,* July 9, 1870; *Galveston Daily News,* July 8, 1870 (second quotation); Houston *Daily Telegraph,* July 29, 1870.

[2] Report of Austin meeting in *Daily Austin Republican,* July 14, 1870; *Flake's Daily Bulletin,* July 29, 1870; *Galveston Daily News,* July 30, 1870.

[3] *Galveston Daily News,* Aug. 3 (quotation), 1870; *Flake's Daily Bulletin,* July 30, 1870.

[4] *Brenham Banner* quoted in *Daily Austin Republican,* July 14, 1870.

[5] *Daily State Journal,* July 15, 1870 (quotation); *Daily Austin Republican,* July 20, 1870; Election Proclamation, Sept. 23, 1870, in *Galveston Daily News,* Oct. 4, 1870.

[6] E. J. Davis to J. P. Newcomb, Sept. 30, 1870 (first quotation), and Davis to Gentlemen [Newcomb and Davidson], Sept. 26, 1870 (second quotation), Newcomb Papers, CAH, UTA.

[7] M. L. Bates to E. J. Davis, Aug. 16, 1870 (quotation); W. H. Howard to E. J. Davis, Sept. 1, 1870, Records of the Governor, Edmund J. Davis, TSLA; W. M.

Waddell to J. P. Newcomb, July 9, 30, 1870, Newcomb Papers, CAH, UTA; *Daily State Journal,* July 3, 1870.

[8] Thomas Sheriff to E. J. Davis, Jan. 1, 21, 1871, Letter Book, Records of the Governor, Edmund Jackson Davis, TSLA.

[9] Voting returns from Secretary of State's office, TSLA.

[10] *Galveston Daily News,* Jan. 24, 187; Winkler, ed., *Platforms of Political Parties,* 124–27.

[11] J. L. Haynes to A. H. Longley, Feb. 12, 1871 (quotation), in *San Antonio Daily Express,* Mar. 5, 1871; *Daily State Journal,* Jan. 31, 1871.

[12] *Democratic Statesman,* May 26, July 4, 20, Aug. 12, 1871; *Tri-Weekly Democratic Statesman,* Aug. 5, 1871; *Flake's Daily Bulletin,* July 19, 1871.

[13] *Democratic Statesman,* Sept. 23, 1871.

[14] *Houston Union,* quoted in *Galveston Daily News,* Aug. 24, 1871.

[15] Davis's speech at Galveston was reported in *Flake's Daily Bulletin,* Aug. 17, 1871 and the *San Antonio Daily Express,* Aug. 9, 1871; the Austin speech was reported in the *Daily State Journal,* July 30, 1871, and the Houston speech in ibid., Aug. 22, 1871. The basic speech was the same in all reports. Unless otherwise noted the quotations come from the account provided in the *State Journal.*

[16] *Galveston Daily News,* Aug. 17, 1871 (quotation); *Flake's Daily Bulletin,* Aug. 17, 1871.

[17] "To the Representatives of the Grand Council, U. L. A., in Meeting Assembled," May 18, 1871, "Circular. Grand Council Chambers, Union League of America," May 19, 1871, L. W. Stevenson to J. P. Newcomb, Feb. 13, 1871, J. P. Newcomb to G. W. Honey, May 25, 1871, J. G. Tracy to J. P. Newcomb, June 1, 1871, G. T. Ruby to Newcomb, June 13, 1871, T. G. Baker to Newcomb, June 1, 15, 26, July 22, 1871, Newcomb Papers, CAH, UTA; *Galveston Daily News,* Aug. 2, 3, 1871; *Flake's Daily Bulletin,* Aug. 3, 4, 5, 1871.

[18] *Galveston Daily News,* Aug. 20, Sept. 5, 22, 1871; *Flake's Daily Bulletin,* Aug. 26, 1871.

[19] *Annals of Travis County,* 52.

[20] A. T. Monroe to Newcomb, Sept. 5, 1871, D. Kelly to John H. Harrison, Oct. 8, 1871 (quotation), Newcomb Papers, CAH, UTA.

[21] J. M. Gibbs to J. P. Newcomb, Apr. 30, 1871 (first quotation), H. C. Hunt to Newcomb, May 2, 1871, A. M. Bryant to Newcomb, Aug. 24, 1871 (second quotation), Newcomb Papers, CAH, UTA.

[22] Wood to James P. Newcomb, Oct. 15, 1871, D. Kelly to John H. Harrison, Oct. 8, 1871 (quotation), W. T. Clark to J. P. Newcomb, Oct. 13, 1871, F. T. Wood to Newcomb, Oct. 18, 1871, Newcomb Papers, CAH, UTA; Election Returns, 1871, TSLA.

[23] For election returns see Carl H. Moneyhon, *Republicanism in Reconstruction Texas* (Austin: University of Texas Press, 1980), 209, 213.

[24] *Galveston Daily News,* Apr. 7, May 22, 23, June 18, 19, 1872; *Flake's Daily Bulletin,* Mar. 26, 1872; *Daily State Journal,* June 19, 1872; E. Degener to J. G. Tracy, May 20, 30, 1872, in *San Antonio Express,* June 12, 1872; Ferdinand Flake to E. M. Pease, mar. 29, 1872, Pease-Graham-Niles Papers, CAH, APL.

[25] *Galveston Daily News,* May 15, 16, Oct. 18, 19, 22, 23, 24, 1872; *San Antonio Express,* May 16, 21, 1872; *Daily State Journal,* May 31, 1872; Winkler, *Platforms of Political Parties in Texas,* 141–43.

[26] *Daily State Journal,* Sept. 27, 1872; J. P. Hogue to J. P. Newcomb, Nov. 11, 1872, Newcomb Papers, CAH, UTA; *New York Tribune Almanac for 1874,* 69.

[27] Texas Legislature, *Journal of the Senate of Texas: Being the Session of the Thirteenth Legislature* (Austin: John Cardwell, 1873), 26–46; *Galveston Daily News,* Jan. 18 (quotation), 1873.

[28] *Galveston Daily News,* Feb. 25, 1873.

[29] Moneyhon, *Republicanism in Reconstruction Texas,* 184–85.

[30] *San Antonio Express,* June 3, 1873; *Weekly Date Journal,* July 3, 1873; *Galveston Daiy News,* May 31, June 13, 1873.

[31] Edward T. Wallace to J. P. Newcomb, Aug. 12, 1873, Newcomb Papers, CAH, UTA; see *New York World,* Aug. 13, 1873, in *Galveston Daily News,* Aug. 21, 1873, for Democratic views on the Republican party's internal divisions; for information on the Brenham Colored Men's Convention see *Weekly State Journal,* July 10, 1871, see also *Galveston Daily News,* July 3, 4, 5, 6, 1873.

[32] *Galveston Daily News,* Aug. 19, 20 (first quotation), 21 (second quotation), 22 (third quotation), 1873.

[33] *Galveston Daily News,* Aug. 22, 1873; Winkler, *Platforms of Political Parties,* 155–57.

[34] *Galveston Daily News,* Sept. 4, 5, 6 (quotation), 1873.

[35] G. T. Ruby to John Ireland, Sept.11, 1873, in *Galveston Daily News,* Sept. 14, 1873.

[36] *Galveston Daily News,* Sept. 17, 1873.

[37] *Galveston Daily News,* Sept. 18, 1873.

[38] *Galveston Daily News,* Nov. 12, 1873; see ibid., Nov. 13, 1873, for speech at Houston.

[39] *Galveston Daily News,* Nov. 14, 1873.

[40] *San Antonio Daily Express,* Nov. 15, 1873.

[41] *Houston Union* in *Galveston Daily News,* Mar. 19 (quotation), 1873; *San Antonio Daily Express,* Nov. 22, 1873; W. P. Ballinger Diary, Dec. 2, 1873, W. P. Ballinger Papers, CAH, UTA.

[42] C. C. Augur to E. J. Davis, Jan. 7, 1874, Telegrams Received, Department of Texas, RG 393, NA; for a detailed examination of the conflict see Carl H. Moneyhon, "Edmund J. Davis in the Coke-Davis Election Dispute of 1874: A Reassessment of Character," *Southwestern Historical Quarterly,* vol. 100 (Oct. 1996), 131–51.

[43] E. J. Davis to U. S. Grant, Jan. 11, 1874, in *Daily State Journal,* Jan. 20, 1874; U. S. Grant to E. J. Davis, Jan. 12, 1874, in ibid.

[44] *Washington Capital* [n.d. 1881?], clipping in David and Harriet Condon Collection; *San Antonio Weekly Express,* Aug. 20, 1874, clippings scrapbook, Newcomb Papers, CAH, UTA.

CHAPTER ELEVEN: THE STRUGGLE FOR POLITICAL SURVIVAL: SEARCHING FOR NEW POLITICAL STRATEGY AND NATIONAL RECOGNITION

[1] *San Antonio Daily Express,* June 6 (quotation), 21, 24, 1874; *Galveston Daily News,* June 3, 11, Oct. 3, 1874; (Austin) *Daily Statesman,* May 29, June 5, 1874; S. A. Hackworth to E. M. Pease, Apr. 27, 1875, Pease-Graham Niles Collection, APL.

[2] *San Antonio Daily Express,* June 21, 24, 1874.

[3] *San Antonio Express,* June 24, 11, 1874; *Galveston Daily News,* Sept. 11, 26, Oct. 1 (quotation), 3, 1874; Boulds Baker to J. P. Newcomb, Sept. 26, 1874, Newcomb Papers, AHC, UTA.

[4] E. J. Davis to President of Chattanooga Republican Convention, Sept. 25, 1874, *New York Times,* Oct. 17, 1874.

[5] *Galveston Daily News,* June 3, 1874; *Daily Express,* Aug. 2 (quotation), 21, 1874.

[6] *Galveston Daily News,* July 30, Aug. 20, 21, 29, Sept. 2, 3, 4, 11, 26, Oct. 4, 1874; *San Antonio Daily Express,* Aug. 2, 21, Sept., 1874; *Tyler Index* quoted in *Galveston Daily News,* Sept. 29, 1874.

[7] J. G. Tracy to U. S. Grant, Nov. 13, 1872, E. J. Davis to U. S. Grant, Mar. 13, 1873, in John Y. Simon, ed., *The Papers of Ulysses S. Grant, Vol. 26: 1875* (Carbondale and Edwardsville: Southern Illinois University Press, 2003), 172 (first quotation), 173 (second quotation); E. J. Davis to B. H. Bristow, Oct. 4, 1874 (third quotation), Morgan C. Hamilton to B. H. Bristow, Oct. 3, 1874, Letters Received, Treasury Department, RG 56, NA; *New York Herald* item in *Galveston Daily News,* Apr. 27, 1865; *San Antonio Daily Express,* Apr. 4, 1874.

[8] Boulds Baker to J. P. Newcomb, Sept. 26, 1874 (first quotation), Newcomb Paper, CAH, UTA; *New York Herald,* Sept. 6 (second quotation), 1874, in *Galveston Daily News,* Sept. 12, 1874; Baker Interview, April 26, 1875, in *Galveston Daily News,* Apr. 27, 1865.

[9] *Galveston Daily News,* Oct. 11 (quotation), 14, 1874; (Nashville) *Republican Banner,* Oct. 13, 14, 1874; *Nashville Union and American,* Oct. 14, 1874; *New York Times,* Sept. 11, 13, 14, 15, 24, 1874.

[10] *New York Times,* Oct. 15 (quotation and Davis speech), 1874.

[11] *Galveston Daily News,* Nov. 4, 5, 1874.

[12] E. J. Davis to Adolph Zadek, Apr. 10, 1875, in *Galveston Daily News,* Apr. 17 (quotation), 1875; Davis to Newcomb, May 2, 1875, Newcomb Papers, AHC, UTA.

[13] Benjamin H. Bristow to Carl Schurz, Apr. 4, 1877, in Frederick Bancroft, *Speeches, Correspondence and Political Papers of Carl Schurz* (New York, G. P. Putnam's Sons, 1913), III, 412 (quotations); "occasional" to Editor, June 28, 1875, Washington, in *San Antonio Daily Express,* July 6, 1875; E. J. Davis to J. P. Newcomb, July 20, 1875, Newcomb Papers, CAH, UTA.

[14] *San Antonio Daily Express,* Apr. 27, 1875; E. J. Davis to J. P. Newcomb, Apr. 21, 22, 28, 30, 1875, Newcomb Papers, AHC, UTA; .S. A. Hackworth to E. M. Pease, Apr. 27, 1875, George W. Paschal, Jr. to Pease, May 10, 1875, Pease-Graham-Niles Papers, AHC, APL; B. G. Shields to Editor, May 4, 1875, *San Antonio Daily Express,* May 10, 1875.

[15] (Dallas) *Norton's Union Intelligencer,* May 1, 8, 1875; *Galveston Daily News,* May 22, 26, 1875; George W. Paschal, Jr. to Pease, May 10, 1875, Pease-Graham-Niles Papers, AHC, APL.

[16] *San Antonio Daily Express,* June 4, 1875.

[17] *San Antonio Daily Express,* June 2, 3, 4, 1875.

[18] J. L. Haynes to E. M. Pease, May 28, 1875, Pease-Graham-Niles Collection, AHC, APL.

[19] Alwyn Barr, *Reconstruction to Reform: Texas Politics, 1876–1906* (Austin: University of Texas Press, 1971), 9; Davis interview in *Galveston Daily News,* Aug. 8, 1875.

[20] Patrick G. Williams, *Beyond Redemption: Texas Democrats and Reconstruction* (College Station: Texas A&M University Press, 2007), 70–76, 111–15; Barr, *Reconstruction to Reform,* 9–10; Seth S. McKay, *Making the Texas Constitution of 1876* (Philadelphia: University of Pennsylvania Press, 1924), 24, 132; *San Antonio Express* in *Houston Telegraph,* Nov. 23, 1875.

[21] *Galveston Daily News,* Jan. 12, 13, 14, 15, 16, 1876; *Galveston Weekly News,* January 17, 24, 1876; *Proceedings of the Republican Convention of the State of Texas, Held at the City of Houston, January 12, 13 and 14, 1876* (Austin: Evening News Book and Job Office, 1876), *passim;* Winkler, *Platforms of Political Parties,* 177–79; *Austin Statesman,* Dec. 14, 1875; *Galveston Daily News,* Dec. 16, 1875; *San Antonio Daily Express,* Dec. 18, 1875.

[22] *Proceedings of the Republican Convention of the State of Texas, Held at the City of Houston, January 12, 13 and 14, 1876* (Austin: Evening News Book and Job Office, 1876), *passim; Galveston Weekly News,* Jan. 24, 1876.

[23] E. J. Davis to C. B. Sabin, Dec. 16, 1875 and Sabin to Davis, Dec. 24, 1875, Pamphlet, AHC, UTA; Davis quotation from *San Antonio Daily Express,* Jan. 29, 1876; Davis letter of February 9, 1876 cited in ibid., Feb. 18, 1876; *Galveston Daily News,* Jan. 12, 13, 14, 15, 1876; *Galveston Weekly News,* January 17, 24, 1876; *Proceedings of the Republican Convention of the State of Texas, Held at the City of Houston, January 12, 13 and 14, 1876* (Austin: Evening News Book and Job Office, 1876), *passim.*

[24] Davis letter of February 9, 1876 cited in ibid., Feb. 18, 1876 *San Antonio Daily Express,* Jan. 29, 1876; *Galveston Daily News,* Jan. 15, 1876.

[25] *Galveston Daily News,* Feb. 16, 17, 18, 21,1876; *San Antonio Daily Express,* Feb. 17, 22, 24, 1876; W. P. Ballinger Diary, Feb. 15, 1876, Ballinger Papers, AHC, UTA; McKay, *Constitutional Convention of 1875,* 183.

[26] *San Antonio Daily Express,* June 21, 1876; A. B. Norton to R. B. Hayes, May 6, 1876, Rutherford B. Hayes Papers, Hayes Library, Fremont, Ohio; Hans L. Trefouse, *Rutherford B. Hayes* (New York: Times Books, Henry Holt & Company, 2002), 66–68.

[27] E. J. Davis to J. P. Newcomb, July 8 (first quotation), July 19 (second quotation), Aug. 15 (third quotation), 1876, Newcomb Papers, AHC, UTA; E. J. Davis to A. Zadek, Aug. 16, 1876 (fourth quotation) Treasury Department Records, RG 56, NA; William A. Welsh to R. B. Hayes, Aug. 28, 1876, Rutherford B. Hayes Papers; Barr, *Reconstruction to Reform,* 32–33; Vincent DeSantis, *Republicans Face the Southern Question* (Baltimore: The Johns Hopkins Press, 1959), 36–65.

[28] E. J. Davis to Committee, Oct. 23, 1876, in *Galveston Daily News,* Oct. 28, 1876; *Galveston Daily News,* Sept. 17, 19, Oct. 22, 24, 26, 28, 29, Nov. 4, 5, 1876; E. J. Davis to J. P. Newcomb, Aug. 18, 1876, Newcomb Papers, AHC, UTA; S. A. Hackworth to E. M. Peae, Sept. 14, 1876, James Shaw to E. M. Peae, Oct. 16, 1876, Pease-Graham-Niles Papers, CAH, APL.

[29] E. J. Davis to Alphonso Taft, Sept. 9, 1876, *Galveston Daily News,* Nov. 4, 1876; D. J. Baldwin to Alphonso Taft, Oct. 11, 1876, *New York Times,* Oct. 22, 1876; *Galveston Daily News,* Nov. 2, 1876.

[30] *Galveston Daily News,* Nov. 8, 1876; Kingston, et al., ed. *The Texas Almanac's Political History of Texas,* 72–75.

[31] E. J. Davis to R. B. Hayes, Mar. 14, 1877, Rutherford B. Hayes Papers, Hayes Library, Fremont Ohio; C. Vann Woodward, *Reunion and Reaction: The Compromise of 1877 and the End of Reconstruction* (Boston: Little, Brown and Company, 1951), 25; DeSantis, *Republicans Face the Southern Question,* 36–65.

[32] J. R. Burns to E. J. Davis, Apr. 9, 1877, *Galveston Daily News,* Apr. 27, 1877; Interview with James H. Bell, *Galveston Daily News,* Apr. 1, 1877.

Concerning Davis's financial situation see E. J. Davis to J. P. Newcomb, Aug. 14, Sept. 11, 1877, Newcomb Papers, SAPL.

"Britton Davis," F. B. Heitman, *Historical Register and Dictionary of the United States Army* (2 vols. Washington: Government Printing Office, 1903), vol. I, 357; "The Texas German and English Academy, 1876–1902," http://www.austintxgensoc.org/records/bickler.php. Consulted 2/24/2008.

[33] E. J. Davis to J. P. Newcomb, May 9, June 4, 1877 (first quotation), July 7, 1877 (second quotation), Newcomb Papers, AHC, UTA; *Galveston Daily News,* July 17, 1877.

[34] *Galveston Daily News,* July 17, 1877, carries catalogue of charges leveled against Purnell; E. J. Davis to J. P. Newcomb, Aug. 9 (quotation), 1877, Newcomb Papers, AHC, UTA; E. J. Davis to J. P. Newcomb, Newcomb Letters, SAPL.

[35] Carrie A. Purnell to R. B. Hayes, Aug. 11, 1877, Hayes Papers, Fremont, Ohio; E. J. Davis to J. P. Newcomb, Aug. 14, 1877, Newcomb Papers, AHC, UTA; see also *New York Times,* Aug. 14, 18, 1877.

[36] E. J. Davis to J. P. Newcomb, Aug. 14, Sept. 11, Oct 2, 17, Nov. 4, 1877, Feb. 1, 1878; E. J. Davis to Stephen Powers, Feb. 11, 15, 1878, James B. Wells Papers, AHC, UTA; "City of San Antonio *v.* Thomas J. Mehaffy, 96 U. S. 312, 24 L. Ed. 816 (1878); J. R. Burns to Nathaniel P. Banks, May 24, 1878, N. P. Banks Papers, LC: J. R. Burns to Rutherford B. Hayes, May 27, 1878, Letters Received, Treasury Department, RG 56; NA; J. R. Burns to John Sherman, July 5, Nov. 14, Dec. 12 (quotation), 1878, John Sherman Papers, Library of Congress.

[37] Barr, *Reconstruction to Reform,* 43–48.

[38] Winkler, *Platforms,* 187–90; E. J. Davis to O. & H. Deitzel, July 31, 1880, *New York Times,* Aug. 9, 1880.

[39] Barr, *Reconstruction to Reform,* 48–49; E. J. Davis to O. & H. Deitzel, July 31, 1880, *New York Times,* Aug. 9, 1880; *San Antonio Daily Express,* Oct. 3, 4 (quotation), 1878; J. R. Burns to John Sherman, Nov. 14, 1878, John Sherman Papers, LC: E. J. Davis to J. P. Newcomb, oct. 5, 1878, Newcomb Correspondence, AHC, UTA.

[40] A.W. Terrell to Ashbel Smith, Nov. 25, 1878, Ashbel Smith Papers, AHC, UTA; Barr, *Reconstruction to Reform,* 52–53.

[41] J. R. Burns to John Sherman, Nov. 19, 1878, R. B. Hayes Papers; Kingston, et al., *The Texas Almanac's Political History of Texas,* 58–62.

[42] E. J. Davis to J. P. Newcomb, Dec. 10, 1878 (first quotation), Feb. 8, (second quotation), July 11, 1879, Newcomb Papers, AHC, UTA; Guy M. Bryan to Rutherford B. Hayes, Nov. 30, 1878, Appointments, Department of Justice, RG 90, NA.

[43] E. J. Davis to E. M. Pease, Dec. 5, 18 (first quotation), 24; Davis to J. P. Newcomb, Nov. 13, 1880 (second quotation), Newcomb Papers, AHC, UTA; E.M. Pease to John Sherman, Dec. 10, 1880, Treasury Department, RG 50, NA; E. J. Davis to Rutherford B. Hayes, Jan. 10, 1881, Hayes Papers.

CHAPTER TWELVE: A NEW POLITICAL DIRECTION

[1] E. J. Davis to John O. Walker, Dec. 11, 1879 (first quotation), John Sherman Papers, LC; *New York Times,* Jan. 23, 1880, 4 (second quotation).

[2] *Galveston Daily News,* Mar. 23, 1880.

[3] *New York Times,* Mar. 25, 31, 1880; *Galveston Daily News,* Mar. 23, 24, 26, 1880; (Austin) *Daily Democratic Statesman,* Mar. 27, 1880; E. M. Wheelock to John O. Walker, Dec. 22, 1879, R. M. Moore to John Sherman, Dec. 23, 1879, John Sherman Papers, LC.

[4] *Daily Democratic Statesman,* Mar. 26, Apr. 1, 1880; E. J. Davis to O. & H. Deitzel, July 31, 1880, in *New York Times,* Aug. 9, 1880.

[5] *New York Times,* Mar. 26, 1880; (Austin) *Daily Democratic Statesman,* Mar. 26, 1880; Winkler ed., *Platforms of Political Parties in Texas,* 196.

[6] E. J. Davis to J. P. Newcomb, May 7, 1880, Newcomb Papers, CAH, UTA.

[7] "Campaign Literature—To the Republican party throughout the United States, Greetings, . . . May 1, 1880, Galveston," [unidentified newspaper clipping], Elizabeth Davis Scrapbook, David and Harriet Condon Collection.

[8] A.D.C. to Editor, Mar. 11, 1880, *St. Paul Dispatch* [undated clipping], Elizabeth Davis Scrapbook, Harriet and David Condon Collection.

[9] *New York Times,* June 8, 9, 1880; Ira Rutkow, *James A. Garfield* (New York: Henry Holt and Company, 2006), 50–57; Garfield quoted in Vincent DeSantis, *Republicans Face the Southern Question—The New Departure Years, 1877–1897* (Baltimore: Johns Hopkins University press, 1959), 135.

[10] *New York Times,* June 9, 1880; Zachary Karabell, *Chester Alan Arthur* (New York: Times Books, Henry Holt and Company, 2004), 40–42.

[11] *New York Times,* April 22, Aug 9 (quotation), 1880; Winkler, *Political Parties,* 199–201, 202–203; Roscoe C. Martin, "The Greenback Party in Texas," *Southwestern Historical Quarterly,* 30 (January 1927), 169; Wooten, II, 242; Alwyn Barr, *Reconstruction to Reform* (Austin: University of Texas Press, 1971), 57.

[12] Barr, *Reconstruction to Reform,* 58–59.

[13] Davis to O. and H. Deitzel, July 31, 1880, from *Texas Post,* quoted in *New York Times,* Aug. 9, 1880.

[14] *Galveston Daily News,* Aug. 26, 1880; *New York Times,* Aug. 26, 1880; for an assessment of the motives of the Central Committee see "A Plot to Divide Texas," *New York Times,* Nov. 29, 1880, p. 4.

[15] "Call for Convention of Boys in Blue," Sept. 27, 1880, New York City, circular in Rutherford B. Hayes Papers; *New York Times,* Oct. 9, 1880; "October 4, 1880 Speech," pamphlet, CAH, UTA.

16 "The Galveston Spectator Suggests," *Galveston Spectator* [n.d.] clipping, "Untitled article," [n.d.], unidentified clipping, Elizabeth Davis Scrapbook, Harriet and David Condon Collection.

17 Barr, *Reconstruction to Reform,* 59; "A Plot to Divide Texas," *New York Times,* Nov. 29, 1880.

18 J. C. DeGress to J. P. Newcomb, Apr. 5, 1881, Newcomb Papers, CAH, UTA.

19 E. J. Davis to J. P. Newcomb, Mar. 8, (first quotation), Mar. 14 (second quotation), 1881, Newcomb Papers, CAH, UTA.

20 E. J. Davis to J. P. Newcomb, Mar. 14, May 4, (quotation), May 14, 1881, Newcomb Papers, CAH, UTA; "Cadet Studies Finished," unidentified clipping [n.d.], Elizabeth Davis Scrapbook, Harriet and David Condon Collection.

21 S. B. Maxey to Guy M. Bryan, Nov. 4, 1881, Guy M. Bryan Papers, CAH, UTA.

22 "A Southern Republican Plea," in *New York Times,* Dec. 27, 1881, p. 1, "Cabinet Speculations," undated, unidentified clipping, (Washington) *Critic,* undated clipping (first quotation), *San Antonio Evening Light,* Nov. 19 (second quotation), 1881, *Austin Citizen,* undated clipping (third quotation), *Union Land Register,* Dec. 2 (fourth quotation), 1881, all clippings in Elizabeth Davis Scrapbook, Harriet and David Condon Collection.

23 *San Antonio Evening Light,* Nov. 19, 1881, clipping in Lizzie Davis Scrapbook, David and Harriet Condon Collection; Lizzie Davis to J. P. Newcomb, Oct. 25, 1881 (quotation), E. J. Davis to J. P. Newcomb, Oct. 27, 1881, Don Cameron to J. P. Newcomb, Nov. 28, 1881, Newcomb Papers, CAH, UTA.

24 E. J. Davis to J. P. Newcomb, Nov. 18, 1881, E. J. Davis to Newcomb, Dec. 27, 1881, Newcomb Papers, CAH, UTA.

25 E. J. Davis to J. P. Newcomb, Apr. 10, June 6, July 4 (first quotation), 10 (second quotation), 1882, Newcomb Papers, CAH, UTA.

26 *Washington Post* in "Liberalism in Texas," *New York Times,* Dec. 12, 1881, p. 1.

27 *New York Times,* July 5, 1882.

28 E. J. Davis to J. P. Newcomb, Aug 10 (quotation), 21, 1882, Newcomb Papers, CAH, UTA.

29 E. J. Davis to J. P. Newcomb, May 11 (quotation), 23, July 24, 1880, Newcomb Papers, CAH, UTA.

30 "To the Voters of the 10th Congressional District, August 1, 1882," broadside in Newcomb Papers, CAH, UTA; "For Congress," [n.d.] unidentified newspaper clipping, David and Harriet Condon Collection.

31 *Dallas Daily Herald,* Aug. 24, 25, 1882.

[32] "The Texas Republican Call," *New York Times,* July 5, 1882, p. 3 (quotation); "Texas Republican Convention," *New York Times,* Aug. 24, 1882, p. 1.

[33] E. J. Davis to J. P. Newcomb, Aug. 31, 1882, Newcomb Papers, CAH, UTA, Paul Casdorph, *History,* 44; Winkler, *Political Parties,* 206–208, 212–14.

[34] Unidentified newspaper clipping, Elizabeth Davis Scrapbook, Harriet and David Condon Collection.

[35] E. J. Davis to J. P. Newcomb, Nov. 8, 11 (quotation), 20, 1882, Newcomb Papers, CAH, UTA.

[36] Lizzie Davis to J. P. Newcomb, Nov. 19, 1882, E. J. Davis to J. P. Newcomb, Nov. 20, 1882, Newcomb Papers, CAH, UTA.

[37] "Manuscript of biographical sketch of Edmund J. Davis written by James P. Newcomb in September 1907," Newcomb Papers, CAH, UTA.

[38] "Manuscript of biographical sketch of Edmund J. Davis written by James P. Newcomb in September 1907," Newcomb Papers, CAH, UTA.

[39] "Ex-Governor Davis," unidentified newspaper clipping [n.d.], Elizabeth Davis Scrapbook, Harriet and David Condon Collection.

BIBLIOGRAPHY

PRIMARY SOURCES

MANUSCRIPT SOURCES

The Dolph Briscoe Center for American History, University of Texas at Austin:
    William Pitt Ballinger Papers.
    Guy M. Bryan Papers.
    Biographical File–E. J. Davis.
    Ben H. Epperson Papers.
    Andrew J. Hamilton Papers.
    James P. Newcomb Papers.
    John H. Reagan Papers.
    Oran M. Roberts Papers.
    Ashbel Smith Papers.
    J. B. Wells Papers.
Center for Austin History, Austin Public Library, Austin:
    Pease-Graham-Niles Papers.
Harriet and David Condon Collection.
Library of Congress:
    Nathaniel P. Banks Papers.
    Benjamin F. Butler Papers.
    William Chandler Papers.
    Samuel P. Heintzelman Papers.
    Carl Schurz Papers.
    John Sherman Papers.
National Archives:
    Generals papers, RG 94.
    Department of Justice, RG 50:
        Appointments.
    Treasury Department, RG 56:
        Letters Received.
        Records of the Division of Appointments, Registers Relating to customs Service Appointments, Records Relating to "Customhouse Nominations" ("K" Series).
United States Bureau of the Census:
    1850, 1860, 1870 Manuscript Census, Galveston County.
United States Congress:
    Legislative Records, "Select Committee on Reconstruction," RG 233.

United States Military Academy Cadet Applications, 1805–1866,
    Microfilm Publication Number 688.
Military Service Records–E. J. Davis File.
Records of the Fifth Military District, RG 393.
Records of the Headquarters of the Army, RG 108 or 107.
Rosenberg Library, Galveston, Texas:
    Edmund J. Davis Letters.
Rutherford B. Hayes Library, Fremont, Ohio:
    Rutherford B. Hayes Presidential Papers.
San Antonio Public Library:
    James P. Newcomb Papers.
Texas State Library and Archives Commission. Archives and Information Services
    Division:
    Texas. Governor:
        Records. Governor Edmund J. Davis (1870–1874).
        Records of the First Two Terms, Texas Governor Elisha Marshall Pease
            (1853–57).
        Records of the Third Term, Texas Governor Elisha Marshall Pease
            (1867–1869).
    Texas. Secretary of State:
        Election Returns.

GOVERNMENT PUBLICATIONS

Gammel, *Laws of Texas.*
Texas. Constitutional Convention:
    Ernest W. Winkler, ed., *Journal of the Secession Convention of Texas.* Austin:
        Austin Printing Co., 1912.
    *Journal of the Texas State Convention, Assembled at Austin, February 7, 1866,
        Adjourned April 2, 1866.* Austin, 1966.
    *Journal of the Reconstruction Convention Which Met at Austin, Texas, June 1,
        A.D. 1868.* Austin: Tracy, Siemering & Co., Printers, 1870.
    Journal of the Reconstruction Conventoin, State of Texas. Second Session. Aus-
        tin: Tracy, Siemering & Co., Printers, 1870.
    Ordinances of the Constitutional Convention of 1866.
Texas. Constitution:
    The Constitution as Amended and the Ordinances of the Convention of 1866.
        Austin: Printed at Gazette Office by Jo. Walker, State Printer, 1866.

Texas. Governor:

>Message of Gov. Edmund J. Davis, with Documents in Relation to Lawlessn-
>aess and Crime in Hill and Walker Counties. Austin: J. G. Tracy, State
>Printer, 1871.

Texas. Legislature:

>Journal of the House of Representatives of the Twelfth Legislature, Adjourned
>Session–1871. Austin: J. G. Tracy, State Printer, 1871.

>Journal of the Senate of Texas: Being the Session of the Thirteenth Legislature.
>Austin: John Cardwell, 1873.

U.S. Bureau of the Census:

>Sixth Census, 1840.

>Seventh Census, 1850.

>Eighth Census, 1860.

U.S. Congress:

>39th Cong., 2nd sess., H. Misc Docs., no. 35. "Memorial on Behalf of the
>Citizens of Western Texas."

>40th Cong., 3rd Sess., H. Exec. Docs., no. 1. "Annual Report of the Secretary
>of War for 1868."

>40th Cong., 3rd Sess., H. Exec. Docs., no. 97. "Report of Commander of Fifth
>Military District on Adjournment of the Constitutional Convention
>of Texas."

NEWSPAPERS

Austin Republican.

Austin -Democratic Statesman.

Austin State Gazette.

Congressional Globe.

Corpus Christi Caller Times.

Dallas Herald.

Dallas Norton's Union Intelligencer.

Flake's Daily Bulletin.

Galveston News.

Harrison Flag.

Houston Union.

Houston Telegraph.

New York Herald.

The New York Times.

New York Tribune.

Northern Standard (Clarksville).

Norton's Union Intelligencer (Dallas).

Philadelphia Inquirer.

Republican Banner, Nashville, Tennessee.

San Antonio *Evening Light.*

San Antonio *Herald.*

San Antonio Express.

Southern Intelligencer.

State Gazette (Austin).

State Journal (Austin).

Tyler Reporter.

Union and American (Nashville, Tennessee).

PRINTED PRIMARY SOURCES

Bancroft, Frederick. *Speeches, Correspondence and Political Papers of Carl Schurz.* New York: G. P. Putnam's Sons, 1913.

Barr, Alwyn. "Records of the Confederate Military Commission in San Antonio, July 2, October 10, 1862," *Southwestern Historical Quarterly,* 73 (October 1969).

Basler, Roy ed., *Collected Works of Abraham Lincoln.* 9 vols. Rutgers, New Jersey: Rutgers University Press, 1953.

Cheesman, Bruce S., ed. and anno. *Maria von Blücher's Corpus Christi: Letters from the South Texas Frontier, 1849–1879.* College Station: Texas A&M University Press, 2002.

Davis, Britton. *The Truth About Geronimo.* New Haven: Yale University Press, 1929.

Hayes, Charles W. *Galveston: History of the Island and the City.* 2 vols.; Austin: Jenkins Garrett Press, 1974.

"Important letter from Gov. Davis," *The New York Times,* Oct. 17, 1874.

Proceedings of the Republican State Convention Assembled at Austin, August 12, 1868. Austin: Daily Republican Book & Job Office, 1868.

Proceedings of the Republican Convention of the State of Texas, Held at the City of Houston, January 12, 13 and 14, 1876. Austin: Evening News Book and Job Office, 1876.

Speeches of Colonel John Burke of Harrison County, in the State Convention Assembled At Austin, February and March, 1866. Austin: State Gazette Book and Job Office, 1866.

Statement and Memorial in Relation to Political Affairs in Texas, by Members of the Late Convention and Other Citizens of that State, Addressed to the Hon. B. F. Butler. Washington, D. C.: McGill & Witherow, Printers and Stereotypers, 1869.

Simon, John Y., ed., *The Papers of Ulysses S. Grant.* Carbondale: Southern Illinois University Press, 1967.

Tabular Statement, General Order No. 19, Showing the Number of Votes Cast in Each County For and Against the Constitution, and for State Officers. Tabular Statement, Showing Number of Votes Cast in Each County for Members of Congress. Tabular Statement, Showing the Votes Cast in Each District for Senators and Representatives. Statement, Showing Vote by Counties for Clerks of District Courts, Sheriffs, Justices of the Peace. Austin: n.p., 1870.

The War of the Rebellion: A Compilation of the Official Records of the Union and Confederate Armies. 128 vols. Washington, D.C.: Government Printing Office, 1880–1901.

Thompson, Jerry, ed. *Fifty Miles and a Fight: Major Samuel Peter Heitzelman's Journal of Texas and the Cortina War.* Austin: Texas State Historical Association, 1998.

Tilley, Nannie M. ed. *Federals on the Frontier: The Diary of Benjamin F. McIntyre, 1862–1864.* Austin: University of Texas Press, 1963.

Williams, Amelia W., and Eugene C. Barker, eds. *The Writings of Sam Houston, 1813–1863.* 8 vols. Austin: 1943.

Winkler, Ernest William., ed. *Platforms of Political Parties in Texas. University of Texas Bulletin No. 53.* Austin: University of Texas, 1916.

ON-LINE PRIMARY SOURCES

Henry Ketzle Diary, http:www.ketzle.com/diary/ accessed March 22, 2006.

Samuel Hayes Letter, http://www.geocities.com/Heartland/2101/hayes-letter. html?200618/. Accessed April 18, 2006.

Patterson Letter, http:www.antiqbook.com/books/bookinfo.phtml?o=cum& bnr=211569. Accessed March 22, 2006.

SECONDARY SOURCES

BOOKS

Anderson, Gary Clayton. *The Conquest of Texas: Ethnic Cleansing in the Promised Land, 1820–1875.* Norman: University of Oklahoma Press, 2005.

Barr, Alwyn. *Reconstruction to Reform: Texas Politics, 1876–1906.* Austin: University of Texas Press, 1971.

Biographical Directory of the United States Congress, 1774–2005. Washington, D.C.: Government Printing Office, 2005.

Blank, Joan Gill. *Key Biscayne: A History of Miami's Tropical Island and the Cape Florida Lighthouse.* Sarasota, Florida: Pineapple Press, Inc., 1996.

Barr, Alwyn. *Reconstruction to Reform.* Austin: University of Texas Press, 1971.

Baum, Dale. *The Shattering of Texas Unionism: Politics in the Lone Star State During the Civil War Era.* Baton Rouge: Louisiana State University Press, 1998.

Beverly, James M. *A History of the Ninety-First Regiment, Illinois Volunteer Infantry.* White Hall, Ill.; Pearce Printing Company, 1913.

Buenger, Walter L. *Secession and the Union in Texas.* Austin: University of Texas Press, 1984.

Campbell, Randolph B. *Grass-Roots Reconstruction in Texas, 1865–1880.* Baton Rouge: Louisiana State University Press, 1997.

Crouch, Barry A., and Donaly E. Brice. *Cullen Montgomery Baker, Reconstruction Desperardo.* Baton Rouge: Louisiana State University Press, 1997.

DeSantis, Vincent. *Republicans Face the Southern Question: The New Departure Years, 1877–1897.* Baltimore, MD: The Johns Hopkins Press, 1959.

Elliott, Claude. *Leathercoat: The Life History of a Texas Patriot.* San Antonio: Standard Printing Company, 1938.

Ewer, James K. *The Third Massachusetts Cavalry in the War for the Union.* Maplewood, Mass: The W. G. J. Perry Press, 1903.

Fletcher, Samuel H. *The History of Company A, Second Illinois Cavalry.* n. p. 1912.

Foner, Eric. *Reconstruction: America's Unfinished Revolution, 1863–1877.* New York: Harper & Row Publishers, 1988.

Fornell, Earl W. *The Galveston Era: The Texas Crescent on the Eve of Secession.* Austin: University of Texas Press, 1961.

Friend, Llerena. *Sam Houston: The Great Designer.* Austin: University of Texas Press, 1954.

Hart, John Mason. *Empire and Revolution: The Americans in Mexico Since the Civil War.* Berkeley: University of California Press, 2002.

Hinojosa, Gilberto Miguel. *A Borderlands Town in Transition, Laredo, 1755–1870.* College Station: Texas A&M University Press, 1983.

Karabell, Zachary. *Chester Alan Arthur.* New York: Times Books, Henry Holt and Company, 2004.

Kearney, Milo and Anthony Knopp. *Boom and Bust: The Historical Cycles of Matamoros and Brownsville.* Austin: Eakin Press, 1991.

Kingston, Mike, *et al. The Texas Almanac's Political History of Texas.* Austin: Eakin Press, 1992.

McKay, Seth S. *Making the Texas Constitution of 1876.* Philadelphia: University of Pennsylvania Press, 1924.

McPherson, James M. *Ordeal by Fire: the Civil War and Reconstruction.* New York: McGraw-Hill, Inc., 1992.

Marten, James. *Texas Divided: Loyalty and Dissent in the Lone Star State, 1856–1874.* Lexington: University of Kentucky Press, 1990.

Moneyhon, Carl H. *Republicanism in Reconstruction Texas.* Austin: University of Texas Press, 1980.

———. *Texas After the Civil War: The Struggle of Reconstruction.* College Station: Texas A&M University Press, 2004.

Nunn, William Curtis. *Texas Under the Carpetbaggers.* Austin: University of Texas Press, 1962.

Procter, Ben H. *Not Without Honor: The Life of John H. Reagan.* Austin: University of Texas Press, 1962.

Ramsdell, Charles W. *Reconstruction in Texas.* New York: Columbia University Press, 1910.

Richter, William L. *The Army in Texas During Reconstuction, 1865–1870.* College Station: Texas A&M University Press, 1987.

———. *Overreached on All Sides: the Freedmen's Bureau Administrators in Texas, 1865–1868.* College Station: Texas A&M University Press, 1991.

Rister, Carl Coke. *The Southwestern Frontier.* Cleveland: Arthur H. Clark, 1928.

Roberts, Oran M., "The Political, Legislative, and Judicial History of Texas for its Fifty Years of Statehood, 1845–1895," in Dudley G. Wooten, ed. *A Comprehensive History of Texas, 1685–1897.* Dallas: William G. Scarff, 1898.

Rutkow, Ira. *James A. Garfield.* New York: Times Books, Henry Holt and Company, 2004.

Smallwood, James M. *Time of Hope, Time of Despair: Black Texans During Reconstruction.* Port Washington: Kennikat Press, 1981.

Spaw, Patsy McDonald. Ed. *The Texas Senate, Volume II: Civil War to the Eve of Reform, 1861–1889.* College Station: Texas A&M University Press, 1999.

Thompson, Jerry D. *Warm Weather & Bad Whiskey: The 1886 Laredo Election Riot.* El Paso: Texas Western Press, 1991.

———. *Cortina: Defending the Mexican Name in Texas.* College Station: Texas A&M University Press, 2007.

Trefouse, Hans L. *Rutherford B. Hayes.* New York: Times Books, Henry Holt & Company, 2002.

Wallace, Ernest. *The Howling of the Coyotes: Reconstruction Efforts to Divide Texas.* College Station: Texas A&M University Press, 1979.

Waller, John L. *Colossal Hamilton of Texas: A Biography of Andrew Jackson Hamilton, Militant Unionist and Reconstruction Governor.* El Paso: Texas Western University Press, 1968.

Wilbarger, J. W. Wilbarger. *Indian Depredations in Texas.* Austin: Eakin Press, 1985.

Williams, Patrick G. *Beyond Redemption: Texas Democrats and Reconstruction.* College Station: Texas A&M University Press, 2007.

Winters, John D. *The Civil War in Louisiana.* Baton Rouge: Louisiana State University Press, 1963.

Woodward, C. Vann. *Reunion and Reaction: The Compromise of 1877 and the End of Reconstruction.* Boston: Little, Brown and Company, 1951.

ARTICLES AND BOOK CHAPTERS

Ashcraft, Alan C. "Role of the Confederate Provost Marshals in Texas," *Texana* 6 (1968), 390–92.

Avillo, Phillips, Jr. "Phantom Radicals: Texas Republicans in Congress, 1870–1873," *Southwestern Historical Quarterly,* 77 (April 1974), 431–44.

Baenziger, Ann Patton. "The Texas State Police during Reconstruction: A Reexamination," *Southwestern Historical Quarterly,* 72 (April 1969), 470–91.

Baggett, James A. "Beginning of Radical Rule in Texas: The Special Legislative Session of 1870," *Southwestern Journal of Social Education,* 2 (Spring/Summer 1972), 28–38.

Baum, Dale. "Chicanery and Intimidation in the 1869 Texas Gubernatorial Race," *Southwestern Historical Quarterly,* 97 (July 1993), 37–54.

Betts, Vicki. "Private and Amateur Hangings": The Lynching of W. W. Montgomery, March 15, 1863." *Southwestern Historical Quarterly,* 88 (July 1984), 145–66.

Brockman, John. "Railroads, Radicals, and the Militia Bill: A New Interpretation of the Quorum-Breaking Incident of 1870," *Southwestern Historical Quarterly,* 25 (October 1987), 105–22.

Campbell, Randolph B. "Scalawag District Judges: The E. J. Davis Appointees," *Houston Review,* 14 (1992), 75–88.

———. "Carpetbagger Rule in Texas: An Enduring Myth," *Southwestern Historical Quarterly,* 98 (April 1994), 587–96.

Cantrell, Gregg. "Racial Violence and Reconstruction Politics in Texas, 1867–1868," *Southwestern Historical Quarterly,* 93 (January 1990), 333–55.

Crouch, Barry A. "A Spirit of Lawlessness: White Violence, Texas Blacks, 1865–1868." *Journal of Social History,* 18 (Winter 1984), 217–32.

———. "'Unmanacling' Texas Reconstruction: A Twenty Year Perspective." *Southwestern Historical Quarterly,* 93 (January 1990), 275–302.

Elliott, Claude. "Union Sentiment in Texas, 1861–1865," *Southwestern Historical Quarterly,* 50 (April 1947), 449–77.

Ewing, Floyd F., Jr. "Origins of Unionist Sentiment on the West Texas Frontier," *West Texas Historical Association Year Book,* 32 (1956), 3–29.

Field, William T. Jr. "the Texas State Police, 1870–1873," *Texas Military History,* 5 (1965), 139–41.

Havins, T. R. "Administration of the Sequestration Act in the Confederate District Court for the Western District of Texas, 1861–1865," *Southwestern Historical Quarterly,* 43 (January 1940), 296–322.

Hunter, John Warren. "The Fall of Brownsville, 1863." In Milo Kearny, ed. *More Studies in Brownsville History.* Brownsville: American University at Brownsville, 1989.

"Life and Background of William Alfred Neale," *Southwestern Historical Quarterly,* 47 (July 1943), 64–66.

Martin, Roscoe C. "The Greenback Party in Texas," *Southwestern Historical Quarterly,* 30 (January 1927), 161–77.

Miller, Edmund Thornton. "A Financial History of Texas," *Bulletin of the University of Texas,* 37 (July, 1916).

Moneyhon, Carl H. "George T. Ruby and the Politics of Expedience in Texas," in Howard N. Rabinowitz, ed., *Southern Black Leaders of the Reconstruction Era.* Urbana: University of Illinois Press, 1982, pp. 364–78.

———. "Public Education and Texas Reconstruction Politics, 1871–1874," *Southwestern Historical Quarterly,* 92 (January 1989), 393–416.

———. "Edmund J. Davis in the Coke-Davis Election Dispute of 1874: A Reassessment of Character," *Southwestern Historical Quarterly,* 100 (October 1996), 131–45.

Sanbo, Anna Irene. "Beginnings of the Secession Movement in Texas," *Southwestern Historical Quarterly,* 18 (July 1914), 41–73.

———. "The First Session of the Secession Convention of Texas." *Southwestern Historical Quarterly,* 18 (October 1914), 162–194.

Shelley, George E. "The Semicolon Court of Texas," *Southwestern Historical Quarterly,* 48 (April 1945), 451–68.

Shook Robert W. "The Battle of the Nueces, August 10, 1862," *Southwestern Historical Quarterly,* 66 (July 1962), 31–42.

Singletary, Otis A. "Texas Militia During Reconstructon," *Southwestern Historical Quarterly,* 60 (July 1956), 23–35.

Smallwood, James M. "When the Klan Rode: White Terror in Reconstruction Texas," *Journal of the West,* 25 (October 1986), 4–13.

Smyrl, Frank H. "Texas in the Union Army," *Southwestern Historical Quarterly,* 65 (October 1961), 234–50.

————. "Unionism in Texas, 1856–1861," *Southwestern Historical Quarterly,* 68 (October 1964), 172–95.

Sneed, Edgar P. "A Historiography of Reconstruction in Texas: Some Myths and Problems," *Southwestern Historical Quarterly,* 72 (April 1969), 435–48.

Somers, Dale A. "James P. Newcomb: The Making of a Radical," *Southwestern Historical Quarterly,* 72 (April 1969), 449–69.

Doctoral and Masters Papers

Carrier, John Pressley. "A Political History of Texas During the Reconstruction, 1865–1874." Ph.D. dissertation, Vanderbilt University, 1971.

Dobbs, Ricky Floyd. "'A Slow Civil War': Resistance to the Davis Administration in Hill and Walker Counties, 1871." M.A. thesis, Baylor University, 1989.

Gray, Ronald N. "Edmund J. Davis: Radical Republican and Reconstruction Governor of Texas." Ph.D. dissertation, Texas Tech University, 1976.

Owens, Nora Estelle. "Presidential Reconstruction in Texas: A Case Study." Ph.D. dissertation, Auburn University, 1983.

Sandlin, Betty Jeffus. "The Texas Reconstruction Constitutional Convention of 1868–1869." Ph.D. dissertation, Texas Tech University, 1970.

INDEX

Locators in *italics* indicate illustrations.